Value-Added Tax and Other Tax Reforms

Value-Added Tax and Other Tax Reforms

Richard W. Lindholm

Nelson-Hall
Chicago

Library of Congress Cataloging in Publication Data

Lindholm, Richard Wadsworth, 1914–
  Value-added tax and other reforms.

  Bibliography: p.
  Includes index.
    1.   Value-added tax—United States. 2.   Taxation—
United States.   I. Title.
HJ5715.U6L55   336.2′71   76–24827
ISBN 0–911012–87–7

Manufactured in the United States of America.

Contents

Foreword   **vii**

Preface   **ix**

1   Government Spending and Taxing   **1**

2   Description of the Value-Added Tax   **27**

3   Basic Taxes Used in the United States   **59**

4   Fiscal Impact Analysis   **99**

5   Economic Growth   **125**

6   Financing a Broad Social Security Program   **161**

7   International Taxation and Commercial Relations   **187**

8   Tax Philosophy for Today   **235**

Notes   **263**

Glossary of Technical Terms   **295**

Bibliography   **301**

Index   **321**

Foreword

The impact our tax system has on the nation's economic and social well-being has been growing as we develop more of an urban society which brings us closer into contact with each other and which of necessity increases the role government must play. In a similar vein, international relationships have also grown closer and have become more interrelated, and therefore international tax relationships become more important.

Professor Richard Lindholm of the University of Oregon, in the discussion in this book, does not suggest the abandonment of a progressive income tax or the graduated estate tax. However, he sees the present or possible future levels of these taxes as having a harmful effect on efficiency, employment, and international competition and as a result, he suggests the desirability of a major new national tax source, a value-added tax which might raise as much as $100 billion a year.

Professor Lindholm has engaged in the analysis of tax problems at the local, state and federal levels of government for over thirty years and has worked to aid in the development of the fiscal systems of a number of low income nations in the world. His experience and background make it particularly appropriate that he present an analysis of value-added taxation for general consideration.

It certainly is, of course, appropriate that we analyze the use of a value-added tax as a possible replacement for some of our existing revenues, or as a source for additional revenues should that become necessary. While there is much to be said in favor of a value-added tax, nevertheless we must recognize that it is a tax on consumption expenditures and as such itself has an important economic impact. Whether this effect is desirable or not would appear to depend upon the combined impact of our different revenue sources, the general level of taxation, and our national objectives.

I believe that Professor Lindholm makes a valuable contribution in his book and in his analysis of the value-added tax without neglecting the political realities of tax reform and the temptations of deficit financing. I recommend it to your study.

Al Ullman, Chairman
Committee on Ways and Means
U.S. House of Representatives

Preface

Everyone is aware that our federal tax system provides the United States government with huge amounts in revenues. These payments are made, or, put differently, these resources are made available, out of the annual productivity of the people of the United States. This basic fact does not receive proper recognition in U.S. tax legislation. The federal tax system, as it has developed through the years, has been designed to collect the needed revenues in one way or another from economic windfalls and realized incomes remaining after a maze of adjustments.

The tax system was, and still partially remains, aimed at the frosting and not at the cake. As anyone who thinks about it for a while will realize, this is no way to go about collecting what has become approximately 30 percent of the gross national product (GNP). No economy generates a surplus of that size, and individual ability to pay loses its meaning when the product collected is produced by giant corporations and when spending arises from provisions of national legislation that are applicable nationwide and may be used directly to increase the well-being of nontaxpayers in a foreign land.

GNP has become the accepted measurement of economic activity and well-being. It alone is a sufficiently inclusive aggregate to cover rather well the total productivity of a society. It also represents the resources that any economy has available to distribute in support of whatever it is going to do. Therefore, any tax system has to draw upon GNP in turning resources over for government use. Since this is an economic fact of life, what makes better sense than to use GNP itself as the base to which a tax rate is applied to provide a basic and important revenue flow? This book accepts this common-sense argument for the value-added tax, which utilizes GNP as it arises in each enterprise as the tax base to which the tax rate is applied.*

*See pages 51–57 for consideration of composition of national income accounts.

The sophisticated pressures bubbling and boiling in the international economic caldron must be considered in making U.S. tax decisions, since we all now live in one commercial world. We are learning this the hard way, and one result was the provisions of the 1962 Revenue Act relative to foreign source income and the no-longer-applicable interest equalization tax and the related guidelines to capital exportation of the same period. Since then international monetary developments and the adoption of the Domestic International Sales Corporation (DISC) tax legislation have demonstrated, along with the actions of the oil-producing nations, that international imbalance is a continuing major economic problem.

The United States stands largely by itself in its approach to taxation, particularly business taxation. The argument of this book is that there is nothing inherent in the U.S. fiscal system that makes it preferable to systems existing in the countries of the European Economic Community (EC), for example. Therefore, if the U.S. approach to taxation fails to provide the support required for America to realize its worldwide commercial and political goals, it is appropriate to consider a change. Consideration of change is also appropriate if the social goals of taxation have shifted from those of the nineteenth century, which were used by tax theorists when the existing federal tax system was formulated.

Once in a while events become so interrelated that one rather dramatic action can cut a Gordian knot that has been restricting action in a number of related fields. The adoption of the Sixteenth Amendment and the introduction of the federal income tax was an example. The use of the income tax permitted the federal government to meet the accepted standards of tax justice while greatly expanding its revenue-raising base. The whole history of America's moving into the world vacuum created by a weakening Western Europe after 1914 seems to flow naturally from the strength imparted to the federal government by the revenue-raising power of the individual income tax with graduated rates.

Today a similar opportunity appears to exist, and again it is fundamentally a tax adjustment that is required.

An acceptable level of government social conscience requires immense revenues, and these same developments reduce the need for individuals to accumulate savings. At the same time, the pressures of technological developments, population growth, and the need for environment preservation require more and more savings. In addition, the non-Communist and to a growing degree the Communist world are becoming a single economic unit united by the operations of the great international corporations and the need for natural resources that are un-equally distributed over the earth's surface.

These developments have been causing serious difficulties. The prob-lems range from bankrupt cities and nations to a continuing deficit in the American international balance of payments. Patchwork reactions have resulted in a cumbersome group of domestic and international fiscal and monetary actions.

It is the thesis of this discussion that through the adoption of a major value-added tax, the United States could progress a long way toward resolution of many of its domestic and international difficulties. This tax, which possesses great flexibility and revenue-raising potential and provides basic economic justice, has become the principal tax of Western Europe and has proven itself in less developed countries as well.

1

Government Spending
and Taxing

The role of government in stimulating economic activity and in cooperating with the private sector in meeting the day-to-day peaceful and military ambitions of people and nations is important and constantly changing. The ancient roots as well as current trends of government spending and taxing must be briefly considered to provide a base for understanding why a major change in the American approach to government finance appears to be in the wings.

The concept of the justice of the free market developed out of a closely controlled society that had become debased and corrupt. The orders of the market to produce, consume and save broke down in the 1930s. Keynesian economics, with its emphasis on money creation through national government budgetary policy, restored the workability of the market economy.

At the national level the United States has remained wedded to somewhat progressive individual income and corporate profits taxes that have become increasingly complicated. As rising government services are demanded to meet big city needs and general social responsibilities, the inadequacy of both the revenue sources and the test of government expenditure efficiency are becoming apparent. Also, the Keynesian-related countercyclical budgetary policy appears to require a revenue stability not found in the existing federal tax system.

HISTORICAL PERSPECTIVE

Through the ages taxation and government spending on government-determined projects has been an important positive or negative factor in the well-being of the residents of a region. Much of the government spending has gone into defensive and offensive military operations.[1] The fact that military spending is so obvious in the public economy and the heroic nature of military endeavors have tended to hide the impact of the relatively peaceful day-to-day pursuit of collecting taxes and spending public funds.

The size of the public economy relative to that of the private economy has tended to increase during periods when a nation is united in pursuit of a clear-cut goal. In the past this united effort has usually existed when the goal was religious or military in nature. Nevertheless, the effective accomplishment by individuals of the myriad tasks required to realize such goals—putting stones in place or replacing broken spears, for example—was basically dependent on economic functions.

Through its tax system the public economy had to collect the funds it needed without destroying individual initiative in the private sector. For example, the government had to be sure that the farmer continued to raise more than he ate, that he brought his grain to town, that the miller made the flour needed by the people of the city, and so on.[2]

Men have been dealing for ages with three basic economic issues—(1) what to produce, (2) how to divide it, and (3) how to produce more. An excursion to the Great Pyramid of Egypt gives some clues to the solutions that were worked out in the civilization of the Pharaohs some five thousand years ago. This immense structure, covering thirteen acres, was built of great blocks of stone, which had to be hauled by unaided human labor from quarries on the other side of the Nile to the construction site. Vast numbers of architects, craftsmen, and laborers worked for the better part of a generation to build it. The cost, in terms of food, shelter, and raw materials provided to the workers, must have been fantastic. Today we see it as no more than a tomb in which the reigning ruler, at his death, could be laid away with proper observance of religious prescriptions to assure his entrance into an afterlife.

GOVERNMENT-DIRECTED ECONOMIES

To the ancient Egyptians, however, the pyramid was much more. It symbolized their power and their organizational ability. Its construction was a highly accepted use of their productive talents, and was an *economic* achievement of great significance.

It is easy to see that royal privilege and religious doctrine had much to do with the decision of what goods would be produced in the Egyptian economy. One might also conclude that the Pharaoh was able to determine the direction of a major share of the productive activity. In fact, the determination of what goods and services should be produced and how they should be divided was made by the Pharaoh, the nobles, and the temple priests. A large portion of production and also of education was aimed at the preservation of the existing Egyptian civilization.[3]

The efforts of thousands were directed toward the construction and maintenance of a widespread irrigation system. The system benefited the ruling class, but it also benefited the common man, for a productive Nile Valley kept them from starving. This was a god-ruled state. Change was very slow. It was also, however, a well-ordered state: it met the basic economic needs of the people and provided employment for everyone on projects considered worthwhile.

In the later civilizations of Greece and Rome free markets for goods and services broadened, and the uncertainties of the market increased. When goods are offered for sale by their producers or by retailers, anyone who has sufficient money can buy them. When buyers show by their purchases that a certain product is in great demand, the price of that product increases and producers are encouraged to bring more to the market. Similarly, when a product goes unsold, its price decreases and producers are discouraged from producing more. With this kind of market, salesmanship becomes very helpful, and consumers must learn to recognize quality and budget money.

Although markets became important in the Greek and Roman civilizations, they did not become the means by which all basic economic issues were decided. For one thing, slaves continued to provide the labor foundation of the economy. They did not earn incomes, however; they were maintained by their owners. Their consumption preferences entered the market only as their owners permitted. For another, legally enforced distinctions of social class often restricted a person's choice of employment.

The relatively powerful free market of early Rome was gradually reduced in scope.[4] The state came to hold immense economic power through regulation of economic activities and through active participation in production, transportation, and even in selling to consumers. The growth of state economic activities seemed necessary to hold the empire together. Though some decisions could still be made by the consumer in the markets of imperial Rome, and though many individual producers might decide for themselves how much to save and invest, the major weight of decision-making lay with the state. In Rome as in Egypt, education was not aimed at technical improvement. Its main function became to show why the current social, political, and religious systems had to be continued.

THE ROLE OF THE PUBLIC ECONOMY

In early medieval times, after the Roman Empire and its state-directed economy had crumbled, trade and the transport of goods were sharply reduced. Roads fell into disrepair, and robber bands roamed the countryside.

Local economies, restricted to the household or manor of one noble or landlord, became the common economic unit. The lord organized the activities of serfs, who could not legally leave the land to which they were bound. The serfs worked their fields and gave a portion of the produce to the lord. In addition, they worked the lord's own land without wages. The lord employed craftsmen to produce the manufactured goods needed on the manor. Decisions on all economic matters rested by custom and law with the lord of the manor. This system, like earlier ones, met basic human economic and social needs. But the price was high. Lord and serf alike were unable to live except according to a prescribed set of guidelines.[5]

Part of the lord's income might be given to the church or to a greater lord to whom he owed allegiance, but he did not produce for the market. His products did not have to compete.[6] He consumed, invested, and produced according to the feudal customs, and *he* received the lion's share. Again, education was aimed largely at justifying the current state of affairs.

Gradually conditions suitable for trade, however, redeveloped. Cities grew and the marketplace again assumed importance. More and more economic decisions were made by buyers and sellers in the market. By early modern times the dynamics of the market were beginning to dictate what was produced and consumed. The market broke through royal regulations and feudal restrictions. The economic system that was developing was called *capitalism,* because private producers used capital, either their own or borrowed from other private owners, to produce goods for the market. The motive for using privately owned capital in production for the market was, of course, the hope of making a *profit*—receiving more than one paid out in the process of producing goods sold on the market.

THE GROWTH OF THE FREE MARKET

The free market grew more important as businessmen gradually escaped old restrictions on their enterprise. The American and French Revolutions were at least partially struggles to free the rising system of capitalism from old royal economic controls.

By the end of the eighteenth century, capitalism predominated in Western Europe and North America. The economists of the period proclaimed the free, competitive market as an automatic mechanism that would resolve all the basic economic issues. Adam Smith's *Wealth of Nations* appeared in 1776, and his theory of the "invisible hand" was gaining favor. Everything would be in order and everything would be done right, but without regulations.

According to the theory, buyers would determine by their purchases what was produced. Sellers would decide how to use their incomes. Producers would supply goods according to the demands of the market and invest capital in the production of goods that would earn the best profits. As producers competed with one another, the search for profits would lead them to use the most efficient methods of production. Wages of labor would be fixed by the supply and demand of labor in the market. Rents charged by landowners and interest charged by persons who loaned money would also be set by supply and demand.

Competition among buyers and sellers of all goods and services in free markets would determine what should be produced, how it would be produced, how income would be distributed, how much could be saved, and for what purposes savings would be invested. The one who prospered most was the one who changed to a better method of distribution or production first—the world would beat a path to the door of the man with the better mousetrap. There was no need for economic decisions on the part of the government, and, in fact, government would upset the whole system if it interfered in economic life.

This is the theory of *laissez-faire*, which held that the state should play a minimal role in economics. All decisions should be worked out by the automatic mechanisms of competitive markets and the "invisible hand" they provided. The concept as developed in the nineteenth century continues to be widely advocated, and the changes introduced during the past eighty years are merely modifications.

NEW ECONOMIC NEEDS

The United States more than the Economic Community (EC) member states claims to be following the theory and practice of nineteenth-century capitalism. The simple economics of the nineteenth century, however, have become the complex economics of the 1970s. This complexity has required the adoption of laws to regulate and guide economic activities and the introduction of government action to stimulate and assist them. Laws and government regulations are necessary because perfect competition among producers and users is very difficult to maintain. Also, competition by itself does not always lead to a socially desirable use of resources or to an adequate degree of economic stability or growth. Therefore, the United States has adopted laws specifying minimum wages and maximum hours of work, setting pure food and drug standards, regulating stock exchanges and investments, and setting guidelines for many businesses.

To stimulate the economy, the federal government, along with state and local governments, is active in promoting opportunities for private enterprise development and investment. Highways and airports are constructed to facilitate movement of goods. Foreign market information is sent to American exporters. Perhaps even more important is the function the federal government has assumed by acting as a sort of balance wheel to the private sector of the economy. In 1946 Congress adopted the Employment Act, which pledged policies that would help create economic conditions conducive to a high level of employment and sufficient purchasing power. The enjoyment of economic prosperity by citizens is a major government goal. It is also one that, as the country learned in the 1930s, could not be provided by the free enterprise system alone. In the 1970s we have learned that it is an elusive goal even when government is actively helping out.

CONCLUSION

The role of government spending and the role of collecting revenues change as requirements for the "good life" as seen by leaders and their followers change. The theory of *laissez-faire* and the necessity for active government involvement in the economy can live side by side. For this to occur, however, adequate revenues must be available for each without destroying the foundation of the economic power of either.

THE GREAT DEPRESSION

Although the private enterprise system, modified by government spending, revenue-raising, and regulation, had never worked perfectly, it had provided a tolerable arrangement for personal freedom and economic progress. In 1930 the Great Depression changed what had become conventional economic wisdom.

KEYNESIAN ECONOMICS

One of the developments that resulted from the depression of the 1930s was the revolution of economic analysis begun by John Maynard Keynes. A fundamental aspect of the Keynesian revolution was the development of a relationship between the high levels of unemployment and low levels of investment of the 1930s and current taxation and monetary policy. The pre-Keynesian monetary policy was not much more than an admonition to keep the monetary and the real rate of interest at about the same level. The approved government posture was a balanced budget financed with taxes that had a minimum unfavorable impact on the level of savings and therefore on the level of private investment.

After the depression and the related economic theories, the United States moved directly to the concept of the balanced budget under conditions of full employment. No one who has worked with the concept has the confidence in its usefulness today that he or she had ten years ago. Experience and rapidly shifting economic relationships have not supported the basic assumption that deficits during recession will be the basis of tomorrow's prosperity.

One critic of the Keynesian approach, Henry Hazlitt, wrote, "So there you have it. The people who have earned money are too shortsighted, hysterical, rapacious, and idiotic to be trusted to invest it themselves. The money must be seized from them by the politicians, who will invest it with almost perfect foresight and complete disinterestedness."

AN ECONOMY BALANCED WITH UNBALANCED BUDGETS

The concept of the unbalanced budget as the economy's balance wheel—or the cyclically balanced budget or even automatic stabilizers, as the Committee for Economic Development (CED) liked to call the policy—brought with it a need to find the money to do the balancing. It was often assumed that the money could be borrowed from individuals and businesses, and it was an accepted assumption of the theory that an excess of private savings would arise at the very time budget deficits were needed to pull the economy back on the road to prosperity. These excess savings, borrowed or perhaps taxed away, would give the government the budgetary support it needed.

If weak economic conditions existed when an excess of savings in private hands did not exist, the stimulation of the government could be safely provided through deficits financed with additional central bank credit. For as Alvin H. Hansen, the great sage of the period, wrote, "There can be no general price inflation until scarcity conditions, owing to full employment, become general over at least a considerable range of industry."[7]

The budget could even be stimulating without incurring a deficit. The concept was called the balanced budget theorem. It became a portion of the political and economic environment of the U.S. known as "the tax and spend program." The stimulation was expected to arise because a dollar of additional government spending would provide more economic stimulus than the concomitant decrease generated by the initial tax collections, because they were made largely by those in the upper income brackets.[8]

The economies of the United States and the world have apparently failed to generate an excess of private savings since the depression. Also, governments have been generally unable to accumulate tax surpluses during periods of boom. Thus federal government deficits of the 1970s could only be financed with a creation of additional monetary reserves. The results were inflation, high interest rates, and a budget that never reached the full employment balanced condition spoken of by Democratic and Republican Councils of Economic Advisers.[9]

The budget as related to taxation and monetary aggregates is not a dead concept. Today, a better level of economic activity continues to be sought through these means. The record, however, has not been as good as expected. One observable result of the experience of the last several years is that a high aggregate level of spending and the use of federal deficits to stimulate the economy no longer enjoy the support they were accorded in the 1960s. The economic malaise has acquired new symptoms, and new complexities have developed in efforts to apply a remedy.

A change in the kinds of things purchased with budget funds at the federal level and an increase in local determination of the use of funds have been suggested as possible ways to make budgetary actions more effective in improving economic conditions. Gross changes in government spending levels and variations in the portion financed with tax collections (without much consideration of type of tax used) have not worked out as many people had hoped.

However, the aim of reordering federal government spending priorities has also run into difficulties.[10] The energy crisis of 1973–1975 and the need for large armament expenditures despite the end of fighting by U.S. troops may have prevented the new revenue sharing and transfer payment approaches from receiving a fair test. Nevertheless, it remains true that "the twentieth century clearly does not offer any comfortable prospect of a smooth functioning economic Utopia."[11]

CONCLUSION

Shifts in fiscal and monetary policy that developed out of the Keynesian revolution are proving to have formidable shortcomings. The cyclically balanced budget together with taxes whose base increases sharply during prosperity and decreases about as much during a recession have not worked together to balance the economy as envisaged.

TAX INEQUALITY AND THE MARKET BARGAIN

The definition of taxable income—that is, the income to which the federal income tax rate is applied—excludes more than 60 percent of what is included in the definition of personal income in the U.S. national income accounts. Because taxable income is so much less than personal income, and because the federal government relies almost completely on taxes based on income, a very high rate must be applied to the income that the law leaves as the taxation base.

In addition, differing tax standards must be applied to taxpayers in differing circumstances, and an effort has been made to assure that differences are fair both horizontally and vertically. *Horizontal justice* refers to equal treatment of persons in about the same basic economic position. (Statistically, horizontal justice is measured by the coefficient of variation.) *Vertical justice* refers to equal treatment of persons in different basic economic positions, based on some measurement of the sacrifice required to meet taxes.

HORIZONTAL INEQUALITY

The creators of the U.S. tax system have done many amazing things in their search for justice through unequal treatment. For example, interest, including that on a home mortgage, and property taxes on the same home are deductible in arriving at taxable income. However, the imputed income from an owner-occupied house made possible by the owner's investment is not taxable income, and capital gains from the sale of the property are not taxable if the owner purchases a similar home within a year.[12] On the other hand, a person who rents may not deduct rent payments from taxable income, and the return from funds that might have been invested in lieu of purchasing a house *is* taxable. In addition, if stock purchased as an investment is sold, any gain is taxable as capital gains even if it is used to purchase stock of another company in the same industry.

In this brief example, the tax law is based on several doubtful concepts. The first is the treatment of capital gains. Are capital gains income? The British until 1965 and the Canadians until 1972 said no, and the Germans continue to say no.[13] Also, are realized capital gains so greatly different from unrealized ones that the latter may never be subject to taxation while those realized bear a maximum tax of 30 percent? Are capital gains that are due largely to inflation or falling interest rates so nearly the same as capital gains that are not related to these factors as to justify the same tax treatment?

The law also is based on a number of doubtful principles in the treatment of interest. Why is the payment of interest on an installment contract deductible from taxable income while the price of the washing machine or television set that was purchased is not? Why is interest deductible as a cost of capital from corporate income in arriving at corporate taxable income while a reasonable return on equity capital represented by common stock is not?

How does capital gain from sale and purchase of similar securities differ from capital gain from sale and purchase of similar residences? Why are long-term capital gains from sale of business property treated as capital gains while losses are treated as regular income? Why is the full value of appreciated property donated to a charity deductible from taxable income that has never been increased by a realization of the capital gain? Why is exchange of property (held for productive use or investment and with an appreciated value) for property of like kind not taxable while a sale and purchase of like property from the proceeds of the sale is taxable?

All these questions relate to examples of the treatment afforded under the U.S. income tax. Each of them apparently arose from efforts to develop justice through inequality of treatment of those with economic power. The United States and other nations using the income tax have been unable to develop a tax "set up so that the burden is the same regardless of the action of the taxpayer."[14] Under the conditions existing in the United States, tax justice, to the degree that it can be defined, consists of everyone's having access to information telling how the law operates. This is a low order of justice. It is based on equal adjustment ability of taxpayers, and in the case of tax law, adjustments are very demanding; the taxpayer may not be able to interpret the law without employing a high-priced accounting or legal tax specialist. Yet this is basically an accurate general description of the kind of horizontal justice existing under the U.S. income tax law and the income tax laws of all nations.

Although relative tax burdens as they have been discussed here come under the general heading of horizontal distribution, many of the considerations also relate to the kind of vertical distribution of tax burdens that exists under the U.S. income tax.

VERTICAL INEQUALITY

The Brookings Institution Studies of Government Finance included a study based on adjusted gross income as reported on 1960 U.S. tax returns. As a measurement of tax-paying ability, gross income has many of the shortcomings mentioned earlier; it is adjusted by adding the excluded capital gains or losses and excludable sick pay and dividends. In the study, the highest tax as a percentage of income was found to be paid by persons in the $100,000-$150,000 income class, not by those in the highest income classes.[15] The income tax as it actually operates is most progressive in the lowest tax-paying brackets; it is nearly proportional for those in income groups between $5,000 and $8,000. It is considerably progressive between $10,000 and $100,000, and progressivity ends at the $100,000 bracket.

The maximum rate on total income reaches 33.3 percent for those receiving $100,000 to $150,000 and is 29.8 percent for those with total incomes over $1,000,000. The average for all income classes is 13.1 percent, which is the approximate rate paid by those with a total income of $10,000. The rate calculated to have been paid by those with total incomes between $4,000 and $5,000 was 9.6 percent.

This picture is very different from the one presented by the 1960 income tax rate structure. At that time rates started at 20 percent and continued up to 91 percent. Today, of course, they start at 14 percent and go up to 70 percent. The reduction of the legal rates has most likely resulted in an approximately equal reduction of income taxes as a percentage of total income.

For the great mass of taxpayers, the income tax works out to be basically a flat-rate tax when calculated as a percentage of adjusted gross income as in the Brookings Institution study. Tax-caused vertical redistribution of income exists if it is assumed that the income bargain is before taxes rather than after taxes, but it is largely between the person with $100,000 or so of realized income before taxes and the person with $5,000 to $10,000 of realized income before taxes. The U.S. personal income tax does not bring about vertical income redistribution of this kind between those with realized incomes above $150,000 and those with realized incomes between $100,000 and $150,000.

The progressive income tax as developed in the United States, even when measured on the basis of gross realized income before deductions, has not made a substantial contribution to improving the income distribution. In fact, it may have increased the degree of economic injustice that had been developed through actions in the marketplace. Actually, the position that realized cash income is the only proper income tax base is not supported by economists who have examined the situation. Nevertheless, it is basic to an administrative income tax and is utilized by all nations using the tax.

UNTAXED INCOME

The horizontal justice problems of the U.S. income tax have become very severe because the tax does not cover all income. Pressure is in the air as never before to move toward a complete coverage of income. A U.S. personal income tax that included all income would require a far-reaching reform and change of the system. Also, a tax-making provision for the deduction of all expenditures and outlays necessary to earn an income would require a considerable increase of personal expenditure deductions and would develop pressures that would cause changes of individual expenditure patterns. If adopted, for example, it would encourage purchase of better food and more preventive and remedial medical expenditures because the expenditure was deductible.

In 1947 William Vickrey of Columbia University produced a study that developed the requirements for horizontal justice. The concluding statement after 395 pages of analysis is as follows:

> If a tax is set up so that the burden is the same regardless of the action of the taxpayer, it follows that there will be no loopholes by which the taxpayer can escape tax. There will be no need to try to circumscribe the avenues of avoidance by detailed and minute distinctions between the treatment to be applied to various possible lines of action, nor will there be any occasion to superimpose upon the law a patchwork of loophole-plugging provisions. In the long run, the correct method will usually pay bigger dividends in simplicity and freedom from unforeseen difficulties than rough and ready approximations.[16]

The virtue of simplicity in the horizontally just income tax has become more admired through the years. However, greater simplicity can also be reached by abandoning the concept of taxation of net income, and it is this approach that seems to be gaining the greatest support. The simplified U.S. income tax returns available for persons with low and middle income are indicative of the trend. The recommended increase of permissible percentage deductions by receivers of higher income, long advocated by Senator Russell Long, chairman of the Senate Finance Committee, is another example. These approaches are a compromise between a low tax rate on a gross measurement of purchasing power resulting from economic activity and a tax levied on income found here and there, the taxation of which is politically acceptable and is therefore identified in tax legislation. The apparent after-tax horizontal unevenness arising from legislative income tax action must frequently be rationalized by some unproven relationship outside the area of equal treatment of economic equals. For example, it is said that if interest on state and local government securities were taxable, the borrowing ability of these levels of governments would be unfavorably affected, or if the private petroleum industry were not allowed an additional percentage depletion deduction before arriving at taxable income, they could not develop domestic oil and gas reserves and our energy shortage would worsen.

AFTER-TAX INCOME

The differing tax liabilities of persons receiving relatively equal before-tax incomes under current tax legislation have been taken into consideration in personal service contracts, investment decisions, and industry development. As a result, a rough horizontal evenness based on after-tax income or after-tax rate of return on capital has been worked out. If it is further accepted that all income-related decisions are based on calculations of after-tax income, then the present differential treatment of before-tax income does not really affect meaningful horizontal income justice. It also follows that any change in the relative treatment of taxpayers who receive different incomes introduces different tax burdens for equally placed persons where none existed before. The resulting horizontal injustice will be gradually worked off as new contracts are negotiated, as the market changes the direction of commitments, and as the values of capital assets are adjusted.

This manner of looking at tax justice, when extended to include vertical income redistribution—that is, the change in the level of income between receivers of large and small income—suggests that in the case of vertical income redistribution, too, it may not be useful to consider before-tax income. Perhaps the general situation throughout our society is that prices, including wage and income bargains, are set on the basis of income after taxes. This perception of the burden of taxes, if taxes are to be used to change rewards as decided in the marketplace, leads to advocacy of a tax policy that constantly introduces new and different taxes or one that does not attempt to redistribute incomes vertically or to treat income equals equally.

It has long been argued that *ad valorem* land taxes do not represent a burden because the price of land is forced down to the point where the rate of return on investment after taxes is the same with the higher tax as before with the lower tax. The relatively high income taxes that fall on the upper-middle-income brackets in the United States may have provided a portion of the reason for the expansion of the portion of the population within these brackets. Or the considerable stability of U.S. industrial prices during the 1962–1965 period may have been assisted by the reduction of applicable corporate income tax rates through accelerated depreciation, the investment tax credit, and finally the reduction of the basic corporate tax rate from 52 to 48 percent.

TAX LEVELS AND WAGE LEVELS

To go back to the impact of taxes on prices, and particularly the price paid for unskilled or partially skilled labor and professional, technical, and even unskilled services, the general argument has run that high income taxes are not adequate justification for wage increases but that excise taxes are. Excise taxes enter the wage bargain because excise taxes, more than income taxes, can be directly demonstrated to cause prices to rise. Until the sharp social security tax increases of 1966, the observable fact that income and social security taxes decrease take-home pay has not been—at least publicly—advocated as a justification for higher wages. Instead, higher prices, sometimes related to excise taxes, have been the basis for wage increase requests.

In the past the rationalization for higher wages has rested largely on three legs—higher prices, high profits, and increased productivity. Surprisingly, the fact that income and social security taxes decrease take-home pay was neglected in the United States until 1966, possibly because of the original and continuing sources of political support for the income tax and the social security system. The original advocates were workers and salaried people, and the original opponents of these taxes were generally business groups and propertied classes.

CONCLUSION

The arguments that identify the undesirable impacts of horizontal inequality in the income tax can also be used to support the desirable vertical inequality of the tax and the collection of taxes with a minimum of social cost. However, if the marketplace, through its determination of value on the basis of after-tax income, eliminates undesirable horizontal inequality, it could, through the same process, largely remove the desired vertical inequality. If this is the case, the basis for general support of the income tax over other taxes because of its closer correspondence to ability to pay is eroded.

THE INFLATION CRUNCH ON STATE AND LOCAL FINANCES

The strength and pervasiveness of general inflation during the past ten years is a major element of the state and local government finance crisis that has resulted in the federal revenue sharing program and an evolving fundamental change in America's fiscal practices. In fact, during this period of inflation the state and local government dollar depreciated more rapidly than did the consumer dollar. This difference in the inflation rate of the dollar the taxpayer used for private purposes and the one he paid in taxes, provides a neglected element in the explanation of the taxpayer revolt and the state and local government finance crisis of 1970. Since then, the shortage of raw materials has made the public dollar, basically a service dollar, relatively stronger but city finances in 1975 were weakened by sharply reduced levels of economic activity and union contracts tied to cost of living.

Government costs continue under pressure and medical care services are an expanding government spending area. The medical dollar became a sixty cent 1958 dollar.[17] On the other hand, the public's love affair with the automobile continued up to 1974 and the purchasing power of the automobile dollar changed hardly at all between 1958 and 1970.

Much of the difficulty that has arisen in the public economy relative to costs is related to a general failure to ask the fundamental question: Do state and local governments get more for their dollars devoted to medical services, education and highways than do private purchasers?

Even when the question is asked, the answer is generally inadequate. Costs and benefits analyses and other relative data of state and local government activity are very fragmentary. Because of the pressure of those who feel government must become more efficient, however, experiments have been initiated that transfer traditional public-sector activities to the private sector and that initiate new decision procedures in the public sector. Private contracts have been let to provide educational services, but fragmentary analyses of the results have not supported the original optimism with which this experiment was met. Attempts have been made to use a planning, programming, and budgeting system (PPBS) to identify how state and local governments can perform more efficiently. The emphasis, as would be expected, is on tasks that are generally acknowledged to be the responsibility of the public rather than the private sector.

Only Pennsylvania has a PPBS in operation, and one cannot be certain at this point whether this is even the right way to improve government policy-making decision processes.[18]

THE THIRTY-EIGHT LARGEST SMSAs

The political pressures generated by the fiscal problems of large metropolitan areas have been very influential in changing the fiscal system of America. The data seem to indicate that the fiscal crisis arose much less from economic conditions than the urgent requests for funds by the city mayors of the period seemed to indicate.

Of course, there are many unique conditions within each standard metropolitan statistical area (SMSA) that account for changes in both expenditures and revenue sources. During 1966–1970, when per capita personal real income (1958 dollars) increased from $2,404 to $2,595, a significant number of SMSAs were reducing per capita real collections from property taxes. Milwaukee, Pittsburgh, and Atlanta increased per capita real property tax collections by 16.0, 16.6, and 15.7 percent, respectively, and stand out as SMSAs that made good use of their basic revenue sources during the period under study. Additional SMSAs with about a 10 percent increase include Boston; Chicago; Columbus, Ohio; Detroit; Los Angeles; New York; and Paterson, New Jersey.

San Francisco alone substantially increased per capita real revenues from its own sources during the five-year period. Between 1966 and 1970 the San Francisco per capita dollar increase was $110, ten times that of Denver. The percentage of expenditures in San Francisco covered by its own revenues rose from 50.4 percent in 1966 to 71.5 percent in 1970.

The general increase of expenditures by the large SMSAs on a per capita real dollar basis was rather impressive. Milwaukee was one of the leaders. Between 1966 and 1970 the per capita dollar general expenditure total increased from $272 to $331, or by $59. Thirty-four dollars of this expansion was financed with outside revenues. The data demonstrate that such increases were generally typical for the thirty-eight largest SMSAs.[19]

The per capita real revenues from local sources in Miami *decreased* by $10 during the period under study. As Miami revenue collections were declining, general government per capita real dollar expenditures of the Miami SMSA rose by $30. The relationship between expenditures and local revenues had largely disappeared. In 1966 four SMSAs (Chicago, Miami, Newark, and Paterson) were covering over 80 percent of general expenditures with revenues from their own sources. In 1970 only Boston was covering over 80 percent of its expenditures with its own revenues.

Chicago's percentage fell from 82.2 to 73.0 percent, Miami's from 80.5 to 67.4 percent, Newark's from 80.9 to 69.4 percent. The decline of Paterson's was the least—from 82.5 to 78.3 percent. Boston ran against the current, proving that it can be done, and increased its local financing of general expenditures from 73.9 percent in 1966 to 82.1 percent in 1970.

The 1966–1970 period brought a number of nagging state and local government fiscal concerns to the boiling point. Developments since then include (1) rapid expansion of the financing of SMSAs with revenues from other than their own sources, (2) expanded use of income taxes by state and local governments, (3) rapid growth of local indebtedness, (4) widely fluctuating interest rates on such debts, and (5) relative growth of state and federal revenue-raising responsibilities. All these developments emphasize that the past ten years have created forces that have changed and are continuing to change the American fiscal system. Although the "patch and make do" approach—the old standby of the past—has not been abandoned, a fundamental change in America's intergovernment fiscal relationships has begun, and more change can be expected.

CONCLUSION

The trend toward the state as the revenue source for traditional state and local government expenditures can be expected to continue. It may result in state collection of statewide property taxes to finance educational costs and for other purposes.

The revenue-sharing program of the federal government has the potential for the initiation of shared or "piggy-back" taxes. Likely tax candidates are the corporate profits tax, the individual income tax, and the value-added tax.

State and local government borrowing difficulties seem to be moving toward resolution through a national state and local government credit agency and reduced capital spending. The credit agency would have access to the U.S. Treasury and will have interest subsidies available. Therefore, it should be able to largely eliminate violent fluctuations in the cost of borrowing by state and local governments. However, as inflationary conditions continued to result in a reduction of the real income of state and local governments the pain became unbearable and a search for a procedure for federal assistance was initiated. The effort stimulated revenue sharing, but this program will need an assignment of substantial tax collections if it is to meet the need; maybe ten times the funds now available. This level of assistance is going to require a new and stable source of federal revenues.

SOCIAL RESPONSIBILITY

The basis of developing a tax policy to fit existing economic realities is found in satisfying what Richard A. Musgrave in the 1950s began to call "merit wants."[20] These are wants of great importance that the market system in many instances could provide but that are carried out by government institutions "because of an unsatisfactory past and present social importance."[21] What we are actually seeing today is a serious challenge of the correctness and validity of marketplace decisions. The decisions of the private sector as to what resources are used and how are being questioned by American society.

Government, through the expenditure of funds, can direct private production efforts. Our so-called military-industrial complex is a result of one kind of stimulation of private production by government spending. The increasing expenditures of the aged with funds from social security benefits are directing private enterprise toward meeting their economic demands.

How large a portion of total demand met by private enterprise should come from government social expenditure sources in a modern industrial state is unknown. If poverty is to be eliminated, if all citizens are to have an opportunity to reach their full potential, and if modern medicine is to be available to everyone, the portion would be high—maybe even higher than in Sweden, where taxes are approaching 50 percent of GNP. Our concern here is not in forecasting the growth or decline of government spending but discovering how the expenditures decided upon can best be financed.

The social welfare generated by marketplace decisions may be less than it could be. In the past the approach to remedying the situation through taxes has been to increase the equality of incomes.[22] It was argued that under conditions of greater income equality, the signals given to the market would do a better job of maximizing welfare. To a considerable extent this has happened, but it has been the income-equalizing impact of government social spending rather than tax collecting that has improved the market signals.

Today's welfare state potentials were not envisaged in the United States when the procedures for social security financing were established in the 1930s. In fact, today's conditions are as different from those existing in the 1930s as those of 1930 were from those of 1795, when one of the first formal efforts was made by government to alleviate social distress.[23] In 1795 the justices of Berkshire, England, met at Speenhamland. Their program provided that if the incomes of agricultural workers fell below a minimum level considered necessary in the interests of humanity, the balance would be made up with property tax funds.

The meeting place was a public house, and a satirist of the day wrote:

> The famous inn at Speenhamland
> That stands below the Hill,
> May well be called the Pelican
> From its enormous Bill.

Assuring adequate wages for the farm worker is still a problem. Sometimes it seems as though the problem is being attacked with procedures not much better than those in use at Speenhamland Inn two hundred years ago. And the bill at the inn is still pelican-size.

The evolving tax system of the United States has been cornering a small portion of the economy and extracting from it the maximum levy. We are gradually taxing less and less at higher and higher rates. Tax policy has become a shell game. The aim is to finance large government expenditures without anyone's suffering a reduction of private resources; or, if there is a reduction, it is because the individual chooses it by deciding to continue to smoke cigarettes or to drive an automobile. The assumption is that the person in question could have gotten along perfectly well without smoking cigarettes or driving an automobile and could have avoided the sumptuary tax. It is, of course, largely a Hobson's choice—one usually has no alternative.

THE INCOME TAX APPROACH

Income means different things to different people. The definition of taxable income provided by the federal individual income tax legislation is quite different from an economist's definition. The sharp distinction in treatment under the income tax between income-producing spending by business and consumption spending by wage earners is unreal. The word *income* as applied to the corporation or any other business has been reduced to a concept of profits. Profits really mean what is left over after paying all costs—from the consumption of business lunches to the depreciation of equipment. For the worker, taxable income is determined after much more limited deductions.

The concepts of taxable income and taxable corporate profits corner a relatively limited portion of economic activity for taxation. The amount cornered—that is, the tax base—gets narrower as special provisions are made for tax-sheltered savings and rapid depreciation. At the same time, the combination of progressive income tax rates and inflation causes real tax rates to go ever higher. A dollar spent to employ expert advice to reduce the income and profits tax base is considered to be a dollar well spent—and deductible, too. Income tax companies have become multimillion-dollar businesses catering to the small taxpayer.[24] The receiver of a large income patterns his life style after his tax counselor's advice. As an expensive revenue-raising device, the total private and public cost as a percent of net revenue from income and profit taxes begins to rival the lottery, the costs of which are said to absorb nearly 50 percent of the gross receipts of ticket sales.

THE PAYROLL TAX APPROACH

At the same time the very regressive payroll tax is continued to finance what is often—but mistakenly—called an actuarially sound social security program. We stand alone among nations in our approach to social security financing. We haven't really budged since President Franklin D. Roosevelt worked out what he considered to be the right approach about forty years ago. Now, finally, payroll taxes are being considered adequate if the collections are only enough to equal outgo. Proposals for expansion and development of social spending, however, continue to rely on payroll taxes as the revenue source, as originally provided in the 1930s. Much more of this later.

The paragraphs above cannot be read without horror and astonishment. How did we get ourselves into this box? A portion of the explanation consists of the taxable income shell game that Congress plays. Another portion of the explanation rests in the considerable conservatism of the tax thinking of American citizens.

Populist and Puritan influences in our society have been important. The Puritan influence shows up in the emphasis on sumptuary taxes; the Populist, in the desire to keep capitalists in line through high individual income and corporate profits tax rates even though the portion of income included in the base has decreased.

Fortune, the well-known business policy journal, concluded in an editorial on U.S. tax and expenditure development:

> What we need, after years of piecemeal and emotionalized debate on business taxes, is a thorough going rethinking of the whole subject. As the pressure of foreign competition rises, as demands for capital grow, inefficiencies and distortions introduced in the U.S. economy by the tax impacts will become increasingly dangerous. . . . A new approach would include serious considerations of such alternatives as the value-added tax, now in use throughout the Common Market.[25]

CONCLUSION

Socially responsible government is expensive and requires a revenue source that bears on the total productivity of the society. This sort of revenue system does not yet exist in the United States.

GENERAL GOVERNMENT SERVICES

The size of government expenditures and the areas in which they should be concentrated are citizen decisions that are continually adjusted according to conditions. The social needs of an urban population are considerably greater than those of a rural one, and they include economic opportunities as well as provision for emergency and welfare financing, police services, sewers, water, streets, and so on.

DECISION-MAKING

Government expenditures are directed by political pressures as well as by the need to perform services effectively. The need to educate children is the prime reason for government expenditures for education. The amount of funding that will go into the core areas of cities, however, is affected by the political pressures generated by inner-city problems. Much of the federal defense spending is outside the control of domestic political and economic groups. The use of tax resources for defense is strongly affected by political and economic decisions of foreign governments.

Foreign influences do not change the basic fact that governments must decide what to buy and how to tax. The actual decisions reflect all the political, economic, and traditional influences that impinge on any government. One result is that it is very difficult to forecast what government will do next. This is not to say that the private economy will act as expected, but it does respond much more predictably than does government. During the past thirty years the major cause of economic fluctuations has been unpredictable instability of a federal government that spends large sums.[26]

The accepted legitimate goal of business is to maximize profits. This goal provides very useful guidelines for the decisions of business leaders and greatly assists the government in forecasting the impact of its actions on business. If opportunities for profit exist in an area, it can be forecast with considerable confidence that entrepreneurs will do their best to organize the capital and labor needed to exploit the opportunity and reap part of the profit. On the other hand, if sales decrease, the business manager will nearly always reduce his costs, even if he must discharge employees.

In the United States, business and government sometimes both want to perform the same service. For example, both public capital (government money) and private capital have been offered to finance the construction of hydroelectric projects along the Snake River in Idaho. More often, however, government prefers to regulate rather than operate enterprises. This is more true in America than in other advanced industrial nations. In Australia, for example, there are two major airlines, Qantas and Trans Australia. Qantas is owned and managed by the Australian government, while Trans Australia is privately owned and managed. Most of the railroad, telephone, and electric utility systems of the world are owned and managed by governments. This is not true in the United States, of course.

Whenever something goes wrong with a private undertaking, it is easy to shout, "Turn it over to the government!" It is much more difficult for the government to remedy the shortcoming. Generally speaking, in a nation in which private undertakings are well managed, government undertakings will be, too. The general attitude of the people toward efficiency and innovation is not limited to the private or the public sector of a national economy. Today the trend in the United States and around the world is much less toward direct government control and operation of economic enterprises than was true twenty or forty years ago. Government regulation is experiencing an upward trend, however, particularly in the area of ecology.

GOVERNMENT SPENDING SHORTCOMINGS

One big set of problems faced by all managers of government activities is largely avoided by private enterprise managers. Private managers can keep their eyes firmly set on the long-run goal of profit maximization. All government economic agencies are to a considerable degree required by law to do the things they do. Often they perform socially desirable and politically dictated services at a loss. They find it difficult to introduce labor-saving improvements. Everyone employed by the government is also a voter, and because every move is protested by some voters, changes in products and prices are sluggish. When compared with these aims and pressures, the private enterprise goal of turning out a product salable at more than cost and priced to maximize profits seems relatively simple and straightforward.

It must not be forgotten that government has been the big research spender in our society. Some 60 percent of all scientific business research and development in the United States is financed by the federal government. Again and again business leaders report that more than one-half of their profits accrue from selling products that did not exist five or ten years earlier. Business has undoubtedly benefited greatly from well-financed government research spending, but it is very uncertain who will gain and to what extent. It was a $300,000 contract by the army to the Morse School of Engineering at the University of Pennsylvania in 1942 that produced the first computer. No one believed this expenditure would spawn a multibillion dollar industry twenty-five years later and initiate a major social revolution.

The products of business are sold in the marketplace. The price must be low enough to produce sales and high enough to cover all costs, including taxes. If buyers are willing to pay a price high enough to cover costs, the product will be provided. If the consumers in the marketplace will not pay these costs, the private enterprise system cannot continue to provide the service or product.

In the public economy, products and services are frequently provided without specific payment. The city fire department does not ask citizens if they wish to contract for its services—the services are free. The cost is covered by funds collected from taxes of one sort or another. Under these circumstances, the concept of the marketplace is not applicable as a method of transferring products or services to the consumer.

COSTS AND BENEFIT ANALYSIS

The question of what should and should not be done by government can best be answered by what is called *costs and benefits analysis*. If benefits are sufficiently clear-cut, like the saving in fire insurance costs through provision of fire protection, the calculation is relatively simple. It is a very complex matter, however, to attempt a costs and benefits analysis of public education for four-year-olds.

For example, the resources of a region might be put to very good use providing medical attention free to all persons between the ages of four and fifty. The benefits would far outweigh the costs. On the basis of a costs-benefits analysis, however, government provision of medical attention to the aged might *not* be a desirable economic policy. Obviously allocation of resources cannot be decided solely on an economic basis.

The basic link between revenue and expenditure that exists in the private economy does not exist in the public economy because goods are not brought to the market to be sold to pay the costs of production and marketing. Because this is true, one does not have a way to put a dollar value on the final social "product," so one has no equivalent to the price of final use private goods. This is all just a way of saying that the basic economic question—How big should government be?—cannot be determined on the basis of a general economic theory.

The "second-best rule" is frequently used to analyze whether or not government should initiate a new program. Under this rule, government should go ahead if its action does not displace a better private use of resources. This method of analysis has a pro-government bias, but it may be the best one available when the convenient measurement provided by the price system of the market does not exist. Measurement of the opportunity costs is basic to the determination of what should be done and who should do it.

FEDERAL SPENDING AND REVENUES

The debt of the federal government and its financial agencies has been increasing at a compound annual rate of over 10 percent since 1969. Although the 1973 growth of federal taxes was twice the growth rate of federal expenditures, the nation continued to experience serious inflationary pressures attributed in part to the federal budget. In 1975 and 1976 federal deficits grew as real dollar revenues fell sharply.

Over one-fourth of the increase in federal receipts between 1972 and 1973 arose from higher payments of social security taxes.[27] These taxes increased as a result of higher rates and higher levels of taxable income. Despite the revenue growth, it is generally believed that the social security system is on the threshold of serious fund shortages.

CONCLUSION

The areas in which the government provides services have remained essentially similar through the years. At the same time, rapid and substantial changes in the functioning of the private sector and in international relations have caused serious shortcomings in financing. Some of these are related to the changes of attitude toward government finance that came about in the 1930s. Others have arisen from the expanding social responsibilities of government precipitated by the rapid growth of urban life and the increased costs of providing acceptable welfare levels. These changes at all levels of government point to the need for a basic tax that (1) uses a portion of all economic production to finance the government's costs of meeting basic social needs, (2) provides a new stability in government finance, and (3) is compatible with international practices.

2

Description of the
Value-Added Tax

The rapidly expanding role of government in the sophisticated urban societies of Europe resulted in the adoption of the value-added tax (VAT) as the basic tax of the European Economic Community. Although the growth of expenditure levels and the need for government services in the United States approximate those of Western Europe, the national tax system remains very largely as it was during the great reform period just before World War I—over sixty years ago.

The value-added tax approaches the finance of government services from the reasonable position that (1) government costs continue from year to year and can only be paid out of current productive activity, and (2) there is no way to determine what economic activity should contribute more or less, so equal payment out of each unit of GNP becomes appropriate.

This highly reasonable approach to a major portion of government finance is achieved through the value-added tax, which has developed not only in Western Europe, but in a growing number of developing nations as well.

DIRECT AND INDIRECT TAXES

Traditional economic theory holds that direct taxes are not included in prices of goods sold but result in a reduction of the after-tax return of those subject to the tax.[1] Income taxes, including corporate, individual, and social security taxes, are generally considered to be direct taxes. The economic burden of these direct taxes rests on the income receivers who pay them. After-tax income is assumed to be reduced from the before-tax level. It is also taken for granted that the income level before taxes is not changed by the imposition of additional income taxes.

Traditional economic theory also holds that indirect taxes, which include all types of excise, turnover, and sales taxes, do not increase prices by the amount of the tax if they are general—that is, if they cover all products. It also holds that prices of products taxed are increased by special excises and that prices of products exempted from the special excise taxes tend to fall.[2]

Property taxes and wealth (asset) taxes generally do not fit into the classification of taxes as direct and indirect. The Organization for Economic Cooperation and Development (OECD) tax classification, however, places property taxes in the indirect tax classification and wealth and death taxes in the direct tax category. John Stuart Mill, the great nineteenth-century economist and reformer, was uncertain about property taxes but seems to have considered them to be direct taxes. The United States Constitution as interpreted considers property taxes to be direct taxes.[3]

DISTINGUISHING DIRECT AND INDIRECT TAXES

The economic usefulness of distinguishing direct and indirect taxes under modern conditions has been questioned but because it is necessary to understand taxation as included in the federal Constitution, the distinction has legal importance. In these days of basic constitutional government, therefore, the legal support acts to buttress the weakening economic support.

In Western Europe the division of taxes into direct and indirect continues to have considerable economic support. In addition, the division is a vital part of the regulations within the General Agreement on Tariffs and Trade (GATT). The participating members of GATT are the industrial non-Communist nations, and the purpose of GATT is to establish operating procedures that will encourage the free flow of international trade. The manner in which taxes are collected and refunded has an important effect on international trade, and therefore GATT has developed tax understandings. The current GATT position relative to direct and indirect taxes is the traditional position developed in Europe in the eighteenth century.

Although the classification of taxes as direct and indirect goes beyond the tax on personal income and the tax on sales to consumers, it is only with regard to these two taxes that the classification is useful. The dichotomy is used in the System of National Accounts (SNA) of the United Nations as a basic concept for treatment of taxes paid in two very different ways and for treating social security contributions separately from other taxes.

The SNA includes in its list of direct taxes regular assessments by public authorities on income from employment, property, entrepreneurship, capital gains, or any other source of income received by individuals, households, enterprises, nonprofit institutions, and others. Indirect taxes are defined by SNA to be those assessed on producers with respect to the production, sale, purchase, or use of goods and services. These indirect taxes are charged to the expenses of production.

Actually, criteria for dividing taxes into direct and indirect do not exist. Nowhere is this conflict more clear and of greater importance than in the allocation of social security payments. The SNA excludes them from both categories (see p. 496).

The problems of distinguishing direct and indirect taxes are so great and the distinction of so little use that the OECD does not use it as a basis for tax allocation. If more were known about tax shifting, a useful method to divide taxes into two categories would be to include as direct all taxes shifted backward, and as indirect all taxes shifted forward.[4]

The U.S. Constitution was interpreted in the famous Pollock cases of the 1890s as prohibiting the federal government from collecting direct taxes, except a property tax allocated on the basis of population.[5] The Sixteenth Amendment, adopted in 1913, expanded the power of the federal government to collect direct taxes. The power is granted in a thirty-word statement:

> The Congress shall have power to lay and collect taxes on incomes, from whatever source derived, without apportionment among the several States, and without regard to any census or enumeration.

The concept of a differentiation between direct and indirect taxes seems to have been clear to those who developed the provisions of the Constitution, but practically no one else dealing with the problem has found this to be the case.

GATT makes the distinction thus: A tax defined as a tax on consumption—an indirect tax—can within the GATT understanding be refunded on exports, and a border tax of an equal amount can be levied on imports. A tax considered to be a direct tax cannot be treated in this manner according to the GATT understandings.

The real importance of the differentiation arises in the area of administration. The amount of tax included in each unit of product or service is much easier to calculate when the tax is a percentage of price than when it is a percentage of wages, profits, or capital. Indirect taxes are therefore easier to use when one contemplates a refund of taxes related to sales. The amount of tax to collect on a particular item or service is also easier to calculate. However, as discussed in the section entitled Value-Added as a State Tax, VAT can be administered as an income tax, and the only major U.S. experience with VAT turned out to be income-based rather than sales-based as had been intended.[6]

CONCLUSION

The differentiation of taxes on the basis of an assumed location of economic burden, or incidence, does not work well in practice. Identification of a tax with a particular article or service, such as a tax based on sales or purchases, is perhaps necessary if tax refunds and special tax assessments are to be made to reach an established goal.

THE CONCEPT OF THE VALUE-ADDED TAX

The theoretical base to which the value-added tax is applied is calculated by adding up the market value provided at each stage of the production and distribution process. This value approximates the payments received by workers, owners, and managers. Therefore, the base of VAT could also be calculated by adding together the incomes of the factors of production.

The production aggregate, with some modification, can be calculated in two ways. One way is to add up the total of final sales for consumption plus investment and government purchases. The second is to calculate the difference between total receipts from all sales and the purchases and rent payments to other firms. This is, of course, the theoretical base to which the VAT rate would be applied.

Every shirt or dress you purchase for your personal use, every machine purchased by business, and every brick purchased by government includes the costs of taxes (government), machines and buildings (investment or saving), interest, rents, profits, and wages. All interest, rent, profit, and wage receipts of individuals are used to spend, pay taxes, or save.

Someone must make purchases in order for someone else to produce consumer goods. Someone must save in order for productive capital to be financed. Someone must pay taxes in order to finance government services. This is the great circle of income and spending. The income aggregate, gross national income (GNI), has not, however, become such a popular term as has the spending aggregate, GNP.

Figure 1 and Table 1 should make the interrelationships in our national income accounts clearer. Figure 1 shows that VAT can be applied to a base consisting of an income aggregate as well as a spending or product aggregate. Table 1 demonstrates that the effect on disposable income available for consumption is the same whether indirect (value-added) or direct (personal income) taxes are used.

Figure 1

National Income Accounts

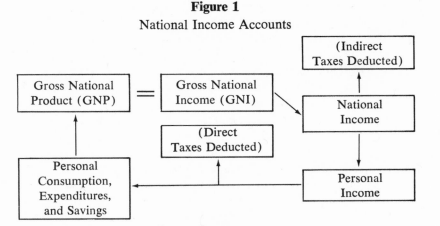

Table 1

Spendable Income Effect of Indirect and Direct Taxes

Item	With Indirect Tax (VAT)	With Direct Tax (personal income tax)
GNP	$1,000	$1,000
Indirect Tax	200	—
National Income	800	1,000
Direct Tax	—	200
Disposable Income	800	800

When VAT is classified as an indirect tax it is collected by the subtractive method. This procedure is used by all the Western European nations using VAT. In a modified form it was the procedure used in Michigan in the administration of the Business Activities Tax, and all the people involved with BAT reported no administrative problems. Because the subtractive procedure has worked, it is explained first.

THE SUBTRACTIVE PROCEDURE

The subtractive procedure basically works with the GNP side of the national income accounts. The base to which the VAT rate is applied is developed out of the gross sales data of firms.

Figure 1 and Table 2 give a convenient summary of the application of the subtractive method. The numbers used are for illustrative purposes. Under the basic subtractive method, which is also called the subtractive/accounts or calculation method, the VAT rate is applied to the difference between sales and purchases. A refined version of the subtractive method called the subtractive/tax credit method is used almost exclusively in actual practice. The basic subtractive method is very simple and appropriate when all sales are subject to VAT and a single uniform rate is used. Under these conditions the subtractive/accounts procedure is preferred over the subtractive/tax credit method because (1) it does not require listing the amount of the VAT separately on each invoice and (2) the amount of the tax being paid by the purchaser is not highlighted; it is buried in the price.

The use of the subtractive/accounts method means that the government has given up the self-policing aspect of the subtractive/tax credit method. The unusual self-policing aspects of VAT extend through all stages of production and sale down to the ultimate consumer of the product or service. Each purchaser or renter of a product or service who is subject to the VAT has an interest in making certain that the full amount of VAT has been paid by the seller, because this total is deductible from the VAT liability of the purchaser. Of course, this self-enforcement feature of VAT is lost when the subtractive/accounts method is used.

The subtractive/accounts procedure is more appropriate for use by a nation with a strong tax-paying tradition. The VAT rate should be low—1 or maybe as high as 3 percent if the subtractive/accounts method is used. This approximates the way the Committee for Economic Development (CED) envisaged the condition likely to exist if the VAT is introduced in the United States. Therefore, the subtractive/accounts

Table 2

Subtractive Procedure for Administration of VAT

Total sales of goods and services	$1,000,000
Plus (+)	
Total interest, dividends, rents, and royalties received	200,000
Inventory expansion	50,000
Total	$1,250,000 (A)
Less (−)	
All other taxes	$ 200,000
Purchases of materials, services, and power from other firms on which VAT has been paid	300,000
Dividends, interest, rents, and royalties paid to other firms subject to VAT	100,000
Inventory reduction	—
Purchases of capital goods on which VAT has been paid	200,000
Total	$ 800,000 (B)

Tax base = A − B
Tax base = $1,250,000 − $800,000
Tax base = $450,000 of value added.
$450,000 x 10% (VAT rate) = $45,000 VAT tax due and payable

rather than the subtractive/tax credit procedure would, under these conditions, be the rational choice for America.

The subtractive/accounts method is demonstrated by the following exhibit of the value-added tax liability at the retail stage.

		1% VAT
Sales	$10,000	—
Less Purchases	2,000	—
Value Added	$ 8,000	$80

This procedure includes in the base to which the VAT is applied all receipts that are not included in the definition of purchases. A broad definition of purchases reduces the value-added tax that must be paid. For example, if interest paid is considered to be the purchase of loan capital and rent paid is considered the purchase of quarters, and taxes paid are considered the purchase of government services, and dividends paid are considered the purchase of equity capital, the VAT base is set at about the minimum level. If this procedure is used, a broad definition of sales is also justified. The interest and dividends received would be sales of capital, and imputed and actual rents received would also be a portion of the sales total. The sales made to government would be included in the total in the same manner as sales to other members of the private sector.

Although financial institutions are generally exempt from VAT, the broad-based approach outlined above would logically include them. A commercial bank would include as sales all interest received and as purchases all interest paid to business subject to VAT. Under this procedure, the interest paid to individuals would be subject to VAT just as retail purchases are.

This approach to VAT is very attractive.[7]

THE ADDITIVE PROCEDURE

The value added is the difference between the selling price and the amount paid to other business firms for supplies and the like. The difference all goes somewhere. It goes to the factors of production—land, labor, and capital—and is called rent, profits, wages, and interest.

One more item accounts for a varying portion of value added, and that is taxes paid. These would include property and excise taxes, but not corporate profit taxes—if profits were included before tax payments, as they should be. When profits are treated in this way, the corporate profits tax is treated more unfavorably than other taxes.

Taxes other than the VAT itself become a portion of the base to which the VAT rate is applied under the subtractive method. This could be true under the additive approach, but generally it has not been assumed to be the case. Therefore, the VAT base to which the rate would be applied would be somewhat less under the additive method.

The additive procedure utilizes the income side of the national income accounts. The amounts (see Table 3) are rigged in the additive approach to give the same VAT base as in the subtractive.

THE NET TURNOVER TAX

The phrase *net turnover tax* is sometimes used in referring to VAT. The title is appropriate when the subtractive procedure of administering VAT is used. The goal of VAT is to collect revenues at the various stages of production and distribution while avoiding placing a heavier tax on one of two goods of equal value. The subtractive procedure is

Table 3
Additive Procedure for Administration of VAT

Employee payroll	$500,000
Total profits from operation	100,000
Net interest	50,000
Total	$650,000
Less (−)	
Net rents and royalties	$200,000
Total value added	$450,000

Figure 2
How Taxable Value Is Added During the Production Process

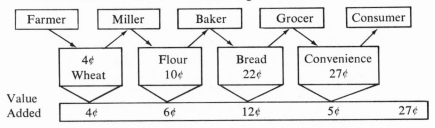

used to apply VAT to spending and to keep the tax burden the same on goods passing through many stages and those passing through only a few. Because it subtracts from sales the amount of purchases from other businesses, the subtractive procedure makes VAT a net turnover tax.

Figure 2 is a common approach that has been used to illustrate the way VAT is applied step by step through the production process. A major weakness of the simplification is its assumption that all taxes collected result in higher prices and none of the amounts collected are financed with lower payments to resource owners of various kinds, from providers of land to those who furnish capital and labor.

THE TAX ON TAX APPROACH

Through the years the French have used the "tax on tax" method of VAT administration. In this approach, the rate is *tax inclusive*. On the other hand, when the tax on tax method is not used, the rate is *tax exclusive*.

The formula used to convert a legislated rate to an effective rate, when the tax is applied to price including tax (that is, when it is tax inclusive) is

$$\frac{T}{100 - T}$$

where T is the legislated rate. Under the former French legislated VAT rate of 20 percent, the formula was

$$\frac{20}{100 - 20} = \frac{.20}{.80} = 25 \text{ percent}$$

When the legislated basic French rate for VAT was 16⅔ percent, the formula was

$$\frac{16⅔}{100 - 16⅔} = \frac{.1667}{.8333} = 20 \text{ percent}$$

The effective rate was therefore 20 percent. The legislated rate of 6 percent becomes a 6.3830 percent effective rate and a legislated 10 percent rate becomes an 11.1111 percent.

Despite the fact that this procedure levies the VAT rate on a price base including VAT, it does not result in a gross turnover tax or a tax that discourages decentralized business ownership. These undesirable qualities are avoided because the tax paid is deductible from the tax due; that is, the application of the rate to a larger base increases *deduction physique* by the same portion of the total at all levels of economic activity.

ZERO RATING

Goods and services are given a zero rating to exempt them entirely from VAT under the subtractive approach. This is done by including the business under VAT, but assessing a zero rate. VAT is not assessed on sales, but all VAT included in prices paid is refunded just as when sales are subject to VAT. If $800 of VAT is paid on $4,000 of purchases, this amount is refunded in its entirety while no VAT is due on sales.[8]

Zero rating under the additive approach would require a refund of an amount calculated by applying the VAT rate to all purchases from businesses subject to VAT. The determination of this amount would be somewhat less definite than under the subtractive approach. Under the additive approach, the exact amount paid by the zero rate business on purchases made would not be set down on an invoice held by the zero-rated firm. This shortcoming would not be a serious problem.

The real difference between zero rating under the subtractive and additive approaches arises from a different incidence assumption that is made between a transactions tax and a tax on payments to the factors of production. It is generally felt that a tax on a sale is passed forward to the purchaser, while a tax on income is not, so the burden rests on the income receiver. Therefore, zero rating under the additive approach, and the resulting payment to zero-rated firms of VAT paid by suppliers, will be seen as more of a subsidy than when done under the subtractive approach.

VAT EXEMPTIONS IN EUROPE

As mentioned earlier, the income tax has become so complicated that even people with modest incomes seek professional help in preparing returns. It is said that no one really understands all the ins and outs of the corporate profits tax. Many of its complications arise from exemptions and special treatments of one sort or another.

In theory, the value-added tax is as simple as any major tax could be in our complicated world; in practice, it is more complex. The Germans have decided to use two rates—one twice as great as the other. The lower rate, for example, applies to the charges for the transport of passengers by railway (excluding mountain railways) and trolley bus and licensed public transport by motor vehicle or taxi (1) within a community or (2) if the transportation distance does not exceed fifty kilometers.[9]

One doesn't need much imagination to visualize the airline people pushing for equal treatment and the mountain railway lobby going to work to rectify an injustice.

HOW TO INCLUDE THE BANKS

Financial institutions, including banks, are exempt from the VAT as used in Europe. The reason arises from the historical treatment of banks relative to taxation plus special problems that exist in the taxation of financial institutions.

Actually, the inclusion of banks under VAT does not require major adjustments. If VAT is administered using the additive procedure, the VAT base of a bank would first include wages and profits, as for any other business. To that total can be added interest and rent paid. In doing this, one assumes that these are payments to the factors of production just like wages and profits.[10]

The use of the additive approach to banks does not cause difficult administrative problems if the additive approach is used generally. All interest and dividends received by a business from another business are deducted after the VAT gross base has been calculated. The amount remaining becomes the base to which the VAT rate is applied.

If the subtractive approach were used (as mentioned on p. 32), all interest received by a financial institution would be considered to be a sale to be included in the VAT base. Interest received would be deductible only if it were included in the VAT base of another financial institution. Interest paid by other businesses would be considered to be purchases that could be deducted if VAT at some stage had been paid. The same approach would apply to rent payments and receipts.

When banks are exempt from VAT, they cannot take credit for VAT paid on purchases or directly add the VAT paid onto their charges. Therefore, even when exempt, the financial community would be paying some VAT.

THE NEUTRAL TAX

A tax is truly neutral when all economic decisions are unaffected by collecting the tax. On the face of it, this makes tax neutrality impossible. Some taxes, however, are more neutral than others.

VAT is favored by those who believe that a neutral tax is good, because then decisions to spend, earn, invest, hire, fire, and borrow are not determined by tax advantages or disadvantages. Under VAT the value as measured by selling price is taxed at the same rate whether it was caused by inflation or by efficiency, whether the money goes into the pockets of a rich capitalist or an average worker. The tax does not depend on how value was created, who created it, or who pocketed it.

Aims of government beyond taking a certain percent of all value added as measured by sales are not achieved through VAT. Although the neutrality of VAT is favored, policy-makers have found it difficult to treat value created in food or included in exports, for example, the same as they treat other created values. Zero rate VAT is universally applied to exports, and lower rates, exemption, or zero rates to food.

It has been argued that if VAT were truly general, including government as well as the private sector, it would be equivalent to a general price increase by the amount of the tax. Therefore, why not just have an unbalanced budget financed with money from central bank credit instead of collecting VAT?

If one takes this position, he must also regard inflation as a neutral tax. The economic consequences of this choice include at least one that cannot be swept under the rug. Inflation directly provides revenue to spend only in the year central bank credit is increased. VAT, on the other hand, provides governments with spending money not only in the year of the price increase but in every year thereafter. The use of VAT, therefore, leads toward a stability that is not directly included in a policy of deficits and inflation.

VAT AND LAND RENTS

The value added to a product or service as it passes through the stages toward becoming a finished commodity includes the price that must be paid to use a certain amount of land and air space and the price required for the right to utilize certain natural resources. The amount paid for the right to remove oil from the ground or to occupy a certain space for raising wheat or to build a house or an office building is *economic rent*. This payment is a cost of production that could be largely funneled into the public treasury through the levy of a tax sufficiently high to remove the economic rents arising from control over flat land, air space, and natural resources.[11] Under either procedure, the cost involved becomes a portion of price and therefore a part of the VAT base under the subtractive method, whether consumption or income is used to calculate value-added tax paying liability.

BUSINESS JUSTICE

VAT is a tax whose base is the full monetary income earned or the full monetary receipts from sale for final use. It does not tax a business organized in one way more heavily than one organized in a different fashion, as does the corporate profits tax. Also, VAT taxes production, sales, or income on a gross basis where it occurs and therefore avoids the need for high rates to produce substantial revenues and avoids the problem inherent in the income tax of determining geographic location of the source of the tax base.

The logic and the basic justice of VAT arise from its two fundamental assumptions: (1) that all economic activity for the market, without exception, requires government assistance and (2) that it is not possible or desirable to assess these costs at each point as they arise. Based on this logic, the best way to tax is to levy a flat-rate tax on value or gross income as it is added and earned. Because it is economic value that is being taxed, the marketplace test of a sale is required before the taxable value can be set under the subtractive method. This is approximately the situation under additive procedure. Therefore, it is the sale that provides the tax base. Under the modified subtractive procedure, the tax payable by any particular firm is reduced by the VAT included on the invoices of its purchases and therefore purchases from those not paying a VAT do not reduce VAT payable. Again, this is the procedure actually used by the industrial nations of Europe.

CONCLUSION

The value-added tax is paid as sales are made and income earned. It includes in its base government costs as these costs affect prices and incomes. The tax has characteristics that encourage a broad base, so it is *not* appropriate if one sector of the economy is to be selected for tax favors or tax burdens.

ROOTS OF THE VALUE-ADDED TAX

The roots of the value-added tax and the theoretical support of the concept are American-made. VAT arose from a desire to generate a neutral tax that would provide substantial revenues without reducing the efficiency of the market system. Because the United States was and is the great free-market nation—increasingly so after the fiasco of the 1972–1973 price control efforts—it was very appropriate that the early examining, explaining, and advocating of VAT be American. Germany has always been interested in VAT, but VAT did not attract German tax scholars as it did American ones.

DATA-BASED ECONOMICS

VAT can be traced to American tax discussions after World War I. It was considered as the replacement for special World War I excise and excess profits taxes. The American heritage of VAT is forgotten when VAT is called a "foreign tax." VAT is as American as apple pie.

In addition to the American belief in the desirability of the free market, a second factor could lead one to expect VAT to be considered first by American economists. Economists in the United States originated the whole business of gathering economic statistics. At the turn of the century, as today, economists studying sound economics that dealt with realities found the University of Chicago intellectual climate stimulating. Thorstein Veblen and his students, particularly the brilliant Wesley Claire Mitchell, founder of the National Bureau of Economic Research, developed the statistics that made possible the calculation of GNP.[12] Once the total current production became measurable, its use as the base for a general business tax was a natural development.

It was in the United States that economics ceased to consist of armchair philosophizing and started on the long road to becoming a real social science. One of the results was the development of VAT—that is, a tax on total production, or a tax that becomes a part of the cost of all consumption. Another was the quantification of expenditure shortfalls that caused depressed economic conditions. In each case, the early American development was grasped and utilized more effectively in Europe than in America.[13]

AMERICAN DEVELOPMENT

VAT has become a principal tax in twelve Western European nations (France, Denmark, Germany, the Netherlands, Belgium, Luxembourg, Norway, Ireland, Italy, Great Britain, Sweden, and Austria). Countercyclical government spending and related economic planning to prevent unemployment through government budgetary policy is fundamental in most Western European nations, but has never been wholeheartedly accepted in this country.[14]

In 1932 and 1933 the Brookings Institution, the prestigious economic research group of Washington, D.C., recommended the adoption of VAT in the states of Alabama and Iowa.[15] In 1964, a little over thirty years later, the institution published the proceedings of a conference entitled *The Role of Direct and Indirect Taxes in the Federal Revenue System*. The conclusion of the conference was that VAT would not be helpful to the United States in developing sound domestic fiscal policy or an improved international economic balance.

Gerhard Colm, a German-trained fiscal expert who became a leading tax specialist in the federal government and the American Planning Association, published an article entitled "The Ideal Tax System" in *Social Research* in 1934. The article described and recommended VAT.[16]

In 1940 Paul Studenski, certainly one of America's most distinguished taxation scholars, concluded that VAT was the ideal business tax. His general philosophical foundation for VAT bears the short title "Cost of Services Variant."[17] He saw VAT to be a neutral tax because wages, rent, interest, and profits (the return to the factors of production—labor, land, capital, and entrepreneurship) each bore the same direct tax burden. He believed that because government services benefited each of the factors of production largely in proportion to income received, the payment of VAT became a collection for government services enjoyed.

Studenski's support of VAT was an expression of a general attitude toward VAT by knowledgeable American students. The early favorable reception of VAT by the tax profession originated in the writings of

T. S. Adams, the father of the 1913 individual income tax legislation. An article of his in the *Quarterly Journal of Economics* supported VAT as the best approach to the taxation of businesses.[18] Adams had previously supported the basic concept of VAT in 1911. This awareness of VAT led to the introduction of Senate Bill 3560 on March 11, 1940, by Senator C. Joseph O'Mahoney. It was a legislative proposal for the introduction of VAT by the federal government.

After the defeat of Japan in World War II, a group of first-class U.S. tax experts was sent to Japan to assist in the development of a democratic Japanese tax system.[19] Headed by Carl S. Shoup of Columbia University, the mission recommended the adoption of VAT by Japan in 1949.[20] In 1950 the Japanese Diet adopted a local government VAT. A variety of circumstances prevented the legislation from being activated, and it was later repealed. A somewhat similar system is currently being used very effectively in Brazil.

In 1953 Michigan adopted a modified VAT and continued to use it successfully through 1967.[21] The tax was re-enacted in 1975 under the title "Single Business Tax." The Business Activities Tax (BAT) was praised by a number of Michigan tax specialists, including A. L. Cornick of the Ford Motor Company and Harvey Brazer of the University of Michigan.

The first American developments took place *before* the French introduced their VAT in 1954. The French VAT is called *taxe sur la valeur ajoutée* (TVA). The French, in the introduction of the TVA, were taking an American and German tax idea based upon modern quantification of production and using it to meet a serious French fiscal crisis.[22] TVA was adopted by France at first as a limited reform of a badly functioning tax system. Later it became the basic characteristic of the French fiscal policy.

The first French economic writer to seriously evaluate TVA was Maurice Lauré in 1952.[23] As early as 1921 Wilhelm von Siemens of the great German steel family wrote of the desirability of VAT.[24] And by 1952 VAT had been a portion of the business taxation bibliography in American university courses in public finance for at least twelve years.

FRENCH ORIGINS

The French general consumption or turnover tax grew quickly out of a luxury tax introduced in 1917 in the form of a sales stamp, part of the highly organized French stamp duty system.[25] As time went on, it was concluded from observation that this general turnover tax rested too lightly on "industrial and business services included in processing and distribution as such."[26] The result was the introduction of a single-stage production tax (*taxe à la production*) in 1936. This production tax used value added as its base and tended to cover more and more production. Between 1953 and 1955 (April 10, 1954, is the official date) the French production tax became TVA, a genuine value-added tax, albeit with quite a few exemptions, including retailing. In 1966 retailing was added. The French originators of TVA in 1954 saw it as part of a philosophy of an economic development plan.[27]

CURRENT ATTITUDE IN THE UNITED STATES

There is no doubt that the concept of VAT grew out of the American economic and business environment. America is the land of economic data and the land of competitive free private enterprise. The prime economic aggregate GNP is calculated by adding up the value of effort at each stage of production. This is also the way the base of VAT is calculated. VAT treats all productive economic activity alike. It does not dictate the use of savings and does not treat the profits of success harshly. VAT does not attempt to favor one business approach over another. It is well suited to an environment of competitive private enterprisers.

The fact that VAT is a native American product and not a foreign import should reduce some illogical opposition to this tax, which has been largely rejected in America and received with such enthusiasm in Western Europe.[28]

The degree of American rejection of VAT varies, as would be expected. In the September 1970 report of the President's Task Force on Business Taxation two of the fifteen members filed a minority report favoring immediate adoption of the VAT. The thirteen other members recommended "that should the need ever arise for substantial additional Federal revenue, the government should turn to the value-added tax or some other form of indirect taxation rather than to an increase in rates of the corporate or personal income tax."[29] The committee did not consider financing of an expanded medical and social security program through use of VAT.

In 1971 the international economic shortcoming of the American approach to business taxation was recognized in congressional legislation establishing the Domestic International Sales Corporation (DISC). This legislation reduces somewhat the taxes carried by American exports, taking one step toward giving U.S. exporters the tax refund assistance enjoyed by Europeans under VAT. However, it has been costly and annual revenue losses of over $1 billion have developed.

A 1973 study of VAT by the Advisory Commission on Intergovernmental Relations (ACIR) concluded that the tax's negative characteristics outweighed its potential for usefulness. In the same year two studies of the International Monetary Fund (IMF) reported favorably on the use of VAT by developing nations.[30]

CONCLUSION

The value-added tax is not a new idea. It developed along with the national income accounts and the realization that government was going to be an important element in the day-to-day affairs of nations. VAT did not receive active political support until the European Economic Community member states adopted it as a basic tax after observing its success in France.

COMMON MARKET'S DEVELOPMENT OF VAT

Never before have a tax study and recommendations had the impact of the EC tax study of 1963. The study group was headed by Fritz Neumark and the reported findings and recommendations provided the basic framework for the introduction of VAT throughout Western Europe and its adoption as a major tax by all EC member states.

THE NEUMARK REPORT

In 1963 the Fiscal and Financial Committee (FFC) on Tax Harmonization in the Common Market issued a report that was destined to be the blueprint for the development of the value-added tax.[31] Carl S. Shoup was included on the committee even though he was not from a member state.

By "tax harmonization" the FFC meant a gradual development of uniform tax practices in the countries of the European Economic Community. The Treaty of Rome that set up the Common Market required action on the tax front. Although FFC considered the entire panorama of taxes in use, it zeroed in on Germany's cascade turnover tax.

The cascade turnover tax was seen to be no match for the French value-added tax. No one could think of a reason why France should give up her advantage, so everyone agreed to adopt the French method as the way to even things up. Today, fourteen years later, the United States is in about the same position relative to the EC as Germany was to France in 1963.[32]

THE COMMON MARKET DECISION

The Neumark Report of 1963 turned out to be the basic guide for the development of tax harmonization among the member states of the European Community. The report pointed out that tax harmonization would strengthen the EC, and suggested that it be initiated in the area of indirect taxation. A careful analysis of the arguments developed in the report as well as the procedures set down for reaching determined goals is very helpful to one interested in understanding the economic impact of taxes in the real world of international economic interaction.

The Neumark Report was directed to a group of nations that was rapidly approaching a complete customs union and that individually made major use of the turnover tax as a source of national revenue. Its applicability to the choices that must be made by the United States, therefore, is surely limited. Nevertheless, as the following analysis demonstrates, the report provides a very useful base for the consideration of (1) the economics of tax harmonization among nations; (2) the economic effect of border taxes and the relationship of this effect to reduced international restrictions of trade and capital; and (3) the potential for growth of indirect taxation through introduction of the value-added tax.

The general aim of EC financial policy as it is included in fiscal policy is to eliminate differences in tax and expenditure policies "which lead enterprises, and, consequently, capital, labor and business to choose to establish in locations other than that which would be naturally or technically the most favorable. Among other things, this includes the elimination of tax havens as well as of tax discrimination based on nationality and often fiscal domicile."[33]

The analysis of the tax collection and expenditure totals of the EC member states concludes that they are sufficiently similar, at least, in the aggregate, that they do not present insurmountable obstacles to the development of a common market.[34] The FFC emphasizes, however, that "in ascertaining possible dislocations of competition which may result in trade between States from public-finance measures, one must take into consideration ... the additional effects ... resulting from the use of tax revenues ..."[35] The kinds of state expenditures most influential in improving the competitive position of a nation are considered to be those made for research and for stimulating exports.[36]

The FFC concludes that although "the total amount of taxes is approximately the same in two countries, a structural difference in fiscal systems ... can ... influence the competitive conditions ..."[37] Nevertheless, some structural tax differences must be accepted because they are deeply rooted in the social or economic habits of the country. The report concludes that inability to remove these structural differences in the way the tax revenues of the different member states are raised need not prevent the establishment of tax conditions that do not materially affect competition. The competitive impact of the disparities in the structures of taxes in different countries could be greatly relieved "if one were to retain the principle of the country of destination . . ."[38] Basically, this means that all taxes on goods exported would be levied by the country of import and that the exporting country would exempt exports of all taxes. A major goal of FFC, however, is the elimination of fiscal frontiers, and this requires abandonment of the principle of the country of destination.

FISCAL FRONTIERS

The FFC kept the turnover tax in the foreground of its discussion of tax harmonization because it was considered the tax having the greatest "direct influence on price formation and therefore on competition."[39] The first basic decision was that all member states having the "multistage gross turnover taxes" should abolish them.[40] Abolition was recommended for the stock reasons that the tax was believed to distort domestic commerce and artificially promote concentration of enterprise. The principal shortcoming in terms of international competition was that exact overall burden could not be calculated and therefore the amount of countervailing levies or refunds was uncertain.[41]

THE PRINCIPLE OF DESTINATION AND ORIGIN

Although the FFC wants to eliminate fiscal frontiers, the fiscal frontier must continue to exist as long as taxes—particularly either net or gross turnover taxes—are levied on the basis of the country of destination rather than the country of origin. When these taxes are levied on the basis of country of destination, neither country is assumed to be particularly concerned with the rate of the tax because the rebate of the tax on exports and the levy of a compensating tax on imports eliminates any direct impact of rate differences. When the net or gross turnover tax is levied on the basis of country of origin, as are income taxes under the present rules of the General Agreement on Tariffs and Trade, then the goods taxed and the rates become important, because rebates on exports and compensatory levies on imports are abolished and the relative international competitive position is directly affected. In addition, when the net or gross turnover taxes are levied on the basis of country of origin, fiscal frontiers can be abolished and a major goal of EC, tax harmonization, can be accomplished. Before establishing the country of origin as the basis for turnover taxes, relatively uniform rates and coverage of turnover taxes must be adopted by each of the EC member states. The FFC recognizes this and recommends the use of a uniform net turnover tax "with the same or almost the same rates."[42] The recommendations on coverage are less precise, and as a result it has not been possible to implement the plan to assess a one percent VAT to support EC, and contributions continue to be made as a percent of GNP.

The principles in the Neumark Report contain an important lesson for U.S. taxation policy-makers. The lesson was learned by the EC, and tax action toward uniform value-added tax rates between member states of the EC is now nearly complete. The lesson was also learned by a number of nations of the European Free Trade Association (EFTA)— Sweden, Norway, and Austria—which have adopted value-added taxes similar to those in use by EC member states.

The lesson is that the United States cannot expect the initiation of the country-of-origin approach in the treatment of indirect taxes, and therefore the abolition of border taxes and tax refunds to exporters, until it also puts into effect a value-added tax with rates and coverage similar to those existing in Europe.[43]

CONCLUSION

Our tax people tend to fight the action that the Neumark recommendations require. The continuation of the status quo is supported by pointing out that exports are only 10 percent or so of our gross national product even under the unusual foreign trade conditions of 1975. Therefore, to have a tax policy determined by international trade considerations would mean a tax situation in which the tail was wagging the dog. This would not be the situation, of course.

If the development in the United States roughly corresponded to the situation existing and evolving in the nations of EC and EFTA, then only a portion of tax policy is set by the indirect tax harmonization recommendations of the Neumark Report. These nations continue to have corporate and personal income taxes. They continue to tax estates, cigarettes, automobiles, and alcoholic beverages, and to levy payroll taxes. They also, however, find it advisable to legislate in the tax field to utilize the basic lesson taught by the Neumark Report. In the United States we are acting as though the tail is not even a part of the dog. The international trade impacts of our tax policy are sufficiently important to justify their inclusion in domestic tax legislation decisions.[44] As a matter of fact, international tax considerations come up year after year as an important portion of Congressional tax-related legislative proposals.

START-UP PROBLEMS AND OPPORTUNITIES

The EC as it has moved to implement the recommendations of the Newmark Report has not found everything to be sweetness and light. One by one each problem has been solved and the final step, a VAT so uniform among the member states that it can be used to finance EC itself, is about to be taken. The harmonization of the major general indirect tax used by EC member states is a major success.

EC MEMBER STATES

The French experience with a general value-added tax goes back to 1954. The German tax began on January 1, 1968. And VAT became effective in Italy and Great Britain in 1973.

In all these nations the value-added tax was introduced into a tax system that included a substantial national excise tax system. The United States, of course, does not make use of a general tax on transactions. Therefore, the experiences and problems of these nations and the EC directives that are aimed at nations using a national excise tax are only indirectly applicable to the problems the United States would encounter through introduction of VAT. Nevertheless, the procedures used and the problems encountered by these major international commercial competitors suggest some answers to questions that arise when one considers the introduction of a value-added tax into the U.S. national tax system. The comparative approach makes concrete, and therefore much more understandable, what is involved in the use of a national value-added tax in the United States.

The basic EC action that provided for the use of VAT by all member states took the form of two directives issued on February 9, 1967, by the Council of Ministers. The first directive provided for the replacement of existing cumulative turnover taxes with a common value-added tax—that is, a net turnover tax—and established the general basis for VAT.

In the first directive the latest date set for a common VAT was January 1, 1970. Of course, the admission of new nations into EC was not included in the timetable, but Italy, an original EC nation, was three years late. Each member state was required to accept responsibility for passing appropriate legislation sufficiently early to meet this deadline.

This directive also required the EC commission by the end of 1968 to set before the council the date and the procedures to be used to achieve the basic aim of eliminating all border taxes levied on imports and all tax drawbacks on exports. If possible, the council was to make its decision on these final matters relative to harmonization of turnover taxes before January 1, 1970.[45] All customs duties on manufactured goods moving between member states were to be removed in 1968. This deadline was met.

The second directive concerned methods for applying the common VAT system. The directive envisaged a very broadly based tax, covering everything down to and including retailing and also covering service transactions.[46]

REMOVAL OF FISCAL FRONTIERS

The ultimate goal of EC tax harmonization relative to VAT is the removal of the member state fiscal frontiers. When this is accomplished, VAT rebates will no longer be given to exporters or to customers in EC member states. It will also result in the elimination of border taxes on imports that are equal to the domestic VAT rate.

When refunds and border taxes are no longer part of the use of the value-added tax by EC member states, VAT will have become a production tax within EC and a consumption tax outside EC. The change required to make a consumption tax a production tax is that the tax not be refunded on exports and not be levied as a border tax on imports.[47]

GREAT BRITAIN

Before the value-added tax was adopted by Great Britain, the National Economic Development Office prepared an excellent study entitled *VAT*.[48] Looking at a portion of this study and applying the same approach to the U.S. tax system provides useful understanding of what is involved in the introduction of VAT into a productive tax system based fundamentally on the concept of ability to pay.

In Britain the opinions of a sampling of the business community showed that they could see little reason for going to a VAT unless it brought with it a simplification of British taxes. British businessmen, like American ones, are finding their tax system entirely too complicated. In Britain a series of new business taxes had been introduced as fiscal crises developed—a short-term capital gains tax in 1962, taxation of company capital gains like income in 1965 and a selected employees tax (SET) in 1966.

A similar situation had arisen in the United States with the foreign portfolio investment tax (1963), the Subpart F and Section 482 of the *Internal Revenue Code* (1962) that tighten restrictions on allocation of profits from international activities, the Domestic International Sales Corporation (1972) that provides corporate tax reductions on earnings from exports, and the reintroduction of the tax credit on investments (1971).

The VAT in Britain is regarded as a new tax to replace a number of taxes, including SET, the purchase tax, and some excises, and to make possible the granting of greater freedom in calculating taxable corporate profits.[49] It is considered to provide the potential for a giant step toward greater tax simplification. Michigan has highlighted this same advantage in readopting a VAT type tax.

THE UNITED STATES

In the United States, where national indirect taxes consist of only a few special excises, the repeal of all indirect taxes except the tobacco, alcohol, and gasoline (TAG) group would absorb less than 10 percent of the collections of a 10 percent VAT. This leads to the possibility of using a national American VAT to finance on a grand basis federal government revenue-sharing with state and local governments, while also reducing federal income taxes.

We could follow the example of Denmark, which took advantage of the introduction of VAT to make major shifts in its tax system. Denmark cut the income taxes on receivers of low income, introduced a withholding income tax system, established higher allowances for those with low incomes, and abolished its wholesale single-stage sales tax.[50]

In the United States a 10 percent broad-based VAT could finance a liberal revenue-sharing program related to the retail sales tax, and have enough funds remaining to reduce corporate income taxes by 50 percent and eliminate from the federal income tax all taxpayers with gross incomes below $15,300 a year. (About 60 percent of persons who currently pay federal income tax would be free of the individual income tax, and would only be paying the social security taxes on their wage income.)

ADMINISTERING VAT IN THE EC

Because VAT (as used in Europe) is collected at each stage of production, those who are about to introduce VAT have occasionally expressed strong fears of administrative difficulties. Experience has not justified these fears. France, with the most complicated of all VATs in effect, has been able to administer the tax with the personnel who were released when small excises were repealed upon introduction of VAT.[51] The changeover from the German turnover tax to VAT was remarkably smooth.[52]

Denmark has been able to retain a single rate and therefore has not found it necessary to use complicated forms. Figure 3 is a translated copy of the administrative VAT form used by Denmark. What could be simpler?

Although VAT evasion is reported in France and Italy, it remains the tax most likely to be administered as the law provides. "The highest-level tax officials of the Danish Ministry of Finance are emphatic in their conclusion that the present value-added tax is far easier to administer than was the wholesale tax. . . ."[53]

THE UNAMBIGUOUS TAX

The nefarious purposes of taxes are known and guessed, but there is also the socially necessary business of financing services needed by society. A tax on net income rests only on the efficient, the lucky, or the monopolistic. A tax on capital stock varies among industries and companies without any real reason. A corporate profits tax is paid only by corporations and a retail sales tax only by those who can't get it "wholesale." The rates of these taxes and their titles fail to demonstrate the relative tax burdens carried by different products and businesses. Different rates of capital turnover and different degrees of vertical integration change the ways the ambiguous taxes rest on industry.

The value-added tax uses a base that can be compared between partnerships and corporations, between different industries and between government jurisdictions.

Whether or not businesses should be used as tax collectors can be argued ad infinitum. However, if businesses are to collect taxes, then a tax that doesn't play favorites is certainly the best kind. VAT uses a base that is commensurable between firms and businesses organized in very different ways and carrying out very different activities. Actually, the VAT base provides a good denominator for any studies that might be made of tax payment ratios.

CONCLUSION

The EC member states and Western Europe have found the movement to VAT easier than they had expected.[54] This has been partially

Figure 3
Danish VAT Form

Value Added Tax
TAX ACCOUNTING

| Date | 1 Purchase price Including VAT | Purchases | | 4 Sales price | Sales | | Comments |
| | | Tax Credit | | | 5 Tax payable | 6 VAT deductible on exports | |
		2 Domestic purchases	3 on own imports				

Value Added Tax
DECLARATION   LETTER

Taxable Period

Kroner (rounded)	Specification
	Tax payable
	Tax deductible
	Tax liable

Official
Paid

194

To
Tax Service
Postbox 297

Copenhagen V

. . . .
Signature

Space reserved

due to careful planning, but in addition VAT has proven to be a way to eliminate a number of tax complications that had previously been considered necessary to meet basic revenue requirements.

NATIONAL INCOME ACCOUNTS AND THE VAT BASE

Personal expenditures for goods and services include all costs of production and distribution, including taxes. This total, as a VAT base, avoids the double counting involved in adding raw materials and capital costs to consumer goods totals, while it includes taxes as a portion of the total of the taxable base. Therefore, the personal consumption expenditure totals, as reported in the national income accounts, provide a fairly good idea of the base available to a VAT adopted by the federal government.[55]

Table 4 shows that about one-fifth of total consumer expenditures consists of food and tobacco. These items must remain in the base if VAT is going to provide large revenues with low rates. A $246 billion difference between the liberal exemption total and the limited exemption total arises largely from the exclusion of food other than purchased meals in the liberal exemption example. These data show that each 1 percent VAT rate would provide between $6 and $8 billion in revenues.

The national income accounts that provide the data used in Table 4 also include data of government purchases of goods and include a system of tax burden allocation. The accounts show that purchases by government are made out of tax payments and borrowed funds; the personal income total of the national income accounts is calculated before the personal income taxes and payroll taxes paid by employees and the self-employed have been deducted. Taxes that have been deducted before personal income is calculated include indirect taxes, corporate income taxes, and social security taxes paid by the firm.

Table 5 provides a summary of government purchases of goods in 1973. Services that do not include the payment of wages and salaries to government employees are nearly one-half of the total. The remainder of the $264.1 billion of federal government expenditures and net state and local government expenditures of $143.9 billion go to meet such payments as social security and the salaries of government workers.

The goods purchased by government are largely consumption goods and are appropriately added to the total of consumer goods purchased. The services provided by government through its employees directly serving as policemen, soldiers, teachers, and so on are not purchased through the price system. However, all government spending must be included in prices of goods and services through the price system, for

Table 4

Estimated Base of Value-Added Tax at 1973 Levels of Consumption

	Personal Consumption Expenditures (Billions)	Estimated Tax Base	
		Limited Exemptions (Billions)	Liberal Exemptions (Billions)
Food and Tobacco	$178.7	$175.0[a]	$51.3[b]
Clothing, Accessories, and Jewelry	81.3	81.2	81.2
Personal Care	12.3	9.7	9.7
Housing	116.4	57.3[c]	57.3[c]
Household Operation	117.5	112.3[d]	79.6[e]
Medical Care	62.7	42.6	—
Personal Business	45.2	16.5[f]	10.4[g]
Transportation	109.2	107.5[h]	107.5[h]
Recreation	52.3	51.3[i]	51.3[i]
Private Education and Research	12.2	—	—
Religious and Welfare Activities	10.8	—	—
Foreign Travel and Other, Net	5.6	3.3[j]	3.3[j]
Total	$805.2	$656.7	$451.6
Inflation 20% to 1976	$966.2	$788.0	$541.9

[a]Excludes only food furnished to government and commercial employees and food produced and consumed on farms.

[b]Includes only purchased meals and beverages and tobacco products.

[c]Total of new investment in housing structures.

[d]Excludes only domestic services.

[e]Excludes domestic services and household utilities.

[f]Excludes services furnished without payment by financial intermediaries except life insurance companies and expenses of handling life insurance.

[g]Excludes items in footnote *f* and legal services and funeral and burial expenses.

[h]Excludes bridge, tunnel, ferry, and road tolls, street and electric railway, and local bus.

[i]Excludes admissions to legitimate theaters and opera; admissions to entertainments of nonprofit institutions; clubs and fraternal organizations, except insurance; and parimutuel net receipts.

[j]Excludes foreign travel by U.S. residents and expenditures abroad by U.S. government personnel, but includes expenditures in the United States by foreigners.

SOURCE: U.S. Department of Commerce, *Survey of Current Business,* July 1974, p. 24.

Table 5

Government Purchases of Goods—1973

Type	Amount (Billions)
Durable Goods	$24.5
Nondurable Goods	24.0
Services	45.7
Total	$94.3

SOURCE: U.S. Department of Commerce, *Survey of Current Business,* July 1974, p. 32.

this is fundamentally the *only* income source businesses and individuals can use to make tax payments. Unless income is received—and income is only received through sale of goods and services at a price—taxes in any real sense cannot be collected.

It is also true, as was mentioned above, that raw materials and capital goods can only be purchased if they can be combined into a marketable product. This, of course, means that again selling prices must provide the funds for payment.

The $1,295 billion gross national product for 1973 is reported to be made up of $1,280 billion of final sales and $15 billion of inventory increases. Basically a final sale can only be made to someone with income. All sales except those made to the final consumer are made with the expectation that income from sales will cover the cost of the purchase. The consumer purchaser does not expect to receive funds for repayment from sale of the purchase in its present form, or as a portion of a different product. There is, however, a direct relationship between the cost of purchases for consumption and the price that must be paid to gain control of the production abilities and resources of the final consumer. This circle of sales and purchases makes up the national income accounts.

NATIONAL INCOME ACCOUNTS ADJUSTMENTS

In order to make the final total of consumer expenditures equal the amount consumers spend, the national income accounts make a long series of adjustments. For example, taxes are deducted to provide income for government spending while decreasing personal income. Another large deduction for depreciation is made very early in the accounts. This provides income along with savings, which are deducted later, to finance all expenditures called *private domestic investment.* The effect of these deductions and adjustments is to develop a certain concept of total personal consumption expenditures. If equal amounts of income were not deducted to represent the cost of investment and government in producing goods and services for final consumption, the accounts would show the consumer had unused income —that is, income that was not used to pay taxes, was saved, or was used to purchase consumer goods. If these amounts of income were not deducted, the definition of consumer goods would have to be broadened to include investment and government spending. This, in fact, is the way raw materials are handled. Raw materials are included as consumption, and a special amount is not deducted from income to cover cost of replacement of natural and human resources used up in production. There is, of course, considerable justification for eliminating as separate quantities both private investment and government expenditures and to include them as a type of consumer spending even as raw materials are currently included. If this were done, consumer income and spending in 1973 would be about $1,280 billion rather than some $805 billion.

The decisions that have been made in developing the logic of the national income accounts arise out of the manner in which our economy actually works. In other words, no one is required to reduce personal income to pay for raw materials or human energy used up. Whatever repayment is made is included in price. This brings one to the two big questions: (1) Do the tax and savings deductions reduce funds available for personal consumption spending? or (2) Is the effect merely to increase incomes to compensate for these deductions?

One can't really say from looking at the data. We do know in a general way that consumer prices and incomes increase when taxes are raised. The same thing occurs when investment increases. It is also true that the logic of the situation leads one to suppose that investment and government spending are financed out of prices paid for consumer goods. If this is the case, the portion of GNP that is in addition to consumer expenditures is largely double counting. Under these conditions, expenditures of consumers have had to expand to make funds available to finance investment and government expenditures. Everyone recognizes this is what happens when the price of raw materials or labor subsistence increases. No confusion exists, because it does not result in an increase of the deductions from GNI as is true when the cost of government or investment increases and taxes, depreciation, and savings increase. When gross investment increases, depreciation and/or savings are expanded to cover cost. When government spending expands, taxes and/or savings (savings because some government spending is from borrowed funds) are increased to cover cost. When the cost of raw materials increases, personal consumption expenditures must also increase, but there is not an equal increase in a "raw materials account" as there is in an "investment account" when savings increase or in a "government spending account" when tax payments increase. Therefore, of course, the total increase is in the consumer expenditure total, and it is not hidden by an increase of other accounts as when investment and taxes increase.

CONCLUSION

The 1973 base for a value-added tax in the United States, as demonstrated with national income accounts, is substantial. Because VAT is a portion of the selling price of goods and services purchased by government from the private sector, the base in 1973 approached $750 billion with limited exemptions except in the housing area, and $550 billion with liberal exemptions in housing, personal business, food, and medical care. The application in the United States of the current 15 percent VAT rate that is in effect in Denmark on a broad base would in 1973 have provided revenues of $75 to $100 billion and in 1976 collections would be $85 to $120 billion. Experience in Europe has shown that VAT provides more revenues than originally forecast. For example, this was reported to be true of the British VAT in June 1974.

3

Basic Taxes Used in the United States

The taxation system of the United States consists of six major taxes: (1) the personal (or individual) income tax, (2) the corporate profits (or corporate income) tax, (3) the property (or real estate) tax, (4) the retail sales tax, (5) the payroll (or social security) tax, and (6) the gasoline tax. To a degree, the use of the personal income and corporate profits taxes is concentrated at the federal government level. The property tax is very largely used as a source of local government revenues and is very closely associated with the financing of education. The retail sales tax is largely used to finance state governments. The payroll tax is used nearly entirely by the federal government and is closely associated with the financing of social security. The gasoline tax started as a state tax to finance highway construction and maintenance after the introduction of the automobile. It was used by the federal government to finance the national highway program introduced in the mid–1950s. In 1975 the tax is taking on new dimensions. It is seen as a means to improve both our environment and our balance of international trade. Table 6 provides collection data by level of government of these six major taxes.

U.S. citizens have always been hostile to taxes. The attitude is associated with the deepest roots of national pride and patriotism. After

Table 6
Collections from Six Major U.S. Taxes
(Billions of Dollars)

	Federal Government	State Government	Local Government
Corporate Profits	38.4 (1973)	4.4 (1972)	—
Gasoline	4.0 (1973)	7.2 (1972)	—
Payroll	60.0 (1973)	2.5 (1971)	—
Personal Income	111.0 (1973)	13.4 (1972)	2.3 (1972)
Property	—	1.3 (1972)	41.0 (1972)
Retail Sales	—	17.6 (1972)	4.3 (1972)

SOURCE: *Facts and Figures on Government Finance,* Tax Foundation, 1973; *Federal-State-Local Finances,* Advisory Commission on Intergovernmental Relations 1974, pp. 7, 8.

all, our very existence as a nation is associated with the elimination of taxes and tax collectors.[1]

In mid-1974, it was popular economically and politically to advocate no increase in taxes and a reduction of government expenditures. The serious 1974 inflation was seen by the people of this disposition as having been caused by the government, although government purchases of goods and services as a portion of GNP have been declining since 1968. This trend was reversed in 1975 as a result of the recession.[2]

Government deficits developed support as the recession and the high unemployment level developed in 1975, even though the high interest rates of over 12 percent in 1974 had often been attributed to government deficit financing. Actually, however, between 1973 and 1974, government as a whole, if agency borrowing is excluded, had been a net provider, not a borrower of funds (in 1975 government was a major net borrower).[3] On the other hand, new business and consumer borrowing, other than for housing, had been very high. In addition, large quantities of private savings went abroad to avoid taxes and to enjoy the higher interest rates of the Eurodollar market.

The increase in prices due to the assessment of taxes—particularly indirect taxes—is seen to be regressive and undesirable. At the same time, higher interest rates and prices to pay for elaborate offices and high executive salaries are not seen as being regressive. Also, the current inflation is not associated with these practices of the business community, and the shortage of funds for new small businesses is not often associated with the fact that large corporations distribute as dividends less than 50 percent of their profits.

We are all aware of areas of inadequate government services, from police protection to the cleaning of streets and sidewalks. The lives of most Americans are being stunted by too low a level of government services. However, few people demand higher taxes to remedy the situation.

Many citizens regard all levels of government as inefficient regulators and uninspired performers of services. People ask (and the answer is assumed), "When you are ill, which would you rather have—a private, professional doctor or a government employee?"

It is within this public economy environment that the fiscal system of the United States has developed and functions.

THE CORPORATE PROFITS TAX*

The legitimate principal goal and measurement of corporate efficiency is profit, yet it is profit that is used as the base of the very high rate Corporate Profits Tax (CPT). Efforts to avoid the full impact of the CPT have developed extremely complicated legislation and regulations. Such a wealth of special deals and pitfalls has been created that the oracles of the Internal Revenue Code must be consulted at each business decision and personal investment decision.

The selection of one particular accounting concept as the base to which a high tax rate is applied, has resulted in continued pleas to Congress for places to locate earnings so they won't be counted in taxable profits. The high CPT rates make efforts to reduce taxable corporate profits, even including yachts and three martini lunches, eminently worthwhile. Possible tax savings justify allocation of the very best corporate brain power to this activity.

Someone has said, "If a mad genius were to sit down to develop a method of taxing business that would maximize uneconomic behavior— the outcome would be the American CPT."

*Bears title Corporation Income Tax. This title is misleading as it gives the impression the base of the tax is conceptually the same as that used by the individual income tax.

CPT in 1968 accounted for about one-half as much revenues as the individual income tax. The sharp reduction of profits in 1970, plus some impacts of the new federal tax legislation of 1969, pushed CPT collections in 1970 and 1971 down to about one-third of individual income tax collections, where they continue to be in 1975. State use of CPT has expanded steadily and the collections are about 10 per cent of the federal total.

At the very time when more government spending was appropriate, because the economy was producing at less than capacity, government receipts were falling, making the expansion of government spending more difficult. In 1971, the concept of the full-employment balanced budget was introduced to make a large federal deficit budget politically acceptable. It is a gimmick that has proved to be disastrous.

Our federal tax system is dominated by the individual income tax and the CPT. These two taxes bring in around 85 per cent of total taxes (when the social security payroll tax, itself a type of income tax, is excluded). No other industrial nation approaches this concentration of revenue raising activity on the income and profits of its citizens and businesses—which means, of course, that America's national government largely neglects expenditures, sales and production as tax bases.

The federal revenue system adopts nearly completely the philosophy of taxing on the basis of what one puts into the economy. It fails as completely to tax on the basis of what is taken out of the economy.

DEVELOPMENT OF CPT

This unique American approach to taxation arose out of the 1913 concept of tax justice, the pressures of the Great Depression of the 1930s, and the revenue requirements of arming and supplying our allies while fighting one major war in the Pacific and another in the Atlantic. The Great Depression developed a great bitterness and an anti-business attitude in America. The depression was more severe and longer here than in Western Europe. We didn't spawn a Hitler, but we were well on the way in the person of Huey Long. What we did do was develop the world's harshest corporate profits and capital gains tax. This anti-business and anti-savings revenue system persevered through World War II and all the cold and hot wars since.

The terrible citizen disappointment over business' failure to provide two chickens in every pot when it was calling the tune is now forgotten. Today it is the promises of government that are going unfulfilled and causing citizen disappointment. These changes have not been fully recognized by legislatures, but as they are felt, the love affair of Congress with CPT and the graduated income tax can be expected to cool.[4]

INCIDENCE

The original popularity of the CPT with economists and the unsanctified arose from its supposed incidence, i.e., location of economic burden. The incidence was believed to rest on profits, i.e., the return to equity capital, and not on wages or prices. It was further believed that providers of equity capital, owners of common stock, could not recover the tax payment by charging higher prices or paying lower wages. The whole house of cards was built on a belief the marginal firm—the no-profit and therefore the non-CPT paying firm—set prices and wages. This may have been true in the days before the corporate giants. It is well known to be no longer the case.

Research observation and theoretical developments built on the research findings have demonstrated the CPT is not absorbed, at least in the long run, by equity providers.[5] It has also been demonstrated that prices are set by the most profitable and powerful firms and not by the usually economically weak no-profit operation. The dominant firms of an industry set prices to reach profit margins considered appropriate. The calculation is based on income after CPT and wages have been paid or estimated, and not before.

The marginal firm under this set of circumstances is a very different creature. It is not the hardy price setter. It becomes the firm being protected by an umbrella erected by the high CPT payer. In the long run the high CPT payments of the stronger and more efficient firms cause prices to be set higher than would be the case without the tax. This takes place during the normal business of setting profit targets. This gradual adjustment to a new CPT situation permits weak firms to charge higher prices than they could if the efficient and high profit firms were not subject to CPT. They are able to survive, at least for a while.

Another source of CPT support was a belief it reduced savings. This was associated with the earlier idea that its incidence was on equity capital providers—the last of the big savers. Lower savings was an economic change to be desired in the 1930s with the prevailing 2 percent interest rates and 20 percent unemployment rates.

Excess savings may again become a problem, but this is not the current expectation. The rebuilding of many cities and the investment needs for environment preservation and urban transportation are a few among the many expected savings absorbers this year and down the road as many next years as can be seen. It looks like all the potential savings that can be generated will be needed by a society bombarded continuously by consumption appeals and enjoying continued improvement in the protection of the individual from loss of income and poverty through sickness or old age. One development decreases ability to save and the other the need to save—a one-two punch that could quite effectively keep savings in short supply.

The present system encourages savings by corporations, for undistributed profits avoid the personal income tax. These savings are not available in the open market to be used by the highest bidder. As a result the efficiency of their use must be suspect. Also this relationship encourages actions that reduce competition and lead to corporate giantness.[6]

Even the attitudes of government and business bureaucrats are changing. The government man is much less likely to consider every businessman an exploiter than was true in the 1930s. Also, business leaders are finally beginning to realize the public sector can be productive, and that its guidelines and regulations are needed to avoid sharp practices and to preserve consumer confidence. These new understandings and economic environment changes tend to lower the acceptability of CPT as a revenue raiser. It has lost favor because (1) national savings levels are not in excess, (2) the incidence of CPT is not certain, and (3) its revenue providing instability is seen to have economically destabilizing elements that may outweigh countercyclical benefits.

Another shortcoming is arising from the favors CPT gives to debt financing relative to use of equity. The individual income tax is applied to corporate profits distributed as dividends (both on common and preferred stock) at the same rate as corporate payments of interest. These same dividends, as corporate profits, have often been already taxed at the high CPT tax rate of between 38 and 48 percent. Interest payments, on the other hand, are deductible from corporate profits (a 1974 proposal would treat dividends on preferred stock largely as is interest) before the CPT rate is applied. The effect is to encourage financing with debt capital and to discourage use of equity capital—a situation unsuited to aggressive entrepreneurship and an economy with substantial discretionary spending ability. Also, the push toward debt financing is increased and as a result the danger of a financial crisis is expanded.

To raise the high revenues needed while using the profit and income base nearly exclusively, Congress cannot treat the CPT as withheld individual income taxes on dividends, i.e., integration with the individual income tax. It is also true that the American approach requires a hard nosed definition of capital gains and the application of relatively high rates which were increased in the 1969 federal tax legislation from 25 percent to 35 percent and efforts to reduce the tax rate on assets held a long time failed. The very heavy American reliance on taxes using profits and income as the base prevents generous tax allowances to businesses that invest in identified desirable areas, e.g., in pollution control facilities and in geographical areas where unemployment is high.

Finally, the American love affair with CPT makes it very difficult to encourage the return of foreign earned profits of American multinational corporations. There exists a very strong Treasury belief that these profits should be taxed at at least as high a rate as domestic profits. This usually requires the payment of substantial CPT and income taxes when earnings are returned home. The homecoming tax welcome is not exactly stimulating, and re-investment abroad is encouraged.

This same profit tax rate situation encourages export of domestic American savings for investment in foreign countries. The effect is reduced multiplier impact on the American economy from investment of savings arising from domestic operations and greater difficulties with the American balance of international payments.

CPT ALONG WITH VAT

The fact CPT is proving to have serious shortcomings does not require it be abandoned. One commentator very familiar with American business practices envisages VAT collections becoming sufficient to reduce the American CPT to a legislated rate of around 35 percent.[7]

The British study of VAT, completed by their National Economic Development Office, does not envisage elimination of CPT. After going over the pros and cons of VAT's replacing CPT, the report concludes: "Whatever the balance of this debate, in practical terms it seems likely that only a very small cut in corporation taxes (or perhaps only the avoidance of some small future increase) would be possible in the immediate future."[8]

Occasionally, American observers have recommended GATT treat the CPT as it does VAT relative to internationally traded goods. If this were done, America's position would be strengthened but would remain inferior. Even if CPT marginal rates were equal in all industrial nations and CPT relative to internationally traded goods was treated like VAT, the producers in America would benefit less than their competitors. The reason for this is that studies show European exporters are the high profit industries of Europe while American exporters tend to be low profit firms. Of course, the tax refund of CPT as a portion of export price would, under these conditions, be greater for European exporters than for American.

American exports tend to be made by U.S. firms that find the domestic market to be unsatisfactory and from agricultural sources that have not been large payers of CPT. They tend not to be firms established to exploit foreign opportunities. On the other hand, the small domestic markets of European nations force them, even the most efficient firms, to consider exports as an important portion of operations. The less efficient European firm is the one forced to stay in his local market.[9] Also, because the calculation of profit rate applicable to a particular export or import is practically an impossible task, the proposal is not really practical.

CONCLUSION

The CPT was developed in the United States as a method of taxing businesses on the basis of ability to pay. However, as the tax has evolved and as market control by large firms has increased and savings shortages have developed, CPT has lost many of the original strengths that were attributed to it.[10] In addition, the need for international tax harmonization and very large tax revenues points to the use of a major VAT and reduced use of the CPT.[11]

THE GASOLINE TAX

The gasoline tax is called the motor fuel tax in government publications because it covers diesel fuel as well as gasoline. Federal, state, and local governments all use the gasoline tax and apply substantial rates in cents per gallon. In 1973 the highest state rate was 10 cents (Connecticut) and the most common rate was 7 cents. City and county rates are not greater than 1 cent per gallon, and the federal rate is 4 cents per gallon.

Federal collections from the gasoline tax are about 57 percent of those of the states. Local government collections are less than 0.5 percent of the state total. The official gasoline tax receipts of state government in FY 1974 were $8.2 billion.[12] This total is about 36 percent of the collections made by states through their retail sales and gross receipts taxes.

The gasoline tax in the United States is a powerful revenue-raiser and is currently worth more than $13 billion a year. The federal gasoline tax rate drops to 1½ cents per gallon on October 1, 1977. The federal highway program expires in 1976. The states apparently stand ready to take up any reduction of federal taxes.

The eagerness of the states arises from the inflation and therefore the reduced value of the cents collected on each gallon. The complete absorption by the states of the federal gasoline tax would approximately maintain the purchasing power of state gasoline tax collections. More revenues will be needed.

The gasoline tax is the showcase example of a tax that was willingly paid because it was largely used to finance highways and highway facilities desired by the users of gasoline. In fact, the state taxes exempt gasoline not used to propel vehicles on the highways.

The current hassle over the gasoline tax has arisen as citizen perception of the potential of the tax has shifted. In a rather vague way, it is becoming generally realized that the consumption of the natural resource oil in the form of gasoline produces economic surpluses. That is, a close substitute of a comparable "cost" is not available. In Europe, for example, gasoline taxes are high enough to result frequently in prices twice those in the United States, yet consumption continues to increase.

Currently, the impact of high-priced oil imports on the balance of international payments of many nations has caused gasoline taxes to be favored as a means of gaining international stability. The high domestic taxes will improve the situation either through reduction of consumption because of higher prices at the gasoline pump or lower prices at the wharf because of reduced charges by oil exporters. The possibility of reduced import prices due to domestic taxes on the imported product is high in the case of oil, because oil is largely a natural resource cheaply extracted and therefore has a very low cost of production, as costs are usually measured.[13]

In addition, some urban planners are coming to the conclusion that high gasoline taxes can help solve urban congestion by moving people out of single-rider cars. The political acceptability of this program and all other proposals for high gasoline taxes has not been fully tested. The relationship of tax payment to taxpayer benefit will be much less direct than that enjoyed by the traditional gasoline tax.

PRICES AND TAX RELATIONSHIPS

One major question is seldom answered: Why is it that taxes are considered fair if levied according to ability to pay, but that prices are considered equitable if set according to cost of production and not when set as high as the market will bear? A rare realization of the many facets of this complicated matter arose during the policy-formation days of the energy crisis that developed in 1973.

Economists pointed out that supply and demand could be brought into balance through sharp price increases or sharp tax increases. Both procedures would have the same immediate effect on decisions of fuel purchasers, but quite different impacts on the economic well-being of the oil companies, the use of additional funds received, and the long-run availability of energy resources. If price increases brought supply and demand into balance, the short-run additional profits could be taxed away with special windfall taxes paid mainly by large oil companies. The amount of taxes collected would presumably be less than if market balance were brought about with excise taxes. However, the windfall tax approach meant that taxes would be paid by large corporations, while much of the excise tax would fall on low- and middle-income individuals.

The use of a windfall tax would not have the simplicity of an excise tax high enough to balance supply and demand. It also would change the tax from one on ordinary motorists to one on big business. Price increases would temporarily become greater than cost and therefore unacceptable. As soon as oil wells of low-cost producers became capitalized at their higher value and new high-cost producers just able to meet expenses at the new higher prices became a portion of the supply, the high price would become acceptable because it would correspond with cost of production.

The relative effect on efficiency of the two approaches depends on whether society favors a small quantity of oil at a high price per unit or a potentially larger quantity at prices that would depend on demand and the cost of expanded supply. Here in a nutshell is a very important aspect of the interrelationship of taxes and prices, and also of taxes and economic growth. The high price and the windfall-tax approach places the after-tax surpluses available for investment and research and development expenditures under the control of the companies supplying oil. These companies would have a larger or smaller amount, depending on the general rate of the windfall tax and tax inducements offered if funds were used for designated purposes.

The levy of excise taxes high enough to equate supply and demand would give the government relatively substantial additional funds. These could be appropriately designated in a variety of ways. For example, a considerable portion, say 10 percent, of the revenues could be refunded to low-income buyers and to others required to purchase a considerable amount of fuel in earning a living. The remainder could be used to meet general revenue needs or allocated to energy development projects.

If cost per unit remained constant and rationing were used, the consumer price index (CPI) and other official measurements of inflation would increase much less than under the price-tax approaches sketched above. In both the price-tax and the rationing approaches, consumers would be induced to seek alternatives to all or a portion of their current uses of fuel. Under the price-tax approach, however, those in low- and medium-income brackets would make the greatest adjustments. Under rationing, it would be those using fuel judged to be least necessary that would make the greatest adjustments. Frequently these would be the more active consumers and those with the higher incomes. This pattern of restriction of fuel use can be substantially modified by establishing an official white market for fuel ration coupons. Under any circumstances the black market would reduce the effectiveness of the rationing procedure and change the pattern of allocation expected from it.

Certainly the points discussed do not cover all the aspects of efficiency that should be considered in this single tax decision of whether or not to levy high taxes on gasoline. One must also consider the effect on costs of substitution of various kinds and in various places, and the problems of enforcement and administration. The ecological impacts of fuel consumption make up an important and unconsidered area of costs that are measured in satisfactions provided by the environment and not in dollars and cents.

CONCLUSION

The gasoline tax shows tendencies to evolve into a natural resource tax rather than a tax to finance benefits enjoyed by the taxpayers. Also, the tax is recognized as having potential impacts on the restoration of livability in cities and the restoration of balance in international trade accounts.

The gasoline tax as used by the consumers of petroleum products has been very different from the taxes collected by the oil-producing nations. The struggle in the future will be by consumers attempting to capture some of the surplus arising because oil is basically a free product.

THE PAYROLL TAX, WAGE BARGAIN AND EMPLOYMENT

The United States is entering a period of careful reconsideration of its social security, medical delivery, and welfare programs. The expansion of these services through government financing seems to be in the cards. By moving in this direction we are not treading on untried paths.

The European industrial nations of the Free World have had considerable experience.[14] They appear to have decided that the best approach, taking into consideration the basic requirement that the private enterprise system must prosper, is to make extensive use of the value-added tax in meeting welfare revenue requirements.

The following discussions analyze the desirability of the European approach. The analyses consider particularly carefully the comparative economic impacts of financing expanded social security, medical delivery, and welfare with the existing payroll tax and with a general and substantial value-added tax.

When considering tax policy in this area, it is well to keep in mind what Couve de Murville, the French minister of finance, did during the French economic crisis of 1968. (Student riots in the streets of Paris triggered a crisis that resulted in a devaluation of the franc.) He dropped the 4.25 percent tax paid by French employers on total payrolls. The revenue lost, and a bit more, was made up by increasing the rates of the French VAT.

The switch was carried out in order to reduce labor costs and make French goods more competitive. The French measure essentially boiled down to eliminating the wages tax and taking an equivalent amount of revenue through a rise in the TVA rates. We have here a procedure for swallowing up taxes that under GATT understandings do not provide for refunds on exports and border taxes on imports because they are direct taxes. The result is an expansion of border adjustments without a corresponding impact on domestic prices.

RELATION TO THE WAGE BARGAIN

The base of the value-added tax (as of all broadly based taxes, whether direct or indirect) consists largely of the input of labor. The wage earners of a modern society are the final users and buyers of production as well as the major receivers of income. VAT, when compared with the payroll tax, is one step further away from labor compensation and one step closer to labor as a final user of production. This difference is of sufficient importance to warrant attention when considering financing social security with a value-added tax.

Under the prevailing institutional economic arrangement, workers have much more control over the wages they receive than over the prices they pay. At least this is the impression one gains from watching organized wage-earner actions. For example, demands for higher wages are frequent, but a labor strike for lower prices is unheard of. It is also true that neither prices nor wages are completely manageable, and the levels of both continue to bear some of the mystery of Adam Smith's "invisible hand."

The introduction of a VAT that provides the additional revenues required to balance the intake and outgo of the portion of the public economy concerned with social security removes this financing further from the wage bargain than is true under a system of payroll taxes. Under a payroll tax system taxes are withheld from wages, and the employer is required to pay a wage-related tax increase each time social security reserves and/or benefits are increased.

The relation of social security payroll tax payments to the wage bargain is apparent in wage negotiation efforts aimed at keeping and increasing the purchasing power of take-home pay. In the United States the rapid increase in the withholding rates of social security with Medicare plus the increase in the maximum salary covered by social security taxes has triggered the increased emphasis. Also, the U.S. tax climate developed by the push for the 10 percent federal income tax surcharge during the last half of 1967 and in 1968 contributed to the increased emphasis on the relationship between tax withholding and the level of take-home pay. When the level of take-home pay gained central attention in wage bargaining, the level of tax withholding became very important.

The payroll tax is much more closely related to cost of labor than is an indirect tax like the value-added tax. To the extent that this affects hiring decisions, payroll taxes have a deleterious effect on the level of employment that is not part of the impact of the value-added tax.

COST OF SOCIAL PROGRAMS

VAT can make additional funds available to general government to permit it to finance a substantial portion of a basic pension program. This must be a major portion of the social-security-financing aspect of VAT. Another social-security-financing role of VAT would be to assure a current revenue base adequate to maintain the purchasing power of the earnings-related portion of a national pension program. A tax-balanced budget continues to bring in its full level of revenue receipts year after year, while a debt-financed budget piles debt plus interest costs on top of each other year after year. The German experience seems to be an example of the use of a broad-based VAT to provide general revenue levels that make the use of deficits unnecessary to finance a national budget that meets government responsibilities reasonably well.

An estimate of the cost of a fully matured national pension and children's allowance program is 16 to 18 percent of GNP.[14] Currently the U.S. level is at only about 9 percent, so expansion in this area can be expected to continue. Sweden in 1962 was at the 9.2 percent expenditure level. Fiscal comparisons—including this one—are always difficult and somewhat inaccurate. There is little doubt, however, that to meet the Western European level in the eight types of coverage identified as appropriate for a fully developed national pension and family allowance program, the United States will need to expand tax revenues dedicated to this purpose substantially.[15]

A study paper of the Joint Economic Committee of the U.S. Congress released in September 1965 presented data relative to social security costs. In Table 7 the United States is shown to be operating at a level considerably below that of the nations of Western Europe. This relative position has changed somewhat during the past nine years as the American social security program appears to have expanded at a somewhat more rapid rate than those of Europe.

Table 7

Social Security Expenditures as Percent of National Income: 1962

Country	Total	Old-age, Survivors', Disability Insurance
Belgium	13.4	4.7
France	13.4	3.9
Germany (Fed. Rep.)	14.4	8.1
Italy	12.0	4.7
Luxembourg	13.7	6.3
Netherlands	12.0	5.7
Sweden	9.2	5.1
United Kingdom	10.6	4.2
United States	4.8	3.6

SOURCE: Joint Economic Committee, *Labor in the European Community,* Washington: United States Government Printing Office, November 1965:11.

WITHHOLDING LEVELS

Payroll taxes great enough to raise 12 or 14 percent of America's national income would most likely have to include all wages and self-employed income in the base. Even when this broader wage and salary base was used, the total payroll tax rate (employee plus employer) would have to reach 17 or 20 percent (assuming the wage and salary tax base was 70 percent of national income).

Rates at the current level for payroll taxes, when added to normal marginal federal income tax withholding rates of close to 20 percent plus a state income tax of 5 percent, cause the last dollar of individual take-home pay to be reduced by about one-third from the level of any labor-management bargain for additional wages. The employer, because of pressure to keep purchasing power, or take-home pay, rising through wage increases, while meeting employer payroll tax contributions, finds the problems related to rising labor costs per unit of production expanded.[16] Labor becomes more expensive to the employer and therefore becomes an item to decrease in the production mix.

When the payroll tax method is used to finance social security, the cost falls where it will have the greatest possible deterrent effect on business decisions to hire additional labor. Payroll taxes "are, in effect, a tax on employment. . . ."[17] On the other hand, the use of a broadly based VAT to meet the basic economic security needs generalizes the cost. As a result, "there has been a tendency for the state's proportion of the total cost to increase in a number of countries and for some schemes to be financed wholly by the state."[18]

It is also true that the payroll financing procedure provides no method of adjusting export and import prices to take into account different national social security costs. VAT can be very effective because the established international practice, formalized in the GATT, is to refund indirect taxes (taxes levied at point of sale) on exports and to collect border taxes on imports equal to domestic indirect taxes.

ECONOMIC IMPACTS

High payroll taxes added to the U.S. tax system, which already uses high personal income taxes and high corporate profits taxes, produce very strong incentives to reduce domestic employment, and domestic sourced income, and profits.[19] One important result of this pressure is an expansion of the portion of American-controlled business activities carried out in foreign nations. Another result is the reduction of domestic mobility of American capital. Efforts to keep taxes down result in minimized payouts to stockholders. This means stockholders have less money with which to purchase new capital issues. Also, the high cost of hiring additional labor and the high pretax earnings required from domestic invested capital reduce the number of attractive new domestic business undertakings.[20]

The theory of the general transaction tax holds that the tax does not affect business decisions or consumer decisions.[21] The theory is violated when rates become different depending on business organization and items sold. The basic nature of the cascade turnover tax (providing lower taxes for integrated industries) was a prime cause of the breakdown of generality and uniformity in the excise tax system of Germany. VAT, by eliminating a variation in tax liability depending on number of turnovers, has added considerably to the generality and uniformity of the transaction tax system of Germany and Western Europe. VAT does not affect business and consumer decisions. It also tends to increase generality of coverage.[22]

Transaction taxes generally carry the "antisocial" taint of being as high on goods purchased by the poor as on those purchased by the rich. VAT has this reputation just as much as a gross turnover or retail sales tax. The use of a value-added tax instead of retail sales or turnover taxes does, however, avoid tax liability differences based on different procedures of bringing identical goods to market. Also, the ability of business firms engaged in any line of production to pass VAT forward in price depends largely on the elasticity of supply and the relative inelasticity of final demand for the product sold.

It is also true that the corporate profits tax and even the individual income tax, everything else equal, are more likely to be shifted forward in higher prices if the amount sold does not decrease sharply when prices are raised and if the supply does not fall rapidly with lower prices. In fact, from this particular point of view, the transaction-based tax, by violating the theoretically desirable tax feature of complete generality and by using its unique ability to grant exemptions for particular products, has a distinct advantage over taxes using the profits or income base, which cannot, or at least do not, exempt profits and incomes earned by producers of a necessity consumed in relatively large amounts by the poor.[23]

There can be little doubt that general EC interest in moving rapidly toward a common VAT was stimulated by the 1954 French development of a value-added tax. The favored position of French industry as seen by other EC member states, under the high French VAT and the application of the destination principle, is as follows:

[the] country of destination principle as presently applied to the turnover tax gives a distinct advantage to France. While the rate of the "taxe sur la valeur ajoutée" (TVA) is very high, the burden of direct taxes imposed on French enter-

prises is correspondingly lighter. Since the detaxing equalization removes the whole TVA from French exports at the frontier, France gives greater tax relief to its efforts than its neighbors . . . Through the operation of the equalization machinery, French goods enjoy a virtual customers' protection. . . .[24]

SCANDINAVIAN WELFARE FINANCING

The Scandinavian countries have progressed furthest toward the provision of basic old-age, invalid, and death benefits from general revenues. General revenues provide 83 percent of the cost of the basic Danish system; they provide 85 percent of the cost of Finland's assistance pensions and 70 percent in Sweden.[25]

All the Scandinavian countries, led by Denmark, have made VAT a major source of general revenues. In Sweden, VAT was very nearly introduced in 1964.[26] The additional revenues required at that time were largely provided through higher rates of the Swedish retail sales tax. The 10 percent Swedish retail sales tax was repealed in 1969 and replaced with a VAT with a rate of 10 percent. The Swedish VAT rate is expected to reach 17 percent.[27]

In commenting on the introduction of VAT, the Danish government pointed out that the tax replaces the sales tax levied at the wholesale level of distribution. The expectation expressed was that VAT would "yield a much bigger revenue" than the sales tax. These additional revenues will permit easing direct taxes "payable to the central government."[28]

CONCLUSION

The introduction of VAT is basically the introduction of a general tax using net transactions or GNP as its base. A major tax on transactions is more than likely appropriate at the national level when 30 to 40 percent of GNP must be funneled through government to finance social security and to provide the goods and services that have become the responsibility of the public economy. Also, a general transaction tax, and particularly VAT, stimulates exports and protects imports, making possible more national independence in setting expenditure policies.

The unfavorable social reputation of a tax using transactions as its base can be only partially erased by numerous deductions and exemptions. In fact, it is perhaps unwise to attempt to change attitudes toward a transaction tax in this manner. There is no logical stopping place short of changing a "general" transaction tax into a "special product" excise tax.

General acceptance is more likely to be found in emphasizing improvement of general welfare through spending of collections.[29] European and particularly German and Scandinavian experience and the new British VAT seem to indicate that a high tax on transactions becomes acceptable only in an informed democracy with citizens possessing a high social conscience when, directly or indirectly, the revenues collected are associated with basic minimum income protection.

The financing of an expanding basic social security, medical delivery, and welfare program from payroll, income, and profit taxes (all direct taxes) places a strain on a tax system limited to these taxes. The introduction of a general transaction tax with substantial rates has overcome this difficulty in many Western European countries.[30]

THE PERSONAL INCOME TAX

Roy G. Blakey and Gladys C. Blakey, in their 1940 history of the U.S. income tax, say the Sixteenth Amendment and the 1913 establishing legislation were "really the result of a great equalitarian movement generated by two prolonged post-war depressions of great severity."[31] Twenty-five years later Richard Goode quoted with approval the *Internal Revenue Bulletin* and saw the 1913 income tax as a response to "the general demand for justice in taxation, and to the long-standing need of an elastic and productive system of revenue."[32]

To the ordinary voters, as Blakey and Blakey saw it, income meant money to spend, and most people were short of money. However, some —the high-income earners—had lots of spending money. Therefore, the thing to do was to tax incomes—but only the big incomes—then those with a shortage of spending money wouldn't have to pay taxes. Goode seems to believe that the voter is a considerably more sophisticated person. More than likely he is wrong, as was the *Internal Revenue Cumulative Bulletin* of 1959, which reprinted a portion of the Home Report of April 22, 1913. The Blakeys are the more persuasive. The mass of the voters favored the income tax in 1913 because they wouldn't have to pay it. Also, they didn't believe the tax would be harmful to the country and therefore indirectly to them. The new taxes to support the federal government were to be paid by those relatively few defined by the law to be subject to the income tax.

A TAX ON THE RICH FEW

The 1913 act was expected to collect taxes from less than 1 percent of the population, and this turned out to be the case. Even as recently as just before World War II, less than 5 percent of the population made out federal income tax returns or were dependents of those who did.

Most purchasers of tobacco and alcoholic beverages, however, were paying a federal tax, and they knew it. Also, tariff duties—the one on sugar, for example—looked as though they increased prices, and the prices were paid for by everyone out of incomes that were too small to meet all the needs of the family.

It has always been difficult to determine definitely how a tax affects prices of goods sold for consumption or prices of goods or labor used in production. The voter to whom the politician was appealing in 1913 was convinced that the things he purchased would not increase in price if 1 percent of the population began to pay an income tax, nor would his personal income decrease. The problems of defining what income was or how income from one source differed from income from another source in ability to bear taxes was an academic question for the 99 percent of the population exempt from the tax in 1913.

The question is no longer academic in 1975 when over 75 percent of the population pay an income tax or are dependents of those who do. Despite this vast increase in the portion of the population directly concerned with what "taxable income" really is, relatively few questions were asked before 1968, when Joseph W. Barr, the outgoing secretary of the treasury, talked of a taxpayer's revolt. But then revolt was in the air in 1968. The crusade launched still hasn't evened things out, and middle income people pay less of their income in taxes than low income taxpayers. Also, the new minimum tax legislation to force the rich to pay income taxes still contains the "executive suite" loophole.

TAX THE OTHER FELLOW

When the voter of 1913 favored the taxation of income, it was usually because the voter would not be paying the tax. If the voter of the 1970s thinks about why he likes the income tax, he must give the same answer, but it is a much more personal question and answer because *he* is the taxpayer. Actually, the question is not being asked in any systematic fashion. Some economists of the United States have been raising the question, but in the United Kingdom not even economists seem to have bothered. The general lack of concern by the average voter as he began paying the tax must have been caused by too many things happening too quickly—the initiation of withholding, the need to finance a big war, inflation, and the introduction of social security all took place within a short, seven-year period. In addition, U.S. private enterprise was still suffering from the scandals and failures that had been securely tied to it during the political campaigns of the 1930s.

The failure of British economists even to consider whether income as defined for setting the base of the income tax also represented tax-paying capacity seems to be due to complete mesmerization. The one hundred years of British tradition had made income and tax-paying capacity synonymous—even to the economists. So in the United States and the United Kingdom the income tax grew—with hardly a challenge —and the efforts to define a basically undefinable concept became even more frantic, and exemptions and adjustments and special provisions became ever more complicated. Then in the United States in 1966, congressional committees began to give up and asked for a simplification reform. They are still asking, but the tax is resistant; one simplification seems to spawn additional complications a few years later as injustices and loopholes appear.[33] New loopholes for the 1980s include provisions for retirement, head of family, minimum tax, and earned income.

MINIMUM SACRIFICE

Actually, as Gunnar Myrdal, the 1974 Nobel Prize winner in economics, has pointed out, the entire theoretical framework of justice used to support the progressive income tax is faulty. This is the case without arguing the merits or demerits of utility and individual satisfactions.

The aim of equating satisfactions or pain of the last dollar earned or spent works at the margin and does not consider total satisfactions. Actually, any value judgments must be concerned with total utilities. Myrdal concludes that "even if subjective value theory could evolve a political rule, this would have to aim at a maximization or a just distribution of *total* utilities and not of marginal utilities."[34]

How can the effect on total satisfactions of a tax-created income equalization or disequalization be measured even subjectively? The heart of the matter is that the plausible justification of income taxes with progressive rates fails even if all assumptions are accepted. Failure arises because marginal utility rather than total utility is considered, and the conceptual job of dealing with total utility is unresolved.

HORIZONTAL EQUALITY OF TREATMENT

The average voter believes that the justice of the income tax rests on its collection on the basis of individual ability to pay. This means to him that those with larger incomes, however measured, can pay a bigger portion of those incomes in taxes without giving up expenditures for goods and services needed for the "good life." Until 1968 the voter believed the income tax to be paid largely by this portion of the population. He will always give little consideration to the way the high and progressive rates goad the capitalist "into irrational and anti-social behavior in order to escape taxes."[35] The effect of taxes on society's well-being because the tax stimulates uneconomic behavior is not yet a portion of the voter's picture of the tax.

A very heavy reliance on a net income of some sort as in the United States makes the allowable deductions or base reduction procedures immensely important. An allowable deduction or a special low rate favors income use of one kind or income of one type. This pushes resources in the direction favored by the tax and encourages income realization in the fashion that minimizes tax liability. The effect is that judgments as to the use of resources become basically uneconomical and tax-determined. No one knows the social cost or the impact on the efficiency of a market economy of high-income receivers acting in a tax-determined fashion. There may be a social benefit; for example, charitable and other gifts might increase because of the fact that they are deductible in calculating taxable income.[36] There may also be a social benefit arising from the pressure toward home ownership arising from the exclusion of imputed rent from occupancy of an owner-occupied home.

These benefits, if they exist, must be weighed against the locked-in effect high income taxes have on successful investments, the pressure they provide for business consumption spending, the reduction of corporate profit distributions, and the like. The social benefit of some income-use redistribution must also be weighed against the horizontal inequality arising from the deductibility provisions allowed in arriving at taxable income.

Persons in the same economic position, one renting and one owning his own heavily mortgaged home, have, as a result of the law, quite different tax liabilities. Also, two taxpayers with identical incomes, one married and one unmarried, find themselves with quite different tax liabilities. None of the benefits provided by the wife are taxable as income, while the purchase of these services by the unmarried taxpayer is not deductible.[37]

Perhaps the way to look at the use of the income tax in both the United States and the United Kingdom is to compare it to the use of feet and inches and ounces and pounds in both countries. It has become a habit that is retained despite the problems and inefficiencies related to the use of the system. However, Australia, the United Kingdom, and New Zealand have abandoned the pound-shilling money system for decimal money. The metric system is on the verge of being generally adopted. One can hope that habit will be overcome in other areas of human action, including the complicated business of defining taxable income. Perhaps France developed a portion of the answer when she introduced the value-added tax back in 1954.

CONCLUSION

The highly touted personal income tax has been a federal tax for over sixty years but has not brought about the redistribution of incomes it was to provide. In fact, the current trend is toward making the tax increasingly a simple percentage of earnings, and its relation to ability to pay is declining.

If the personal income tax is unable to redistribute income, much of the justification for enduring all the administrative problems of the tax is also eliminated. The problems related to horizontal equality, the definition of taxable income, and the weakness of the nineteenth-century concept of minimum sacrifice have become too serious to be swept under the proverbial rug.

THE PROPERTY TAX

The development of the *ad valorem* property tax as a local tax in the United States grew out of three taproots: (1) the state reliance on local officials to administer the tax, (2) the need for local revenues to finance free public education, and (3) the belief that state government expenditures could be financed with new taxes administered by state officials. The concept of property taxation arose out of the eighteenth-century revolt against the power of the landlord. Both Adam Smith and David Ricardo identified land rent to be a distributor's share that could be taken by the state without reducing economic growth and productivity.

ADMINISTRATION

Although the states have, and some continue to make extensive use of property tax revenues, none of them directly assumed the burden of administering the tax.[38] State laws governing assessment of property values were passed, but a body of state assessors to administer the law was not a part of the legislation. The states relied on local township or in some cases county assessors, usually elected officials, to search out taxable property, place a value on it, and sometimes to collect taxes due, and sell properties on which taxes were delinquent. This general rule was abandoned by many states in the assessment of selected properties—for example, those of public utilities and banks. In the areas where the states did assume responsibility for the full administration of the property tax, the administration was generally superior.

The property tax, which started as a state tax with Ohio providing much of the leadership, soon became a local tax source to support developing local governments.[39] The states retained legal control over the tax, however, through constitutional provisions and state legislation. This continues to be rather largely the legal position of the property tax. This, of course, corresponds with the subordinate position of local governments in the state-local government relationship.

The failure of the states to take over the property tax and administer it as a state tax was an important element in drift of the tax toward local use, where the real administration took place. Local administration has also usually meant unprofessional administration.[40] The deep involvement of local government servants with property tax administration and their inability to solve the problems of this tax made local governments hesitate to experiment with other types of taxes. Also, their inferior legal position *vis-à-vis* state governments made experimentation difficult. On the other hand, the deep involvement of local officials with the property tax, and a general lack of experience in administering other taxes, caused local government officials generally to feel that the property tax was the tax best fitted to their needs. As a result, a general consensus arose among property tax administrators that was consistent with the theoretical position of the academic community: The revenue source best suited to local government use was the property tax. It followed that states should *not* collect a property tax.

DEVELOPMENT BETWEEN 1880 AND 1936

By the 1880s the older states such as New York were busy developing state revenue sources that were independent of the property tax. The business corporations were the first economic institutions to be identified as independent state tax sources. State inheritance taxes came along at about the same time.

The pressures for spending between 1870 and 1914, and the fact that the services to be provided by this spending were centered in the local community, created an appropriate environment for the property tax to move toward local governments and away from the state. The changes recommended to accommodate the fiscal requirements were called "segregation." Segregation, which was first recommended in 1886 in Illinois, provided for the abandonment of the property tax as a source of state revenues. Advocates felt that the state revenue needs could be met by a group of indirect taxes.

Segregation would involve separation of the tax sources used by state governments and those used by local governments. The policy recommendation was meant to establish for state and local governments what largely existed between the federal and state governments. The program was recommended by tax reformers as a .method of improving the property tax.[41]

During the last twenty years of the nineteenth century and the first twenty years of the twentieth century, a basic change took place in the fiscal systems of state and local governments. The property tax was no longer to be a basic concern of the state government. The states were going to develop indirect taxes and use their powers of incorporation to meet their revenue needs.

All the discussions of the period assumed that the expenditures best carried out by state versus local government would remain as they were at the turn of the century. It was also taken for granted that the expenditures administered by each level of government would be financed by taxes administered by that level of government. Neither the idea of grants-in-aid between state and local governments nor the distribution for local government use of state-collected revenues entered significantly into the considerations. It was assumed that primary education, the major growing expenditure, would remain firmly rooted in local government, as would road construction and maintenance and the provision of welfare assistance. Higher education was largely supported by the private economy, with the state area limited to teachers' colleges and cooperation with federally assisted land-grant colleges.

This was the situation as the economy and American society moved placidly along from 1910 to 1930 (with some frivolity and violence induced by war and prohibition). Then came the sharp deflation of 1933, and the property tax frequently couldn't meet local expenditure requirements.

DEVELOPMENT SINCE THE 1930s

The property tax, which had gradually become only a local government tax, proved in the depression years not to have the basic revenue stability that tax theorists had identified as one of its few basic good characteristics.[42] Jens Peter Jensen, writing in the late 1920s, took the regular collection of property taxes as being assured and discussed delinquency only as the result of economic decadence of a limited area, taxpayer carelessness, bad tax collection procedures, or unrealistic expenditure programs.[43] Jensen recognized the vital importance to the performance of local government services of regular collection of the assessed amounts, and he wrote that "if a cog slips in the machinery and the assessment or the collection or both are delayed, the situation becomes extremely critical."[44] He didn't visualize many of the cogs' being frozen through severe and continuing deflation. The types of pressure resulting in sharp reduction of property tax collections from 1932 to 1937 were not considered in Jensen's very careful analysis of the tax.

The deflation crisis of the 1930s largely completed the elimination of the property tax as a source of state revenues. State aid to local school districts was the major new element that developed at this time. It was introduced first in only a few states as a temporary procedure but rapidly became more widespread and turned out to be very permanent indeed.

Basic property tax collections for state use have continued in New Jersey, Nebraska, Montana and Washington with scattered amounts in other states, arising largely from the application of state property taxes to public utilities. It is calculated that property taxes going to state governments amount to somewhat less than 3 percent of state revenue collections.[45]

Today the local government reliance on the property tax remains great; the tax provides around 80 percent of the tax revenues of local governments. Local source tax revenues are a decreasing portion of local government budgets, however. In Ohio the property tax became nearly completely a local tax source as early as 1902.[46]

The Suggested Property Tax Legislation prepared by the Advisory Commission on Intergovernmental Relations has moved a long way toward greater state control of property tax administration. However, the next step after state control—a uniform state property tax levy— is not taken. It would appear that this shortfall is politically dictated and does not rest squarely on the direction of the commission's analyses of state and local government expenditures and revenues.[47]

The advisory commission points out in developing the case for a state property tax that "a main defect of the separation of sources policy that assigns the general property tax to be levied by local governments for their basic support is the failure of the distribution of taxable property in a state to coordinate with the cost of local government."[48] The commission's report goes on to point out all the problems that separation of tax sources has developed. For example, it has seriously hindered metropolitan planning and encouraged inefficient subdivision of local government.

The impractical idea of developing what has come to be called "economic balance" in an area as small as a school district or township is being recognized for what it is. Sufficient property values do not exist in all areas to meet the revenue needs for average local government services. The realization of this impossibility is the source of the original popularity of establishing state foundation programs in the area of local education finance. The fact that property of equal value bears unequal tax payments in support of public education vitiates the program. Yet this is the case "when wealthy school districts can meet the foundation by levying less than the mandated rate or are guaranteed specified amounts of state aid regardless of their high fiscal ability."[49]

THE JUSTICE OF THE PROPERTY TAX

The literature on public finance attempts to justify large property tax collections from households of modest means because the funds collected are spent for education. The argument typically points out that the value of property increases with the productivity of the population and that this productivity is substantially increased by a good education. In addition, education is identified as a way to increase the incomes and well-being of those in lower-income brackets. The benefit to property from school expenditures is of quite a different sort than that which arises from the city's employment of policemen and firemen.[50]

Most expenditures supported by property tax collections other than that for education benefit property owners directly, and the tax can be justified on that basis. The benefit theory of justifying tax payments has been applied to the consideration of property taxation because tax philosophers since the days of John Stuart Mill have seen that taxation, to be just, must be supported by the benefits enjoyed by the taxpayer or must be levied on the basis of ability to pay.

The property tax could not qualify as a just tax on the basis of its relationship to ability to pay, for direct property tax payments do not vary in any regular way with personal income adjusted for costs of earning the income and family responsibilities of the income earner. Nevertheless, the property tax was collected; it had many good characteristics; and a portion of the receipts was used for roads, fire protection, and the like. The benefit justification seemed appropriate, but it had to be expanded to include the indirect benefits of education, which absorbed 50 percent or more of the collections.

The benefit justification could not rest on the education benefit directly enjoyed by families who paid property tax and who had children going to schools supported by taxes collected on the assessed values within the local school district. Actually there is very nearly an inverse relationship between the number of children going to school from a family and that family's property tax payments.

The indirect benefit of educating the children of families in a neighborhood undoubtedly has an economic value to everyone in the neighborhood. It is also true that the education of children in areas other than where real estate is owned has an economic worth to the out-of-state or out-of-district property owner and property taxpayer. However, it is very doubtful whether this economic value of general education is peculiarly associated with real estate ownership. This point is at the heart of the matter.

If real estate does not gain in some outstanding way from general education, the justification of property taxation for education on the basis of benefit is not acceptable. It is not acceptable because the benefit of real estate from education is not unique. Any revenue source providing funds for education would have the same degree of justice gained from this type of benefit as that enjoyed by a tax on real estate. If the portion of property tax revenues going for education must rely on this type of benefit justification, it becomes a tax inferior to the sales or income tax. For the sales tax has additional justification as a tax on the quantity of the fruits of the society a taxpayer has enjoyed.[51] The income tax also is levied according to ability to pay as measured by taxable income after permitted deductions.

THE JUSTICE OF LAND VALUE TAXATION

The basic justice of the taxation of land value does not rest in the ability of the owner to pay, although this ability usually does exist. Nor does it rest to any special degree on any benefits the land enjoys from government expenditures. Neither benefits nor ability to pay is a sufficient justification of the property tax as a major revenue-raiser when it is compared with VAT or the income tax. For the property tax to be a just tax, it must receive major support from another source. Such support exists for the portion of the property tax resting on land values. Land amounts to 30 to 50 percent of the total value of real estate.

Land is among those goods and services that are necessary for man's development and used by all men but that are not produced day by day. Other examples of such goods are water, air space, sunshine, rainfall, and fish in the water. These goods, with the exception of land and water, have little economic value because they are not generally susceptible to exclusive use and control.[52]

Land, on the other hand, can be set aside for exclusive use. The person who controls land not only benefits from the minerals and fertility of the soil but through use of earth space enjoys air, sunshine, and rainfall, none of which have a cost of production. The quantity of land available is limited because the size of the earth is finite.

The limitation is much sharper when particular uses of land are to be met. The limitation of quantity causes the price for control to be bid up. The increased value is created by the expansion of land uses. This expansion arises from the needs of the people, which become effective demand through the increase of per capita and aggregate incomes.

In addition to its location value, land has productive value. Minerals are extracted from the land, and the basic quality of the soil plus manmade fertilizers, pesticides, and seeds, and sometimes artificially supplied water, combine with the climate to produce foods and fibers. These products from the soil give a value to land as well as providing payments for capital, management, and labor. The control of land is the basis for the development of a market value. This value consists basically of the capitalization (see glossary) of the income represented by the difference in the average cost per unit of output of the land and that of the land just able to produce with total costs of fertilizer and the like covered by selling price. The latter land is no-rent land, which means it is also free land because no one would be willing to pay a price to control it.

The levy of a tax on land does not in any quantitatively important sense decrease the amount of land. Taxation only can change the use made of land and therefore the quantity of land allocated for various purposes. The closer the tax comes to collecting the full surplus arising from the best economic use of land, the closer the tax comes to forcing the best use of the land. To reach the goal of various amounts of tax depending on the surplus productivity of a piece of land over free land, it is not necessary to set a variety of tax rates applicable to different parcels of land. All that is required is that a uniform tax rate be applied to the market value of land as determined by a combination of recent sale prices and the application of competent valuation procedures to develop what is called *constructive market value*.

ECONOMIC IMPACTS

Under the current system of property taxation and expenditure in effect in the United States, the formation of property taxation districts including only a small number of persons, or only people during the day, or people requiring a relatively inexpensive package of services, can sharply reduce the portion of the economic rent arising from the land that is collected as property taxes. The United States has hundreds of tax districts existing largely for the purpose of removing property from the tax base of a populous nearby school district or residential area.

This establishment of separate tax districts to avoid assessment of property taxes on expensive structures and equipment may be desirable, for it could stimulate capital investment for an expansion of the productivity of workers and the general economic growth of a region or the nation. Low taxes on land value cannot have this justification because the cost of land is not made up by adding the various costs required for its production, except in a relatively minor sense or under unusual circumstances, such as where usable land is created by filling a swamp or cutting off a hill. Therefore, the quantity of land in aggregate is not determined by the uses to which it can be put that will be sufficiently productive to cover necessary costs, of which property taxes are one. The quantity of structures and equipment is affected by the relation between cost and price, but this is not true of land.

The *ad valorem* property tax assessed on land values acts to reduce the income the land provides to those controlling it. The reduction of income would take place in all instances except where for one reason or another the full economic price had been avoided until the tax based on land value was increased.

CONCLUSION

The property tax was originally designed to provide most of the tax revenues of state governments. The development of free public schools financed by school district revenues brought the property tax down to the local level of government. Currently, the pressures for equality in school financing are bringing the property tax back to the state level.

Another development is the realization by many students of taxation that the portion of the property tax base consisting of land is very different from that consisting of structures and personal property. As a result of this realization, serious consideration is being given to greater use of service charges and to the use of a land value tax (LVT).

THE RETAIL SALES TAX

The retail sales tax came largely out of the depression.[53] The fabled dependability of the property tax failed, and the states enacted retail sales taxes to finance their basic services. Again in the post–World War II period, higher education costs arising from the earlier "baby boom" brought forth renewed state retail sales tax legislation.[54] At this time local governments, particularly cities, began to use the tax to supplement property tax collection.[55] In 1974 the retail sales tax was used by all states except Alaska, Montana, New Hampshire, and Oregon.

THE REGRESSIVE CONCEPT

The retail sales tax has been called a regressive tax. The term *regressive* connotes undesirability, and this connotation remains when the term is used in reference to taxation. Regression means going back to a previous place or state. Popularly, the word means going backward—that is, becoming worse.

In taxation, the term *regressive* is used correctly to refer to tax payments that decrease as a portion of the tax base as the base expands. A regressive sales tax would require reduced payments as a portion of sales as the value of sales increased. For example, a sales tax with a higher rate on a small purchase than on a large purchase would be a regressive sales tax. Also, a property tax that is based more nearly on the full value of a modest residence than a luxury one is correctly labeled a regressive property tax.

The term *regressive* as applied to tax policy does not contain the concept of regression. It does not mean going backward, either in terms of shifting the economic burden to the producer rather than forward to the buyer or in terms of reducing well-being or forward progress.

Frequently the unmodified word *regressive* is used in a tax discussion to refer to family or personal income payment regressivity. The tax, whatever the base used, is said to be regressive because the portion of personal income going to pay the tax increases with the lower the income. When *regressive* is used in this way, the assumption is that whatever base is being taxed, the tax is still being paid out of some definition of family or personal income, and that the possessor of the income being reduced can be identified. In addition, a necessary condition of the analysis is that economic well-being or ability to pay taxes approximates the gross size of this income. However, any careful consideration of tax regressivity in this sense also requires adjustments of income to take account of the costs of the basic needs of the receiver and his or her dependents. Also, the income base, since the development of the concept of permanent income, needs to be adjusted to take account of lifetime income expectancy, and simple annual totals cannot be used. Finally, wealth holdings capable of meeting tax liabilities are not adequately accounted for in personal income totals, and a procedure to take this into account is needed before true taxpayer ability is related to taxes paid.

SHIFTING THE ECONOMIC BURDEN

When the retail sales tax is said to be regressive, all the conditions that were briefly mentioned above must be kept in mind when evaluating the charge. The retail sales tax does not use income as its base, and the tax is paid to the tax collector by the merchant and not by the purchaser. This tax has been seen to be passed forward by the merchant to his customers, and these customers absorb the burden themselves and do not, in turn, shift the tax to their employers or their landlords.

Although this additional complication of considering tax shifting by the consumer is important in assessing the retail sales tax as income-regressive, it is less so than first appears to be the case. For if the same employees who shift the tax in higher wages are consumers of the goods taxed, the shift to higher wages may only bring the tax back again as higher prices. However, it is also true for the retail firm and for all firms paying higher wages that the pressures from increases in selling prices and wage payments may not balance out in such a way as to preserve profits. Maybe lower rents will be negotiated and the income of landlords will be reduced.

The retail sales tax could be shifted in a great variety of ways. On the face of it, the tax is a proportional levy based on retail price. The tax payment itself is not the source of the income regressivity generally accepted to be characteristic of the retail sales tax. The regressivity arises because existing data demonstrate that persons in lower income brackets generally spend a larger portion of their incomes than do those in higher brackets. Therefore, the proportional tax on retail sales applies to a generally larger portion of a smaller income because a larger portion of that income is used for retail purchases. On the other hand, retail purchases total a generally smaller portion of a high income.

The regressivity label borne by the retail sales rests largely on the data on the use of income of those in the lower and upper income brackets. In addition, it is assumed that the greater portion of income saved by those with higher incomes is not spent on taxable items. Of course, if you go back through the labyrinth of the previous discussion, you will have some doubts as to the soundness of the assumption that goods and services purchased by whoever borrows or spends the savings of the receivers of high income avoid the burden of the retail sales tax.

What is purchased as an investment may cost more because the employees making it have bargained for higher wages to pay the retail sales tax on their purchases; also, in a number of states, the retail sales tax applies to some machinery and office equipment.

Nevertheless, and despite all these uncertainties, some of which change with the economic climate, it is still a useful generalization to consider the retail sales tax as income-regressive. It does not follow, however, that every tax paid at the time a sales transaction is completed is a regressive tax.

In order to reduce the regressivity of the retail sales tax, thirty states in 1973 exempted purchases of medicine, and twenty states exempted "food for human consumption off the premises." Seven states also use the personal income tax to reduce the regressivity of their retail sales tax by granting limited income tax credit. When income is sufficiently low and retail sales taxes paid are high, this can result in a negative income tax; that is, rather than paying income taxes, the taxpayer receives a payment to further reduce net retail sales taxes paid.

ADMINISTRATION

The administration of state sales taxes becomes more and more difficult as the rates increase. Higher rates make it more worthwhile to evade the tax. Retail stores, by reporting smaller sales than actually made, can avoid bankruptcy. The retail sales tax evaded by marginal merchants becomes the difference between staying in business or closing the shop.[56]

Out-of-state sellers are always tempted to sell directly to users to avoid retail sales taxes. When the sales tax rate is low, prospective in-state purchasers find tax evasion worthwhile only on large purchases. The existing 5 and 6 percent rates make evasion worthwhile to purchasers of smaller items, and this in turn reduces voluntary cooperation by out-of-state sellers. Under these conditions, as was demonstrated to be true in Sweden, farmers and upper-income groups work out procedures to make many purchases wholesale and evade the tax. The already regressive retail sales tax becomes even more regressive.

The immense impact of advertising and modern distribution procedures have combined to make possible sales in states without locating a branch or sending a salesman or even establishing a warehouse in the state. Sales made under these conditions are not great enough for a state to require registration and reporting of sales.[57] The effect of this situation is that sales made to residents of another state are exempt from the sales tax of the state in which the firm is located and are not taxed in the state where use takes place. The result is tax-exempt sales unless the buyer reports the purchase to his state's tax authorities. The result is tax injustice.

There is also the troublesome business of meeting the requirements of the sales tax legislation of the various states. States use many variations in coverage, rates, and filing times. The effect of this is to place a considerable burden on the small or medium-sized business firm making interstate sales.

OUT-OF-STATE SALES

It has been suggested that states tax out-of-state sales of their domestic firms just as they tax in-state sales. Under this procedure, if an out-of-state purchaser is asked to pay a use tax by his state, he will be relieved of liability to the extent that he can prove he paid a sales tax to another state. Although most states already grant credit for out-of-state sales tax payments, they nevertheless continue to exempt sales made to out-of-state customers. Under these conditions, for out-of-state sales to be taxed, they must be taxed under the use tax of the resident state of the purchaser. The use tax is difficult to administer and is generally collected only when applied by the selling firm or when the item purchased requires a license for use—an automobile, for example.

If taxation of out-of-state sales were the general practice, a mixture of the origin (source) and destination principles would exist. The origin principle is followed to the extent that an out-of-state sale does not benefit from tax exemption. The destination principle would be followed when additional taxes were collected by the state of the consumer if taxes paid were less than those charged in the state of the seller. Because of these difficulties, state use of the retail sales tax is approaching a crisis situation.

The developing problems in the area of retail sales taxes have been recognized by Congress and by the states themselves. To date, Congress has not developed a program to solve these problems and to relieve the burden placed on the American international balance of trade by the state approach to indirect taxation.

CONCLUSION

The retail sales tax is the cause of considerable inefficiency in the carrying out of economic activities in the United States. The justification of the development of the tax during the "Great Depression" and its expansion during the great surge in primary and secondary education costs in the 1950s and 1960s no longer exists. Nevertheless, use of the tax at the state level continues to expand.

The collection of a value-added tax at the national level with revenues returned to the states on the basis of retail sales or on the basis of the location of the source of the value added taxed by VAT is an alternative that needs to be studied.

THE VALUE-ADDED TAX AS A STATE TAX

The crux of any serious proposal to introduce VAT as a state tax is the determination of how interstate business is to be treated. This requires a consideration of the base and the tax liability calculation procedure to be utilized.

The VAT legislation of Michigan (1953–1967) and that proposed in West Virginia treated this subject differently. In addition, there are two other appropriate approaches that a state should consider in framing its VAT legislation. In this discussion the Michigan and West Virginia legislation is considered first. Next the basics of the two other VAT administration techniques appropriate for state use of VAT are described.

Michigan stayed basically with sales data in calculating the tax base of VAT. West Virginia, on the other hand, stayed with cost of sales. In the terminology of VAT, Michigan used the subtractive method and West Virginia the additive method. Again using VAT terminology, Michigan used the product base and West Virginia the income base.

MICHIGAN

The base of the Michigan VAT was calculated by making itemized allowable business deductions from gross receipts.[58] The deductions in arriving at the base are important for what they *do not* include as well as what they do include. Wages and salaries paid were not deductible. Depreciation was not deductible if claimed on furniture, fixtures, equipment, or any other tangible personal property. Dividends paid on preferred and common stock were not deductible nor were profits of a business. The large deduction for most taxpayers was the cost of purchases from other firms.

Michigan companies doing business in another state allocated their VAT taxable base to Michigan through application of the conventional three-factor formula—property, payroll, and receipts (sales). The percentage of the firm's total of each of the three elements included in calculating the base allocable to Michigan was added and divided by

3 to determine the portion of the base of VAT to which the tax rate was applied.

The approach Michigan took relative to VAT is the same as that followed relative to the allocation between states of business taxable income under the corporate profits tax and the individual income tax. The *Armco Steel Corporation* vs. *Department of Revenue* decision (359 Mich. 430), 1960, established the Michigan VAT to be an income tax. The effect of this decision was to permit Michigan to treat interstate transactions under their VAT as other states were treating the business income base for their income and profits taxes. The legality under the Commerce Clause of treating VAT like a retail sales or a gross receipts tax was not considered.

If VAT were treated like an ordinary state retail sales tax, all the goods subject to the sales tax sold in Michigan by out-of-state firms could have been subject to a use tax. Under this approach, the VAT rate would be applied to total sales of an out-of-state firm in Michigan and the VAT burden on Michigan sales of in-state and out-of-state firms would be uniform. Under the income tax, or formula, approach used in Michigan, if the out-of-state firm had a minimum of property and payroll in Michigan, the VAT rate on the sales of the out-of-state firm in Michigan was only about one-third as high as on sales of a firm operating nearly entirely within Michigan.

A Michigan firm making a very large portion of its sales outside Michigan under the three-factor formula would pay a VAT rate on total receipts that would be about two-thirds of the rate of a firm carrying out all its activities within the state. The Michigan VAT rate applicable to an out-of-state firm making all its sales in Michigan was about one-half as high as the rate applicable to a Michigan firm making all its sales outside Michigan.

Under the Michigan approach a wheat farmer exporting his wheat out of the state would have to pay VAT on two-thirds of the base that would be taxable if sold for final use within the state. The same relative VAT burden would exist for other firms making nearly all their sales to out-of-state customers.

WEST VIRGINIA

The proposed West Virginia VAT was very definitely an income tax. The law provided for the taxation of "value added income of business."[59]

The base of the tax was (1) interest payments except those made by financial institutions on savings accounts, (2) rentals or other payments required to be made for continued use of possession, (3) compensation paid for personal services rendered by employers and officers, (4) all taxes imposed that are measured by income except the portion of the social security tax paid by business, (5) contributions to employer-provided trusts and profit-sharing funds.[60]

The West Virginia legislation did not work down to a VAT base by allowing and not allowing certain items to be deducted from a receipts total. It directly identified the income items to be included in the tax base. It used the income or additive approach all the way.

West Virginia broke away from the Michigan halfway house VAT which used sales as the base but administered the tax as though income were the base. If the West Virginia legislation had become effective, it would without question have had to use the well-established procedures of distributing interstate income of businesses.

THE DESTINATION PRINCIPLE

The approach of the Michigan VAT law has not been followed by the Common Market countries and other Western European nations. They have all followed what is called the destination principle.

This approach attaches VAT much more closely to the article than does the Michigan procedure. It moves VAT toward being a tax on the selling price—that is, a transaction tax. The fact of VAT's being a tax on total receipts or sales is taken more seriously under the destination principle than under the Michigan method.

The collection of a use tax on goods imported into a state at a rate equal to a state's retail sales tax is an acceptable procedure in American interstate tax relationships.[61] The American relationship of the use tax to the retail sales tax is the basic equivalent of the Western European relationship of the border tax to VAT.

The use of the destination principle on goods produced within the state using VAT would mean that goods sold outside the state would be exempt from a state's VAT. On the other hand, firms producing outside the state but making sales within the state would be liable for the full VAT rate, just like in-state firms.

The idea of the collection of a use tax on interstate sales is well established. Although the use tax is related largely to the state retail sales tax, this does not mean that its applicability is limited to consumer out-of-state purchases. Many state retail sales taxes include machines and building materials as a portion of their base. Therefore, these industrial goods are frequently subject to the use tax. However, sales of raw materials are not included, nor are general sales to those who are not the final users of the goods. Because the legal basis of the use tax is the concept of coming to rest in a state, the coverage is only of interest in identifying how the tax works in practice.

A VAT treated as a sales tax would require application of use taxes to a wider range of sales than the present use tax covers. Even so, a use tax related to VAT does not appear to violate the basic concept of a use tax as a tax equal in rate to the local tax and justified because the goods come to rest within a jurisdiction where the local tax is applied.

The Michigan VAT procedure of allowing the deduction from gross receipts of goods purchased is not fundamentally different from the accepted practice in the levy of use taxes. When the use tax is related to the retail sales tax, if the state use tax is paid, the goods are not subject to the state retail sales tax.

A state adopting VAT could decide to apply VAT as a transactions tax and to follow only the border tax portion of the destination principle. Under this approach goods produced in the state and sold outside the state would continue to be subject to VAT. This would violate the general principles under which the retail sales and use taxes operate. Generally, sales made to customers living outside the jurisdiction are not subject to a retail sales tax. However, this procedure is not dictated by constitutional difficulties. It is done rather to encourage sales to nonresidents.

The fact that a nonresident paid a retail sales tax when he purchased an item does not exempt the goods from the application of the use tax by the state of residence. The nonresident purchaser should have requested exemption from the sales tax under the law of the state of purchase.

The real question relative to a state VAT that applied a border tax on imports but did not exempt exports is: If this procedure were used by a number of states, would its possibility of double and multiple taxation violate constitutional law?

THE ORIGIN PRINCIPLE

If a border tax were not levied on goods and services sold within the state by out-of-state producers, and if goods and services sold out of the state by in-state producers were taxable, a state VAT could be levied on the origin principle—that taxes are paid to the jurisdiction where production takes place. In utilizing this procedure, a state would be assuming that other states levy relatively as heavy a burden on their producers as the VAT state does on its own businesses.[62]

RECOMMENDED STATE VAT

Actually, if a state were to initiate a VAT, it would appear desirable for the legislation to avoid both the Michigan and the West Virginia approaches. The Michigan legislation required out-of-state sellers in Michigan to calculate a relatively complicated income concept to which the ratios were applied to allocate the VAT base for taxation. The West Virginia legislation avoided much of this problem. The new 1975 Michigan *single business tax act* uses basically the approach used under the 1953-1967 VAT type tax, called the *Business Activities Tax* (BAT).

Both Michigan and West Virginia had retail sales taxes when they passed VAT legislation, and the retail sales taxes were not repealed. This provided an inducement to both legislatures to move toward the income-type VAT. This pressure does not exist in states that would substitute a VAT for their retail sales tax or who do not use a retail sales tax. Therefore, a VAT in a state without a retail sales tax could be a real production- and sales-based VAT.

It does not appear as though any real problems of constitutional law would arise from the full application of the destination principle to a VAT enacted by a state. A sales-based VAT on imports into the state could be collected like a use tax. The businesses producing and selling goods in the state would be able to deduct from their VAT liability both (1) VAT paid as a border tax (use tax) on purchases from out-of-state businesses and (2) VAT included in the invoices of purchases within the state. All sales outside the state could benefit from a refund of VAT paid.

CONCLUSION

The use of the income-type VAT like that proposed in West Virginia would permit levying VAT on both exports and imports. As indicated in the discussion of the Michigan law, however, it does grant some favors to out-of-state sellers and somewhat hurts domestic producers with out-of-state as well as in-state markets.

The best approach for a state introducing a VAT seems to be the adoption of a modified destination procedure. VAT would be collected on all sales within the state. If the sale were made out-of-state to come to rest within the state, the use tax technique developed under the sales tax would be used. However, sales made for out-of-state destinations would bear the same VAT burden as in-state sales. The base of VAT would include all receipts from sales of domestic firms plus all sales of out-of-state firms coming to rest in the state using VAT. Double taxation could be avoided by providing for the refund of VAT on out-of-state sales to customers located in states using VAT.[63]

4

Fiscal Impact Analysis

Certainly one of the more persistent attitudes toward the value-added tax is that prices and unemployment would be increased if a portion of the individual income tax and the corporate profits tax were replaced with a VAT.

A good illustration of this myopia is provided by two government publications, one prepared by the United Kingdom and the other by the United States. The UK study called the *Richardson Report* came out in 1964.[1] The U.S. study was distributed ten years later and is called the *ACIR Report on VAT.*[2]

The UK study assumes out of hand that the replacement of corporate profits taxes with a VAT would raise prices by the same percentage as the VAT tax rate. No consideration is given to the effect on prices and investment of the elimination of CPT or of possible backward shifting to lower profits, lower land rents, lower wage increases and increased efficiency arising from the introduction of VAT.[3]

The ACIR study hedges somewhat in its introductory statement which goes like this, "The consumption value-added tax would lead to an equivalent rise in prices, assuming the tax would be fully shifted forward and that its introduction would be accompanied by an accommodating monetary expansion."[4] However, the study assumes without doubt that the money supply will increase and higher prices will prevail, because if this didn't happen unemployment would ensue and that would be much worse than inflation. Also, the study assumes the reduction of taxes that would take place if VAT provided only replacement revenues, would fail to develop either a downward pressure on prices or a stimulant of economic activity. In line with this way of thinking, it is assumed higher income or payroll tax withholdings do not trigger higher wage demands and no consideration is given to the rather well-established position that higher corporate income tax rates either reduce investment or force up prices to the levels required for normal after-tax profit rates, more than likely some of both.

The British thinking relative to tax sources some ten years earlier must be partially responsible for the continuing UK economic difficulties. It seems rather too bad that we are following in their footsteps.

An approach can be made to understanding the desirable and undesirable features of the value-added tax as a major national tax by looking at the tax's impact on basic achievements that are used to judge tax policy. In the sections that follow, VAT is considered in relation to prices, revenue sharing, tax justice, employment and economic growth.

PRICES

It is generally considered desirable to levy taxes that do not increase the prices of goods and services purchased largely by the poor and lower-middle-income groups and therefore avoid an increase in the inequality of distribution of income and wealth.

PRO

The prices at which goods and services are available are affected by the costs of government services. However, the pressure is not always toward higher prices as is so often assumed. For example, if services purchased with tax funds are considered, costs for a given level of satisfaction may be decreased by more than the taxes collected increased costs. In addition, VAT as a tax has a number of cost-decreasing elements, and its price impact is not limited simply to passing the tax forward as an add-on to the seller's price.

As VAT becomes an additional business cost, the firm can bargain to decrease other costs as well as bargain to increase its prices. The likelihood of these actions is questioned by those who ask, if the shifts are made after the tax, why they weren't made before the tax by a business firm anxious to maximize profits. If one concludes that change is not possible merely because a tax is levied, one is left with a tax paid out of wealth or out of profits in excess of the amount required to attract and hold capital. Under these conditions the effect of VAT would be the same as one would expect from personal income or corporate profits taxes.

On the other hand, the introduction of a VAT can be assumed to trigger changes in the prices of labor, raw materials, and capital and/or changes in prices of goods and services sold. The assumption that prices are increased by the amount of the VAT means that costs are also increased by this amount and that the profitability of the firm is maintained only if the quantity sold is not decreased by the price increase. Former sales levels can be maintained at the higher price levels only if permitted by an expanded monetary velocity and/or money supply.

The complex of relationships between prices and sales affected by an increase of tax collections through the use of VAT leaves many opportunities for a variety of impacts. The possibilities do not differ widely from those available to a business firm adjusting to an increase of payroll taxes or corporate profits taxes. Upward monetary adjustment along with any tax increase can ease adjustment to the new situation by making price increases easier.

The principal difference in VAT adjustment is that the tax increase has not affected the cost of one particular factor of production. The higher payroll tax has increased the cost of labor, and the higher CPT the cost of capital. Because of the selectivity of payroll taxes and CPT, each brings about pressure to reduce labor or capital used. The placing of a special tax on payrolls and profits, with a rate that differs between the two, tends to reduce efficiency by causing a less than optimum use of labor or capital. This is not true of VAT with its theoretical uniform coverage and uniform rate. This uniformity and universality makes the tax neutral in its effect and therefore does not upset the basis of making optimal decisions.

If a payroll tax and a profits tax were introduced at a uniform rate, they would largely amount to an additive VAT. The economic neutrality advantage of a VAT could be gained by increasing existing payroll taxes and decreasing corporate profits taxes until their rates were equal.

CON

The assessment of a general tax on the sales price, which is the base with a subtractive VAT, makes a price increase by the amount of the tax very nearly automatic. The business firm realizes that everyone has to pay an equal percentage of price as a new tax. This assures him that he can increase his price by this amount without sacrificing a share of the market.

These higher prices will cause additional unemployment unless VAT replaces taxes on profits, causing a stimulation of investment, or unless a countervailing monetary policy is put into effect. Also, one has no assurance that investment will be expanded because taxes on profits are reduced. The reduction of sales through higher prices may counter the investment stimulant of lower profits taxes. Also, the disadvantages of monetary ease to stimulate investment or sales may outweigh VAT's fiscal strengths under conditions of great inflationary sensitivity.

Payrolls and profits as a portion of cost vary from firm to firm. Therefore, the collection of more revenues from one or the other of these taxes affects firms unevenly. The result is that the adjustment required by a new, less general tax is frequently made through greater efficiency and reduced costs. Therefore, additional revenues collected in this partial manner are less likely to increase prices than is revenue provision through a national VAT.

GENERAL

The introduction of VAT in Holland was accompanied by a considerable price increase; in Germany price effects were largely absent. The currencies of both countries have increased in value by about the same amount relative to the American dollar.

These experiences and those of Belgium and Denmark in introduction of VAT seem to indicate that economic conditions existing at the time of introduction affect the price impact of VAT. Price stability has apparently been assured by having a system of price controls in effect when VAT is introduced and later gradually removing them. Once VAT is introduced, it apparently provides considerable relative price stability to internationally traded goods, as demonstrated by the general upward valuation of many of the currencies of countries using VAT.

All taxes increase prices and/or decrease incomes. Sometimes it is reasoned that taxes increase production by putting into productive use resources that would be idle if the tax were not collected and spent.

Under these probably unusual conditions, a tax increases incomes while prices could fall or remain unchanged.

The taxation of personal income or business profits is often believed to decrease incomes of persons or firms paying the tax. The taxation of production or sales is often considered to cause price increases. The taxation of land is usually assumed to decrease rent income, to increase the efficiency with which land is used, and to decrease the price of land.

A subtractive VAT becomes due when a sale is made, and an additive VAT when income is realized. But the tax as a percent of total sales actually paid by the seller with a check to the Treasury varies according to what portion of the sales price is made up of purchases from other firms. The influence of this variation must be uncertain, but it perhaps reduces the extent to which VAT affects prices in the manner expected of a general tax covering all sales and all incomes under conditions where some monetary easing can be expected. Therefore, the likelihood that prices will increase by the same percentage as the VAT rate is decreased.

THE GERMAN EXPERIENCE

In January 1969 the *Neue Westfalische Zietung* of Bielefeld, West Germany, commented on how VAT had worked out during its first year. It was the conclusion of the article that the tax did not cause an overall price increase. The rule of thumb used by the government when introducing VAT, that one-third of prices would increase, one-third remain the same, and one-third would decrease, proved to be correct.

TAX THEORIES

The diffusion theory is an approach to a general theory of the burden of taxes. The theory teaches that the burden of taxes is always carried by the economically weak. The distribution dictated by relative economic strength is not changed by type of tax. Another general theory of incidence developed by the physiocrats, a group of French economic analysts of the mid-eighteenth century, saw the incidence of all taxes resting on the landowner, for he was the only person producing a *surplus*. In the 1970s the general equilibrium approach to a broad-based tax concludes that this type of tax does not have an incidence.

In the 1920s E. R. A. Seligman of Columbia University identified what he called the *transformation impacts* of taxes. Transformation came in two shapes, both good.[5] The first kind was the increased effort that taxation generated. The effect, of course, was increased productivity because of the tax. The second kind was the improvement in productive techniques induced by particular methods of assessment.

Somewhat later, A. C. Pigou, the British public finance giant, developed the *announcement effect* as an aspect of tax incidence. In his book, *A Study in Public Finance*, published in 1947, announcement effects were described as the effects of a tax arising from the expectation of a change in the rate of a tax being applied to a base that the taxpayer could control to a greater or lesser degree.[6] It refers to the effect on economic plans and actions arising from a shift in kind, coverage, or rate of tax.

The diffusion theories—the physiocratic theory, the transformation impact, and the announcement effect—all accepted the idea that the economic impact of a tax went beyond the fact that the taxpayer made a payment to the government. The additional impact of a tax arose through shifting. Analysis of the shifting of a tax is required if the incidence is to be found. Each of the theories outlined so far has within it an assumption of shifting.[7]

The assumption of the GATT provisions that a tax on an article raised its price is called *forward shifting*. The assumption that individual income taxes reduce disposable income rather than causing higher wages and unchanged disposable income is *backward shifting*.

Forward shifting of sales and excise taxes was the general assumption until several American taxation theorists challenged the idea some twenty years ago.[8] They pointed out that taxes on articles—sales taxes —could be shifted backward as easily as, or perhaps even more readily than, taxes on profits and incomes. After all, they pointed out, when only the tax is considered, and government expenditures and the level of monetary activity are not changed, taxes reduce effective demand. When effective demand is reduced, the prices and incomes received by workers and capitalists decline. This means, of course, that the tax is not shifted forward in higher prices but rather backward in lower costs —that is, lower income to workers and owners.[9]

OBSERVATION OF TAX EFFECT ON PRICES

General observation of the current economic situation leads one to conclude that it is take-home pay and profits after taxes that are meaningful. Therefore, every effort will be made by the taxpayer and his representatives to prevent a reduction of these amounts because of a tax increase. It is also true that the introduction of VAT would cause all businesses to attempt to increase prices enough to pay VAT. In both instances ability to achieve the aim depends on aggregate demand. If the level of aggregate demand—that is, the ability to purchase—is falling, both direct and indirect taxes get shifted backward through lower prices or unemployment. When markets are strong, forward shifting is more likely.[10]

Degree of transparency is another idea related to shifting and incidence of taxation. The higher the degree of transparency of the tax— that is, the buyers' knowledge of the actual amount of the tax—the greater the shifting. The retail sales tax, being most transparent, would be most easily shifted; next would be VAT, and then CPT. The least transparent is the *taxe occulte*—a tax included in price because of taxed items used in the production process.[11]

A few more points are worth mentioning. It is sometimes thought that a medium-rate tax is more likely to be shifted forward than a low-rate tax or a relatively high-rate tax. The idea is based on the likelihood that producers would absorb a low-rate tax and that consumer purchases would fall off if the tax rate were high.

Taxation incidence and shifting is a fascinating area of conjecture. The whole business is not even considered in prices paid and charged in the private economy. Public economy development of the idea undoubtedly arose from the early interest of economists and moral philosophers in tax justice. This in turn is related to efforts to make the burden of taxes heavier on the well-to-do than on the poor.

If there is any general conclusion arising from empirical studies of CPT, it is that in the short run it reduces profits and in the long run it increases prices.[12] This conclusion translates into a tax that is inflationary. Without CPT, money would not have to be so easy to stimulate investment, and prices as a result would not be so high after production got under way. Also, in the long run profits are a cost of production that must be covered by prices charged.

In 1967 William Verity, president of Armco Steel Corporation, wrote to the House Ways and Means Committee that the proposed 10 percent CPT increase would force his company to raise prices substantially or sharply cut back on the investment program.[13] He might have added that his international competitive situation would deteriorate with a CPT increase, because he could not deduct it from export prices or place a border tax on imported steel, as could be done if VAT were introduced.

Indirect taxes are paid only if they are shifted backward on you as a supplier or forward on you as a purchaser. The tax does not apply to the enjoyment of leisure, and therefore encourages it. This leisure statement needs to be modified if purchases are needed to enjoy leisure or if a reduced payment for services forces the expenditure of more time or effort to maintain an accustomed standard of living.

Individual income taxes also encourage leisure as a use of time. The benefits of leisure are not taxable. Again, the tax may force more work, and therefore less leisure, to reach acceptable income levels.

It would seem that indirect and direct taxes combine to increase the attractiveness of idleness. Or maybe they combine to push one to work harder to enjoy a given level of private-sector consumption and savings.[14]

A general or broad-based tax such as VAT is sometimes considered to be a tax without burden—that is, without incidence. This is true if it is assumed that all incomes or prices remain in the same relationships to each other after the tax as before. The tax has not placed a burden on anyone, because no one is relatively worse off. Under these conditions, the incidence arises entirely from expenditure. The individuals or groups benefiting least from government expenditures financed with the collections bear the incidence of the tax. An interesting idea: burdenless tax but burdensome expenditures.[15] Actually it fits in well with the role assigned to VAT.

PROBLEMS OF PROFIT SHARE AND RATE RETURN

The corporate profits tax, the major tax paid by business to the federal government, is also used by some thirty-five of the fifty states. The tax rate is applied to taxable corporate profits. In considering the incidence of this tax, the major point of emphasis is on what the tax has done to profits as a percentage of national income, as a rate of return on investment, or as a percentage of business sales. Recently considerable attention has also been given to the effect of corporate income taxes on prices. The data support the general conclusion that when rate of return on capital is used as the basis for the analysis, the CPT does not reduce profits because the historic rate of return has not fallen as corporate profits taxes have increased. The general conclusion, when profits are considered as a portion of national income and sales, is that profits are a decreasing portion of the total and therefore that profits have been decreased by the increased rates of the corporate profits tax.[16] In brief, this is where the analysis of incidence of the corporate income tax as indicated by profit trends rests.

Economic theory has always differed considerably relative to the incidence and therefore the shifting of the corporate income tax that takes place in the long run. A fundamental reason for the uncertainty has been the difficulty of determining how the CPT has affected the quantity of capital in the long run—that is, the quantity of investment. Economists have differed much less in their theories on the incidence of the CPT in the short run, because the short run has been defined to mean that the quantity of capital is not changed.

PRICE-SETTING AND PROFIT MAXIMIZATION

Traditional marginal economic analysis teaches that if firms are maximizing their profits, or are attempting to do so, before a tax measured by corporate profits is imposed, the new tax gives them no reason to change their prices. The price and output that will yield maximum profits before the tax is levied will yield maximum profits after the tax is in effect. Any increase in prices by a firm operating at its optimum point will reduce profits before taxes and will leave it with smaller after-tax profits than it would earn at the old price.

Certain qualifications of the incidence conclusion of this type of analysis have usually been conceded. One is that the self-restrained monopolist or oligopolist will find in the tax increase an excuse for exercising market power and might raise prices when the tax is increased. In order to believe that in the short run the corporate income tax is shifted to prices so that the incidence does not fall on profits, one must believe that pricing in the American economy is dominated in the short run by the decisions of restrained oligopolists or that price theory and its conclusions are irrelevant to the understanding of market behavior.

The results of a number of studies that have asked businessmen how they set prices have revealed that in many cases prices are set to earn a certain target profit and not to maximize profits, as traditional price theory assumes through its assumption that price is set where marginal revenue equals marginal cost. Also, several econometric studies that include factors other than the relation of prices to the CPT have been completed. One of these concluded that in the short run the incidence is shifted to prices and does not rest on profits as the traditional approach concluded. In the case of this study, the period included and the way in which other elements affecting prices were treated have been seriously criticized, and therefore the unique finding cannot be accepted at this time. Another econometric study using quite a different approach arrived at a tentative conclusion that corresponds roughly with that of the traditional findings based on marginal price theory. A final and actually most ambitious economic study seems to conclude the corporate income tax actually increased after-tax corporate profits.[17]

MORE DETAIL ON LONG-RUN INCIDENCE OF THE CORPORATE INCOME TAX

Time-series-based analyses of the incidence of the corporate income tax are studies of its long-run incidence. Data from these analyses are available and have been the subject of a number of commentaries.[18]

A study comparing profits as a percentage of corporate value added during 1922–1929, when the CPT rate was about 10 percent, with

1948–1957, when the corporate tax rate was about 52 percent, shows that corporate profits *before* CPT rose only from 19.2 percent to 22.6 percent. It is estimated with less reliable data that corporate income after taxes as a percentage of corporate value added was 16.0 percent during the 1922–1929 period and only 12.7 percent during the 1948–1957 period.

The conclusion that seems to follow from these data is that as CPT rates increased the share of corporate value added—that is, gross national product—arising from profits decreased. However, this type of comparison necessarily assumes that the share of corporate value added consisting of profits was affected only by changes in the corporate income tax rate. Obviously, a number of other factors also affect profits as a share of value added. One of these factors was a substantial increase in the ratio of sales value—aggregate sales—to value of capital employed. This relationship is called *capital turnover*. The increase of sales per dollar of capital permits a smaller profit portion of the sales dollar to provide an equal or larger return to dollar of capital.[19]

A reliable study shows that the increase in the after-corporate-tax earnings per dollar of investment has been due to the added efficiency per dollar of capital in terms of dollars of sales. This same change could have arisen from the development of administered prices aimed at a profit goal. The data themselves do not reveal whether the rise of dollar value of sales per dollar of capital was due to increased capital efficiency or ability to increase prices.

It is well known that a significant portion of postwar corporate profits was associated with price increases and inflation, with inventory profits accounting for much of the price-related profits. The net rate of return on the total capital base of all manufacturing corporations is calculated to have been 7.6 percent during 1927–1929, when the statutory rate of the corporate income tax was 11 to 13.5 percent; it was 6.3 percent during 1936–1939, with corporate statutory rates of 15 to 19 percent; it was 8.5 percent during 1955–1957, with a corporate statutory rate of 52 percent.

It is obvious that the findings of none of these studies can prove that net corporate profits would not have been much higher in the 1950s, for example, if corporate profits taxes had not increased to the very high 52 percent rate. It is of interest in terms of corporate profits as rate of return on equity capital, that students of the subject not particularly interested in the incidence of the corporate income tax have completed solid studies to explain why corporate profit rates are what they are without attributing much of a role to corporate income taxes.

For example, one study of before-tax corporate profits during the postwar period (1947–1959) found variations to be determined by fluctuations in the net markup and to be related to variations in the level of output. Another study explained corporate profits, before taxes and before depreciation allowances, over the two periods 1923–1941 and 1946–1959 as a function of GNP originating in the corporate sector, the year-to-year change in that GNP, capital stock valued at current prices, and effective corporate tax rates. However, effective tax rates turned out to be statistically insignificant. The conclusion of this study was that corporate profits taxes had their incidence on corporate profits and that the expanding rate of return after taxes was due to a shortage of capital. Bringing in the impact of the corporate income tax on the quantity of capital made this a long-run study.

CONCLUSION

The shifting of a tax backward onto lower rents, profits, interest, and wages rather than forward into higher prices is a real possibility in the case of the use of VAT. It is also true that a tax directly placed on income may result in higher prices through successful efforts to maintain incomes.

Theories of where the burden of a tax rests vary considerably. The great variation is perhaps largely due to the fact that economic conditions affect where the burden of a tax rests. In other words, the burden of a tax changes over time.

The theories and empirical work in the area of the effects of taxation are not very satisfying. The weaknesses arise from the difficulty of isolating the taxation effect from other economic, political, and social changes. Nevertheless, efforts aimed at understanding how taxes affect our society are very useful, because they at least force one to look beyond the name of the tax or the one who makes the actual payment to the government.

REVENUE-SHARING

Much of the current dissatisfaction with revenue-sharing by the federal government arises because people in one section of the country feel that they are asked to provide assistance to another area that for one reason or another is not adequately utilizing its tax base. Also, central city areas that need assistance see much of their economic surplus being drained off through high federal taxes paid by major corporations located within their borders. Both of these situations create rather deep-seated objections to really significant federal revenue-sharing.

PRO

A major national value-added tax becomes an important portion of a viable revenue-sharing policy because it is a procedure for providing funds needed to finance the program while eliminating the serious shortcomings of the retail sales tax. In addition, revenue-sharing based on VAT collections can truly allocate the revenues to the geographic location where the production took place, and in this way sharply reduce major shortcomings arising from financing revenue-sharing with income and profit taxes already badly needed to meet federal spending obligations. VAT at the national level can be used to replace state and local retail sales taxes and in doing this also allocate revenues to localities responsible for producing the base taxed. The unique characteristics of VAT that make it the ideal tax for the EC are also needed to make revenue-sharing in the United States a really viable and major program.

A national value-added tax of 5 percent collected on a broad base would provide substantially greater revenues than are now being collected by all state and local retail and gross receipts taxes. In 1975 a 5 percent VAT of the type envisaged would provide over $50 billion of revenues. This is more than double the amount expected to be collected by all state and local general retail sales and gross receipts taxes. The annual revenues available for revenue-sharing, taking into account revenues given up through repeal of state and local sales taxes, would annually total over $25 billion. This is many times the annual amount currently available under revenue-sharing. The introduction of a national VAT would assure substantial revenues for distribution to state and local governments for uses determined by those governments.

The retail sales taxes of a number of states include machines and equipment that are used to carry out business activities. These taxes become a portion of business costs that increase prices, which are the base to which the retail sales tax is applied. This "tax on tax" situation is avoided by VAT, which provides for the deduction of tax paid on machines and materials purchased from other businesses. This characteristic makes VAT a net turnover tax, and it is a strength of VAT that caused the EC to adopt it as the basic revenue-raiser.

The payment of revenue-sharing out of collections from a national VAT also eliminates the very complicated group of retail sales taxes in use by state and local governments. A national VAT provides a substantial reform of the general excise tax system while financing a substantial revenue-sharing program from increased tax receipts without higher rates. At the same time it increases the international competitiveness of American products. Revenue-sharing financed with borrowed funds or from taxes that cannot be refunded on exports or applied as border taxes on imports creates balance of payments problems on both the capital account and trade account sides. These side effects of financing government expenditures of all types can be partially or completely avoided through use of a national VAT.

A revenue-sharing program financed with national VAT revenues avoids the difficulties of returning personal or corporate income tax collections to the area where they were earned. Income from investments and business profits goes to the area where the legal control rests, which is frequently different from the area that was their source. The income and profit taxes are paid from this other location and not from the geographic area where the activity giving rise to the interest, dividends, pension, and profits took place.

CON

To give the federal government the right to levy a national VAT to finance revenue-sharing would take away from state and local governments their second most important source of tax revenues. Whether VAT was used to replace state and local sales taxes or was levied on top of the existing state and local sales taxes, the result would be about the same. In both instances federal demands on the transaction tax base would take away the freedom that state and local governments now have in the use of this approach to raise revenues.

The federal government is already dominant in the use of the personal and corporate income taxes. If it takes over the taxation of transactions as well, it would destroy state fiscal independence and federalism as we know it. Financing revenue-sharing through use of taxes that go beyond traditional federal sources would destroy the reduction of centralism and federal domination that was a principal purpose of the originators of the revenue-sharing concept. To accomplish its purpose, revenue-sharing must decrease the revenues available to the federal government for setting expenditure priorities and increase the ability of state and local governments to do this. The use of a national VAT to finance revenue-sharing maintains the ability of state and local governments to set spending priorities while reducing their control over the revenue source. Therefore, the net result of the change could be regarded as a reduction of local government control.

GENERAL

The United States is an economic unit. In fact, the entire developed world is fast becoming an economic unit. This unification into one functioning economy of millions of people and thousands of square miles has been made possible by technical data-gathering and communication developments. Economic practices and institutions are in the process of adjusting to these changes. Taxation procedures are one area of great importance in which adjustment is required and is beginning to take place. To an unknown extent at this stage of development, revenue-sharing is a political euphemism for the initiation of more centralized, uniform, and efficient revenue-raising procedures for the finance of spending responsibilities best carried out and determined at the state and local government levels.

Revenue-sharing initiated without new general financing will have to compete for funds with programs that have definite spending goals. Each of these spending goals has a strong political base and a group of ardent supporters. Revenue-sharing, because of its general and necessarily indefinite spending purpose, will encounter difficulty in competing effectively. As a result, revenue-sharing without a strong tax base dedicated to its financing is very likely to be pretty anemic and uncertain, and also increases the power of Congress because it can withhold as well as give, as we are learning in 1976.

THE POSITION OF RETAILERS

The careful study entitled *The Value-Added Tax in the United States —Its Implications for Retailers,* by the American Retail Federation, arrives at the general conclusion that VAT could be added to the existing American retail tax system without great inconvenience.[20] This is the conclusion of the study despite the decision not to include VAT in the quoted retail price but to have it quoted as an add-on similar to the retail sales tax.

In the study VAT is envisaged as a tax of 1 to 3 percent to furnish needed federal government revenues. After considering various other ways of raising the billions a 3 percent VAT is likely to provide, the ARF concludes that VAT, even though it is a new tax, is the best approach.

The study concludes that the retail industry would not be hurt by the addition of a federal VAT at the 3 percent level, even if state and local retail taxes remained unchanged. The study did not consider the procedure of introducing VAT as a method of eliminating all the administrative costs and difficulties associated with some forty-seven different state retail sales and use tax laws and at least that many court interpretations. The advantage of simplicity arising from the elimination of state variation would benefit retailers only indirectly, and therefore their unconcern for this aspect of possible development is understandable.

The only detailed study of American taxation of retail sales in relation to interstate compliance was completed in 1965. The conditions summarized in the conclusion at that time have not materially improved. In fact, any state uniformity advance has perhaps been destroyed by expansion of local retail tax legislation and higher rates. The *State Taxation of Interstate Commerce* report concluded that "in terms of its effect on compliance, the prevailing patchwork is likely to produce reluctance and resistance rather than the high degree of voluntary compliance which comes from clearly evident rules."

In addition, "for the states, the situation implies the loss of revenue. For the individual businessman, it implies an uncertainty as to his liability which may be resolved only at his own expense."[21]

It just could be that VAT will provide the answer to the growing retail sales and use tax nightmare.[22] In fact, the use of the VAT "out" could also be very helpful to the federal government in applying a VAT rate high enough to have a substantially favorable impact on the balance of international payments and at the same time cause a reduction of business costs consisting of the 20 percent or so of sales taxes levied on purchases for business use. A reduced increase in the national total of indirect taxes (new VAT collections minus repealed sales taxes) could provide the same international benefits as a VAT levied without repeal of retail sales taxes.

By having VAT provide replacement for revenues given up in state and local retail sales taxes, the federal government's VAT rate can be appropriately set at about 2.5 percentage points above what would be acceptable with an unchanged state and local sales tax situation. Also, of course, the administrative costs of the eliminated state and local sales taxes could be saved, and if the federal government were going to introduce a VAT, even though state and local sales taxes were continued, the additional administrative costs of applying a higher rate would not be great.

At this point, one can only hope that what seems to be good taxation sense is also appealing to private and public decision-makers. A tax is a tax for all of that—so why not make it as simple as possible?[23]

CONCLUSION

Funds for revenue-sharing are not available at the federal level, and as a result the program is uncertain and the available funds are inadequate. VAT at the national level dedicated to revenue-sharing, with each state deciding whether it wishes to eliminate its retail sales tax and/or increase other taxes, has great potential.

TAX JUSTICE

To Adam Smith (*Wealth of Nations*, 1776), a tax was just if it met the four maxims of taxation, i.e., equality, certainty, convenience and economy. By equality Smith meant contribution to government "in proportion . . . to the revenue which they respectively enjoy under the protection of the state." In addition, Adam Smith considered it just to have lower taxes on profits where risks were involved than on land rents where risks were minimal.

David Ricardo largely agreed with Adam Smith, but he went further with the idea that the landlords were the one group that could be taxed without increasing costs or decreasing production. (*On the Principles of Political Economy and Taxation*, 1817) He felt that additional taxes on land rents would largely result in reduced expenditures on luxury consumption goods, which would have very little undesirable effect. On the other hand a tax on wages would increase prices and a tax on profits would reduce capital formation.

John Stuart Mill (*Principles of Economics*, 1848) also believed in equality as did Adam Smith, but to Mill equality meant equality of sacrifice by the taxpayer. He believed in a highly progressive tax on those receiving an income above a certain minimum level required to maintain an acceptable scale of living.

Henry George (*Progress and Poverty*, 1879) advocated the position of Ricardo and Smith. Taxes that fell upon the rent of land were the only good taxes because only the economic rent arising from control of land was a true surplus.

C. F. Bastable (*Public Finance*, 1903) advocated tax rates that were proportional and did not change with the size of the base. Taxation based on benefit would lead to regressive rates and progressive taxation to equate sacrifice is like a ship without a rudder. Taxation of the "very poorest is a sad necessity" which is "not inconsistent with justice."

J. M. Keynes (*The General Theory of Employment, Interest and Money*, 1936) reasoned that until full employment was experienced, taxes that caused a redistribution of incomes from the high to the low, "may prove positively favorable to the growth of capital" and are therefore desirable.

Richard A. Musgrave (*The Theory of Public Finance*, 1958) postulates tax justice or equity to consist of treating equals equally. When horizontal equality exists under a tax system as much has been done to obtain tax justice as is feasible.

ABILITY TO PAY

The relation of a tax payment to ability to pay is frequently calculated by taking all those receiving a certain income and calculating the ratio of this income to taxes paid. When this is done, those receiving a windfall income fall into a higher income bracket than normal. Also, those who are new to the labor force or aged are receiving a lower income than normal and of course, there are always those who for one reason or another found it to be a bad year.

The young worker is a user of considerable credit to permit higher consumption levels. The middle-aged person is a saver and a repayer of borrowed funds, particularly of borrowings to finance housing. The aged person is consuming at a higher rate than justified by income, and through imputed housing spending and other consumption is "living off" savings.[24]

A tax that is an equal portion of the production of the nation becomes a tax that corresponds with changes in the level of permanent income. The permanent income of a family or an individual is dependent on the productivity of society. As long as the normal distribution of the age of the population does not vary greatly, a uniform tax on production is a good approximation of a proportional tax on normal income.

The payments of this type of tax, for example, a value-added tax, related to incomes of the moment, turn out to produce high ratios for the low income receivers and low ratios for many of the high income recipients. This apparent regressivity arises because of the life cycle of income and saving. If permanent or normal income is used as the base to which a VAT is related, the regressivity is wiped out. The use of the production of a society as the tax base corresponds to the taxation of the permanent income of the society.

The ability to pay of a taxpayer is affected by many conditions; often these cannot be established until time has passed. A successful musician may appear to have a great taxpaying ability but a sudden change in musical tastes or an accident reducing the quality of performance will quickly and sharply reduce current income and at the same time lifetime taxpaying ability. Although procedures providing for income averaging can reduce the injustice inherent in this approach to taxation, the complications involved in working out acceptable approaches nearly defy administration.

The use of VAT as a general indirect tax provides a tax paid by income receivers as a constant percent of products and services purchased and enjoyed. The tax is based on ability to pay to the same degree as purchases represent economic affluence. VAT does not fall on savings as does the income tax, and therefore to the degree that savings measure economic well-being, a general indirect tax such as VAT is weaker as an ability-to-pay tax than is an income tax. This conclusion must be modified by the additional future well-being, to be expected by the additional investment per worker VAT assures by its encouragement of saving. Also, VAT avoids the reduction of productive effort that an income tax encourages by leaving leisure as a high rate tax free alternative use of time.

The holding of wealth represents taxable taxpaying ability, which is not reached by the income tax except as income is realized. On the other hand, the wealth itself as used to purchase goods and services is reached by VAT.

The ability-to-pay concept of justice is related to the general belief that the provision of a greater equality of income distribution is good, and that this can be brought about through taxes paid largely by the wealthy and the large income receivers. A tax payment related to a benefit enjoyed receives its justice from its similarity to the payment of a price that approximates the cost of production.

PRO

Because one does not consider it unjust when the other costs of production are carried as an unequal portion of income or wealth of the users, it is also logical to accept the fact that some of the fourth factor—government—costs be distributed on the basis of use of production, and not to be concerned with the income or wealth of the purchaser and the percentage the price happens to turn out to be of the level of these measurements of affluence. VAT becomes a cost like wages and rent to be included by business people in making their pricing and other management decisions. The economic burden of the payment of VAT as a portion of price is distributed in the same manner as the other costs of goods and services purchased.

The value-added tax is an impersonal tax. It is not suited to making distinctions based on number of dependents, type of business ownership or usefulness of the product or service including VAT in its price. These special characteristics of VAT make it a procedure to raise substantial government revenues without affecting the efficiency of consumer or business choices. VAT is neutral and does not favor pop drinking over coffee drinking or cooperatives over corporations, or, for that matter, if the full theoretical base is used, churches over dance halls.

The basic justice of VAT rests on the fact that *all* activities require the support of government. Just how much this is for each activity cannot be accurately set. One can, however, be certain that in a modern society the cost of government assistance is greater than that assessed by a VAT with a rate of 10 or 15 percent. The portion of government costs recovered by VAT is done in a manner that leaves individuals and businesses free to make profit and satisfaction maximization decisions without being influenced by tax considerations. VAT provides a stable government revenue base that possesses the basic justice of the price system. An important desirable impact of government using a revenue base of this type is that it reduces the general fiscal burden to be carried by taxes with aims in addition to those of raising revenues.

CON

The levy of VAT is very similar to the levy of a tax on consumption. The business firms paying VAT pass the amount forward in higher prices. This forward shifting (as illustrated in Chart II) continues until the consumer makes his purchase, but stops there because people don't have a cost of production that can be passed along in higher wages and pensions. The consumer therefore becomes the final payer of VAT, and here is where the economic burden comes to rest.

The low and middle income consumer is able to save only a small portion of income received. Ninety-five to 100 percent of the income is spent for food, clothing, housing, etc. On the other hand, the upper income and rich consumer saves 15 to 25 percent of his income. The effect of this situation is to make payments of a flat-rate VAT covering all income and production, a larger percentage of the income of most poor and low income receivers. A tax that takes a higher percentage of the income of the low income receivers than of the middle and high income receivers is labeled a regressive tax.

A regressive tax is an unjust tax because the collection rate is the heaviest where each dollar of payment involves the greatest sacrifice. The result of the use of a tax with this sort of burden is to fail to collect taxes so that satisfaction sacrifice in tax payment is minimized.

GENERAL

The effect of a tax on the economic well-being of a society should be judged in terms of the role it plays within the general fiscal system. The introduction of VAT does not require the abandonment of income taxes with progressive rates or prohibit the introduction of wealth taxes, also with progressive rates—taxes that are paid largely by the rich and the high income earners.

In Sweden, the fiscal system allocates a very large portion of production for government use, but the general welfare is also very carefully guarded. A major Swedish revenue source is VAT. The collections from VAT are very important in meeting the very high costs of government-provided social services enjoyed directly and indirectly by all segments of the population. Without the large relatively neutral VAT collections, the costs of Swedish social programs would run the danger of making the Swedish private economy inefficient, and unable to meet the demands placed upon it.

THE DECLINE OF THE INCOME TAX

It is in the 1970s that the underside of the "according to ability-to-pay income tax" rolled to the surface all too visibly. The extrapolation of the doomsayers would predict an inability of government to finance itself as the faith of the people that the income tax was an ability-to-pay was destroyed.[25] However, human events and trends seldom follow the scientific curve, and therefore the loss of high levels of government service in many areas and growth in others cannot be forecast from an inability of the progressive income tax to extract the same level of buying power from the private economy.

The new 1975 German income tax structure is an example of one legislative approach. The revenues raised are to be reduced by DM 9 billion during a period when the cost of everything purchased by government is increasing at least as rapidly as the rate of the general inflation. The DM 9 billion is being given to low and average income earners, and everyone raising a family is to benefit from tax deductions or equal payments to those not paying an income tax because the family's taxable income is less than about $12,500 a year.

The ability of Germany to reduce income tax collections while prices are rising and required government services are not declining exists because of their very productive value-added tax and the growing collections from the national wealth tax. The income tax under this type of fiscal development becomes a tax paid only by those in the middle and upper income brackets. In fact, at the same time as large numbers were being taken off the income tax rolls the top income tax rate and the income tax starting rate were increased from 54.6 percent to 56 percent, and from 22 percent to 30.3 percent, respectively.[26]

The reduction of personal and corporate income tax rates of the

United States, at the same time as the need for government financed services has not been decreasing, has taken place with only the payroll tax available to make up somewhat for the reduced effectiveness of the income tax in providing federal revenues. The evolving situation has resulted in the use of large federal government deficits, rather than tax collections, to meet expenditure fiscal needs.[27]

CONCLUSION

The basic justice of VAT is that all activities producing goods and services for the market and for enjoyment by purchasers utilize some government services. These services have a price tag that cannot be set without excessive administrative cost. Therefore, it is just to allocate a portion of the total cost of government as a percent of the cost to be paid as a portion of the price to be paid to enjoy the satisfactions of consumption.[28]

The income tax under conditions where both a wealth and value-added tax exist becomes the appropriate tax for use only at the middle and upper income brackets with a maximum rate set to avoid reduction of willingness to produce and with inducements to encourage savings, i.e., exemption from the income tax of capital gains reinvested within a brief period of time.

EMPLOYMENT

The level of employment is related to the cost of employing a person. This cost consists of wages plus social security taxes and also more than likely contributions to a pension fund plus a medical program. Level of employment is also related to the portion of savings of American individuals and businesses that are invested in domestic enterprise. This amount is certain to be reduced if foreign profit opportunities look better than domestic, and if large government deficits eat up private savings. Finally, foreign competition can take away jobs if American exports bear more domestic taxes than American imports. This tends to be the situation if America's competitors use VAT but America doesn't.

PRO

A national value-added tax assessed on a broad base will provide over $10 billion per 1 percent of rate. A VAT of 10 percent would therefore provide $100 billion of tax revenues for the federal government. This is a sum sufficiently large to be of great assistance in meeting the financing needs of social security expansion and of permitting a reduction in the level of taxes arising from the corporate profits base.

Both lower social security collections and lower taxes on profits would tend to expand employment levels. The lower social security taxes would reduce the costs related directly to all current employees and all future employees. Under typical conditions, this would mean more employees could earn their wage cost, and therefore more could be hired. The lower taxes on profits would make domestic investment opportunities appear relatively more attractive and therefore stimulate expanded domestic investment. Also, lower taxes on profits make additions to plant and equipment possible that higher taxes would have forestalled.

Domestic employment levels in all areas are directly and indirectly affected by the quantity of exports relative to imports. In the 1970s, for the first time since the nineteenth century, U.S. imports of goods and services began to be greater than exports. International commerce resulted in a reduction of domestic employment. The four-fold increase in the price of imported oil has worsened a bad situation. The reasons for this situation cannot be established with certainty, and the period of time for which it will continue cannot be forecast. However, the substantial expansion of American expenditures to finance our Vietnam involvement, the growth of domestic income-maintenance expenditures financed without the development of indirect taxes, and the major use of borrowed funds must have been important causal elements.

If a 10 percent national VAT had been introduced in 1966 or even as late as 1969, much of the need to increase domestic costs through high interest rates and an inflated money supply could have been eliminated. The avoidance of these important causes of two-digit inflation would in itself have been very helpful in preventing an international situation that worked to reduce employment levels. In addition, the use of VAT would have made possible a refund on exports of the amount of VAT collected and an equal border tax on imports. A comparable situation with a government budget financed with borrowed funds was not possible without the dollar devaluations of 1971 and 1972.

Increases in payroll taxes since 1969 have been considerable, and new higher rates are continuing to be proposed and legislated. The same amount collected through VAT does not immediately increase employer costs of employment. Because VAT is paid at the time of sale rather than at the time of employment (as are payroll taxes), the employer under VAT is not committed to paying higher taxes until products are sold. Under a payroll tax, the payment is required before income is expanded. This difference changes the payment from one out of a generated flow of funds to one out of cash balances. As a result, funds collected with VAT become much less an additional cost of employing a worker and much more another element of general costs to be met out of sales.

CON

The levy of VAT reduces employment by increasing wages through price increases generated by each firm in adding the tax to sales prices. Because a large portion of a firm's value added consists of wages, a large portion of VAT is really only a tax on wages. In addition, the VAT included in the price of capital goods can be deducted from VAT due on sales; this causes the value-added tax to encourage use of capital rather than labor.

The firm purchasing new capital equipment to be used in its production processes will always have a considerable amount of VAT to be deducted in calculating VAT to be paid into the U.S. Treasury. On the other hand, a labor-intensive firm does not have this deduction available, and therefore its VAT payment check is a larger portion of its total sales. As a result, VAT tends to weigh relatively heavily on labor-intensive businesses, and this fact acts to reduce employment opportunities.

To the extent that taxation caused the tight money and inflation of 1966, 1969, and 1974, the later unemployment, and the development of an uncompetitive American industrial system, these were caused by a failure to increase conventional tax rates and to close loopholes in the application of the tax on corporate profits. The introduction of VAT might have been a better approach to maintaining sound employment levels than large-scale borrowing, but the effect would be far less than what could be gained by a more complete use of individual income and business profits taxes. Income and profits taxes can be collected without increasing costs and therefore do not develop additional pressures for higher prices as is true when VAT is used. Therefore, income and business profits taxes can maintain international competitive conditions without the need to levy increasing border taxes on imports, as is permitted when VAT is used.

Finally, the increase in unemployment is due to savings in excess of domestic needs and therefore a reduction of aggregate demand in the next period. These excess savings have been invested overseas, so most of their effect on demand and employment is in foreign nations rather than in the United States. To the extent that taxation can be effective, this undesirable situation can best be remedied by higher and tighter taxes on individual incomes and business profits.

GENERAL

If taxes use only income and profits as the base, a level of collections great enough to meet expenditure demands of a modern industrial state requires rates so high that pressures to narrow the base become unbearable. The reduced base further diminishes the revenue potential, causing either a starved public economy or a public economy that absorbs a large portion of individual and business savings through government borrowing. The result is an expanded public debt and a shortage of capital to meet private investment needs plus a rising dead weight burden of taxes used to pay interest costs.

POLITICAL ECONOMICS

America's great crisis of underutilization of human potential took place between 1930 and 1939. Times were bad. Prices were comparable with those of the panic years of the 1870s. Business profits had practically disappeared. Graduates of law schools were finding work as part-time service station attendants. The economic system had apparently stabilized without a return to good times.

Unemployment in 1929 was estimated to be only 3.2 percent. By 1931 the percentage of the labor force out of work was calculated to be 15.9 percent. By 1933 it had reached 25 percent and it was still at the 17.2 percent level as late as 1939. Unemployment in America was not licked until the factories added labor to fill European munition orders for World War II and men were needed for the expanding armed forces.

Early in January 1942, the National Resources Planning Board advocated government action to keep full employment after the war. Congress feared that this policy would require planned inflation, and the board was ordered dissolved. Nevertheless, President Roosevelt on January 11, 1944, proclaimed "the right to a useful and remunerative job" as the first of a new economic bill of rights.

Thomas E. Dewey, the 1944 Republican candidate for president, declared, "If at any time there are not sufficient jobs in private employment to go around, the government can and must create job opportunities, because there must be jobs for all in this country." This goal of jobs for all and the government as an employer of last resort was widely discussed as desirable postwar policy.

THE EMPLOYMENT ACT OF 1946

Because of their recent experiences, people greatly feared a return of unemployment when the war drew to a close in 1945. Congress went right to work framing legislation to guarantee that unemployment would never again be a serious problem. On February 20, 1946, President Truman signed the Employment Act of 1946. The declared national policy established in the legislation is included in its Section 2:

> The Congress hereby declares that it is the continuing policy and responsibility of the Federal Government to use all practicable means consistent with its needs and obligations and other essential considerations of national policy, with the assistance and cooperation of industry, agriculture, labor, and State and local governments, to coordinate and utilize all its plans, functions, and resources for the purpose of creating and maintaining, in a manner calculated to foster and promote free competitive enterprise and the general welfare, conditions under which there will be afforded useful employment opportunities, including self-employment, for those able, willing, and seeking to work, and to promote maximum employment, production and purchasing power.

The post–World War II unemployment so confidently expected and forecast by experts did not develop. Little credit for this unexpected favorable turn of events can be given to the Council of Economic Advisers, which was established under the Employment Act. In fact, the effectiveness of the council fell so low in 1953 that its survival was in serious doubt and Congress cut its appropriation to the bone.[29] In the next year, 1954, unemployment doubled. Obviously, the problem of maintaining an economy that offered everyone jobs was still unsolved, and the council was saved.

The provisions of the Employment Act did not bring forth specialized economic machinery to maintain a high level of employment. Thus, the goal of the most active advocates of the legislation was not and still has not been realized. Rather, the intent of the federal government to set policies that maximized employment was established and remains in effect. The act did, however, establish a council that keeps an account of the health of the economy and provides the president with a source of a current general interpretation of economic data generated by many government and private sources. It is unfortunate that almost from the beginning the council has been kept occupied with day-to-day economic brush fires. As a result, it has expended too few resources in long-range economic analyses, and after thirty years has not developed economic machinery to eliminate waste of unemployment and shortage of purchasing power. The unexpected severe inflation of 1973–1974 demonstrated clearly the need for a new approach to economic analysis. "Economic models based on closed systems with investment and consumption neatly combining to generate income no longer work."[30]

CONCLUSION

The value-added tax used as replacement for a portion of payroll, personal income, and corporate profits taxes has the potential of increasing employment by stimulating savings and investment and reducing the out-of-pocket costs of employing a worker. Also, tax rates become too high to administer if the needs of a modern industrial nation are to be met through use of only income and profits as a tax base.

Full employment continues to be important but legislation to reach the goal has not been adopted. Therefore, acceptable employment levels continue to rest on general fiscal-monetary policy.[31] The flat rates of VAT and their production of constant or reduced purchasing power during inflation provide a useful inducement to a government price stability policy. The personal income tax and its graduated rates act to increase real resources of government during inflation, and therefore tend to encourage an inflationary policy, and a fiscal policy consisting largely of reducing tax rates.

5

Economic Growth

The desirability of economic growth is being challenged here and there. Despite these expressed qualms, economic growth generally speaking continues to be considered desirable if properly directed and controlled.

Economic growth in our society arises largely from investment in productive undertakings of individual and business savings. A productive investment is defined as an undertaking that can produce a product or service that will be purchased at a price that returns a profit. This capitalistic process can be interrupted or stimulated by the tax system in use and by government expenditures.

The expenditures of government for education, transportation, research and development, and general improvement of efficiency are vital to economic growth. To perform these functions properly, a government cannot be worried about deficits and the need to initiate higher rates on taxes that tend to force a reduction of investment and saving and a deficit in the international trade balance.

PRO

If a national value-added tax is used in the United States to provide $100 billion or so of revenues, a substantial and relatively stable revenue base has been provided. A decline in economic activity of the type typically experienced in a downturn of the business cycle will not sharply reduce revenues flowing from this tax source. As a result, large deficits will not arise to force the government to abandon projects that are not directly aimed at meeting the problem of unemployment. It is also true that revenue stability is generally helpful in maintaining all kinds of activity in the government sector, including the responsibility of being employer of last resort.

A large, recession-caused government deficit, which tends to arise when capital gains and business profits provide a large portion of the tax base, reduces confidence in the monetary unit. The use of a major VAT mitigates a considerable portion of the unfavorable impact on economic growth that always arises from monetary uncertainty. The concept of the built-in cyclical flexibility of the federal budget has proven to provide surpluses that tend to cut off economic growth during the boom and large sterile deficits that fail to stimulate economic expansion during a recession.

In the mid-1960s economists of Great Britain and the United States became aware of the relatively greater economic growth rate of Western Europe. Their analysis led to the general conclusion that a portion of the cause of this situation was the expanding use of indirect taxes, and particularly of VAT, in Western Europe. VAT was having this effect because (1) the revenues it provided were permitting more liberal administration of business profits taxes; (2) the rebates it permitted on exports were stimulating the growth of the international sector; (3) the level of investment from private and public sources was increased; and (4) savings were stimulated and their use in more productive ways was encouraged. These four impacts were difficult to prove with data, although attempts were made. The proof of the pudding was in the eating, and Western Europe was experiencing a more rapid growth of productivity and per capita income than was the United States or the United Kingdom.[1]

Studies of the taproots of economic growth have pointed to government spending on education and social development programs to be fundamental. This is well illustrated in the stimulation of agricultural productivity through government-financed education programs. As society has become more complex, the need for this kind of government activity has undoubtedly increased. At the same time, the cost of performing required services has multiplied.

The results of education and research are difficult to measure, and programs must have long-term support before they produce desired results. The shortage and instability of federal funds arising largely from personal income and business profits taxes have worked to reduce the level, stability, and effectiveness of America's people development efforts. In turn, this has reduced the soundness as well as the rate of economic growth. A VAT, with its built-in revenue-providing stability and its large revenue-producing capability, cannot help but assist in remedying this reason for the underdevelopment of the full potential of American citizens.

CON

Economic growth takes place to meet effective consumer demand for goods and services. When more is purchased by consumers, business investment expands to meet the demand. Economic growth is held back by the shortage of ability and willingness to purchase on the part of the consumer and not by shortages of savings and investment. It is the shortage of markets and not the shortage of investment that retards economic growth.

The value-added tax retards rather than stimulates economic growth because it reduces the consumer's ability to purchase. VAT is passed forward in higher prices on consumer goods, and as most consumers save very little, the effect of VAT is to decrease sales.

The United States tends to save more than it can absorb in useful private investment or government deficits. This fact is demonstrated by the large outflow of American investment funds to other nations. The way in which these savings excesses can best be reduced through taxation is by emphasizing the taxation of business profits, high incomes, and the large estates of the rich. When this is accomplished, the full multiplier effect of the investment of all savings arising in America will be available to stimulate the growth of the United States economy.

To the extent that the relatively rapid economic growth of Western Europe arose from its tax system, the growth took place because conditions were quite different from those existing in the United States. Western Europe was short of capital and savings, so encouragement to save stimulated economic growth. The large importation of capital from America during the 1960s and 1970s demonstrates that this was the situation.

The use of VAT in Europe, instead of making more funds available for government spending on education and research, has stimulated income-maintenance expenditures. Social security and Medicare-type spending does not stimulate economic growth except to the extent that it may cause workers to be less aggressive in their wage demands or to be more willing to spend their earnings. Lower wage demands increase profits and savings when lower profits and savings would be desirable.

GENERAL

The evaluation of the economic growth of a nation as measured by the growth of its GNP has many shortcomings. An advanced industrial nation finds its expansion efforts concentrated in such areas as services and environmental preservation. Here productivity increases slowly and the benefits arise so largely outside the marketplace that measurement of value through the market system is impossible. When this is true, benefits as measured by GNP equal cost. Opportunity to equate price and benefit independently, as sale in the market does, is largely absent. No one has yet found a method to measure gross national human satisfaction. Yet this intangible is pretty much what human striving in the economic sphere is all about.

VAT FOR LOW INCOME NATIONS

The development of the third world is dependent on greater economic efficiency. It was thought for many years that because the levels of unemployment were high the development process could be hastened through deficit finance.

The approach has failed and instead of improvement the frequent result has been disorganization and inefficiency caused partially by prices that didn't function to encourage and allocate production to expand efficiency. Inflation and efforts to use direct controls, however, did develop. In these circumstances the raising of taxes that did not discourage investment while providing substantial revenues became necessary. The value-added tax has proven to be helpful.

BRAZIL'S ICM[2]

The ICM, Brazil's value-added tax, was enacted to decrease inflation that was retarding economic growth. It is a state tax and varies somewhat between states. However, the structure is basically the same in all states because the central government prescribed most of the basic features. The revenue provided is given credit for slowing down the Brazilian inflation and contributing to the nation's economic development.

All states apply a uniform flat rate equal to the rate ceiling on out-of-state sales. This ceiling is 19 percent. The rate on in-state sales can vary a bit and is 18 percent in the northwest and 17 percent elsewhere. These rates are tax inclusive, and were decreased by several percentage points in 1974. Only goods are included in the base. The base is further narrowed by excluding what are called essential foodstuffs. However, the two basic items of the Brazilian diet—rice and beans—are not included in the list. In 1971 machinery was moved from partial exemption to outright exemption. And in 1974 domestic industrial equipment was made subject to a zero rate.

Services are excluded from the ICM system because they are included in a municipal service tax levied on gross receipts of service businesses of all types. These taxes are the "property taxes" of Brazilian cities.

Construction is exempt but not the construction materials. Also, agricultural machinery is exempt. However, no provision for exemption is made in the trade sector, and businesses, no matter how small, are included under the ICM system. The ICM is collected from the small businesses under a *forfeit* procedure.[3]

Mineral inputs into manufacturing are not deductible, but oil refining is exempted for ICM purposes. Also, books, newspapers, and printing paper are exempt industrial areas. Finally, industrial exports are exempt, as are domestic purchases of industrial machinery. The border tax levied on imports excludes imported machinery.

The introduction of ICM as a federally controlled state tax in Brazil has proven to be a great improvement over the former turnover tax. It imposes more discipline by reason of its self checking feature and also through its "catching up" feature; it taxes value added that may have escaped at a previous stage.

OTHER LESS DEVELOPED COUNTRIES' (LDC) USE OF VAT

A number of LDCs have seen VAT to be a procedure for increasing the coverage and revenue productivity of their sales taxes. For example, several French speaking African countries have adopted modified forms of VAT.

The VAT legislation adopted varies considerably. In Senegal and the Ivory Coast VAT extends to only a small portion of merchandising activity beyond the manufacturing and import stage. This approximates the coverage of VAT when first introduced in France in 1954.

Despite coverage shortcomings, as Tables 8 and 9 demonstrate, VAT has become the best revenue producer of the transaction taxes used by LDCs as it has become for developed nations. In 1970 revenues varied from 10 to 30 percent of total tax revenues collected, and there is every indication that any LDC introducing VAT can expect collections to grow more rapidly than the general economy. This aspect of VAT can be very helpful to an LDC needing to provide additional and expensive government services as the cities grow and modern industrial facilities are established.

As was noted earlier, all of the developed countries' use of VAT currently provides for a full credit against VAT due on sales, of the VAT included in the purchase price of business equipment and machines. This practice has not been taken over by LDCs in any general way.

This difference in the application of VAT to capital goods of LDCs from what is the practice of developed countries arises partially because labor is abundant and capital is usually imported. Imported capital goods are, of course, the equivalent of importing additional labor—in this case congealed labor—and if imported, none of the congealed labor has been provided by domestic workers. In addition, most LDCs already have in place a program to encourage and subsidize capital investments considered helpful.

None of the LDCs using VAT have completely followed the European practice relative to investments of imported or domestically produced capital. In Africa the practice is to give credit for industrial goods but to refuse it on transportation equipment. In Ecuador and Uruguay only investments in fixed assets are eligible for full credit. In Brazil the tax credit route for industrial goods has been abandoned for an outright exemption. The exemption is a zero rate type, similar to the exemption benefit enjoyed by exporters.

One of the more helpful economic development potentials of the introduction of VAT by an LDC is the inducement it provides to the improvement of business accounting records. VAT requires the issuance of accurate invoices and the accumulation for the tax period of invoices showing type, value, and source of all purchases and sales. This for many businesses of LDCs is a giant step forward in getting on top of the operation. It is also true for many small businesses that the requirement is too much to be handled without excessive hardship. Under these circumstances the forfeit system is used.

Agriculture has been recognized as the economic area that has been least effectively developed by LDCs. It is also the product producing

Table 8

Value-Added Tax Rates in Selected Developing Countries
(in percent)

	Reduced	Normal	Increased	Services
		Applied to sales exclusive of tax		
Ecuador		4.0		not taxed
Malagasy Republic	6.0	12.0		
Uruguay	5.0	14.0		
		Applied to sales with tax included		
Brazil (states)		16.0–17.0		not taxed
Ivory Coast	7.5	15.0	30.0	
Morocco	12.0	15.0	20.0	7.5
Senegal	4.0	9.0	25.0	8.5

Table 9

Selected Developing Countries: Value-Added Tax (VAT) Revenue
as a Percentage of (1) Total Government Tax Revenue
and (2) Gross Domestic Product, 1968–70[1]

	Percentage of Total Tax Revenue			Percentage of Gross Domestic Product		
	1968	1969	1970	1968	1969	1970
Brazil (states)	30.8	28.9	28.4	8.5	8.4	8.1
Ecuador	—	—	10.3[2]	—	—	1.1[2]
Ivory Coast	29.8	29.1	27.4	5.7	5.4	5.4
Malagasy Republic	—	20.9	19.0	—	3.2	2.7
Morocco	18.8	23.9	24.8	3.0	4.2	4.5
Senegal[3]	20.9	17.7	22.3	3.3	3.2	4.0
Uruguay	9.8	13.2	16.0	1.2	1.7	2.1

SOURCE: "The Value-Added Tax in Developing Countries," *International Monetary Fund Staff Papers*, July 1973, p. 340.

[1]Government tax revenue is that of the central government, exclusive of social security payroll taxes, except for Brazil where it covers revenue of federal, state, and local governments. The VAT revenue includes that of supplementary tax on services levied by the same level of government, where applicable.

[2]1971.

[3]Fiscal years ending 1969, 1970, and 1971.

industry that has been least affected by VAT. In Europe a "global credit offset" device is applied to sales of farmers. The effect is to permit purchasers to claim VAT credit as though the farmer had paid it at the established rate for agricultural products. However, the farmer is unable to benefit from tax credit earned on goods purchased subject to VAT. This procedure is followed in Europe to avoid placing on farmers the obligation of keeping records. Of course, the need for this type of lenient treatment is even greater in LDCs for the small farmers, but this is not the case with the large plantation operations.

VAT legislation, by not requiring a tax payment by the farmer upon sale of his production, has avoided economic inducement for the farmer to sell outside normal channels. On the other hand, because VAT picks up total value added as its base, the original exemption does not result in a loss of total revenue based on the value of agricultural production. Therefore, VAT possesses several strengths as an agricultural tax appropriate for economic development. It encourages commercial agriculture while extracting from agriculture the revenues needed to meet government costs of a developing nation.

The use of VAT by LDCs has proven to be the best transaction tax approach. VAT can provide substantial revenues while encouraging domestic production and minimizing the potential of favoritism. Also, VAT has not proven to be too complicated for LDCs; and when administered in combination with the income tax, the result is better administration of both taxes and a more rapid development of record keeping procedures by domestic economic units.

Also, VAT, by developing a stable basic revenue source, reduces the need to finance through inflation. And perhaps inflation, through excess liquidity, is the economic impact least needed for economic development—especially by the LDCs.

CONCLUSION

The development of the full potential of the population is encouraged by the steady revenue of VAT and the reduction of the taxes on incomes increases the economic inducement to earn. On the other hand, VAT in Europe tends to be spent more on income security than income expansion.

The successful use of VAT in Brazil and several other less developed countries is very encouraging. Apparently VAT can be helpful in reducing the debilitating effect of high inflation rates. Also, VAT's encouragement of equity financing can increase the soundness of new business investments in these low per capita income countries.

BUSINESS TAXATION HARMONIZATION

Economic analysts, including the earliest writers, have wrestled with the problem of whether businesses are taxpayers or tax conduits. The development of conglomerate business enterprises operating in many nations has caused observers to doubt any simplistic theory of how business price policies are affected by taxes.

Currently business taxation analyses are deeply concerned with the impact of a tax system on economic growth and efficiency. The United States in very recent years has become a heavy user of tax gimmicks of one kind or another to stimulate investment and to hold capital at home. The United Kingdom and Western Europe generally are old hands at this type of tax activity. It is called *tax dirigism,* and it is the use of business taxes to encourage the private sector to carry out national economic goals.

BUSINESS TAXING EFFECTS AND TRENDS

Mr. A. Rubner reports that the overwhelming majority of economists and economic organizations favored the British tax reform of 1949, which levied a punitive tax on dividends paid out and a very light tax on earnings withheld by the corporation. The wide differential between rates on profits retained and rates on profits distributed was considered to be fair.[4] The British differential profits tax was also considered to be good because it would increase corporate investment by encouraging lower dividend payments with increasing funds available to corporate managers. This didn't turn out to be the result, and the tax was abandoned. It was reintroduced in 1965 in a different form, however, perhaps because of the U.S. example. And now ten years later a new approach has again been introduced.

Under the earlier legislation in the United Kingdom, large companies apparently continued to increase dividend distributions while closely held companies took advantage of the lower tax rates on undistributed profits. The net result was an expansion of dividend payments. In 1958 the British abandoned their punitive tax on dividends and adopted the unified profits tax, which was replaced in 1965 with a corporate tax favoring undistributed profits. The new legislation adopted in 1973 taxes retained profits the same as distributed profits, including the withholding tax on dividends or the tax credit imputed to the shareholder.

The British experience in taxation of corporate profits and the current policy demonstrate the development of tax legislation based on a theory that turned out to be wrong, as statistics can prove a case. The error appears to have been related to lack of knowledge of what determines corporate dividend policy and of the influences affecting the market value of a company share of stock. Finally, Parliament underestimated the impact of corporate raiders on dividend payout, and overestimated ability of company managers to utilize their firm's undistributed profits.

CAPITAL GAINS

Germany, with some exceptions, continues to operate under a theory that capital gains are not taxable and capital losses are not deductible.[5] In the German revenue bill of 1964, capital gains realized from the sale of business assets are included in the annual profits and are taxed at normal rates. However, if certain business assets have been used in a business in Germany for six years or more and are sold, and if certain other business assets are acquired either the year prior or two years subsequent to the sale of these assets, then any gain realized need not be recognized.

The Germans argue against capital gains taxation because of its locked-in effect and because the tax "penalizes changes in investments or portfolios, and thereby retards or even inhibits the sensitivity of the market."[6] Sweden, Japan, the United States, Italy, Holland, and also France, in a complicated way, tax capital gains, but at reduced rates. The general basis used for determining how much lower rates should be on capital gains than on regular income is the length of time the asset has been held prior to sale.[7]

The variations in the accepted theory of whether capital gains are income, and, more important, the question of whether and how they should be included in taxable income, are basic theoretical hurdles in developing international tax harmonization. As in the treatment of dividends, the variation is closely entwined with the legal separation of the corporate entity from the owners and the degree to which this separation seems appropriate in the application of economic legislation, particularly tax legislation.[8]

The heart of the theoretical problem is the definitions of capital gain and capital loss. The heart of the economic decision to include or exclude capital gains as a portion of taxable income is how it will affect the functioning of the capital marketplace. The heart of the political aspect of inclusion or exclusion is how it will affect the general acceptance of the justice of the tax system.

It was not until 1921 that the term *capital gain* was introduced into federal tax law. Neither then nor now has economics or accounting developed a definition of a capital gain or loss that can be used as a basis for tax legislation.[9] To include capital gains as a portion of taxable income involves an arbitrary decision that taxing capital gains is good for the country and good for the effective functioning of the internal revenue system. The fact that successful democratic industrial nations have made divergent decisions on the matter, and the absence of a well-developed concept, must make any reasonable observer willing to reconsider any particular treatment of capital gains in the tax legislation of a particular nation.

For use in applying the income tax rate, the Germans seem to feel no compunction in developing a definition of income that has little relation to any economic or accounting concept of income. This is perhaps as it should be. When this attitude is accepted, the treatment of capital gains becomes just another decision to be decided largely along tax dirigism lines. On this basis, economics and administration requirements should have something to say. After all, David Ricardo wrote: "Political economy is only useful if it directs governments to right measures in taxation."[10]

If the comments of the serious writers on the subject of U.S. capital gains taxation are to be accepted, the finding must be that on both fiscal dirigistic and administrative grounds, capital gains and losses should not be considered in calculating taxable income.[11] The political support for inclusion, which is tied to tax justice and tax progression, remains unaccounted for.[12] When they are brought into the discussion, one must conclude that capital gains should be treated like regular income with some additional averaging provisions.[13] This may require lower maximum rates for individual income and corporate profits. This approach seems to require the application of the tax to gains realized when property becomes a gift or is included in an estate at the death of the owner.

The French treatment comes much closer to individualizing capital gains. More than likely this is inherent in the "treatment like other income" approach. In the United States we have isolated capital gains from sale of a residence. Favored treatment is given, even though the general capital gains rate is less than the regular applicable income rate. In the Netherlands business related capital gains are taxable at the regular income tax rate, but capital gains of a purely private nature, such as the sale of a house or private investments, are tax free.[14] Germany doesn't really tax capital gains but does use a wealth tax.

BUSINESS TAXATION AND THE FIRM

The final bothersome theoretically oriented difference in domestic business income tax systems of the industrial nations winds itself in and out between all generalized tax impact and incidence discussions. It is the way in which a tax on a business firm should affect the firm. In the U.S. and Canada, and to a lesser extent in the United Kingdom and Sweden, business taxation is basically getting the money where it is, with little concern for growth of capital or directing business developments. In line with this approach, there is a frequently repeated British story. Reportedly, in 1937 Neville Chamberlain, then chancellor of the exchequer, was called upon to explain the British corporate income tax (then known as the national defense contribution). Said he, "It seemed to me the natural thing was to go where the money was."

To other industrial nations business taxation is an important means for the government to encourage pre-determined business goals while collecting needed revenues. Advocates of this approach see nothing wrong in giving a firm a tax break if it seems necessary to keep it operating. The first approach sees government tax policy as having no responsibility for a healthy industry. Here government's concern is limited to avoidance of political difficulties and collecting the required revenues.

The difference in attitude arises from the general differences as to how government and business should cooperate. The relationship is not unlike that between church and state. In the United States complete separation is claimed to exist, and it does. The situation is not changed, because church properties are exempt from property taxation and donations are deductible from taxable income. In other Western democracies churches receive operating revenues from the government. In these countries freedom of religion also exists, but differently from in the United States.

It is true that there are private and public economic sectors in Germany and France as in the United States. However, the line between the two is not as sharply drawn. Church and state, or business and state, are not black and white in most of the rest of the world. The philosophical separation of government from business that exists here results in a government attitude toward business not unlike that between the keeper and a wild animal at feeding time. This separation shows up in the U.S. attitude toward business taxation and increases the problems of international tax harmonization and using a tax system in the United States compatible with international economic interaction. American government officials are wary of getting cozy with business. Government officials of most other countries feel it to be necessary, if business and government are going to cooperate effectively. Also, American businesses frequently play their role in this unrealistic drama to the hilt. They pretend that meat thrown by the keeper is actually game that they caught on their own in the forest primeval.

TREATMENT OF DEPRECIATION

The U.S. Treasury and Congress have, within the last several years, completed a 90-degree shift in the treatment accorded depreciation as a deduction from taxable income. The basic element in the change is a movement away from the long-held position that taxable income should correspond to the generally accepted accountant's or economist's definition of income. In the United States there continues to be a nervousness about establishing an amount as the base for the corporate profits tax or an income tax assessed on partnerships and single proprietorships that has little or no relation to profits as defined by economists and accountants. The separation of the concept of taxable income from that of economic or accounting income in the United States has been hastened by tax legislation relative to depreciation and tax credits for investment outlays in 1954, 1962, 1964, 1966, 1967, and 1972. In 1972 the term *job development credit* was introduced.[15]

In Germany the basic philosophy of taxation has long separated what is appropriate for a tax base from what is appropriate for dirigistic tax policy. This is accepted without backward glances. The United States is still uncertain, and Americans are nervous about the use of tax credits or accelerated depreciation. German legislation, to speed up the fight against water and air pollution, grants permission to deduct 30 percent and 50 percent, respectively, of construction costs (in addition to regular depreciation) for investment in these areas. The legislation was given a nine-year time limit.[16] In the United States, a similar program is discussed with qualms.

THE NEED FOR A STABLE TAX

The reduction of taxable income (and indirectly, taxes) of those firms who are doing immediately what they would be required to do in the near future through application of police power is an uncommonly directive use of a depreciation allowance. Whether it will be the direction of the development of depreciation allowances generally cannot be foreseen. The device is, of course, only appropriate when corporate income taxes are relatively high, business profits are good, and the government has stable tax sources based on transactions. Also, government must be sufficiently dynamic to want to make certain that some action does take place.

Both France and Italy have, in the past, included in their depreciation allowances tax legislation providing for raising the depreciable value basis to take account of reduced purchasing power of the monetary unit. Both countries abandoned the practice when their price levels became relatively stable. The German provision for depreciation since 1956 has permitted "the setting aside of reserves for price increases under certain conditions," and this provision has not been repealed.[17] German businessmen are permitted to establish a "going concern value" called *Teilwert* in setting the value of a specific capital good acquired through merger or in a similar fashion. This concept is so vague that adjudicating the tax becomes a matter of administrative discretion.[18] In the United States and the United Kingdom the total value that can be deducted as depreciation in calculating taxable income has always been held at the original purchase price. Secondhand machines purchased, however, could always acquire a value for depreciation purposes equal to the price paid by the purchasing firm.

The innovations or techniques that nations have introduced to provide some sort of rule for the speed of deducting depreciation very nearly runs the full range of possibilities.[19] None of the recent regulations or legislation evidences a deep concern for preserving a depreciation deduction in arriving at taxable income that is equal to actual loss of value of capital equipment in the production process. On the other hand, neither is there a willingness to permit deduction of capital expenditures as material and labor expenditures are now deducted in arriving at income subject to the corporate profits tax. The harmonization of the corporation income taxes of the EC countries would require uniformity in treatment of depreciation as a portion of the job of making corporate profit taxes equal.[20] The importance of the task would decline materially if split corporate income tax rates and integrated profits and personal income tax systems were to become complete and the general rule. For under this procedure a large portion of any tax saving from lower corporate profits due to increased depreciation deductions is apt to reappear in higher dividend payments as a portion of profits and higher tax payments by stockholders.

INVESTMENT DECISIONS AND THE "MONEY ILLUSION"

An investment must be very productive to produce dollars after taxes that are greater by 5 or 6 percent than the number invested. A 6 percent after-tax return on a $1,000 investment in a corporation subject to the 48 percent corporate profits tax, by a person at the 48 percent personal income tax level, requires a before-tax return of $150 of profits. A payout of 15 percent on each $1,000 invested to give very minimal returns to the investor reduces sharply the areas where capital can be expected to go.

First, to make 6 percent a satisfactory return, the risk must be very low. Also, of course, the rate at which the purchasing power of the dollar is decreasing must be low or must be quickly and fully represented in a rising market price for the shares. Therefore, merely preserving the monetary value of an investment requires a normal capital return rate taking the degree of risk into consideration, plus the rate of inflation.[21]

Because the rate of return is calculated by applying current dollars to previous dollars, units of unlike values are used as though values were uniform. An increase in return that is no greater than the rate of inflation has not increased the income produced by the investment. Because progressive income tax rates are based on nominal dollar increases, however, they extract a larger portion of income received as a return on an investment as prices increase.

The condition sharply reduces the ability of society to meet investment needs out of current savings. Savings are developed instead through inflationary central banking policy. A more benign tax treatment of the income earned from investments can remove much of the current reliance on the money illusion. And it would be *good* if it were done.

CONCLUSION

The differences in the tax handles used by the leading trading nations around the world are significant today and will remain so for some time to come. A tendency for greater uniformity arises from tax administrators' observing the effectiveness of different approaches and adopting those that seem to work out the best. Also, because the Treasuries of all modern nations are faced with the job of making available for government use between 30 and 50 percent of GNP from economies that carry out their activities under very similar conditions, the tax collecting processes are forced into similar channels. The major forces for divergence of national tax treatment arise when taxes are used as a tool to attract desired economic advantage or when the rules for determining tax justice differ sharply. These have also proved to be the elements of disparity in business taxes among the fifty states of the United States.[22]

SELECTION OF THE TAX BASE

Irving Fisher, the great Yale University economist of the 1920s and 1930s, developed a strong case for looking at consumption as income.[23] He regarded the saving or lack of saving by an individual to be the change in the value of his wealth between two periods. Consumption was to be calculated by adding income to wealth at the beginning of the first period and deducting from this total wealth at the end of the period.

Nicholas Kaldor has on occasion favored a type of VAT, but his great love is the expenditure tax. His best-selling tax book, *An Expenditure Tax,* argues mightily that expenditures of individuals are a better tax base than incomes.[24] It is Kaldor's opinion that British economists have been completely mesmerized in their efforts to define income. He considers these efforts a waste of time; for to him income is undefinable. To Kaldor's mind, much too little has been done on the usefulness of income, however defined, to measure ability to pay taxes.

Kaldor's conclusion that it is expenditures that measure tax-paying ability is closely allied with Fisher's idea that income was enjoying satisfaction, which meant consumption. Tax-paying ability of a society is uppermost in Kaldor's mind, while Fisher looked at individual satisfactions. Kaldor has recommended the expenditure tax to underdeveloped countries—India, for example. He recommended use of expenditures as the tax base because savings under this procedure are not taxed twice as they are when income is the base.[25] An expenditure tax rests on savings only to the extent that the cost of capital is always a part of the selling price of goods and services.

Kaldor's position that income as a concept is undefinable would be disputed by William Vickrey. Vickrey, a Columbia University tax professor, wrote a book that defines income in such a fashion that taxpayer action cannot reduce taxes payable.[26] When this is accomplished, all income is included in the tax base and horizontal equality under the income tax law is achieved. The pages and pages devoted to developing income as a foolproof tax base are quite unnecessary when expenditures or consumption is the base. These are relatively straightforward aggregates. Income is not (see p. 12).

The differing tax liabilities of persons receiving relatively equal before-tax incomes is a real-world situation. It has been included in the decision-making processes in setting personal service contracts, investment decisions, and industry developments. The result is a rough horizontal evenness based on after-tax income or after-tax rate of return on capital. If it is further accepted that all income decisions are made on the basis of after-tax return, the different treatment of before-tax incomes does not affect the really meaningful horizontal income justice, which is after-tax horizontal equality. It also follow that any change in the existing relative tax treatments of receivers of different incomes introduces different tax burdens for equally placed persons where none existed before. The new horizontal injustice created through income tax changes will be gradually worked off as new contracts are negotiated, as the market changes the direction of commitments, and as the values of capital assets are adjusted.

This manner of looking at tax justice, when extended to include vertical income redistribution (that is, the change in the level of income between receivers of large and small incomes) requires consideration of whether it may also be true here that it is not useful to consider before-tax income. Perhaps the general situation throughout our society is that prices, including wage and income bargains, are set on the basis of the after-tax situation. This perception of the burden of taxes, under conditions in which taxes are to be used to change the rewards from those decided in the marketplace, leads to advocacy of a tax policy that constantly introduces new and different taxes. If this is not done, one should be honest and admit that the tax system does not attempt to redistribute incomes vertically and does not worry about treating income (however defined) equally (see pages 78–79).

VAT does not attempt to change market decisions. The aim of VAT is to be neutral in the vertical sense and to avoid horizontal inequality arising from different methods of organizing business activities.

THE TREATMENT OF SAVINGS

Sometimes taxation of individual expenditures is seen to provide for the exemption of savings from taxation and therefore to violate neutrality. There can be no doubt that S (savings) $+ C$ (consumption) $= Y$ (income), and if only the C portion of Y is taxable, savings are not taxed. Frequently this relationship is expanded by concluding that I (investment) is not taxed when VAT paid on capital goods purchases is deductible in arriving at the VAT a firm owes the government, and therefore VAT is not neutral but favors capital spending—that is, saving. This conclusion is not appropriate, for the selling price of goods, the VAT base, includes the cost of capital along with all other costs.

The conclusion that *is* appropriate is that VAT does not tax savings twice as does the income tax.

THE EFFECT OF USE OF FUNDS

The United States, in expanding its social security program, will be placing additional burdens on income as a tax base, and this base is already overburdened in a comparative international sense. The situation arising from federal and state use of income as the base for corporate, personal, and social security taxes points to a need to reexamine the emphasis placed on income taxes by the federal government. This reexamination must also consider expenditure developments and its relation to the use of taxes to provide greater economic justice.

It seems reasonable to argue that where government expenditures are oriented toward eliminating poverty and providing social security, the method of tax collection can concentrate much more completely on development of the economic base than in a situation where taxes are expected to perform some of the basic tasks of social justice. The United States is now moving into the social justice area of spending at a rapid rate, and this makes it appropriate to consider the introduction of a basically new philosophy of federal taxation. It is also true that the federal individual income tax has *not* developed into the instrument of economic reform and income redistribution feared by its opponents and expected by its advocates. Rather, the tax is a politically acceptable and administratively workable method of gathering together large revenues for use by the federal government.

The policy purpose of taxation based on ability to pay is to collect as taxes a larger portion of the incomes and perhaps wealth of the middle-income groups and the rich than of those of the poor. Because in all societies, until the modern affluence, the number of poor people has been much larger than the number of middle-income or rich people, popular support for ability-to-pay taxation has been dominant. Taxation based on corporate net income and personal income gives the impression that the government has the ability to collect taxes according to ability to pay while this is not an obvious characteristic of taxes based on production or sales.

IWP (income, net wealth, and property) taxes are theoretically adaptable to relatively high tax collections from the rich. IWP taxes are oriented toward redistributing income. They are levied to increase the well-being of the poor by reducing the well-being of the middle class and the rich.

In the United States, especially since the 1930s, the income redistribution potential of taxation has been pushed more actively than in most other countries. Despite one of the world's highest maximum individual income tax rates and the inclusion of capital gains in taxable income, plus what must be the best income tax enforcement organization, the progress made toward the goal of more equal income distribution through tax collections has been disappointing.[27] In recognition of the shortcomings of progressive income tax rates in redistributing income, Germany has very nearly abandoned their use.

The democratic method of helping the poor is rapidly shifting from taxing policy to spending policy.[28] The size of the economic pie has increased rapidly and continuously since World War II. This new economic stability and expanding productivity point toward democratic governments' spending to maintain the income of citizens throughout life and spending to increase citizen education and productivity. Under the circumstances of the present and the visible future, the role of taxation in a democracy will be to provide stable revenues while encouraging economic growth within a framework of close international interaction. This type of tax goal does not require the U.S. government to continue its historical tax attitudes favoring use of only those taxes that are aimed through collection at a redistribution of incomes.

VAT TAXATION OF CORPORATE PROFITS

In Europe the introduction of VAT coincided with the elimination of the turnover tax. In the case of Sweden it was the retail sales tax that hit the dust. In the United Kingdom it was the purchase tax and the selective employment tax. In Italy taxes going back to the Roman Empire were wiped off the books when VAT was adopted in January 1973. And Michigan is replacing inventory taxes with its new "single business tax."

U.S. economic opinion-makers, including Herbert Stein, chairman of the Council of Economic Advisers in 1973, conceive of VAT as being a replacement for the corporate profits tax.[29] Why this should be expected in America when it has not been the case in other industrial nations that have adopted VAT requires some explanation.

Perhaps the principal reason is political. VAT has been adopted, recommended, and explained by U.S. business groups such as the Committee for Economic Development, Herbert Stein's former employer. Labor and consumer groups have rejected VAT out of hand and have therefore failed to explain how VAT could be used to replace social security taxes and state retail sales taxes. In Europe this basically political polarization of attitude does not exist.

LIVING WITH INFLATION IN TERMS OF TAXES

The income and profits taxes, because they are paid largely by savers, provide the need to bring about forced savings (finance investment with an expanded money supply) to meet the capital needs of a modern economy. Therefore, traditional income and profits taxes either encourage inflation or lead to use of government surpluses to finance capital outlays.

Taxes as a cost of production, such as VAT, increase costs and develop cost-push price increases. Equilibrium is restored when receipts and government expenditures get into balance and each VAT-paying firm has exercised its market power in efforts to pass the tax payment backward or forward.[30]

The use of income and profits taxes, by cutting deeper into real savings as inflation continues, fails to produce an equilibrium. There is a constant savings shortage forcing monetary expansion. Under VAT, the savings to production ratio is not changed as inflation continues and therefore the economy finds it easier to right itself.

FISCAL ATTITUDES

The German economists of the mid-nineteenth century, unlike the classical economists of Great Britain, did not believe that government was unproductive. The teachings of these British economists continue to affect the thinking of us all. In 1855, however, a German contemporary of the founders of classical economic thought wrote a powerful essay demonstrating that government spending and government debt had as great a chance to be as productive as private spending and borrowing. His name was Carl Dietzel, and he typified the difference in the attitude of government toward business and business toward government that prevails in Western Europe and the situation existing in the United States and to a lesser extent in Great Britain.[31]

Government and business look at each other as competitors in the United States. In Europe they are closely integrated and supplement each other. This difference in attitude is certainly a partial explanation of the greater attention paid to housing and social programs in Europe than in the United States. In Japan government and business also cooperate very closely. The similar attitude in the United States deteriorated rapidly during the depression of the 1930s. Government and business cooperation increased again during World War II. This new relationship became the military-industrial complex—not a very useful area of understanding to build on to develop the cooperation required to deal with such problems as urban blight.

CONCLUSION

Serious consideration should be given to the position that decisions on negotiations of all economic matters are carried out on an after-tax basis, and therefore the levy of an additional tax always affects the price that is agreed upon. The stronger member of the economic bargain will usually be able to cause most of the burden of any tax to be carried by the weaker member.

Because of this relationship, taxes have not been very helpful in raising the incomes of the poor. The expenditure of revenues collected, however, appears under conditions of a vigorous democracy to have a real potential for reducing economic equality. This is particularly true when government and business work as partners and not as antagonists and when conditions are right for enjoyment of relative price stability.

VAT AS A BUSINESS TAX

Although there isn't a free lunch counter in the world, there are two types of prices. One price is used to meet labor and capital costs of production. Another price is developed through bidding for control over land and natural resources. The role of price in the second function is one of allocation of scarce resources. The second cause of higher prices is perhaps reduced by the levy of VAT. Certainly VAT does not stimulate this cause of higher prices. In the future it is quite likely this second cause of price increases will become of increased importance.[32]

CHARACTERISTICS

The value-added tax is frequently called a regressive tax. The basis for the opinion seems to be another common statement: "VAT is a type of sales tax." Here the word "sales tax" is often interpreted by the general reader to mean a retail sales tax like the one in effect in his state. This often seems to be the actual intent of the writer, for if it were not, he would not say in the next sentence that VAT is a regressive tax.

Actually, VAT is very different from a retail sales tax, while at the same time it is a tax that becomes payable when a sale is made. VAT is perhaps better understood when regarded as a tax on production rather than a tax on sales. VAT is a tax on production collected at the time a sale is made. Ideally, each producer—whether producing a service, as does the barber, or steel cutting equipment like the production of the tool maker—is subject to VAT on the sales price when money changes hands. The tax is not limited to sales made at retail; therefore, the tax is not limited to goods and services purchased by consumers.

VAT is also a tax paid by the seller of investment (capital) goods and the price of these goods is met out of savings.

Neither is VAT a turnover tax, although it has many of the characteristics of this type of tax. It is more correctly identified when the word net is placed before turnover. Also, the adoption of the value-added tax in Europe has gone along with the abandonment of the cascade type of turnover tax.

A business is liable for the VAT rate applied to its gross sales, just as under the cascade turnover tax. However, under VAT, he can deduct from the tax due that VAT that he has paid on goods and services purchased for use in the business. This means that no tax deduction is made just because goods were purchased from another business.

Because VAT is conceptually a tax on value added which is also the basic building block of GNP, the base of the tax amounts to the gross productivity of the economy that passes through the marketplace. It is also equal to gross income, as product and income are the two sides of the same conceptual coin utilized by the national income accounts.

Sometimes it is easier to break away from a well-entrenched position, such as the belief that a tax on sales is regressive, if the object under consideration is viewed from another perspective. In the case of VAT, looking at the base as the income going to the factors of production, rather than as a percentage of selling price less credit for VAT paid on purchases from other firms, has this effect. No longer does VAT possess the characteristics of a sales tax, but instead it becomes a proportional tax on the amounts paid to the factors of production for carrying out the production activity. A tax on income appears to have the taint of regressivity only if the rates are higher on incomes received by factors having low incomes and little wealth than on others. This, of course, is not true of a flat-rate VAT. The general practice of exempting small firms from VAT works toward a reduction of the VAT payments made by those of modest means and tends to make VAT somewhat progressive in its impact. Also because the VAT rate can be lower on food it is a business tax that can favor those with low incomes. This is not true of the CPT which is assessed at the same rate on a bakery as on a producer of luxury goods.

DIFFERENT TYPES

It is difficult to set down in words why a VAT based on income payments seems to be so different from a VAT based on transactions. One is forced to conclude that the difference exists because the location of the economic burden of a tax varies depending on the way it is administered. The VAT levied on transactions is assumed to increase prices on consumer goods and is borne by consumers. The VAT levied on income payments proportionally decreases income paid to the factors—land, labor, and capital.

The transaction-type VAT used in Europe is called the *consumption* variety. This type of VAT provides for the same treatment of VAT paid on capital goods purchased as of VAT paid on raw materials or any other purchase for business purposes. The deduction of VAT paid on capital purchases at the time of the original acquisition avoids problems inherent in attempting to allocate capital to production during the life of the capital good. If the deduction of VAT paid on capital goods was completely disallowed, the value contributed by investment to the price of the final product or service would bear a double burden—once when sold as a machine and once when included in the price of the consumption good. To follow this procedure would be to take away from VAT a considerable portion of the advantage it possesses as a net turnover tax.

LOCATION OF BURDEN

The consumption variety of a transaction or subtractive VAT at first glance looks like a tax that very obviously favors capital purchases. The deduction of VAT paid on capital goods is seen to be the equivalent of the exemption of savings from VAT. This appearance has given it the consumption designation. Savings or investment can only be judged exempt from this type of VAT to the extent that new increments of investment are in excess of investment levels of previous years. In a relatively stable economy, this difference would not be great, and during stages of reduced investment levels, VAT deductions would be less than the VAT included as a portion of the capital consumed in the productive process.

Although all this is true and was known very well by British economists who wrote the British study that provided the basic analyses used in writing the U.K. value-added tax, they concluded that the tax would be regressive and recommended procedures to eliminate the impact of this regressivity.

The income regressivity of VAT is seen to arise largely from the imposition of the tax on food purchases. Despite the failure to consider any possibility of VAT reducing incomes of landowners and others unable to control supply, the general finding is that "there is little substance to the fear that the substitution of a VAT, certainly if applied at two rates and with food and certain other exemptions, would be so inequitable as to be incapable of correction by way of quite small adjustments in direct benefits such as pensions or family allowances."[33] It is regrettable that the study does not consider an additive type of value-added tax. If it had, it would have been hard pressed to explain how the economic burden of a single-rate value-added tax with a very broad transactions base differed from a flat-rate tax using all payments to land, labor, and capital as the base.

If it is true, as some claim, that the American social security tax is an economic burden carried entirely by receivers of taxable wages, then one would expect an income-type VAT to have a similar effect. However, a VAT would include in its base all wages, no matter how high, and also all other incomes, including land rents, originating in businesses. Therefore, as a first approximation, one is justified in believing that a broad-based tax collected at a flat rate on all incomes of factors used by a business results in lower income to the factors by the amount of the tax. Those who claim that a broad-based VAT is borne entirely in the price of consumer goods must come to grips with the inconsistency of the results arising from the analysis of economic burden and therefore of the regressivity of a value-added tax on factor income and one on transactions.

Looking at the burden of taxation from what, for lack of a better name, I will call the *utilitarian macroeconomic point of view,* the disutility of a tax consists of the effect its collection has on the level of satisfying goods and services available for human enjoyment. A shorthand expression of the idea is: How will a tax affect economic growth? This group of tax concepts enters into consideration of the regressivity of VAT when a longer view is taken of how taxes affect income and consumption levels. For example, a tax collected largely from middle-level to low-level wage earners (as is the social security tax), rather than from profits, may assure more investment and rising productivity. The larger pie increases income to be divided among the low- and middle-income earners by more than it was reduced through tax policy. In other words, a regressive tax in the first instance increases savings, a large portion of which will be used for productivity—expanding investment. This is also the generally anticipated impact of the introduction of VAT as a replacement for a separate corporate profits tax. This expectation assumes that a tax on corporate profits is to a considerable degree paid out of profits and is therefore progressive and a reducer of savings because profit receivers are savers.

Maybe all one can conclude with regard to the regressivity of VAT is that like all taxes, with the possible exception of the land tax and the lump sum tax, both of which have the potential of siphoning off only monopoly returns, VAT has an uncertain economic impact. "No one can claim VAT is an ideal tax. There is no such animal."[34]

VAT AND INFLATION

Resolution of the quandary seems to point toward some disaggregation, which in this instance requires some consideration of how our society reacts to a tax change. A value-added tax would most likely be introduced to replace current taxes. In that case, the taxes selected for replacement become important. If VAT is to be used entirely to provide sufficient revenues to keep the federal budget in balance, another set of considerations enters into the analysis. Under the latter circumstances a value-added tax in 1973 would have been used instead of an expansion of the national debt by $20 billion. In 1974 it could have been used to reduce income taxes of wage earners, and thus reduce pressures for higher wages. In 1975 it would have prevented the sharp decrease of revenues in real terms.

Under conditions of a savings shortage, which appears to be the normal current condition, a large government deficit requires inflationary monetary conditions. It is frequently said, but apparently not believed, that inflation is the cruelest of taxes.

THE VALUE-ADDED INCOME TAX

Although VAT developed in Europe as a net turnover tax to replace gross turnover taxes and certain basically transaction-type taxes, the value-added tax in concept is as closely associated with income as to product or transaction.

When the French were moving toward a general value-added tax from a more limited production tax, they realized that the accepted operating procedures of the General Agreement on Tariffs and Trade did not exactly fit the characteristics of VAT. Therefore, some twenty years ago the French went to considerable pains to include words in the written provisions of the GATT understandings that have smoothed the way for treating VAT in the same manner as the gross turnover tax had been traditionally handled. As a result of this effort VAT was given the attributes of a tax on consumption and therefore a tax to be levied on the destination principle and not the origin principle. This meant that the tax could be collected as a border tax on imports and refunded on goods and services exported.

The GATT position rests on the idea that there is a fundamental difference between a tax paid by business that is measured by sale and one that is measured by generated incomes. The alleged difference has usually been supported by appeals to the portion of taxation incidence theory that finds taxes on sales causing equal price increases and taxes on income reducing incomes received. It is also true that administration of tax refunds and border taxes can be carried out in a manner easier to check when they are tied to sales price than when they are a percentage of income. More than likely the administrative convenience of applying the destination principle to a tax measured by sales price is actually more important than the guidelines of GATT indicate.

Most observers of business taxation do not attribute much importance to whether the base of a tax is sales or income. In fact, in Michigan, the VAT law contemplated the use of sales as the base, but because of the problem associated with subtracting purchases, most of the businesses calculated value added from accounting information, such as wages paid, profits earned, and net interest and net rents paid, and this was accepted by the Michigan tax officials. What is important in business taxation is the breadth of the coverage, the degree of rate uniformity, and the manner in which the tax is applied to imports and exports.

COVERAGE, UNIFORMITY AND ADMINISTRATION

There can be no doubt that a value-added income tax can have as broad coverage as a value-added transaction tax. However, it is also true that the variety of rates as developed in the French VAT become generally unworkable under a value-added income tax. In order to apply a lower rate to one commodity of a company under a value-added transaction tax, all that is really required is to keep track of these sales and apply the lower rate. The tax due from these sales is then added to the tax liability arising from the sale of other products; the VAT paid on goods and services purchased is deducted from the total; and a check for the remainder is sent to the Treasury.

Under a value-added income tax with different rates for different products, the wages and profits, plus other incomes arising from each product, must be calculated and the appropriate rate applied. This is a more laborious process than with rate variation under a value-added transaction tax. For this reason, one would expect support for one general VAT rate to be stronger under a value-added income tax than under the traditional VAT.

Most observers have recommended the use of a minimum number of VAT rates, and the Danish VAT has been praised frequently for both its broad coverage and its use of only two rates—one basically for food and one for everything else. On the other hand, a variety of rates makes it possible to give some direction to consumption and protect some goods and services from the full impact of the cost of government. It would seem that a value-added income tax, by encouraging a single rate but not making multiple rates entirely impossible, fits very well with the generally accepted understanding of a "good" VAT.

Therefore, a value-added income tax fits in very well with a number of important conditions a tax on business must meet. There remains the international treatment it can expect. When VAT is no longer tied to the sale, the refunding of the tax on export sales is going to require an acceptance by GATT that all the incomes arising from the sale—that is, the full price of the export—have been included in the income base subject to VAT when sold domestically. Making certain that this is largely true should not be a very difficult task for GATT.

The acceptance of the destination principle for a value-added income tax means some abandonment of the close relationship that exists under the traditional VAT between the tax and the particular item exported. It is quite possible that loosening this relationship will cause some protests. For example, an item exported might have been produced to a considerable extent in another country. Proof might be required that a border tax equal to the product's value at import had been paid before a refund of the full VAT rate would be permitted. This, however, is nearly the same situation as under a traditional VAT. There is a principal difference, however—the base of the border tax is price, while the base of the export refund is income arising domestically from production and sale of the product and the border tax paid on included imported parts that was based on CIF (cost, insurance, freight) price.

The use of CIF price as the base of the border tax and income as the base for the tax refund on exports appears to be a violation of equality of treatment. This, however, is not really the case, and the use of the CIF price as the base for the border tax is nothing more than a convenient procedure to be used in making a value-added income tax work in this area like the traditional VAT.

INDIRECT TAXES AND THE TOURIST BUSINESS

If a nation or state uses largely direct taxes—income, profits, payroll, and property taxes—and the incidence is borne by the taxpayer, as theory holds, then tourists in the country or state enjoy police protection and other government services without having to pay for them. On the other hand, if VAT or other indirect taxes cover most of government costs, then tourists pay their share of government expenses as they consume on their visits.

If things really worked out this way, unfair competition for tourist business would require the state with an indirect tax to sell its money to tourists at an exchange rate below the official rate or the state with a direct tax to charge tourists a higher price for its money than that charged to importers of its goods. Because a higher rate would bring on all the trouble associated with an official rate above street rate, the procedure of a discount to tourists to countries with indirect taxes would be the preferred procedure to equate the competitive situation. When this is done, tourists are subsidized by the regular inhabitants of both countries.

Turkey, for one, has done this, and tourists before the 1970 devaluation of the Turkish lira were granted an advance refund of consumption and indirect taxes in the form of a flat 33.3 percent increase in quantity of Turkish lire received for their money.[35]

France and other countries have tried to give tourists a discount on purchases equal to indirect taxes. It hasn't worked, or perhaps it has worked too well. Frenchmen and others borrowed passports to establish foreign checking accounts to purchase at the discount, no-tax price.[36] In France it all ended on October 1, 1970. France, a big indirect-tax country, however, did not work out a substitute procedure as Turkey did. This means the United Kingdom, with a rather high direct tax, is subsidizing its tourist business, at least in this respect, much more than France.

PAYROLL TAX AND EMPLOYMENT LEVELS

A well-established tax concept teaches that placing a tax on the employment of labor in the form of a payroll tax does not act to reduce the use of labor relative to the use of capital. The common perception that this is not the case arises because observers fail to realize that capital is in fact embodied labor, and therefore the costs of capital increase along with higher labor costs.[37]

It is obvious that this cost relationship between capital (embodied labor) and direct use of labor breaks down when the machines are imported from another nation. This is the common situation in less developed nations, and therefore payroll taxes increase unemployment and increase capital intensity of nations relying on imported capital equipment.[38]

Much labor is employed to accomplish tasks that cannot be performed through use of capital. Either labor is employed to do the job, or the job isn't done. In this area payroll taxes paid by the employer reduce the level of employment.[39] Here again, well-received studies have concluded that the payroll tax paid by the employer reduces wages by the amount of the tax, and therefore the tax does not increase wage costs.

If the laborers used to produce capital goods are employed by employers paying a payroll tax, while workers producing consumer goods have employers not subject to the tax, the level of employment would be pushed above the level that would exist if no payroll tax existed. Of course, this same tendency toward expanded employment would exist if labor unions of the capital goods industry were able to keep their wages higher than those prevailing in the consumer goods area.

If employers reduce wages by the amount of the payroll tax they pay, which should be possible if all employers are required to pay the same tax, then costs and employment levels are not affected by the payment of the tax. This approach returns one to the old economic effects conundrum. In this instance, the question becomes: If wages can be reduced after a payroll tax is levied, why weren't they decreased before the tax? The only answer seems to be that things just don't operate that way. After all, the same question could be asked of higher prices of automobiles after the price of steel and labor has been increased.

COMPLICATIONS OF VAT

The French retailer has found VAT to be very troublesome. The difficulty arises largely from the four different rates the French use. In addition, there are at least eight different ways in which these four rates are applied. The nations adopting VAT during the past several years have learned from the French experience and use one rate as in Denmark and Sweden with variations in the base or two rates as in Germany.[40] The U.K. value-added tax got a little more complicated.

The temptation to use more than one rate is strong, for the desire is likely to be rooted in the value system of a people. In France, for example, there are two rates applicable to chocolate. Baking chocolate, the most respectable form, bears a VAT rate of 7.5 percent (the reduced rate). Other chocolates are taxed at a 17.6 percent rate (the intermediate rate). Pastry, which sometimes includes baking chocolate, is taxed at 23 percent (the standard rate).

The complications of varying rates to the French supermarket are perhaps less than is the case with the retail sales tax in the United States, where some items are subject to the retail sales tax and some are exempt. This is true because the VAT rate is included in the price, and the cashier needn't bother with the tax rate differences. The clerk stamping prices on items also needs only know the price set and needn't worry over the portion consisting of VAT or any other tax. The manager or the central office must wrestle with various rates, and they find them to be bothersome.

CONCLUSION

Although one is tempted to think of VAT as nothing but a retail sales tax with a new name, to do this is to deny the impact of the method of collection in the setting and offering of prices. The examples of the application of VAT under the number of circumstances considered in the discussions of this section demonstrate that VAT is more like the payment of interest. Like interest costs, it becomes a portion of all business decisions. The impact varies from industry to industry and between countries. Generalizations are only marginally helpful, but one that seems appropriate is that VAT fits in pretty well with the needs of a country that is using up its savings on large government deficits and foreign investments, that finds its international trade frequently in serious deficit but doesn't want to lead the way to a sharp reduction of international economic freedom, and that is facing a considerable demand for social services during a period of rapid inflation and large fiscal deficits.

Taxation for Economic Stability

In 1967 Germany enacted a Stability and Growth Law. The legislation authorized the government to vary corporation profit and individual income taxes by 10 percent in either direction as the cyclical situation dictated. This legislation also authorized a 7.5 percent investment tax credit during a recession and the power to curtail depreciation allowances in a period of boom.

American governments have talked about built-in fiscal cyclical stabilization like that of Germany. It has been the theme of many academic discussions of fiscal policy for better economic stabilization. However, achievement has been minimal. The flexibility that has existed in the U.S. investment tax credit has not been well received by the business community. Nevertheless, it will undoubtedly continue as an important portion of U.S. fiscal policy.

The fiscal freedom, both legislated and environmental, enjoyed in America is much less than that enjoyed by the German government. Much of the difference is explained by the closer German government contacts with industry and the very nearly complete dependence of the American federal government on individual income and corporate profits taxes.

A German stability and growth law in America would accelerate the already overly sharp decline of tax revenues during an economic downturn. The size of the resulting deficit is too dangerous to be risked, even to avoid a depression.

The utilization of VAT would encourage American fiscal experimentation. The availability of a revenue source with the immense, stable base of VAT reduces fear of recession-induced revenue shortages and a dollar and gold crisis. As a result, in an economic downturn it becomes feasible to sharply reduce income tax rates to encourage investment and saving. On the other side of the fiscal coin, expenditures can be increased to stimulate demand because the principal revenue-producing base remains relatively stable. The solid revenue source provided by VAT prevents fiscal economic stabilizing actions from causing monetary speculation due to disastrous fiscal deficit levels.

The current (1976) deficit of the federal government has prevented anything but a casual consideration of additional tax cuts to supplement those of 1969. There is little doubt that high unemployment and the low level of the industrial production index point to the need for a more vigorous policy. Despite the conservative fiscal approach, the deficit shows signs of getting out of hand. Government costs continue to increase due to inflation and added welfare demands. At the same time, stable to falling profit levels fail to provide a base for additional CPT revenues, and reduced overtime pay and unemployment hold back income tax collections despite rising hourly wage levels.

THE COUNTERCYCLICAL BUDGET

The famed built-in cyclical stabilizer of CPT is not performing up to expectations. The deficits of sharply reduced federal tax takes, in real terms, which are in the wings in 1975, turn out to be frightening rather than stimulating. Foreign monetary experts look at our deficit potential, wring their hands, and wonder about the soundness of the dollar. Financiers see the situation forcing the Federal Reserve System to increase the money supply too rapidly, requiring a later sharp tightening. The construction industry finds the Treasury bidding away savings to cover its deficit, causing a shortage of financing for new housing.

To put it bluntly, the countercyclical budget policy, once the darling of economists Walter Heller and Herbert Stein and the big-business association called the Committee for Economic Development, has lost much of its former allure.[41] It is incompatible with a monetary policy that is designed above all to avoid alternating feast and famine. Milton Friedman's recommendation of a steady expansion of money at a 4 percent rate may be dead, but the desire to play it safe—monetarily speaking—is not.

CPT is even faulted during the prosperity phase of the cycle. The large tax collection increases during prosperity stimulate government spending when the private economy is already demanding all available resources. The policy of a countercyclical balanced budget has created a constantly stimulating spending budget. It also prevents private investment from carrying out its full potential for stimulating private economic growth. During prosperity high tax rates on profits reduce savings to finance private investment growth. During a recession large borrowings by the Treasury push up interest rates, making both equity- and debt-financed investment less attractive.[42] The U.S. action in 1971 providing for accelerated depreciation dangerously increased a rising deficit. This type of action, or even bolder responses to economic conditions, could have been made earlier if the relatively stable revenues of a VAT had been available.

On the other hand, the deficit of the depression makes economic stimulation policies difficult to carry out. Big spending added to an already big recession-caused deficit encounters difficulties. The same deficit makes tax-cutting legislation appear to be wild-eyed and irresponsible. Nevertheless economic realities have forced action of this type.

The big advantage VAT gives Germany is a stable basic source of revenues that fluctuate only moderately as the levels of employment and profits change. This permits action to reduce taxes on profits, perhaps through more liberal depreciation allowances, to stimulate investment.[43] The action will be effective because the government is not at the same time bidding away savings to cover large deficits arising from sharp reductions in tax collections.[44] Real savings become business investments, and the German government does not become burdened with ever larger annual interest payments on outstanding government debt.

In November 1968 Germany demonstrated in practice what had been all too infrequently pointed out as a useful international adjustment characteristic of VAT. Because of her strong export position, Germany was then under severe pressure to revalue the mark upward. She relieved this situation by reducing by 4 percentage points the VAT refunds on exports subject to standard rates. This made German export firms less competitive in the international markets and also increased her net tax collections.

The additional revenues became available to the government to mitigate any hardship caused by a less competitive export position, or for any other purpose. Later, after revaluation of the mark, when German exports needed stimulation, the VAT refund to exporters was restored. Under floating exchange rates, VAT adjustment to affect flow of funds would appear to remain useful, as demonstrated by French tax adjustments of 1973.

This approach also has advantages under certain circumstances when devaluation appears to be appropriate. Using VAT in the manner illustrated by the 1968 German action is a way to enjoy an exchange rate adjustment mechanism that does not stimulate the in-and-out flow of international hot money. A nation can benefit its international economic situation and avoid the generally undesirable devaluation impacts of a change in the value of deposits and securities quoted in a definite number of monetary units.

As long as something like the Articles of Agreement of the International Monetary Fund exists, these opportunites for international adjustment provided by VAT would be even more helpful to the United States than to other nations. The U.S. dollar continues to be the monetary unit in terms of which the value of all other currencies is defined.[45] Therefore, any change in the value of the dollar places immediate pressure on the value of all other currencies. It is nearly impossible to change the relative value of the dollar in terms of most currencies through any type of exchange flexibility, including floating exchange rates. At the same time, since 1948 the dollar has suffered from devaluation of the currencies of eighteen of the twenty leading export nations.

More than likely the only way the dollar in the 70s can be given some real international flexibility is through fiscal action. This was seen in the area of capital transactions, when the interest equalization tax was introduced. This may have been the wrong approach, and it is no longer in effect. VAT, however, by reducing the need for high taxes on income and capital, can be genuinely helpful in the capital accounts area of our balance of payments. It could also increase the effectiveness of the Domestic International Sales Corporation provisions to encourage production in the United States for export. Or maybe DISC, which is estimated to have cost $1.07 billion in fiscal 1975, could be repealed.

When our government decides to provide additional social security coverage, or to liberalize Medicare or to expand mass transportation, tax collections or new borrowings are needed to foot the bill. The effect is higher costs for the goods produced in America. If VAT is used to provide the funds, the prices on our exports would benefit from tax refunds, and a border tax could be placed on imports to replace revenue lost and to keep domestic firms operating.

SPENDING EFFECTS

The impact of more government spending varies with the manner of expenditure. For example, government spending to train more skilled workmen could reduce costs by increasing productivity and destroying labor shortage bottlenecks. The same result could arise from the building of a better transportation system.

Other types of government spending are basically consumptive in nature. The government raises taxes to finance increased old-age pensions or to increase the size of its army. These expenditures turn up only very indirectly, if at all, in expanded efficiency. They increase costs, because the taxes raised to cover the spending must be covered in prices charged. On the other hand, the expenditure of the funds provided by the taxes makes little or no contribution to production efficiency.

In the United States higher prices on domestic production because of higher taxes also mean higher prices on exports. This, however, is not the situation in Europe, as VAT rates have been raised to cover directly or indirectly additional government expenditures. The VAT taxes paid are refunded on goods exported. This means that a generous domestic social welfare program can exist without creating international trading difficulties.

It is also true that high VAT rates can protect the good life. A high national level of government spending for consumption can be undermined by imports from countries with a low level of government services. A high-rate VAT makes possible a border tax of an equally high rate. The effect of this is to place as high a government cost in the price of imported goods as is included in prices of domestic goods. With a floating exchange rate, VAT holds up the value of the international value of the domestic currency while helping to make domestic producers competitive.

When VAT provides a large portion of a nation's revenues that nation enjoys considerable freedom in setting expenditure levels. The destination principle prevents low costs of government in foreign nations from making it difficult to have a high service level of government domestically. A nation that uses direct taxes to finance much of its government spending sacrifices much of its freedom to expand services and to innovate in the area of fiscal policy.

John Kenneth Galbraith in his advocacy of a higher level of public living has correctly pointed out that "the incidence of public service is similar to that of the progressive income tax."[46] VAT, a tax that treats all production of the private sector in the same way, is not a progressive tax. However, its use to expand public service or to maintain the level achieved makes the impact progressive. Using this approach, one might conclude that VAT used to finance additional social services was more progressive than a graduated income tax used to finance a supersonic transport (SST).

FISCAL RESIDUA

The application of the destination principle makes VAT the tax of fiscal freedom. The theoretical analysis of the destination principle finds some of its support in the concept of *fiscal residua*. The term *fiscal residua* refers to the benefits of the spending of the taxes collected.

Taxes levied on goods sold for domestic consumption are available to finance government expenditures that benefit consumers. Therefore, the collection of the same taxes on goods exported as on goods consumed domestically amounts to the collection, by the amount of the fiscal residua, of higher taxes on goods exported. The consumers of the country of export benefit from the spending of taxes levied on these goods, but the tax is paid by the importer. The importer, to the extent that he pays (in price) the taxes of the exporter nation, is paying for services that cannot benefit him.

The concept of fiscal residua and all other considerations of the effects of tax expenditures are frequently excluded from tax analyses.[47] In fact, the inclusion of expenditure considerations muddies the water of efforts to locate the burden of taxes to such an extent that efforts to locate the burden become fruitless. When taxes are considered in terms of personal sacrifice and expenditures in terms of personal satisfactions, the best approach is to examine separately the benefits of expenditure and the burdens of tax payments.

Efforts to commingle the two remain an unscientific endeavor, but this fact should not prevent every person who thinks a bit about taxing and spending to consider the relation between them.

CONCLUSION

The writers responsible for developing the concept of *fiscal residua* were able to make progress toward combining taxes and expenditure benefits because taxes were considered only as a portion of the costs of consuming. This approach of making taxes impersonal arises naturally out of the consideration of VAT, for VAT is a very impersonal tax that is very much involved in the impersonal production process.[48]

VAT increases freedom in the public spending level and increases choices for economic stabilization.

6

Financing a Broad
Social Security Program

The federal budget's provision for transfer payments increased by 67.5 percent between 1970 and 1975 and the dollar total is now over $130 billion and is increasing at a $10 billion a year rate. This is little over one-third of federal expenditures. The transfer total includes payments to qualified retired and their dependents plus payments under social security to the disabled, sick and unemployed plus contributions to federal civilian and military retirement programs and financing of the food stamp program plus Medicare. When state and local government programs are added in, transfer payments accounted for 13 percent of disposable personal income. The impending adoption of an expanded medical delivery program financed with federal revenues will at the very least maintain the growth rate experienced by this category of government expenditures during the past five years.

The value-added tax possesses the potential of providing a substantial portion of the funds required, while avoiding a sharp reduction of work incentives, investment and saving inducements, and the competitiveness of American goods in the world markets.

CURRENT SETTING

In 1950 basic amendments to federal social security legislation sharply reduced the closeness of the relationship between benefits and payments. The shift substantially increased benefits paid to dependents, and full benefits were offered to workers with only six quarters of covered employment.

ORIGINAL PHILOSOPHY

A look back to 1950 is useful for just a moment to gain perspective in looking at current conditions. For in that same year Lewis Meriam wrote:

> A system that provides a minimum health and decency benefit only, whether the benefit is paid to all regardless of resources or only to those in need to the extent of their need, would not require the elaborate and costly paraphernalia of insurance.[1]

The paraphernalia is still here and is growing; how expensive it is, one can't really say—maybe not more than 1 percent of disbursements —but that amounts to $1.6 billion. Undoubtedly, the introduction of the computer has sharply reduced the administrative costs envisaged in the 1950s. But who in those salad days, when the social security tax rate paid by employer and employee was 1.5 percent, could become excited when Willford I. King expressed the opinion that all social security tax payments were wage costs and are borne by the wage earner and that the insurance idea also promoted a very regressive tax?[2]

Back then Congress was so opposed to using revenues other than those from social security taxes to finance an expanded benefit payment program that they voted to eliminate a 1943 provision authorizing appropriations to the program from general revenues. Legislation adopted at this time also provided for a 3.25 percent rate to be paid by employer and employee at the distant future date of 1970. Also, when this maximum rate was set, no provision was made to increase the base above the first $3,600 of wages.

So in 1950, as in 1939, the amendments to social security legislation destroyed a portion of the insurance-reserve accumulation concept of the original legislation. Benefits were immediately expanded, but higher tax rates to make the new levels actuarially sound were postponed, and nothing was done to reduce the income regressivity of the funding.

The heart of the fiscal difficulty inherent in our original social security program, and perhaps inherent in any social economic guarantees, lies in what is sometimes called the *intergeneration transfer of resources,* and the weakness of the monetary unit in performing its function of being a "store-of-value." In addition, it is difficult to reduce the real level of social benefit once a commitment is made, even though the value of the monetary units paid in has decreased and the relative size of the group to receive benefits from current production has increased. There can be little doubt that the concept of voter economic priorities (VEP), which Howard R. Bowen in 1948 saw as the big area of economic analysis for the future, is with us today.[3]

One very important aspect of VEP revolves around procedures to be used in financing social security and the portion of current production that is to be allocated to this goal. Expenditure developments of governments to assure consumption levels have largely destroyed the original relationship between contribution—i.e., direct tax payments—and benefit rights. This new relationship between individual payment and benefit received removes much of the need to rely on payroll financing. The extent of this development without a conscious policy decision to move in this direction is demonstrated in the expansion of federal health and welfare programs.

For example, in fiscal year 1973 about $26.7 billion was budgeted for federal government health spending in a wide range of programs scattered through the budgets of many different federal agencies.[4] During the same period, about $7.6 billion or 28 percent of this total was collected as medical insurance (MI) or hospital insurance (HI).[5] Table 10 shows the growth of these programs at the federal government level during recent years. The HI tax rate is now 1.8 percent of covered wages and is a portion of the overall social security tax rate.

The five-year period from 1965 to 1970 was one of rapid expansion of national income maintenance programs of the member states of the Economic Community and the United States. The rapid inflation, combined with efforts to raise real income maintenance levels for the expanding group eligible for benefits, has resulted in severe pressures on established financing arrangements.

U.S. SOCIAL SECURITY BENEFITS AND TAX DEVELOPMENT

In 1965 the primary insurance amount (PIA) received by a covered individual reaching sixty-five was $44 and the maximum $168. In 1974 the minimum PIA had risen to $93.80 and the maximum to $412.40. The political pressures for increased benefits are continuing. The law

Table 10

Federal Government Spending for Health, 1965-1973

Fiscal Year	Amount (Billions of Dollars)
1965	5.2
1967	10.8
1969	17.0
1970	18.5
1971	21.0
1972	24.0
1973	26.7

SOURCE: Representative Robert H. Michel, House Appropriations Committee's Subcommittee on Health.

now provides for an annual adjustment to correspond with cost-of-living and wage changes. It is estimated that the annual cost of the 1974 increase was $8.55 billion. To raise the funds required to finance on a current basis the $8.55 billion of additional social security benefits to the aged and their dependents requires a combined payroll tax increase of about 1.5 percentage points, assuming the maximum wage on which taxes were paid is $10,800.[6] However, by 1976 the maximum wage tax base had increased to $15,300 and the end has not been reached, for benefits were increased by 9 percent in mid-1975 and by another $5.5 billion in 1976.

During the period 1950–1970, total social welfare expenditures under all public programs increased from 8.9 percent of GNP to 15.2 percent. During the same period social security tax collections increased from 4 percent of personal income to 8.9 percent.[7] The doubling of the importance of these very large programs during this twenty-year period made their economic impact tremendous. Also, the reduction of tariffs and the convertibility of currencies, plus the introduction of the value-added tax by EC member states, substantially increased the international effect of the levels of U.S. social security financing. Finally, the current annual rate of increase of social security taxes and contributions is about 15 percent.

In 1965 only the first $4,800 of wages was subject to the payroll tax to finance old-age and survivors' insurance (OASI) and disability insurance (DI). The combined rate was 7.25 percent, and the maximum amount withheld from wages was $124. Another $124 was paid by the employer.

In 1972 the social security tax rate was 10.4 percent on the first $9,000 of wages—a maximum amount withheld from the employee's check of $468, and a similar maximum paid by the employer.

In 1976 the first $15,300 of wages is included in the base, and the combined rate is 11.7 percent. The maximum amount withheld from wages is $895.05, with a similar amount paid by the employer, making the annual total cost $1790.10. Additional revenues are expected to come largely from increasing the wage base rather than from higher rates. These taxes based on wages raise the funds used by social security to make payments (OASI) to the aged and their dependents plus disability and hospital insurance (DI and HI).[8] An expanded health insurance program financed from payroll taxes would require both higher rates and a higher salary base.

In ten years the maximum tax payments by employer and employee based on payroll have increased from $248 to $1790.10 (11.7 percent of $15,300). While this seven-fold increase was taking place in the United States and social security payroll taxes were increasing rapidly as a portion of federal tax collections, the European payroll tax situation was more stable.[9] In the United States, payroll tax rates and the payroll base have been increasing rapidly at the same time as inflation-dominated income increases were raising the graduated income tax's withholdings from a given level of real income. In Western Europe, the collections from VAT permitted substantial reductions of personal income tax payments to compensate for inflation-caused higher rates. This was done despite higher general-purpose spending.[10] Of course, it was expanded VAT collections that made this possible.

If it is assumed that payroll taxes result in reduced wages by the amount of the tax, the rapid growth of payroll taxes in the United States has not affected America's relative international competitive position.[11] If this assumption of incidence is not accepted, and instead a full forward shifting in prices of the payroll tax is accepted, then in these days of floating exchange rates, the international value of the U.S. dollar is decreased by the added cost of payroll taxes, causing a decrease in U.S. terms of trade.

NEW PHILOSOPHY DEVELOPING

The current policy has provided for higher social security tax collections. Only if wages are unaffected and collections are spent as raised to expand employment would this procedure be acceptable when international trade deficits exist alongside domestic unemployment.[12]

A program to utilize VAT to change the financing of a major portion of the American social security program cannot be accomplished directly under the procedures established by the General Agreement on Tariffs and Trade (GATT). Instead, the goal is reached indirectly by making the collections from the value-added tax a portion of general revenues; the addition of these revenues will permit payment of current social security tax rates while at the same time total income withheld from wages to pay income taxes can be sharply reduced.

The incidence of VAT is no more certain than that of payroll taxes, corporate income taxes, or, for that matter, personal income taxes. The advantages VAT has over these other taxes arise because (1) it is a tax collected at the time of sale, (2) its basic structure provides for the netting out of taxes paid prior to final consumption use, (3) it can within the rules of GATT be applied as a border tax on imports and refunded on export sales, and (4) the amount of tax applicable to a unit of product sold can be accurately determined.

VAT is not a payment made between the wage contract and take-home pay. Therefore, it does not reduce the psychological effect of the wage payment as compensation for work completed. Also, VAT is not a tax on efficiency, as is the corporate profits tax, nor is it a tax that induces uneconomic resource combinations as does the income tax.

The international effect of the use of VAT by the United States would be to harmonize American taxes with those of Europe. Therefore, the introduction of VAT as a major U.S. tax would correct rather than cause misallocation of domestic American resources dedicated to produce for foreign markets from domestic or foreign production centers.

The concept of the individual providing his own security through forced tax payments, required payroll allocation, or individual retirement plans—so strong in the past—is being found wanting.[13] It has prevented neither the development of economic uncertainty nor insecurity. What seems to be needed are fiscal procedures for guaranteeing to everyone the basics of a decent standard of living and at the same time permitting middle and upper income earners to adopt uncomplicated procedures to preserve the purchasing power of their savings.

The question of whether the income floor can be provided without reducing incentives to strive for economic improvement is asked much less frequently now than a decade ago. On the other hand, much more doubt has developed of the ability of governments to preserve the purchasing power of the monetary unit. In fact, again as this is being written, it appears that productivity levels high enough to assure basic economic living standards are possible only under conditions of a rapid decline in the value of the dollar. The security of the poor appears to require the insecurity of the middle income receivers that arises from inflation. VAT, by not cutting sharply into savings and not encouraging wasteful spending by business because it is deductible, and at the same time providing substantial and steady revenues under conditions of price stability, appears to be an answer to much of the enigma of the current economic interrelationships.

For the first time in history it has become realistic, despite some current shortages, for many nations to give primary emphasis on how to use productive facilities rather than on how to expand the production potential. This level of affluence has not yet been reached in Russia. The USSR has laws "Concerning the Intensification of the Fight Against Persons Who Avoid Socially Useful Work and Lead an Antisocial Parasitic Way of Life" (to quote from a 1961 Soviet law).

INFLATION IMPACT

As pointed out above, the provision of economic security to middle-income earners is related to a second basic citizen economic issue, i.e., the cost of living and inflation. It is only among the poor and the very rich that talk about the rising cost of living is not the chief economic topic. The subject is not new. The French scholar and lawyer Jean Bodin, speaking of the rising French prices of the sixteenth century, said in 1568 that currently depreciation "ruined the state and the poor." A scholar could make the same comment on the current American scene.

The social and economic impacts of changes in the cost of living vary from family to family and among individuals. A careful study comparing change in economic well-being of people in different economic situations between 1960 and 1964, a period of very little inflation, and between 1964 and 1968, a period of considerable inflation, has produced findings somewhat at variance with what had been generally thought. Of all workers, only certain professional groups, such as accountants, attorneys, engineers, and chemists, improved their economic position more rapidly in 1964–1968 than in 1960–1964. Only those holding assets consisting of houses and land benefited more during the inflation years. Also, persons relying very largely on social security for their income found their economic position in 1964–1968 improved over what it was in 1960–1964.[14] The political support for inflation, if based on relative improvement of economic position as demonstrated by this study, would come from the independent professional groups and the recipients of social security.

CONCLUSION

The benefits received by the aged from a social security program are transfers for consumption of the economic productivity of the active members of the community. This creates a basic political problem when before the transfer burden arises voters approve benefits to be paid at some future date through a reduced scale of living of the economically productive members of that future period.[15]

If there were some way for current producers and voters to set aside consumer units equaling a given quantity of housing, food, and the like, much of the problem could be solved for most middle-income earners as the original social security act envisaged. This, however, has not proved possible. The only apparent working alternative is for each working generation to contribute to the aged and dependent the portion of current production that turns out to be politically acceptable.[16]

INDIRECT USE OF VAT

Up to 1970 the relative situation of the United States in the use of general revenues to finance its social security program remained about as shown in Table 11. Since 1970 American income security spending has increased sharply.

In fiscal year 1975 general revenues were used to provide about $31.5 billion of funds to support federal income security programs. An additional $89.7 billion was collected as payroll taxes.[17]

These totals represent increases much greater than those taking place in most of the countries listed in Table 11. It has also meant that tax funds required for this area of expenditure have expanded significantly. The rapid expansion has not, however, caused a shift in American financing practice toward greater use of indirect taxes to finance general expenditures, as is evident in the European nations using VAT.

INTERNATIONAL COMPARISON

The data of Table 11 are no longer current. The publication titled *Social Security Programs Throughout the World* provides current general information on the sources of social security system funds.[18] However, the information does not include data on expenditures and financing other than those of the social security system. Because income maintenance expenditures may take many forms, as has been true of health expenditure expansion in the United States, for example, the

Table 11

Government General Revenues and
Revenues of Social Security Sector for 1959–1960

Country	Non-Employer Payments to Social Security Sector as Percent of Government Current Expenditures	Percent of Social Security Receipts from Government as Employer and Transfers*
United States	2.7	14.2
Spain	5.0	12.0
Portugal	6.3	17.5
Japan	7.8	25.5
Netherlands	8.7	18.0
Switzerland	10.2	23.0
France	10.6	26.6
Italy	13.5	26.8
Austria	15.3	38.4
Norway	15.3	45.1
Germany	15.8	31.9
Finland	18.2	49.6
United Kingdom	19.1	56.5
Belgium	20.7	38.9
Canada	22.2	69.1
Iceland	24.4	63.1
Ireland	26.8	83.9
Sweden	27.4	68.3
Denmark	33.7	78.8

SOURCE: *International Monetary Fund,* 14, pp. 528, 530.

*Transfers cover special taxes allocated to social security, state participation, and participation of other public officials.

comparison of the social security financing situation in 1971 and 1964, as set down in *Social Security Programs Throughout the World,* does not provide a complete picture of the change that has taken place.[19] In addition, because the data reported in that publication do not give changes in income tax payments of lower- and middle-income citizens, one cannot determine whether payroll tax increases were largely or entirely compensated for by income tax reductions or by a failure to increase income taxes to maintain the direct tax portion of an expansion of general revenues. Of course, it is necessarily true that VAT collections become a larger portion of the total when the direct tax portion declines in countries adopting VAT.

ASSISTANCE OF VAT

The situation in Norway is perhaps typical of the change arising on the introduction of VAT. The retail sales tax had been introduced in Norway on July 1, 1935, at a rate of 1 percent and had been gradually increased so that by 1969 its effective rate was 13.64 percent. On January 1, 1970, a value-added tax at 20 percent was introduced. The revenues from indirect taxes as a percentage of Norway's gross national product increased from 13.6 percent in 1969 to 16.3 percent in 1970 and 16.4 percent in 1971. During the same period income taxes other than payroll taxes decreased from 13.3 percent of national income in 1969 to 12.0 percent in 1970 and 12.8 percent in 1971.[20]

A similar relationship is demonstrated by the revenue trends of West Germany. Direct taxes on corporations and households totaled 54,980 million deutsche marks in 1968 and 66,010 million DM in 1970. During the same two-year period, indirect taxes, collected nearly entirely from VAT, expanded from 55,810 million DM to 76,160 million DM.[21]

The expansion in the use of VAT permitted expanded government spending for general purposes, as well as for social security, without bringing about price shifts that would reduce exports and stimulate imports. In the words of the Norwegian Royal Ministry of Finance and Customs, VAT "offers one possibility of reaching a more neutral competitive situation both internally and internationally."[22]

Table 12 provides the distribution for the year 1965 of the financing sources for the social security programs of the then six EC member states. The summary is developed from data reported in *The Cost of Social Security* published by the International Labour Office in 1972. More current data are not available and can be constructed only with considerable difficulty.

All the EC member states in 1965 were rather substantial users of general revenues to finance their social security programs. The portion arising from general revenues was highest in Luxembourg (23.8 percent) and lowest in France (8.6 percent). In the United States general revenues were not used in 1965.

Because interest received by social security funds is paid as a result of ownership of government securities, interest amounts are also in a sense funds from general government revenues. Table 12 shows the revenues from this source received by EC member states varied from

Table 12

Portion of Social Security Financing
Arising from Principal Sources (1965)

Source of Financing	Belgium	France	Germany	Holland	Italy	Luxembourg
Employer Contributions	51.1	71.3	47.9	42.0	60.0	40.9
Employee Contributions	23.1	19.0	30.7	42.2	14.7	24.0
General Revenues	21.0	8.6	18.1	7.9	19.2	25.8
Return on Investments	4.3	0.2	2.6	7.6	2.8	8.3
Other	0.5	0.9	0.7	0.3	3.3	1.0

SOURCE: *Indicateurs de Sécurité Sociale* (Brussels, Commission des Communautés Européennes, 1971), p. 33.

7.6 percent in Holland to 0.2 percent in France. In the United States about 3.5 percent of old-age and survivors' insurance trust fund revenues came from this source in 1965.

Income maintenance expenditures by American local and state governments from general revenue sources are rather large. On the other hand this practice is largely nonexistent among EC member states. Because of this situation, the United States contribution from general revenues to support income maintenance programs is relatively understated.

In 1965 all of the EC member states were utilizing general revenues to finance their social security programs, but the variation in the use of general revenues between the EC member states was considerable.

INTERNATIONAL TAX PRACTICES

Western European and particularly the European Community tax development is proving VAT to be an indirect tax that admirably meets the economic and political fiscal needs of the times. In demonstrating this effectiveness VAT is also becoming a major revenue base for Western Europe's very substantial social security programs.[23]

The large additional revenues being provided by VAT to the nations using the tax, and expected by the nations planning to introduce the tax, are not used to finance social welfare benefits directly; such financing, however, is the indirect effect. Social security benefits are indirectly financed with VAT expansions because income tax collections need not be raised or may actually be reduced. Increases in general government expenditures can be met from the additional VAT revenues provided. As a result, higher payroll taxes to finance social security become possible without increasing total tax withholdings from wages. In this manner, additional general revenue funds become available indirectly to cover general social security spending. Also, when the VAT revenue base exists, social security benefits can be increased by reducing their inclusion in the income tax base, as in West Germany. Again, it is the higher added collections from VAT for general revenue purposes that make higher after-tax social security benefit payments possible.

As has been pointed out, one of the desirable features of all indirect taxes, including VAT, is its refund on exports and its application as a border tax on imports under the principles of GATT. This feature, the destination principle, is lost under GATT if VAT or any indirect tax is used directly to finance social welfare. Therefore, the European and other users of VAT avoid directly identifying the revenues it provides with social welfare expenditures.[24] (See pp. 179–182).

CONCLUSION

The funds required by a social security program cannot be directly financed with VAT if VAT is to continue to benefit from GATT understandings as they apply to indirect taxes. However, VAT collections can indirectly provide social security financial support without abandonment of GATT indirect tax treatment. As social security costs have been increasing in Western Europe the financing needs have been to a considerable extent provided by VAT collections that have permitted lower income tax collections for general fund purposes. This has permitted higher payroll taxes without increasing total withholdings from wages.

ECONOMIC JUSTICE, SECURITY AND GROWTH THROUGH TAXATION

One would be hard pressed to locate an economic or social problem for which someone hadn't devised and advocated a tax solution. Many of these "solutions" arise as methods of giving an economic advantage by granting relief from the effects of the progressive individual income tax and high corporate profits tax rates. Others, like the "negative income tax," use the word *tax* because welfare spending has fallen into such disrepute.

Perhaps efforts to set up some kind of tax inducement to attract industry and to entice industry to stay and expand while meeting normal government costs have absorbed the greatest amount of time and mental anguish. The devices tried include rapid depreciation, tax exemption the first several years, and financing with bonds on which the interest is not included in the federal taxable income base.[25]

The success of the efforts has varied widely. In most cases the result has been to reduce sharply, for a while at least, the impact of high income and profits tax rates adopted by political bodies.

Undoubtedly, the economic problems that need to be set right make a long laundry list. The value-added tax does not lend itself to meeting these goals through tax gimmickry. It does, however, by providing a stable and substantial revenue source, permit reasoned approaches to government problem-solving actions involving tax favors.

U.S. TAX AIDS

The U.S. tax system extends many favors to persons based on the source of income, the way income is used, and the position of the taxpayer in business, the family, and the general social structure. The first effort to quantify the extent of favors extended through special provisions of the federal individual and corporate income taxes was reported in 1969 by Secretary of the Treasury J. W. Barr.[26] The amounts and sources were set down, but no effort was made to determine the final benefactor of these provisions. The phrase "tax expenditures" was used to identify these benefits.

The idea since then has become a portion of what is identified in the current literature as the public grants economy. The phrase "tax expenditures" has been abandoned, and "tax aids" has been substituted. A concept very closely associated with public grants and tax aids is tax incentives. The concept "tax aids" is broader than "tax incentives" and includes items that are not concerned with altering the allocation of resources. The aim of tax incentives is to alter the impact of the tax so that "undesirable" impacts are removed without a substantial reduction of the total revenues provided by the particular provision.

The concept of tax aids is closely associated with the topic of loopholes—or "breathing holes," depending on your position relative to the particular provision. Although one cannot verify that a close relationship exists between tax aids and loopholes and the level of tax rates, it is reasonable to assume such a relationship exists. When the rate of a tax is high, the pressure to find relief is strengthened and the need to grant relief to certain persons and certain groups to avoid difficulties or hardship becomes obvious.

In the United States there is some indication that the pressures for high rates and then the expansion of the number and value of tax aids have run their course.[27] As a result, the question is being asked more and more frequently: Wouldn't the economy be better off if taxes used had lower rates and fewer deductions and special provisions?

If one takes the position expressed by President Nixon in his tax message to Congress in 1969, then tax aids must be evaluated on the basis of cost-benefit. Not much progress has been made in evaluating straight government expenditures on a cost-benefit basis, and the problems of doing this with tax aids are considerably more formidable. For example, the tax aid may make a contribution to what is generally considered to be tax justice—such as the standard deduction—but on the other hand the benefit per individual is greater for receivers of high incomes than for low-income taxpayers, and, of course, those not paying the income tax receive no benefits. Under these circumstances, is the cost-benefit relationship best served by reducing the justice of the tax system by eliminating the standard deduction, increasing direct family assistance a bit while also reducing the minimum income tax rate?

The standard deduction benefits the large family household with a substantial income. It benefits much less the one-person household with a substantial income. Very little benefit is granted to the large family with a modest income.[28] If it were removed, tax rates could be cut, which would give greatest benefit from the current situation to the one-person household. The large family with a substantial income would have their position worsened and the low-income family would be about where it was.

FAIR TREATMENT UNDER TRADITIONAL TAXES

Tax justice is difficult to calculate as a result of these difficulties— plus a very important basic question that is not frequently mentioned, i.e., What is the proper comparable position—tax liability before the aid or after the aid? The tax aid concept takes the position—apparently without any qualms—that a man enjoying a tax reduction is receiving an aid and that it is unnecessary to calculate whether this aid reduces taxes below those of others with a similar ability to pay. For example, no effort is made to go beyond reported current income in calculating taxpaying ability. The relation of age, wealth and the source of income in establishing the relative tax burden of taxpayers is not considered.

The tax aid concept is very elusive, and now that it has been around as a calculated figure ($6.150 billion in 1969 and an expanded version provides a $74.605 billion total in 1974), it seems to be less helpful than was first believed.[29] However, if it is another source of general dissatisfaction with high tax rates on a narrow base, it will have served a useful purpose.

The property tax and the sales tax are also used to extend tax aids. In fact, it is unlikely that any relatively general tax is free of implicit grants. The property tax is cluttered with exclusions for one group or another. Recently the owners of property in the urban fringes have been able to persuade state legislatures that urban sprawl can be reduced if land around urban areas is assessed at only its farm use value.[30] The sales tax often excludes food, nearly all services, and certainly pharmaceutical products.

The exemption of food is said to make the incidence of the retail sales tax proportional. Of course, high-income people buy better and more expensive foods than those with low incomes; nevertheless, food purchased at grocery stores is a much larger portion of the budget of the low-income receiver, so its exemption removes the nasty label "regressive" from the sales tax. No one really worries if the exclusion results in higher prices of food products, because food purchases are increased when the sales tax doesn't have to be paid.

The property tax has been generally conceded to be a bad tax, one reason being that it was income regressive. Recent studies have concluded that the property tax is not income regressive and may actually be somewhat progressive. At the same time as this new evidence is becoming a portion of the literature, the states are rapidly adopting major property tax aids. For example, the circuit breaker is being rapidly adopted by the states as a reform of the property tax's income regressivity problem, a problem that apparently does not exist.[31]

The Advisory Commission on Intergovernment Relations (ACIR) has been advocating the introduction of the "circuit breaker." A circuit breaker is aimed at extending an implicit grant to those occupying as a homestead, property of such a value that the property tax exceeds a legislated maximum percentage of income of the homeowner. Recently, some states have also made this tax aid available to renters by assuming that 25 percent or so of rent paid consists of the cost of property taxes. More than likely the growing unpopularity of the property tax is due to the great increase in the number of home-owners and the relative decline in the number of renters.[32]

This kind of implicit grant provided by the older homestead exemption and the veteran's exemption was adopted to help the unfortunate and those who have risked their life for the nation. In addition, it was viewed as a way to make the property tax more popular with the voters. This approximates the rationale for the circuit breaker, also.

Now that the circuit breakers are in, they are proving to be rather costly. What programs will be cut and/or what taxes will be increased to cover the costs of the circuit breaker? If it is the total of welfare expenditures that is reduced and sales tax rates and coverage that are expanded, the poor are not likely to be better off. However, perhaps it is all worthwhile if the property tax gains additional political support as it becomes even more of a tax paid by the middle-income receivers and the wealthy.

THE ECONOMIC LAW OF INTERNATIONAL TAX HARMONIZATION

An economic law of international tax harmonization would go like this: *Under conditions of approximately equal levels of taxation, the general indirect tax proportion must be equal to that existing in other nations having competing firms.*

Failure to follow this law establishes conditions of international economic imbalance that are not self-corrective. The producers of the nation experience continued inability to compete with manufacturers in nations granting tax rebates and collecting border taxes. The high income and property taxes required to balance the budget because of low collections of indirect taxes cause capital to seek investment in other areas. This outflow increases the domestic cost of capital and works further to bring the international balance of payments into deficit.

The use of a downward floating exchange rate to avoid the tribulations of violation of the economic law of tax harmonization sets the stage for direct controls, quotas, and general beggar-thy-neighbor policies. The harmful effect on useful international economic relations is particularly destructive when the nation is a large international trader and investor, such as the United States. Also, international monetary weakness reduces confidence and therefore increases speculative action against the currency whenever adverse conditions arise. Finally, a decline in the value of the currency of a creditor nation, such as the United States, reduces in foreign purchasing power the value of all foreign investments stated in the currency of the investor and of relatively fixed income payments from abroad also stated in the currency of the investor, and increases the dollar burden of foreign debts and payments requirements stated in units of foreign currencies.

The harmful effects of violation of the economic law of international tax harmonization are very real, and they work out in a particularly harmful manner when the violation is by the United States with all of its international economic responsibilities.

COMPARATIVE TAX LEVELS

Between 1970 and 1971 the per capita tax collections of the United States as developed by the Organization for Economic Cooperation and Development (OECD) increased from $1,404 to $1,409. This was an increase of 1.38 percent during a period when the Consumer Price Index increased from 116.3 to 121.3. The other nations of OECD reported much greater tax collection increases. The United Kingdom, with the next lowest increase rate, experienced a total tax revenue increase expansion at a 5.25 percent rate, and France, next in line, had a 9.45 percent increase. All the other countries reported tax revenue increases above 10 percent. The largest increases occurred in Norway and Turkey with 20.31 and 33.67 percent increases, respectively.

The total per capita tax revenues of a number of OECD countries in 1971 were in excess of $1,000. However, only Sweden (with $1,847) and Denmark (with $1,539) were in excess of the U.S. level of $1,409. The other nations with total per capita tax revenues over $1,000 were Belgium, Canada, France, Germany, Luxembourg, the Netherlands and Norway. Only Turkey, Spain and Portugal had lower total per capita tax revenues than Japan, where the total was $432 in 1971.

The tax level in the United States has not been increasing as rapidly as in the countries of Western Europe. As a result, income for private expenditure has been expanding relatively rapidly in America. Total U.S. tax revenues, including social security, were 28.06 percent of GNP in 1972. In Sweden the percentage was 43.89 percent; Germany, 35.97 percent; France, 35.80 percent; and Japan, 21.09 percent.

SOCIAL WELFARE PAYMENTS

The effect of a liberal state program of pensions and special financing of medical and housing costs of the aged is to increase lifetime income levels. Between 1966 and 1974 the percent of those over 65 below the poverty level decreased from 28.5 percent to 14.2 percent. This in turn reduces the income regressivity of taxes tied to expenditures, for the aged make up a considerable portion of the no-saving below-average income receivers. A tax related to expenditures collects a larger portion of income but not of consumption of the old and the young and a smaller portion of income of the middle-aged but, of course, the same portion of consumption. If the analysis goes one step further and includes the tax included in the cost of capital goods, a tax based on expenditures that do not select goods consumed by the poor for taxation must be proportional.

On the other hand, the U.S. social security contributions are very directly paid by the low-income worker. These taxes are paid only indirectly by the aged as prices are increased as a result of the payroll tax.

Denmark, Norway and Sweden are substantial users of VAT, which is a major contributor to general revenues of these countries. General revenues in turn provide ⅚ of the cost of the Danish government's aid to the aged; the level is 85 percent in Norway and 70 percent in Sweden.[33] Under this arrangement the two large groups with low incomes contribute equally to costs. In the United States with only payroll tax available, the burden on the low-income young to finance social security is relatively heavy.

CONCLUSION

Fiscal systems have been developed and modified in many ways to help particular groups enjoy a "decent" share of the economy's productivity. The areas of action include tax programs to attract investment and to stabilize and stimulate particular industries. The size of these programs varies from country to country.

The ability of the U.S. to finance social security, while also carrying out its fair share of other programs that are tax oriented, has been limited by the lack of a broad based production tax.

FINANCING SOCIAL SECURITY WITHIN GATT UNDERSTANDINGS

It has long been recognized that a nation able to subsidize exports increases the extent to which it can follow an independent domestic economic policy. The enjoyment of a high degree of freedom from international economic restrictions is very attractive. However, the subsidization of domestic export industries to gain additional international economic freedom easily becomes flagrant. In addition, the desired aim of increasing international economic freedom is neutralized if competitors in other nations are granted the same favors by their governments. The role of the international rules administered by both the International Monetary Fund and GATT under these circumstances is to prevent the introduction of new export subsidies and import restrictions. The procedures accepted are usually based on the practices of Western Europe. It is the expectation that each nation will take advantage of approvals granted when to do so will improve its general economic position.

An important portion of Western European international economic relations consists of a highly developed general indirect tax system that after World War I grew into the very productive gross turnover or cascade tax. Since 1954 this European indirect tax system has evolved into VAT. It is also true that the nations with basically direct tax systems, such as Great Britain and Ireland, adopted VAT in 1973. Also, the quantities of revenues being raised from this portion of the tax systems of Western Europe are increasing. For example, the German and Swedish rates were increased in 1971. A general rate of 15 percent is expected.[34]

The development in Western Europe of both VAT and an expanding social security system is closely related to international competitiveness within the "rules of the game" as understood by the membership of GATT. This can be made clear by quoting and commenting briefly on some of the basic articles and amendments included in the GATT understanding.

EXPORT TAX REFUNDS

The contracting parties to the General Agreement on Tariffs and Trade (GATT) provided in the ninth supplement of *Basic Instruments and Selected Documents,* which contains decisions, reports, and so forth of the sixteenth and seventeenth sessions, a specification of what was meant by the prohibition of export subsidies contained in paragraph 4 of Article XVI.[35]

The Working Party considered the text of a draft declaration that was based on a proposal submitted by the government of France, the same nation that initiated the development of VAT in 1954. Among the practices identified in the effort made by GATT to define what constituted export subsidies was in part (c) The remission, calculated in relation to exports, of direct taxes or social welfare charges on industrial or commercial enterprises.[36] This provision was introduced to avoid subsidy through making a portion of wages paid a refundable cost of production.

The general definition of a subsidy was tackled by the contracting parties in the writing of paragraph 4 of Article XVI:[37]

> as from 1 January 1958 or the earliest practicable date thereafter, contracting parties shall cease to grant either directly or indirectly any form of subsidy on the export of any product other than a primary product which subsidy results in the sale of such product for export at a price lower than the comparable price charged for the like product to buyers in the domestic market.

The provisions of part (d) of this GATT working party report modify this general concept of subsidy to provide for the generally accepted *destination* concept of where the burden of taxes should rest.[38]

> (d) The exemption, in respect of exported goods, of charges or taxes, other than charges in connection with im-

portation on indirect taxes levied at one or several stages on the same goods if sold for internal consumption; or the payment, in respect of exported goods, of amounts exceeding those effectively levied at one or several states on these goods in the form of indirect taxes or of charges in connection with importation or in both forms . . .[39]

The detailed listing by the working party of practices considered to be giving of subsidy was not directly challenged by the contracting parties. Also, a willingness to implement paragraph 4 of Article XVI on the basis of working party reports and attached annexes plus some special waivers (but none of these waivers were relative to [c] and [d]) was given by Austria, Belgium, Canada, Denmark, France, Germany, Italy, Luxembourg, the United Kingdom and the United States.[40]

The provisions of (c) combined with (d) make it an export subsidy, which is prohibited, if direct taxes, i.e., personal or corporate income taxes, payroll taxes, or other special types of welfare charges paid by businesses, are refunded to exporters. The provisions are not explicit as to whether refunded welfare charges paid by individuals employed by the exporting firm would be considered to be export subsidies. The failure to do this leaves a considerable loophole, which will certainly be gradually exploited. However, it is also true that GATT is not an enforceable contract. The contracting parties agree to work together within the spirit of the General Agreement.[41] The spirit would seem to consider the refunding of a special tax, whether levied on individuals or businesses and used directly to finance social security or welfare, to be a subsidy when refunded on exports and an import restriction when levied as a border tax on imports.

TAXES ON IMPORTS

The attitude of GATT toward taxation is further spelled out in Article II 2(a), Article III, 2, and Article VI, 4 of the General Agreement.

The provision of Article III, 2, is given first because Article II 2(a) refers to it.

(a) on import equalization charges or taxes:

Article III: 2

The products of the territory of any contracting party imported into the territory of any other contracting party shall not be subject, directly or indirectly, to internal taxes or other internal charges of any kind in excess of those applied, directly or indirectly, to like domestic products. Moreover, no contracting party shall otherwise apply internal taxes or other internal charges to imported or domestic products in a manner contrary to the principle set forth in paragraph 1.

The provision of GATT was briefly violated in 1971 by the American 10 percent surcharge on imports. Under the rules of GATT the surcharge could not be extended beyond an emergency period without also levying a 10 percent tax on domestic production. Also, the funds collected could not be *directly* used to finance social welfare programs.

With respect to items on which tariff concessions have been negotiated, GATT Article II prohibits any import charges above the agreed and "bound" rate. A special exception is made, however, for border tax adjustments in Article II: 2(a):

> Nothing in this article shall prevent any contracting party from imposing at any time on the importation of any product: a charge equivalent to an internal tax imposed consistently with the provisions of paragraph 2 of Article III in respect of the like domestic products or in respect of an article from which the imported product has been manufactured or produced in whole or in part.

EXPORT SUBSIDIES

The GATT's general opposition to export subsidies is contained in Article XVI: 2:

> (b) on export tax rebates:
> The contracting parties recognize that the granting by a contracting party of a subsidy on the export of any product may have harmful effects for other contracting parties, both importing and exporting, may cause undue disturbance to their normal commercial interest, and may hinder the achievement of the objectives of this Agreement.

GATT does not, however, contain an outright prohibition of export subsidies or of import taxes. Instead, it requires countries to notify each other of such subsidies or import taxes. (Article XVI: 1). Regarding export subsidies for primary products, the GATT holds that they should, if possible, be avoided and when granted they should not be used to obtain "more than an equitable share of world export trade in that product" (Article XVI: 3).

GATT assumes that indirect taxes are shifted forward onto the buyer, and that the incidence of direct taxes is on the income earner and does not become a part of price. This concept of tax incidence gives GATT nations making a substantial use of indirect taxes a considerably greater ability to prevent international pressures from having an effect on domestic government spending decisions. As mentioned above, governments generally find that this gives them additional freedom in domestic economic policy.

However, the flexibility in the use of the destination principle does not adhere to taxes tied directly to the financing of income maintenance programs. Under the GATT understandings, it is not possible to enjoy the advantages of the destination principle and use VAT to finance income maintenance programs directly. Revenues from the use of VAT must be used to cover costs of general programs and in this way reduce the need for personal income taxes and corporate profits taxes. This development makes room for additional payroll taxes without increasing direct tax payments or increasing direct taxes by a lesser amount. VAT using nations are able to do this and gain the advantages. The United States and other nations that do not use VAT are unable to do so.

GENERAL CONSIDERATION OF SOCIAL SECURITY FINANCING

A theory of the burden of the taxes or contributions made to a government system to provide payments to the aged has not been developed.

The *social burden* of a tax or social insurance contribution is located in the impact of transfers between income levels.[42] The *economic burden* of a payment is in the impact on the level of productivity. Neither one of these basic concepts of tax burden can be accurately measured.[43]

To demonstrate the relationship between indirect taxes used for general purposes and the financing of social security, let it be assumed that Germany by the introduction of its value-added tax increases the revenues raised from indirect taxes by 30 percent. These additional revenues permit a reduction of the low-bracket individual income tax by 3 percentage points. As this is taking place, a decision is made to increase old-age, invalidism, and death benefits. The new financing required to do this is provided through an increase of the payroll tax by 2 percentage points, divided equally between employer and employee. (See pages 170–172).

In this example, the additional indirect tax collections arising from VAT permitted a reduction of low-bracket income taxes. The reduction in the need for income taxes to finance general government activities provided the financing for the expanded social security program. The higher payroll taxes, as a replacement for the income tax reduction, provided a method of utilizing the additional value-added tax funds for social security purposes. If the fundamental point of this illustration is accepted, any increase in the portion of a nation's revenues arising from indirect taxes through the introduction of VAT amounts to the financing of a portion of the social security costs from a general indirect tax. This would be the case even if social security benefits were increased and income tax rates remained the same or were increased, as long as VAT provided a larger portion of general government financing. When the indirect tax increase arises from a national VAT, taxes that must be covered by export prices are decreased and taxes included in import prices are increased.

If the general budget is in deficit prior to allocating funds to the social security account, then any funds made available are borrowed funds. If new taxes are collected to meet the demands of the social security account, these taxes are directly related to social security financing. If, however, revenues from the general account are used to meet the social security account deficit, no particular general tax can be identified as being the one financing social security benefits above payroll tax collections.

The use of borrowed funds to finance the social security account might in some cases lead to higher taxes in the future to pay off the indebtedness. In all cases, though, the borrowing would require new tax revenues to cover additional interest charges. These taxes, although in a real sense as directly related to social security financing as a tax with revenues allocated to support social security payments, are much less likely to be considered social security financing.

The allocation of revenue support of social security payments becomes complicated even when no attempt is made to develop a reserve. Only the general nature of the source of funds used that are in addition to payroll taxes can be identified. No particular tax of the group contributing to the general fund can be singled out as the one helping to finance social security benefits. Therefore, VAT revenues contributing to the general fund should not lose their ability to benefit from the destination principle.

GENERAL REVENUES VS. PAYROLL TAXES IN REVENUE FINANCING

First, the use of reserve financing requires at least partial acceptance of the contributory principle. This means that benefits are at least partially determined by contributions that can be associated with the economic activities of the beneficiary. Under these conditions a portion of the tax payment is the equivalent of saving. It is a reduction of disposable income. It has not contributed to higher costs and has, in fact, perhaps reduced prices through a decrease of current consumption and an increase of current savings.[44]

The basic complication of reserve financing arises from the difficulty of setting payments accurately over the contributing life of the average contributor. As was previously pointed out, an important aspect of this difficulty arises from a desire to keep real benefits from declining as the purchasing power of the monetary unit declines. There is no acceptable way to preserve the purchasing power of earlier contributions under conditions of inflation other than adding to the fund receipts above those originally contemplated.

These additional receipts could be raised on the contributory principle as were the original payments. In this case their impact would most surely approximate that outlined above. On the other hand, the additional funds needed to keep real benefits from declining could come from general revenues.

The use of general revenues to prevent a decline of the purchasing power of benefits in a mature reserve-finance-type social security program utilizing the contributory principle becomes involved in all the interrelations discussed above for a pay-as-you-go program that does not utilize the contributory principle. In addition, there is the problem of identifying exactly what the additional funds from general revenue are to accomplish.

It could be argued that in providing these revenues society is replacing social security fund resources it originally took away through inflation. This would be rather accurate if the social security taxes under the contributory principle were increased to keep their real burden constant. If this were not done, general fund revenues to maintain purchasing power of benefits should be regarded as payments of additional social security benefits and therefore salary supplements. The rules of the game agreed upon through GATT would then label the tax refund an export subsidy.

There is also the situation which arises when real benefits are increased under a reserve-finance program using the contributory principle when the program fails to increase payment levels adequately to cover these added obligations. The general budget under these conditions is contracting an indebtedness equal to the difference between contributions plus the earnings from these contributions and the payment obligations. This type of indebtedness differs from indebtedness that may arise under a pay-as-you-go program in two important respects. First, interest payments are not required as the debt accumulates. Second, the debt is much more likely to be at least partially retired through higher taxes.

No portion of this type of debt would be retired if, when benefits go above fund reserves, the revenues to finance the benefits are entirely raised through general government debt expansion. On the other hand, if the government used social security fund reserves for operating expenses, the payment of benefits above current collections at a later date would require increased general revenues. These could not be classified as taxes to finance social security, as is the case when new taxes are initiated to meet benefit requirements under a pay-as-you-go system. The taxes raised would really be to finance general expenditures previously financed through social security collections greater than benefit outgoes. Under these circumstances, general revenue taxes are used for general purposes. The collection is postponed because social security reserves had been used to cover general government expenditures.

The GATT rules relative to social security and welfare benefits financing possess a number of potential interpretations. Until the United States develops a major national VAT, its international economic position will be worsened as the importance of social security expenditures and value-added tax collections of other nations result in liberal interpretation of the GATT prohibition of destination principle benefits to revenues collected to finance income maintenance. There is little doubt but that the source of general revenue funds affects the manipulation of the very sizable government costs of income maintenance programs.

CONCLUSION

Income maintenance expenditures of the federal government show every indication of continued expansion. Payroll tax rates combined with personal income and corporate profits taxes appear to be separating income earned from income received to such an extent that the relationship between them is being endangered. Also, the GATT understandings prevent these taxes from being used indirectly to remove much of the burden of social security costs in the area of internationally traded goods and services.

The value-added tax has become a major revenue source of the nations in Western Europe. The development was partially the result of the realization in each country that VAT could be very helpful in meeting income maintenance demands. The use of VAT has permitted revenues for general purposes to expand so that personal income and corporate profit taxes could be moderated and modified to accomplish economic goals. This in turn permitted higher payroll taxes and corporate contributions to meet social security costs without increasing direct taxes paid by individuals and companies.

The federal government makes very little use of indirect taxes. This type of U.S. tax program plus the movement of European industrial nations towards the use of more indirect taxes has reduced the degree of international harmonization existing between America and Europe. This situation increases the difficulty of developing a general expenditure and income maintenance program in the U.S. without being very much aware of the international economic impacts. These impacts do not appear to be removed by floating exchange rates but only tend to be less obvious because a single crisis does not arise.[45]

7

International Taxation
and
Commercial Relations

Perhaps a good way to introduce this in-depth consideration of taxes and international commercial and financial relations is to remind the reader that all sections of the American population are in one way or another involved in competition with foreign economies in the struggle for capital, jobs, and markets. This economic reality has been much more generally recognized in recent years because of the rapid shifts in the international prices of oil, grains, and the dollar. When the immediate impacts of these dramatic events have subsided, it will be easy to act as though our dependence on successful international commercial and financial competition did not exist—but it will still be there.

INTERNATIONAL PRICE COMPETITION

On January 1, 1968, in line with the tax harmonization program of the EC, Germany adopted VAT. The rates were higher than those of the cascade turnover tax that was repealed, and the expected revenues permitted other fiscal adjustments.

The rate on all transactions except food and professional services was set at 11 percent. The *New York Times* (December 1, 1969) estimated that the effect was a devaluation of the mark by 3 to 4 per- cent. The American trade negotiation representative estimated that the change amounted to a devaluation of 2 to 3 percent.[1]

It is always difficult to pinpoint what has caused an international strengthening of a national currency. For example, strengths may be entirely relative and due to policies of other nations. It is a matter of record, however, that Economic Minister Karl Schiller identified the "stormy" growth of exports in 1968 as causing an economic growth rate of 7 percent rather than the 4 percent that was forecast.[2]

VAT AND PRICES

Because VAT is a kind of general indirect tax, the traditional con- clusion is that VAT is not shifted forward and does not cause an in- crease in the general after-tax price level. The experience with VAT in the United States seems to support this position. The Michigan BAT was levied by the subtractive method. (It is of interest that it was de- clared to be a direct tax by the Michigan Supreme Court.)

Although the Michigan tax was an incomplete value-added tax, it did provide significant revenues and was administered in an open econ- omy. Michigan manufacturers were in competition with producers from states using a state corporate income tax. The record does not show that Michigan producers were put at a price disadvantage even though the VAT caused the total state tax take from state manufac- turing activities to increase.[3]

VAT, levied on an additive basis (with the base made up of the amounts earned in wages, profits, interest, and rents), definitely re- sembles a flat-rate income tax withheld at the source. And when levied by the subtractive method, as in Europe, the basic situation has not really changed, for this is just another method of arriving at the total while making it easier to exempt capital goods that are purchased by a firm.

When VAT is calculated on each invoice, the tax is being calculated on a subtractive basis. When this procedure is used, the amount of the tax can be seen by the purchaser as a tax payment figure. The addi- tive method makes VAT more like the corporate profits tax; the amount of tax included in the price is unknown. How this difference affects the incidence of a business tax is difficult to determine.[4]

The TVA of France was developed over a long period. Its impact on prices during its introduction was blurred by the 1958 devaluation of the French franc. The original adoption of TVA took place in 1954 and was introduced to a limited extent as early as 1949. The impact seems to have been deflationary, perhaps because it reduced the likelihood of budget imbalance and expanding central bank credit.[5]

During 1968, the year Germany introduced the value-added tax, German prices were apparently more stable than those of any other major industrial nation except Italy.[6] In the late spring of that year, the U.S. corporate income tax was increased. During the six months after this action, industrial prices increased at a more rapid rate than during the same six-month period of the previous year.[7] In both nations many factors other than tax shifts were influencing prices. Nevertheless, the changes of price level in two nations with quite different tax legislation shifts must be considered significant. It also supports the theory of what to expect from the impact of the two taxes on savings levels.[8]

INTERNATIONAL TREATMENT OF DIRECT AND INDIRECT TAXES

The General Agreement on Tariffs and Trade permits quite different international treatment of taxes categorized as indirect than of those categorized as direct.[9] Direct taxes are not refundable; indirect taxes are. And border taxes may not be levied on imports to compensate for domestic direct tax collections.

Indirect taxes on exports can be refunded, and border taxes of an equal level may be assessed on imports. VAT is treated the same as special excise taxes or gross turnover taxes. GATT assumes that all indirect tax collections are reflected entirely in the price of the goods. It makes no differentiation between general and specific indirect taxes. This position on taxation incidence flies in the face of accepted indirect tax theory.

Basically, the GATT conclusion regarding the tax rebate on exports rests upon two assumptions: (1) that in some way the general price level can increase through the imposition of a general excise tax and not from the levy of special excises on selected products, and (2) that the levy of direct taxes depresses the return to the factors of production and does not result in price increases to permit maintenance of after-tax income levels.[10]

These basic GATT assumptions are also the basis for the collection of compensatory border taxes on imports and the disallowance of similar treatment with regard to direct taxes. The development here is based on logic similar to that justifying tax rebates on exports. In addition, the principles of destination and origin enter the equation. Indirect taxes have generally been collected on what is called the principle of destination and direct taxes on the principle of origin (source).

Under the destination principle taxes are paid by the country where final use of the goods takes place. This means a rebate of turnover tax on exports and the levy of compensating taxes on imports. Under the origin (source) principle taxes are paid where the production occurs. Such taxes are not rebated later, because goods are exported and compensating taxes are not levied when they are imported.

This difference of treatment seems to stem from the fact that governments were impressed by the portion of total profits and income earned at home but paid to residents outside the country. It was further assumed that collecting and not-refunding the direct taxes on these incomes would neither affect the gross size of the incomes nor would it increase the cost of production, and thereby decrease the competitiveness of domestically produced goods nondomestic with the capital and maybe skill. Finally, through tax treaties and a general understanding of a proper treatment of foreign-earned income brought back by investors, the direct taxes paid abroad have been allowed as a deduction from domestic tax liabilities based on grossed-up income increased by the amount of the tax paid.

KALDOR'S MODIFIED VALUE-ADDED TAX

A rather different value-added tax was suggested by Nicholas Kaldor as a possible approach to the encouragement of labor intensive U.K. industries and improvement of the British balance-of-payments situation. In a chapter titled "A Memorandum on the Value Added Tax" of his *Essays on Economic Policy*[11] he suggests a value-added tax in addition to the existing U.K. tax system, and not as replacement, or as a basis for reducing any of the taxes currently collected. The proceeds of the tax would be used to finance an industry subsidy to assist in covering wage and salary costs. The wage subsidy and the related value-added tax is an alternative to devaluation of the British pound or a reduction of the rate of economic growth.

The tax liability of each firm would be calculated in gross terms as follows: The rate would be applied to the sales total after deducting export sales. From this one would subtract the value of all goods and services purchased domestically from firms operating in the United Kingdom. The tax liability up to this point is further reduced by the subsidy due the firm based on a uniform subsidy rate applied to the total wage and salary payments of the firm. If the firm had substantial export sales, and wages and salaries represented a large portion of its total costs, the quantity of subsidy for which the firm would be eligible would exceed the amount of tax liability.

The economic impact of the value-added tax and the wage and salary subsidy would be to encourage expansion of the portion of total sales exported and to encourage sales effort in this direction by firms having wage and salary costs as a higher portion of total costs than the typical U.K. firm. On the other hand, the tax would tend to increase domestic prices of goods that are largely consumed domestically and that utilize a relatively small amount of labor in their production. It would tend to decrease domestic prices of goods that are exported in considerable quantities and that also utilize considerable labor. The overall impact on the domestic price level should be approximately neutral.

Because wages are likely to be somewhat lower in nonmechanized and labor-intensive industries, and, because these industries, if they export, will receive a net government subsidy under this value-added tax scheme, the net effect would be to increase the earnings of some lower-level wage earners or to decrease a firm's wage cost. Economic equality would very likely be somewhat increased by the introduction of a value-added tax of this type with its associated wage subsidy. Because all former taxes are continued, no additional economic inequality would arise to counteract the income-equalizing effect of the scheme.

Kaldor's proposed tax is a means of financing a wage subsidy with eligibility determined by portion of production exported and size of the wage and salary budget. It is only indirectly a subsidy of exports and probably would not violate the provisions of GATT.

CONCLUSION

It is doubtful whether quantitative studies or theoretical developments will ever lay to rest the question of how different taxes paid by business affect prices.[12] The wider and more intensive use of VAT by the trading nations of the world and the treatment this tax is accorded by the nations of GATT must combine to force adoption of new tax laws of two general types: (1) the worldwide adoption of VAT at relatively uniform rates and/or (2) the introduction of international trade and capital restrictions by non-VAT nations.

APPLICATION OF THE DESTINATION AND ORIGIN PRINCIPLES

The 1974–1976 United States general trade negotiations are being carried out somewhat along the lines of the Kennedy round that was completed twelve years earlier. The period since 1964 has been filled with international economic changes, but most of them, even including the devaluations of the dollar, or perhaps more correctly the revaluation of the currencies of the major industrial nations, were seen as possibilities when the Kennedy round was negotiated.

Border taxes, the value-added tax, the destination principle and the relationships among them were realized in 1964.[13] Other concerns were considered much more important, however, and it was these concerns that were given a high priority by the American negotiators; the new studies of the incidence of the corporate profits tax were not yet digested.[14] The economic effect of indirect business taxes like the value-added tax was still considered to be shifted forward in higher prices. On the other hand, the corporate profits tax, a direct tax, was assumed to be largely shifted backward in lower profits and maybe lower wages, too, also possibly in higher prices in the long run.

Ten years later, with billion dollar government to government barter deals and the possibility of beggar-thy-neighbor exchange rate policy through dirty floats, a concern with the harm done to freedom of trade by quotas, tariffs, and border taxes is likely to seem like nitpicking. On the other hand, it is also generally recognized that if a better job had been done to maintain established competitive positions, the need to make the impossible big decisions could have been avoided.

International tax harmonization and domestic tax incidence were passed over lightly in the Kennedy round.[15] No one can be sure how important this neglect has been in the deterioration of international economic relationships that has proceeded through the years. What is important is that because of the potential international impacts of the oil cartel and the high price of gold, the day-to-day impact of border taxes levied on U.S. exports will again be neglected.

The tax rules under GATT are basically limited to (1) consideration of the direct effect of expenditures of taxes that result in product export prices lower than domestic prices, (2) the refund of taxes that are shifted forward, and (3) the levy of border taxes with rates equal to domestic indirect tax rates. Although this tax-trade-price impact can be demonstrated to be much too limited, it is a concept that produces an amount that can be measured with reasonable accuracy and therefore can be monitored. In addition, it is an area of government fiscal actions in which the acceptable approach is pretty well established. It is international fiscal policy according to the destination principle.

FUNDAMENTALS OF THE DESTINATION PRINCIPLE

The destination principle, and its justification of border taxes and tax refunds on exports, owes a considerable portion of its acceptability to the theory that the benefits of tax expenditures are neutral and to the concept of the forward shifting of indirect taxes. The tax refund on exports is justified because the revenues collected from the tax would not be available to provide services for the taxpayers who are the consumers of the exports but would increase prices paid. On the other hand, indirect taxes collected on goods sold for domestic consumption are available to finance government expenditures to benefit the consumer taxpayers. Therefore, by using these concepts of expenditure benefits and forward shifting, the collection of the same taxes on goods exported as on goods used domestically amounts to the collection of higher taxes on exports than on goods consumed locally. That is, taxes are paid on exports by citizens of a nation not benefiting through consumption of public goods financed with taxes paid. It is also true that when taxes are collected on exports, the consumers of the exporter country benefit from expenditure of revenues provided by the taxes, but they don't benefit from the consumption of the goods taxed.

In this very complex fashion, one can reason that the collection of the same taxes on goods produced and exported as on goods domestically produced and consumed amounts to the collection of higher taxes on exports than on goods not exported. Taxes paid by consumers of imports, through forward shifting of taxes on exports, are used to finance services provided by the government of the exporting nation. On the other hand, border taxes paid by importers provide funds to finance services they can enjoy.

PRODUCT TRADE AND RESOURCE ALLOCATION

If the destination principle is utilized by all nations relative to all their taxes, then as far as the free flow of trade is affected by taxes, the producer utilizing the fewest private resources producing in the nation with the largest public sector will be supplying all users, if resources are used approximately as efficiently in all economies. Under these conditions, other nations using the product will levy border taxes equal to the taxes borne by products produced in the importing country. The effect of the border tax is to allocate to imports the costs of production met by government spending in the importing nation, and not the higher amount that under the conditions assumed here is spent by the nation of export.

The tax refund on exports and the border tax on imports, administered in this fashion, encourage the use of government resources to meet worldwide needs for the product. Under these conditions resource allocation need not be pushed away from most efficient resource use.

If the traditional and most efficient producer were a relatively large user of private resources, however, it would take some time to make the adjustment required for production to be centered where real costs were minimal.[16]

The tax harmonization program of the European Community proposes that the destination principle for indirect taxes be abandoned between member states but continued between member states and third countries. The new situation, because it will make indirect tax rates and procedures considerably more uniform within the EC than they are now, has been considered a move toward greater tax harmonization. The new indirect tax uniformity could generate less as well as more trade among member states and a less or more efficient use of resources than that which existed when considerable variation in indirect taxes existed, and the destination principle was uniformly utilized.

For example, if the nation exporting product x were an efficient producer that had a highly developed public sector financed with indirect taxes, and if the principal importer were a nation with a relatively low-level indirect tax, the condition before harmonization would have been more favorable to nondomestic consumers than would be true under harmonization with uniform indirect tax rates. No longer would the low-tax nondomestic consumer of product x benefit from a larger refund of indirect taxes than were assessed as border taxes. If the demand for product x were rather elastic, imports would decline and the number of persons employed in the production of x would decline. On the other hand, if the relative use of indirect taxes of the exporters and importers of product x were reversed, employment and consumption would be stimulated.

ORIGIN PRINCIPLE FUNDAMENTALS

The nearly exclusive use of the tax origin principle (no refund of taxes on exports and no border taxes) by one producing area and the considerable use of the tax destination principle by another is close to the situation that is developing between the United States and the European Community. Exports will be stimulated from the country using the destination principle to the country using the origin principle, but not on the basis of most efficient use of resources. For trade to be in balance, factor or production costs, including taxes, will have to be considerably less in the country using the origin principle than in the one using the destination principle. This is another way of saying the balance of trade between the two areas will require a reduction of the terms of trade of the nation making use of the origin principle —that is, labor and capital will receive less per unit of export. Put in terms of exchange rates, the tax relationship requires the currency of the country using the origin principle to be relatively undervalued. This in turn encourages foreign investment in the country using origin-type taxes and a relatively lower scale of living because of higher-priced imports and lower-priced exports.

Because this tax-caused economic relationship is frequently misunderstood, it is worthwhile to consider it in some detail. If the cost of product x is $C + T$ (T equals taxes and C all other costs) and these costs are equal in the two countries A and B, and if both countries use the origin principle relative to taxes, each country will produce the product x it requires.[17] Whether this situation corresponds with that of best allocation of factors relative to product x cannot be determined because we do not know what other uses could be made of factors used to produce x in countries A and B.[18]

If the situation is changed only in that A utilizes the destination principle and B keeps the origin principle, the cost of x produced in A becomes C to B while the cost of x to A users remains at $C + T$. The cost of x produced in B remains $C + T$ to domestic and foreign users. Under these conditions the consumers of x in B begin to purchase their x in A rather than from domestic producers.[19]

Taxes paid by producers of x for local consumption in A and B have not been changed, but their relative international competitive position has been affected. Country A, by having a tax system capable of using the destination principle and by taking advantage of this opportunity, has improved its international economic competitive position.[20] A will be selling x more cheaply and B will be offering x at the same price, but A will be adding a border tax to this price. Consumers of x in B will purchase more from A, and consumers in A will purchase less of x from B.

The price A pays for products from B will increase its tax receipts because of the collection of a border tax. In turn, its tax receipts will be reduced by the refunding of taxes on its new market for x in B. The higher price A pays for imports will tend to reduce its consumption of imports, and the lower prices of exports will tend to stimulate exports. Balance can be restored by reducing the value of the monetary unit of B, which is another way of saying reducing what can be purchased abroad for an hour of labor in B. This situation cannot be remedied by increasing hourly wages in B, for this would counter the cure of devaluation adopted in B to meet the new competitive conditions arising from the introduction in A of a tax system that can make use of the destination principle.[21]

CONCLUSION

The economic and philosophical bases of the destination and origin principles are a complex group of assumptions regarding tax and expenditure incidence. These have become less acceptable through the years as the result of the findings of new studies.

The application of the destination principle causes an unequal impact of a given tax level on international economic competitive conditions. If the destination principle is eliminated, however, it would not eliminate the difference in the impact of a given level of tax collection that arises from differences in efficiency of expenditure, and the variation of the impact of the same tax under different administrative procedures. Because it is an unnecessary additional element restricting freedom of economic exchange, it seems appropriate to consider elimination of the destination principle as a basic element in GATT treatment of taxes in relation to general export subsidies and compensatory border taxes. In addition, the destination principle acts to interfere with the free choice of fiscal measures by the electorate of the various nations of the world. It is partially responsible for the rapid adoption of VAT in Western Europe.

INTERNATIONAL COST COMPARISONS

In international economic affairs, VAT can do in the fiscal area pretty much what a central bank can do in the monetary area. A central bank is able to protect the functioning of the domestic monetary system from outside disruptions and can moderate foreign influences that might cause deflation or inflation. VAT does the same in the fiscal area. Expansion of government expenditures financed with VAT does not get reflected in prices of exports. Also, additional costs falling on domestic producers to cover domestic government spending must also be paid on imports. International impact insulation of domestic fiscal and monetary actions permits greater domestic economic autonomy. The U.S. Federal Reserve, combined with VAT, can become more effective in preventing the thwarting of independence in national economic policy by foreign influences.

EXPLOITING GATT FOR INTERNATIONAL TRADE ADVANTAGE

It is sometimes argued that the United States can acquire the international advantages arising from the use of VAT by changes in exchange rates. Higher VAT rates, it is pointed out, have international effects similar to devaluation of the dollar. For a number of reasons this is an example of a misleading generalization.

First, VAT affects only goods and services (and services to only a minor degree), while a devaluation affects all international transactions. For example, all debts or interest contracts stated in U.S. dollars are reduced by devaluation but not by an increase of VAT. A devaluation would also increase the cost of all foreign commitments stated in foreign currencies, while the introduction of VAT would have no effect. A devaluation of the dollar increases the cost of imports but doesn't provide revenues.[22] VAT, on the other hand, increases the price of imports and also provides revenue to compensate for the revenue loss arising from the export stimulus through VAT refund. Finally, it is doubtful whether the dollar can really be devalued. This is true even though the International Monetary Fund changes the relation of special drawing rights (SDR) to the dollar. Other currencies, as we have seen during the past several years, tend to keep their exchange rates fixed in terms of dollars. Therefore, what has been often called the 1972 devaluation of the dollar has really amounted to an upward valuation of a small number of strong currencies.

Open international competition by the producers of the world is an important portion of our abundance. A vital aspect of sharing a continuing abundance is the trading of nations on an equal footing—particularly the United States, the world's leading commercial nation. The development of VAT by Germany has placed U.S. sellers to Germany in a disadvantageous position.

For example, prior to the adoption of two-fifths of the Kennedy round of tariff reductions and Germany's 11 percent VAT, the percentage increase in U.S. price due to cost of entry into Germany was as follows for the listed products:[23]

Aluminum Ingot	14.3
Toaster	28.2
Vacuum Cleaner	22.8
Rotisserie	29.9
Steam Turbine	15.9

Afterward, the percentage increase in U.S. price due to cost of entry was as follows:

Aluminum Ingot	21.5
Toaster	34.0
Vacuum Cleaner	27.4
Rotisserie	36.8
Steam Turbine	21.4

This business of attempting to summarize the impacts of entry costs on international economic exchanges is very complicated. The examples given are nothing more than that. With the reduction of customs duties, border taxes have been increased through adoption of VAT. The United States, without VAT, finds itself in a less harmonized position, as far as costs of entry go, than was true before the Kennedy round. It is also true that by adopting a major VAT the United States could remedy the situation (1) without bringing about beggar-thy-neighbor responses, (2) while improving the balance and productivity of its national tax system.[24]

The position of the United States in trade negotiations considering the effects of taxes has not been sufficiently tough. For example, for some reason the United States clings to a system of valuation of imports, to which tariffs and border taxes are applied, based on cost at point of export. Every other important industrial nation (excluding Canada) uses cost at point of import. The result of this stubbornness is to reduce the effectiveness of U.S. tariffs and border taxes by at least 10 percent (measured by the U.S. Department of Commerce at 7.4 percent in January 1974).[25] (See pp. 228–234.)

Another example is the current GATT understandings. These give every appearance of being negotiated by the United States when the problem was a dollar shortage and not a dollar abundance. A heavier use of indirect taxation by Europeans existed then as it does now. A carefully negotiated arrangement would not have granted the favors of the destination principle to indirect taxes.

The GATT regulations and the U.S. import valuation procedures "are not sacrosanct and should be susceptible to change."[26]

One of the largest and least recognized methods of improving sales of a nation's producers (without causing inflation by raising earnings of consumers or by increasing costs of raw materials through international devaluation of its monetary unit) is to reduce government costs included in exports and increase government costs included in imports. The name of the game is "playing the GATT tax rules."

It was the Treaty of Rome that established the operating procedures of the European Community. The rules in the area of taxation very closely followed those already drawn up by GATT. The member states, well aware of the shortcomings of GATT's tax arrangements, began to take care of the difficulty immediately.

Fritz Neumark, the German tax sage of Frankfurt, established in his famous 1965 study that tax harmonization was the route to follow.[27] Also, the first big area to harmonize was the general taxation of transactions. The French had widened the original GATT tax shortcoming in the 1950s and had demonstrated to everyone's satisfaction that the value-added tax was the best vehicle for all to use. The official documents of EC, from the Neumark Report on, reflect the official position that tax harmonization was necessary and that the first big step was the use of a uniform VAT by all EC member states.

UNFAIR EXPORT PRACTICES

The Tariff Act of 1930 provides for the levy of countervailing duties on imports from nations that have granted economic favors to an industry exporting to the United States. GATT rules and provisions outline what are considered to be a subsidy of exports. Basically, any favor directly granted on exported goods, other than the refund of indirect taxes, could come under the tent of export subsidy.

In the past, the United States has been very hesitant in making use of the power it possesses to equalize competitive conditions between imports and domestic goods. Now conditions are changing, and the famous Italian tomato paste case of the mid-1960s has become the forerunner of a general policy rather than an isolated incident.

On February 10, 1973, countervailing duties were imposed on steel-belted radial tires produced by the French-controlled Michelin Tire Company in Canada. The Canadian government had granted the firm low-interest loans and favorable property tax rates. Also, three-fourths of the total production was exported to the United States. Later the U.S. Steel Corporation failed in its 1975 appeal based directly on VAT export refunds.

EARLY THEORIES THAT WERE WRONG

In 1958, when EC was young and the United States looked around and saw no one who could challenge her supremacy, a group of dangerous policies were advocated. For example, Raymond F. Mikesell wrote, "I reject the view that a European Common Market is likely to result in a free trading bloc maintained by high tariffs and other restrictions against the outside world."[28]

The free trading bloc exists, and the common border tax provided by a uniform VAT of around 15 percent is only a few years away. Common restrictions, quotas, and what have you are currently being applied with great vigor to agricultural imports. And the high price of gold and the reduced value of the U.S. dollar have made American agriculture products cheap to Russia and other food deficit nations.

EXPORTATION OF CAPITAL AND JOBS

Classical economics taught that the outflow of $1 million of savings to be invested in a foreign country decreased domestic investment by $1 million. Keynesian economics has emphasized that the multiplier effect of $1 million of domestic investment is such that gross domestic product (GDP) will expand by several times the amount of the investment.

On the other hand, investment in the foreign country expands its GDP directly by $1 million and through the impact of the multiplier the GDP increases by several times the original investment expansion.

As an American interested in a sound domestic economy, one is justified in asking: Why isn't capital exporting something that should be minimized?

THE TREATMENT OF TRADE WITHIN THE EC

The value-added tax is expected to be established soon in all the member states of the EC at relatively uniform rates and with approximately the same tax base. This state of affairs is the next goal now that VAT has been adopted by all member states. When it is realized, the business of zero rate on exports to member states will be abandoned, and border taxes on imports equal to domestic VAT rates will be eliminated.

The member states are very much aware of the need for uniform VAT legislation and established as a second council directive a set of procedures for applying the tax.[30] In fact, because certain services are so closely related to prices of goods traded, they are listed in an appendix as services that must be covered by the regular VAT rate of a member state.

Product source countries not belonging to EC must compete in member state markets after having paid border taxes. The result will be that only imports from outside EC will provide budgetary revenues. These products will be competitive only if they have benefited from a tax refund from the country of production, all other things being equal. If this is the case, one would expect an EC member state to favor imports from a non-EC source.

On the other hand, if one member state exported to another, it would not have to refund the VAT tax to the exporter as it does with exports to destinations outside EC. Therefore, the treasury would benefit and favor exports to other member states.

These fiscal imports of a mature EC value-added tax would tend to cancel each other. But if an outside trading nation had not harmonized its tax by adopting a VAT with rates similar to those of EC member states, it would of course face a border tax hurdle when selling within EC that would not exist between member states.

U.S. TAXATION OF FOREIGN INCOME OF AMERICAN COMPANIES

The world point of view comes down hard in favor of neutrality in the taxation of foreign income. However, like so many concepts, neutrality means different things to different people. For example, it is really very hard to refute those who argue that tax neutrality is impossible without basic tax harmonization. Others, however, consider international neutrality requirements to be met only when taxes are the same to all.

The EC, in their very active struggles to develop tax harmonization, are certainly demonstrating a belief that tax neutrality is unattainable without tax harmonization. Americans, because of their income tax fixation, have on occasion defined neutrality as (1) enforcing the same tax rate on income wherever earned; (2) having the tax liability arise when income is earned; (3) allowing full tax credit for income taxes paid to a foreign government.[31]

CONCLUSION

Open international competition, which is so important to the economic well-being of the world, requires equal treatment of government costs. When one group of countries refunds taxes on exports and levies border taxes on imports, either this must be stopped or all countries must be able to act similarly.[32]

The understandings of GATT have worked to prohibit the United States from carrying on international trade on the same basis as the EC member states. This has been and continues to be the situation, largely because the United States does not utilize a major value-added tax as do the EC member states.[33]

TAX-RELATED U.S. INTERNATIONAL COMMERCIAL RELATIONS

BASIC POSITION I: VAT WITHOUT BORDER TAXES

The average of U.S. exports and imports accounted for 5.9 percent of GNP in current prices during 1968–1970 and 4.9 percent during 1960–1962, but increased to 10 percent in 1975 when the domestic economy was down and grain exports were unusually large. Under these conditions, the United States can extend a substantial subsidy of exports with only a small increase in taxes paid as a percentage of GNP. If the tax is assumed to increase all prices uniformly, this also means a small price increase.

Therefore, U.S. exports could benefit from a 15 percent subsidy at a cost of 0.75 percent of GNP. If the incidence of financing is assumed to rest on prices, the value of the dollar in the purchase of domestic goods would decline by less than 1 percent and all U.S. exporters would receive a subsidy of 15 percent of the market price of their foreign sales.

Nations such as Japan, the Netherlands, and Germany have averages of exports and imports of 10.7, 49.2 and 21.9 percent, respectively, of GNP in current prices. Therefore, the fiscal cost to them of subsidizing exports becomes a much larger portion of GNP. The reflection of this cost in their prices would cause the domestic purchasing power of their monetary unit to decline several times that of the American dollar for each purchasing power unit of tax refund financed with domestic revenues.

The cost of substantial export subsidies by industrial nations that are much more committed to international trade than the United States is so great that financing through a tax on imports becomes very nearly a necessity. For if the needed revenues were raised from taxes on domestic production, a substantial portion of the upward impact of the export subsidy on employment levels would be dissipated. On the other hand, the levy of additional taxes on imports encourages domestic production of goods that do not compete well with foreign products, while they carry much of the budgetary burden of the export subsidy.

The value-added tax, with reduced rates on certain socially desirable goods, zero rates on foods and some raw materials, and substantial border tax levies on equipment and selected raw materials, has done the job needed to carry out an export subsidy program for the EC member states.

As mentioned earlier, the United States, because of the relatively small portion of its GNP exported, would not find it necessary to place a heavy burden on domestic production to finance a substantial export subsidy. Therefore, the United States does not have the same need for a compensating border tax on imports to meet the costs of export subsidies (or general tax refunds) as do the nations exporting a much larger percentage of GNP. However, this country may wish to do it on some products—for example, oil, under current conditions.

The need for large compensating revenues by the nations with relatively large exports arises when the VAT is refunded on domestic products exported just as if a straight subsidy of 15 percent (average VAT rate) were paid. Also, the refunding to U.S. exporters by the federal government of 15 percent of the selling price of exports (as a low estimate of domestic taxes included in selling price) would be an offer of a subsidy to U.S. exporters much like that enjoyed by EC exporters. However, the cost as a percentage of U.S. GNP would be much less than for EC member states. It would require an allocation of fiscal costs equal to only 0.75 percent of GNP if all exports enjoyed the refund.

The relatively favorable export subsidy position of the United States, arising from the $90 of production for domestic use available to support each $5 to $10 of exports, provides opportunities that should be used in international trade negotiations. This advantage, when exploited to reduce foreign import restrictions, will become a force for the expansion of international trade and a reduction of the use of relatively inefficient producing units around the world to get around and behind border taxes.

BASIC PROPOSITION II: CONTRIBUTION OF
DOMESTIC INTERNATIONAL SALES CORPORATION (DISC)

The introduction of DISC by the United States on January 1, 1972, was a watershed. DISC provided fiscal inducement for the first time to U.S. domestic production for foreign sales. In doing this, it introduced the subsidy of exports as a part of U.S. international commercial policy.

The DISC legislation provides a subsidy of varying amounts for a limited portion of U.S. exports. The largest subsidy is provided to medium-sized companies exporting a product that is of considerable per-unit value on which a substantial profit is made, and that can be made more profitable by promotional activity. The selection of this portion of exports for subsidy arose from a combination of several basic elements included in the legislation.

First, it was necessary that subsidy be granted on exports that provided employment to urban organized labor, and companies favored are basically of this sort. Second, the approach needed to have the support of Congress, and this required that multinational corporations not be favored over medium-sized businesses. Third, the first step toward domestic sourcing of foreign sales needed to be taken without treading too heavily on the toes of the interests of other commercial nations as represented by the GATT understandings.

The companies that can benefit most from DISC have in general taken advantage of the opportunity. Because demand has been strong and the value of the dollar has been sharply decreased in most European countries and in Japan, the export subsidy provided by DISC has not generally been the cause of a decrease of U.S. dollar export prices. Instead, DISC has been utilized to expand working capital levels, to assure export profitability, and to finance greater efforts to expand market potentials.

Generally speaking, even before the introduction of DISC, the export sales of this class of firm were increasing more rapidly than domestic sales. This was causing a number of them to consider the desirability of establishing subsidiaries within the EC. A combination of increasing domestic production efficiency as the company worked down the "experience curve" and the subsidy of DISC has caused investment in foreign production to be delayed.

BASIC PROPOSITION III: REDUCTION OF TAX FAVORS TO
U.S. FOREIGN SUBSIDIARIES

Many multinational corporations are American. The rapid expansion of the foreign-based production facilities of these firms has given rise to a galaxy of difficulties at home and abroad. It is also true that the development itself has been to a considerable extent the result of border taxes and other import barriers of other industrial nations. In addition, foreign production by American companies was stimulated by the overvaluation of the dollar, the relatively favorable U.S. tax treatment of foreign-source income of multinational corporations, and tax inducements offered to American investors by countries desiring to attract new industries.

As early as 1918, when the corporate income tax existed only in the United States but the personal income tax was well developed in the United Kingdom and the Scandinavian countries, the American government adopted and pressed for worldwide usage of the tax credit procedure as a method of avoiding double taxation of foreign-source income. The development of the corporate income tax since that time, in both higher rates and national coverage, has made the tax credit procedure as a method of avoiding double taxation of foreign-source income of much greater importance to business decisions than was originally envisaged.

In 1971 multinational corporations repatriated to the United States some $66.4 billion of income and paid corporate income tax to the United States on this income at an average rate of about 6 percent. Although legislative efforts have been made to prevent exportation to sales subsidiaries at prices below cost to avoid profit allocation to the

United States and the accumulation of these earnings where taxes are minimal, the results to date are not impressive.

One piece of proposed U.S. trade legislation provides for the elimination of the tax credit procedure to make the corporate income tax like all other foreign taxes. It is being vigorously fought on the assumption that taxes based on taxable corporate income are shifted backward onto profits. In addition, it is quite correctly pointed out that much of the development of foreign production facilities arose because (1) American investment capital was treated more generously abroad than domestically, (2) barriers to importation and sale of "Made in USA" products were substantial, and (3) the home country tax collection efforts on foreign-source income of domestic companies of other nationalities is minimal.

BASIC PROPOSITION IV: IMPACT OF
DEVALUATION ON U.S. COMPETITIVENESS WILL DECREASE

The devaluation of the dollar has been highly inflationary domestically, but this impact is only now becoming visible. When normality returns in the worldwide demand for manufactured products, the relative value of the dollar will have to decrease again, or the current American industrial competitive position will be weakened. Also, the relatively greater cost increases in the United States in late 1973 and 1974 because of the high dollar price for services and materials with worldwide prices is undermining the U.S. competitive position without any overt action on the part of the other industrial nations on the money markets. A renewed outward flow of dollar savings as currencies of other nations go through another period of revaluation is a possibility.

A balanced international trade position arising from these adjustments has some undesirable characteristics. For example, a relatively rapid increase in the dollar cost of oil and other basic raw materials places upward price pressure on all domestic goods. This push toward inflation takes place without an increase in employment opportunities. In addition, the relationships developed encourage the export of domestic capital because (1) the international value of the monetary unit is likely to decline again; (2) foreign production costs are down due to relatively cheap raw materials; and (3) labor unrest and upward wage pressures due to a relatively higher cost for food and shelter are likely to increase.

On the other hand, an American international trade balance developed with export subsidies rather than devaluation avoids, at least partially, many of these difficulties. For example, the relative domestic currency price of neither imported nor exported raw materials needs to increase. Lower prices on raw material exports will reduce profit-increase-induced wage increases. In addition, as DISC has demonstrated, export subsidies can be largely limited to industrial products containing a substantial urban labor input.

A large part of the failure of the United States to balance its international trade accounts prior to 1975 and to hold American sourced funds for domestic industrial investment arises from border taxes and other import restrictions imposed by the governments of other high income industrial nations. These restrict the international flow of goods between nations and decrease welfare levels. (It is assumed that welfare is maximized under conditions of full employment with goods produced most efficiently the ones most likely to be exported.)

The import restrictions of the major industrial nations are only partially explained on the basis of a desire to enjoy a balance in the international trade accounts. A very important additional consideration is the domestic political need to enjoy a high level of employment. Employment in export industries where productivity at the very least is somewhat greater than in make-work projects is an economical way to meet politically necessary employment levels.

Prior to the oil crisis the decrease in the value of the dollar had coincided with an improvement in the international balance of U.S. trade. A tendency to accord a cause effect relationship is probably largely misplaced, at least the record of the commercial politics of the nations making the purchases does not seem to lead to this conclusion. Rather, the purchases have been made from the United States because prosperity and/or crop failures have caused temporary shortages to arise. These shortages have expanded American sales rather than the price reductions due to devaluation. If this is the true situation—and the fact that European and Japanese sales representatives appear to be generally selling U.S. products at the predevaluation prices is a strong indication that this is the true situation—then U.S. sales can be expected to drop sharply when production abroad again equals consumption abilities.

Of course, it is also true that rising incomes of the industrial nations have caused them to demand products not produced efficiently domestically. The quantities of these sales are likely to continue, and this continuation will be partially caused by the lower prices of these products due to dollar devaluation. Quotas, border taxes, and domestic use regulations, however, can be expected to work to keep U.S. products out where the domestic production capacity is not being fully utilized, e.g. as in the case of steel in 1975. This is sound national economic management as long as economic policy must operate within the assumption of full employment. Of course, sophisticated adoption of this policy also requires active efforts to develop areas where productivity of workers can be sufficiently high to meet international marketing demands. The U.S. devaluation policy seen in this light becomes something less than ideal. Rather than devaluation, a procedure was needed to permit the purchase of imports with a dollar maintaining its relative value among the world currencies while the prices of exports shifted as demand and supply conditions dictated. To do this would have required sharp restrictions or quotas on imports of manufactured products by the United States until the other industrial nations had removed their import hurdles. The high level of prosperity around the world until mid-1974 made action along these lines relatively easy. Although this policy was partially initiated for a time, it was not accompanied by a big enough subsidy threat. Only the DISC approach turned out to be available.

DEVALUATION AND UPWARD VALUATION THROUGH TAX SHIFTS

On November 19, 1968, Germany and France announced that devaluation of the franc would be prevented by German value-added tax action.[34] The German VAT rate was 11 percent. This meant that all German exporters received an 11 percent refund and all imports carried an 11 percent tax applied to value including customs duties and transportation costs. The German government, by cutting the refund of VAT on exports, could increase prices and therefore decrease exports. Also, by decreasing the border tax on imports, the price of imported goods could be decreased, making them more competitive on the German markets.

A German banker was quoted as saying that the action would prevent an upward valuation of the mark and that those speculating by selling francs for marks would suffer a loss. This would make them "less eager to speculate in the future." A German economist said, "If a change in the flow of international payments is desired, alteration of border tax adjustments is favored to exchange rate change, because the result constitutes a smaller, less permanent jolt to the status quo."[35]

BASIC PROPOSITION V: REALISTIC TAXATION OF
MULTINATIONAL CORPORATIONS

The taxation of multinational corporations (MNCs) has become important because these very substantial American enterprises are earning much of their profits from foreign sources. The consistent growth of profits and sales of many corporations during the past ten years has depended on sizable international operations that have tended to be countercyclical. Therefore, tax collections from MNCs can be expected to help stabilize the tax receipts from the corporate income tax and the dividends paid by MNCs to help stabilize the incomes of their stockholders.

Gillette, as an example, earned 31 percent of its net income abroad in 1972, and profits abroad were 40 percent higher as a percentage of net income than at home. The business growth of H. J. Heinz came 46 percent from abroad in 1972, and again profit growth was somewhat more rapid. Net income from sales abroad for Xerox has been growing over 40 percent annually since 1967, while domestic net increased at a 10 percent rate.

The taxable income from foreign sources reported in corporate tax returns of U.S. corporations has increased from $3.725 billion in 1962 to $7.177 billion in 1966. The foreign tax credit claimed (which, of course, decreased dollar for dollar the taxes payable from foreign-sourced income) was $1.565 billion in 1962 and $2.861 billion in 1966.[36]

The integrated petroleum industry accounted for a declining share of taxable income from foreign sources—44 percent of all taxable income from foreign sources in 1962 and 37 percent in 1964. During the same period, mining (which consists largely of petroleum) claimed an increase in foreign tax credits from $328,763,000 to $346,363,000.[37] By 1966 this total had grown to $564,225,000.

TAXATION OF FOREIGN OIL COMPANY OPERATIONS

The 1962 Revenue Act provided for an increase in the taxes collected by the United States on the international business of American companies. This was not the effect of all provisions of the legislation, however. The "gross-up" provision of the 1962 legislation substantially expanded tax payments for most American MNCs. It required that taxes deemed paid by corporations in developed countries be included in U.S. taxable income and therefore subject to U.S. income taxes. On the other hand, the 1962 legislation permitted MNCs to take into account in calculating foreign taxes for which a tax credit on U.S. taxes due can be taken, taxes paid other than those attributable to after-tax profits. Widening the concept of foreign taxes paid on which foreign tax credit could be taken has been particularly important for MNCs engaged in the petroleum business.

The inclusion of taxes other than those assessed on after-tax profits had the effect of making all direct taxes paid eligible as a tax credit against taxes due on income taxable by the United States. A major result of this change was to make the large royalty payments to Saudi Arabia, Venezuela, Canada, Iran, Libya, and Kuwait deductible from taxes payable to the United States rather than an expense that reduced the level of profits (taxable income).

Another aspect of the new tax relationship that developed out of the 1962 legislation was that MNC profits earned in developed countries were treated differently from profits allocated to less developed countries. The provision for the gross-up that increased taxes paid to the United States applied only to earnings and taxes allocated to developed countries. Developed countries include Western Europe (except Finland), Canada, Hong Kong, Japan, New Zealand, Australia, South Africa, and all countries in the Sino-Soviet Bloc.

As a result of these two provisions of the 1962 Revenue Act, the MNCs engaged in the petroleum business were able to include royalty payments as tax credits against taxes due to the United States and were also not required to gross up these taxes. However, this did not result in much tax saving because oil companies decided to operate international oil activities through branches to retain the tax benefits of percentage depletion. Percentage depletion was removed in 1974 and many foreign oil operations have been nationalized, eliminating some royalty payments.

The treatment of royalty payments as direct taxes eligible for treatment as tax credits against income taxes caused oil companies to become by far the largest users of this feature of the U.S. tax code. In the mid-1960s, annual taxable income from petroleum-dominated mining was about $1 billion. The U.S. income tax in 1964, before credits, was $452 million; after tax credits it was $106 million.[38] Although this figure is low, one must keep in mind that these companies carried out their foreign operations through branches and therefore benefited from the depletion allowance. At this time the depletion allowance was 27.5 percent of the gross income from the property, with a maximum of 50 percent of net income.

The tax encouragement for American MNCs to develop their oil resources outside the United States has been very substantial. The program was a tax stimulus to expand petroleum production abroad and to worsen the U.S. international balance of payments. The 1973 nationalization of foreign oil properties plus U.S. tax legalization of 1975 largely eliminated the tax related inducements.

STOPPING SOME INTERNATIONAL LEAKS

A considerable portion of the Internal Revenue Code concerns itself with efforts to collect taxes on foreign economic activities of American individuals and corporations. Also, taxes are used to shore up the U.S. balance of international payments. An example is the Interest Equalization Tax (IET) on September 2, 1964, retroactive to July 18, 1963. This tax was labeled a temporary measure to discourage American investment in developed nations but continued to be extended each time the expiration date arrived. Finally, in 1973, the rate reduction to 0.25 percent made the impact of the tax minimal, and in January 1974 the tax was repealed.

The theory of IET is that by increasing the cost of American capital to users in developed nations, the outflow of U.S. capital can be decreased. The tax aims at increasing this cost by about 1 percent. The law was difficult to administer. Canada protested and was exempted from its provision, and other special deals were accepted.

Until 1973, there were capital export maximums on corporations and financial institutions of the United States. The Department of Commerce and the Federal Reserve Board had the responsibility for enforcing rules limiting the amount of foreign investment under what was called the Voluntary Foreign Credit Restraint Program.

Under Section 483 of the Internal Revenue Code, the Treasury continues to work hard to prevent transfer of profits from domestic operations to foreign affiliates. The effort is aimed at preventing the sale of U.S.-produced products to foreign affiliates of American companies at a price below what would exist under an arm's-length transaction.

Why must this effort be put forth? The answer is simple: because tax rates on profits in America are higher than in other countries. Why? The reason is that U.S. governments collect somewhat less taxes than the governments of other countries, but much less use is made of indirect taxes. The effect is to force the United States to legislate higher taxes on profits and incomes, which in turn cause businesses and individuals to work out procedures to decrease profits and income allocated to the United States.

The tax legislation aimed at the removal of the difficulties is complicated and it isn't working. Currently an effort to require the allocation of more research expenses to foreign operations is being carried out by the Treasury. As a result, today we hear proposals to decrease imports into the United States sharply. In addition, legislation is introduced to set quotas on various products. The enjoyment of the benefits of international free flow of goods and capital is being threatened. With regard to the deteriorated international economic relationships, it is of interest to note what a former member of the Federal Reserve Board wrote. "In my experience, few, if any, international policy matters were weighed carefully by either the Board or the FOMC."[39]

SHAM TRANSACTIONS

The actions of MNCs to reduce their tax liabilities in the United States, their home country, are often the subject of outrage—as well they might be. All too frequently, however, the stories of their actions fail to emphasize that the whole business could be cut out if the United States sharply reduced reliance on the corporate income tax and the personal income tax with high rates and provision for many deductions.

If the United States continues to emphasize profits and personal income in its approach to taxes, it must be prepared for elaborate schemes by taxpayers to minimize these levies. For example, the determination of the transfer of title and therefore the location of future profits is one example of a legal nicety that can remove profits from the reach of the IRS.

An illustration of the way a profitable MNC can operate is the case of *U.S. Gypsum Co.* vs. *U.S.* (304F. Supp. 627 (1969).

U.S. Gypsum Export, Inc., a wholly owned subsidiary of U.S. Gypsum, made profits of over a million dollars a year and had only two employees. U.S. Gypsum Export gained title to the gypsum ore in Canada during the period between the time it hit the end of the conveyor belt and the time it fell into the hold of the docked ship owned by a Panamanian subsidiary of U.S. Gypsum. During this brief ownership period (perhaps less than a second) USG Export was paid 50 cents a ton by U.S. Gypsum.

This was done because USG Export qualified as a Western Hemisphere Trade Corporation (WHTC), and this 50 cent payment was really a procedure based on title transfer of removing 50 cents a ton from the full impact of the U.S. corporate tax. Instead these excluded profits were subject to the lower WHTC rate.

The law does not permit U.S. Gypsum to pay more than the going rate for the transportation services provided by its Panamanian shipping company, which is not subject to a corporate income tax by Panama. However, ocean freight rates are so volatile that it is next to impossible to determine whether the lowest competitive shipping rate was paid. In this instance, it was determined that payments were 10 percent above the competitive rate, and taxes plus penalties were assessed. Also, the WHTC privilege was withdrawn from USG Export.

The tax havens of Bermuda, Liechtenstein, Efate (an island in the New Hebrides), and Switzerland all show the need of MNCs to locate a tax-free and safe place to be used as the country where title to income and assets can be placed. In addition to not levying taxes, the authorities of the safe haven nation must be able and willing to enforce secrecy, and the legal system must be sufficiently competent to apply the laws of the area, which must provide absolute property rights. Finally, the local citizens must be law-abiding.

The continuation of the present sharp differences in tax levels around the world requires that liability to tax be set by a basic economic action rather than the mere location of title. The United States, through some very complicated tax legislation under Subsection F of the Internal Revenue Code, has moved in this direction, but very clumsily.

CONCLUSION

The United States, because of the size of its domestic economy relative to quantities of exports and imports, has the ability to refund taxes on exports without levying border taxes on imports. To follow this policy would stimulate production by U.S. companies at home and keep import prices low.

The tax treatment of MNCs has become the source of much irritation and manipulation. The difficulty arises largely from the use of the corporate income tax. The regulations of the IRS attempting to deal with this problem are very complex. The weakness of the entire effort has recently been highlighted by the relatively low U.S. taxes paid by a number of very prosperous MNCs, including oil company conglomerates.

INTERNATIONAL TAX HARMONIZATION

The international economic game is played, as we have seen, within man-made rules and guidelines that have evolved through the years. In order to have a chance of success, a nation must gather the necessary tools for truly competitive behavior.

HARMONIZATION PROBLEMS

Denmark is an example. The country adopted VAT partially to meet domestic needs for more revenues. It also adopted VAT in order to "harmonize" its tax system with those of the European Community countries.[40] Later, of course, Denmark joined EC. One is justified in believing that Danish tax harmonization was more than a necessary "putting the house in order" before joining EC. *Harmonization* was the word used to refer to the acquisition of the necessary tools to match those of other nations playing the economic game under the established international rules of GATT.

Actually, harmonization was needed by Denmark to protect its economic position. Danish economists saw the country as gaining much of the required harmonization if it introduced VAT. This being the case, why should Denmark delay in the adoption of VAT until membership in the EC? Denmark jumped the gun, so to speak, and became the second nation in Europe to make major use of VAT.

When a country uses only direct taxes (more or less as the United States does), expanding an expenditure program brings about relatively serious international repercussions.[41] If the increased spending is financed with taxes on high income or profits, savings tend to migrate to other nations because investment in foreign nations becomes more attractive. If the additional spending is financed with borrowing, private construction and investment will be diminished. It is also possible for monetary reserves to be considerably expanded through central bank purchase of government securities, and the danger of price increases and international speculation against the nation's monetary unit increases. If the spending is financed with wage taxes, take-home pay is decreased, bringing demands for higher wages, but no opportunity is created for refunds on exports or border taxes on imports of the higher costs.

A nation that uses largely direct taxes and adopts an expansionary expenditure program must worry about the program's impact on the international balance of payments.[42] This is also true of a nation using VAT, but to a much smaller extent. The worries are less because (1) much of the cost of the expanded expenditures will also be paid by importers as border taxes, and (2) prices of exports will reflect little of the cost increase because of the rebate of domestic taxes on goods exported. Another reason VAT makes a nation's economic life easier is the relatively large amount of revenue that can be generated with small rate increases. There is no doubt that it is easier to increase revenues by $5 billion with a 0.5 percent tax rate increase than with a 3 to 4 percentage point increase of the income tax on certain brackets. The pain is spread over more people and is less when the rate increase is small. In addition, the serious problem of threatening the economic well-being of a particular company or industry can be largely avoided.

TAXING PARTNERSHIPS

One of the impacts of taxing on the basis of legal organization rather than economic output is found in the tax treatment of partnerships. This aspect of nonhomogeneity in taxation between nations is of sufficient importance to be briefly summarized.

Common-law countries such as the United States use the personal approach, which allocates all income to the partners. The partnership is considered to be no more than an income conduit, and the partnership as an entity does not have a taxable income. This basic principle is subject to some variation and modification.

In the United Kingdom the standard income tax rate is collected and paid by the partnership, and individual partners are responsible for the surtax. In Australia a penalty rate of about 50 percent is applied to the income of partners without effective control over their income. Basically this Australian penalty rate is aimed at the practice of reducing income tax under progressive rates by dividing partnership income among minor members of the families of active partners.

Germany, Luxembourg, the Netherlands, Norway, and Switzerland use the personal approach as in the United States, but they make provision for treating a partnership like a corporation. This option is available to partnerships limited by shares.

A somewhat similar approach is demonstrated by the "tax-option" corporation in the United States. When this option is taken, a corporation is taxed as a partnership and avoids paying any corporate income tax on its profits. In other words, the partnership enjoys all the tax benefits of being organized as a corporation, but its net income is taxable only from the shareholders and is not subject to the corporate income tax first. Of course, the income is added to the total taxable income of the shareholder whether distributed or kept within the corporation.

The French, who also apply the personal approach, make a great effort to be neutral. A general partnership can choose to be taxed as a corporation or as a partnership with all income allocated to the partners. Because of the current high corporate profits tax rates, the choice is nearly always the partnership.[43]

Some countries use an entity approach to tax partnerships; for example, in Japan and Korea normal corporate rates apply to partnerships. To discourage accumulation of income within the partnership, special taxes are levied on undue revenue withholdings of closely held partnerships.

The entity approach is popular in Latin America and is used with some modification by all the nations. For example, in Mexico and Brazil a flat tax is applied to all organizations engaged in carrying out business activities. The legal differences between a corporation, a partnership, and a single proprietorship do not affect the applicability of this tax. Venezuela uses the same general procedure and applies the same progressive tax rate to all business firms. A special low rate has been legislated for small partnerships and individual proprietorships, however.[44] Central American countries also employ the entity approach to business taxation. The only exception is small partnerships in Nicaragua, which are taxed under a personal approach.

Spain and Portugal treat partnerships like corporations, although partnerships enjoy some special advantages with income from foreign sources. Here it is evident that economic substance plays a large role in establishing tax procedures and legal differences are of minor importance. The use of the schedular income tax tradition in Spain, Portugal, and the former colonies of these nations seems to explain much of this difference and the use of the entity rather than the personal approach.

The treatment of global income of a partnership under the personal approach and domestic income under the entity approach is found in Italy and Chile. Belgium modifies its entity approach by applying the personal approach to small partnerships. This Belgian treatment of partnership bears a similarity to the U.S. tax-option corporation. In both instances the aim is to eliminate the tax effects of different legal forms of organization.

The approach of Finland, where a partnership is taxed at the same progressive rates as are ordinary families, is unique. It has arisen naturally out of the Finnish practice of treating the family as the income tax unit. Here the personal approach has broadened to a family approach, and the partnership acquires the same degree of entity as the family under the tax legislation. Where family partnerships are common the procedure is roughly just and administrative effort is minimal.

The variety of ways in which partnership net income is taxed arises from the lack of uniformity as to a business's ability to pay taxes as a percent of net income as defined by tax legislation. None of the procedures briefly outlined is considered to be satisfactory. They all tend to discourage efficiency to the extent that efficiency is measured by net income. They also encourage high wages for partners and other means of avoiding taxes, including payment by the partnership of interest on loans not needed for operations. Finally, basic equity is lost if progressive rates are used when those benefiting from the income of the partnership cannot be identified with certainty.

REDISTRIBUTION THROUGH THE INCOME TAX

As long as there is some chance of moving from poverty or semi-poverty to wealth, income redistribution aspirations of society will be limited. If doubt about the possibility of greatly improving one's situation becomes very strong, the equalitarian actions of the society become much more intense. Such doubt strengthens the demand for redistribution. In a modern, relatively democratic society the result is likely to be a demand for taxation on the basis of ability to pay, translated into a progressive income tax.

However, these efforts to equalize economic positions or, stated differently, to increase the reasonableness of people's aspirations toward economic improvement, are largely self-defeating. The progressive income tax, instead of improving economic equality through more equitable income distribution, fossilizes the existing inequalites of wealth. The tax acts to decrease the opportunities for new rich to arise and therefore the reasonableness of society's belief in upward mobility.[46]

TAX INFLATION

People are likely to react to increases in prices due to pollution control and ecological considerations financed through a VAT in the same way as they do to another surge of inflation. That is, they demand further self-defeating increases in monetary incomes.[47]

Inflation is defined in a number of ways. Generally, the idea of price increases due to currency expansion dominates the explanation. The reasons for the currency expansion go beyond the definition of inflation and become part of the explanation of why it occurs.

One frequent explanation uses the term "cost push." The cost of labor increases, and prices are pushed up because the producers have to pay higher wages.

THE CED POSITION

As has been mentioned, the replacement of the corporate profits tax with a VAT has been advocated on occasion by American business groups.[48] In 1966 the Committee for Economic Development, which at that time employed Herbert Stein, recommended a low-rate VAT for the United States. The proposal was aimed at cutting back the tax burden on equity capital by reducing the corporate profits tax with the revenue loss made up with a new VAT.

The CED position did not envisage VAT as a method of bringing the U.S. international payments into balance. The report relied on Stein's studies and beliefs, which were published in the *American Economic Review* and which concluded that the use of VAT would not improve the U.S. international payments position.[49]

This finding was based on the fact that VAT was viewed only as a tax sufficiently high to permit the United States to cut its corporate profits taxes to the European level, for it was assumed that if the United States eliminated its corporate profits taxes, the Europeans would do the same. The CED concluded that a reduction to the European level would amount to a U.S. advantage of only 2 percentage points because this was the amount by which U.S. corporate profits taxes exceeded the European level.

The CED therefore considered VAT to be a minor element in setting international competitive conditions. The impact of taxes on capital flows was entirely ignored. Also, the tax advantage of VAT was examined as a portion of aggregate production rather than as a stimulant to marginal export sales. This was also the approach used when considering the effect of the border tax on imports that VAT made possible. Finally, VAT was not considered as a revenue source that would make possible reduced major tax payments by low-income people, for example, reduced social security and withheld income taxes on wages. Neither was VAT seen to have considerable impact at the margin in determining where production would take place.

USING TAX TREATIES TO CHANGE TAX PAYMENTS

Tax conventions or treaties are a method of gradually, maybe too gradually, developing an international economic environment in which tax considerations are of less importance in determining international economic decisions. They also have the potential of creating tax stimulants to direct international movement of funds to selected areas for selected purposes. The tax conditions under which modern industrial economies thrive seem to be remarkably similar in the nations of the world. Here is a base conducive to international tax uniformity and also to the development of tax incentives to attract economic activity. The tax treaty can help do both, but the dominance of the second goal may act to retard the speed of movement toward the first. Both tendencies are very evident in the use of the device by the United States.

The tax convention is related to economic growth policy through its effect on the location of new investments. The overall effect of tax conventions of the United States has been to encourage capital outflow by reducing the tax burden on U.S. capital invested in foreign areas. On the other hand, tax conventions encourage the domestic inflow of the earnings from these investments by reducing or eliminating the relative additional tax burden borne by repatriated foreign earnings of U.S. capital and citizens. During most of the post–World War II period, U.S. international policy has been to encourage foreign investment of U.S. capital. The tax conventions of the period reflect this aim. The country's economic posture in the international environment has been one of excessive foreign investment. The current posture is basically less consistent with the areas of effectiveness of tax conventions than was the previous international posture; however, a desirable goal is still to bring foreign earnings back to this country.

THE TAX TREATY TOOL

The tax treaty is perhaps fundamentally a method of encouraging foreign use of American resources. Today this sort of stimulation seems to be appropriate only in underdeveloped areas of the world. It has a yet undetermined potential, however, in the development of international tax harmonization. The United States has not actively utilized tax conventions in this way, but the Organization for Economic Cooperation and Development has made some progress through the development of a draft model convention, first published in 1963 and in a slightly revised form in 1974.

THE OECD MODEL TAX CONVENTION

One of the activities of the League of Nations in 1921 was to begin a program to assist its members in their efforts to eliminate international double taxation of business income. Double taxation in this sense refers to the imposition of comparable taxes in two or more countries on the same taxpayer in respect to the same income during the same period. International double taxation was seen to have harmful effects on the exchange of goods, services, and capital between countries. The work by the League of Nations resulted in the first bilateral tax treaties to avoid double taxation in 1928, and the work has been carried forward by OECD. The development work of OECD has rested on the Model Conventions of Mexico (1943) and of London (1946).

The member countries of OECD are the nations of Western Europe plus Turkey, the United States, and Canada. Japan did not become a full member until 1963. The OECD countries have believed that increasing economic interdependence and the growth of international business operations generally require better methods for resolving differences related to double taxation.[50] It is also generally felt that the coverage of international tax law must expand and that as far as possible the national tax systems of the major trading nations of the world should be harmonized, as should the provisions of the various bilateral tax conventions.

The number of tax conventions has grown very rapidly from about twenty in 1939 to fifty-six in 1955, about seventy in 1958, and nearly ninety in 1964. In addition, revision of tax conventions is a continuing process. The very number of these international tax conventions has made tax convention harmonization necessary if the treaties were not to result in confusion so great that international economic relations would be harmed rather than assisted. The method of harmonization developed by the fiscal committee of OECD is the creation of a model bilateral international tax convention draft. The draft, which consists of thirty articles, is aimed at making available for negotiating countries a workable treaty to solve the international problems of double taxation, largely of income and capital. If all the OECD countries use the draft, it will create a uniform basis for solving the most common problems of the double taxation of international business income and make a start on harmonizing the direct tax systems of the world.

Chapter III of the draft convention, which is entitled *Taxation of Income* and includes Articles 6 through 21, contains the core of the OECD model convention. A number of the articles of Chapter III are appropriate for consideration in this volume.

Immovable Property. Article 6 settles the question of the taxation of immovable property. The right to tax this property is given to the country in which the property is situated.

Permanent Establishment. Article 7 establishes the right to tax business profits in accordance to the criterion of the permanent establishment. The article says that the permanent establishment must be treated as an enterprise distinct and separate from the central office of the operation. This means that profits of the entire operation may not become a portion of the tax base used by a nation in which a branch is located. It also means that if the company does not have a permanent establishment within the country as defined in the draft model convention, its profits may not be subject to taxation by the second country.

In the United States the problem of defining a permanent establishment is important in the efforts of individual states to collect the corporate income tax from out-of-state corporations doing business in the taxing state. The OECD model tax convention has defined the permanent establishment for purposes of international taxation and has also identified what shall not be deemed to be a permanent establishment in Article 5:

The term "permanent establishment" shall include especially:

(a) a place of management;

(b) a branch;

(c) an office;

(d) a factory;

(e) a workshop;

(f) a mine, quarry, or other place of extraction of natural resources;

(g) a building site or construction or assembly project which exists for more than twelve months.

The term "permanent establishment" shall not be deemed to include:

(a) the use of facilities solely for the purpose of storage, display, or delivery of goods or merchandise belonging to the enterprise;

(b) the maintenance of a stock of goods or merchandise belonging to the enterprise solely for the purpose of storage, display or delivery;

(c) the maintenance of a stock of goods or merchandise belonging to the enterprise solely for the purpose of processing by another enterprise;

(d) the maintenance of a fixed place of business solely for the purpose of purchasing goods or merchandise, or for collecting information, for the enterprise;

(e) the maintenance of a fixed place of business solely for the purpose of advertising, for the supply of information, for scientific research or for similar activities which have a preparatory or auxiliary character, for the enterprise.

The article contains other materials relating to what shall and shall not be considered a permanent establishment and thus what brings the operation under the corporate income tax laws of the second country. One additional point requires explanation:

An enterprise of a Contracting State shall not be deemed to have a permanent establishment in the other Contracting State merely because it carries on business in that other State through a broker, general commission agent or any other agent of an independent status, where such persons are acting in the ordinary course of their business.

This provision has become an issue of considerable importance in the drafting of tax treaties with less developed countries.

Allocation of Net Income. The international problem of determining whether a corporation can be subject to the taxation of its net income is much like the interstate problem. Within the United States, the problem was somewhat clarified by the provisions of Public Law 86-272, as amended, passed by Congress in 1959. OECD in its draft convention has been much more forthright than the provisions of the law or those of state legislation binding the actions of the various state tax commissions.

The major difference between the taxation of corporations among states and among countries under the provisions of a bilateral treaty following the OECD draft is that a second country can only include as taxable income profits arising from the permanent establishment, assuming it to be a "distinct and separate enterprise," while the states can allocate a portion of the profits of the whole organization to each state in which it is determined to be doing business on the basis of a legally acceptable formula. Also, much more business can be done in a second country under the OECD draft convention than can typically be done in a second state before the corporation would be considered to have a permanent establishment.

Article 8 states that only the country including "the place of the effective management" of transportation companies may tax the income of the operation.

Article 9 provides for the reallocation of profits to the extent that the books of the company do not properly do this and since 1974 similar adjustments are required by contracting parties.

Interest, Dividends, and Royalties. Articles 10, 11, and 12 are concerned with the particularly knotty problem of the allocation of dividends, interest, and royalties. The practices of the member countries vary widely, but, because of the growing importance of the international movement of these incomes, harmonization of the rules was very important. Countries are divided between those that favor determination of tax liability on the basis of the country of residence of the receiver of income and those that favor determination of tax liability on the basis of the country of source of income. The compromise was to give the exclusive right to tax royalties to the nation of the recipient's residence and to divide the right to tax dividends and interest between the country of the recipient's residence and the country of the source of the income. In addition, the tax rate that can be levied by the country of source of income is generally 15 percent of the gross amount of dividends and 10 percent of the gross amount of interest. Also, provision is made for exemption of dividends and interest by the country of source in an actual negotiated tax convention between two countries. These apply since 1974 only if the recipient is a beneficial owner.

Capital Gains. Article 13 concerns the taxation of capital gains. Gains from the sale of immovable property may be taxed by the country in which the property is situated. Capital gains from the sale of intangibles are taxable only in the state of residence. If it is the general practice of the country, capital gains from the sale of certain moveables are taxable in the country of location.

Personal Income. Articles 14 through 21 are concerned largely with the taxation of income for personal services. For example, if a person lives in one country and works in another, and if the two countries have negotiated a treaty under the OECD model draft convention, the right to tax is given to the country in which the services are performed. A great variety of problems arise in this area.

Article 14 established the concept of fixed base in the case of independent personal services as the substitute for permanent establishment.

Article 15 sets the general rule of taxation where work is done but exempts certain employment of short duration and the performance of certain government functions.

Articles 16 and 17 relate the general rule to members of company boards, public entertainers, and professional athletes.

Articles 18 and 19 provide that pensions and similar income from past activities are taxable only by the country of residence.

Article 20 provides that payments to students or business apprentices for the purpose of their maintenance or education or training abroad shall not be taxed in the country where they are temporarily residing for such purposes. And finally, Article 21 states that the general rule of taxation of income in the country of residence applies to all income not expressly mentioned.

GENERAL COMMENT

The OECD draft for use by countries in negotiating bilateral tax treaties is an important step toward developing sound procedures for the taxation of international business operations. Of course, the sound and reasonable provisions of the OECD draft convention will be useless if actual negotiated treaties do not use the provisions or if tax conventions are not negotiated between countries at all. It is expected that the new modernized model will speed up negotiation of tax treaties. The work has found favor in the international business community and the

Council of the International Chamber of Commerce has called the OECD work "a valuable and promising advance in the struggle against double taxation."

Additional work must still be done in this area if business is to carry out its activities across international boundaries efficiently. For example, much more needs to be done to determine the interaction between the draft convention provisions and domestic tax laws and the evasion of taxes that may arise when a third country is not a party to the tax treaty.

INTEREST INCOME IN INTERNATIONAL TAX TREATIES

The manner in which interest income is treated in tax treaties and the difficulties inherent in working out uniform rules for the taxation of this income make it a topic worthy of additional consideration. Here one encounters unusually sharp national differences of tax treatment resulting from differences in attitude and differences in the basic national tax system.

Interest is likely to arise as an international net payment from a poorer area to a richer one. The interest income could be taxed at the source, at the residence of the receiver, or at both. Also, the capital loaned may have arisen in a country different from the country of residence of the receiver. International tax treaties have used a variety of approaches.

In the 1957 tax treaty between Italy and the Netherlands, taxation of interest paid is reserved exclusively to the nation in which the recipient has his residence. This was also true of the 1957 tax treaty between Denmark and the Netherlands, the 1953 treaty between France and Norway, the 1957 treaties between Denmark and France, and the 1952 treaty between the Netherlands and Sweden.

Sometimes taxation is shared between the two nations involved. This is the case of the Denmark–Switzerland treaty of 1957, the United States–France treaty of 1956, and others.

Other treaties provide that the nation where the interest has its source taxes it at the ordinary rate, and credit for this tax payment is given by the country of the recipient's residence. Tax treaties with this provision include the 1931 agreement between Belgium and France, the 1956 treaty between Italy and Sweden, and the Franco–German Treaty of 1956.

Sometimes interest paid on indebtedness secured by mortgages on immovable property is reserved to the country in which the property is located. This is a provision of the Netherlands–United Kingdom tax treaty of 1948 and of the Netherlands–Switzerland treaty of 1951.[51]

OECD RECOMMENDATIONS

A study committee of OECD reported that all member countries tax interest arising in foreign countries and paid to their residents, that two-thirds also tax interest arising in their territories, and one-third exempt interest at the source from taxes.[52]

The result has been the recommendation of a compromise by the general committee of OECD .The compromise sets a maximum level at which interest paid to a nonresident may be taxed by the country of the source. There was, of course, a difference of opinion as to the maximum rate to be collected, but 10 percent received the support of a large majoriy. The country of residence of the interest recipient would be expected to take into account the tax levied in the country of source. The result of the compromise is a division of the interest tax base between the country of source and the country of residence of the recipient.

The provisions of the OECD draft treaty have been a substantial forward step in facilitating international business operation. The difficulties in harmonization of interest taxation are far from completely resolved, however. Other problems of nearly infinite complexity must be dealt with.

The treatment of "the force of attraction of the permanent establishment" is a good example. The OECD draft treaty extends to the country of location the right to tax as it wishes any interest arising from the operations of a permanent establishment. This right, as noted above, is not extended in the case of interest not related to permanent establishment. What if the owner of a permanent establishment that is the source of an interest payment to a treaty country actually lives in a third country? Must the country in which the establishment is located rather than the country of the owner be considered the country of the interest source? The OECD draft treaty has answered yes.[53] The draft does not take account of the situation where both the owner and the interest receiver are residents of a treaty country, but the loan was used for a permanent establishment in a third country.[54] In fact, the problem of the interest element in annuities has not been resolved by the OECD draft; neither has the return from various kinds of debentures and bonds possessing profit-sharing rights.

RECONSIDERATION OF APPROACH

In looking at ways in which OECD has treated interest in the draft treaty, the obvious conclusion is that the problems related to taxation of interest have not all been resolved. It also seems that perhaps the method of attack is wrong. The approach has been influenced by older ideas that formerly were useful but that are largely troublemakers in the modern world. For example, the division of property income into such various types as interest, royalties, and dividends follows old separate paths that might better be considered one road. Another old idea is the different treatment accorded movable property and fixed property, and the influence accorded to a fixed establishment and the power to tax at source.

It would, of course, be impossible to modernize the concepts of tax treaties until the tax legislation of individual countries was brought into line with basic economic differences appropriate for use as taxation handles. Such modernization means considerable national action aimed at cutting away complicating legal distinctions that have prevented national as well as international tax harmonization progress. There is some evidence that the U.S. government is concerned and is now searching for ways to provide some leadership toward useful understandings of both international and interstate tax goals. It isn't so evident that the United States is making progress toward harmonization and simplification of its own tax system.

In the foregoing discussion, interest as income to be taxed was considered in some detail as an example of the tax difficulties and complications that arise between national governments sharing a business operation in one way or another. These problems are going to become ever more serious if much of the ancient legal and conceptual heritage is not swiftly cut away by national tax leadership; at least this seems to be the lesson taught by American experience with the taxation by states of the income of interstate corporations.[55]

The whole process of negotiating bilateral treaties is slow, which also makes for lack of uniformity, because in each treaty negotiated there is a great temptation to make certain changes from the draft convention because of claimed special conditions. Just as the negotiation of tariff changes has become a multilateral activity through GATT and the Kennedy Tokyo rounds, so the negotiation of tax conventions could be taken out of the bilateral stage. The Council of the International Chamber of Commerce has recommended progress in this direction, and both the EC member states and the countries of the European Free Trade Association have noted the desirability of using the OECD draft as the basis for negotiating among their members a multilateral treaty to eliminate double taxation of business activities carried on in more than one country.

GENERAL PRACTICE RECONSIDERED

The problems to be met and cracked by tax conventions have been limited to those arising from direct taxes and to some extent death taxes. The tax convention has not been used in the consideration of double taxation through use of indirect taxes. In the past this area has been considered inappropriate, because the location of the economic burden of direct taxes was thought to be much more doubtful than that of indirect taxes. Also, in the case of indirect taxes, there was the internationally acceptable procedure of levy on the basis of the principle of destination, which at least eliminated the formal problem of international double taxation because taxes allocated to goods exported are rebated and a compensatory border tax is levied on imports.

The OECD uniform tax conventions make no provision for the general use of the destination principle in the treatment of direct taxes. The general principle, to the extent that one exists in the international treatment of direct taxes, is that of origin. The income tax is generally applied by the country in which the income originates—the one where economic activity took place—and the country of origin does not reduce the tax it collects because the income is taxed again by the country in which the receiver of the income lives. The general aim is to make the total applicable direct tax rate equal to the rate applied by the country having the highest rates. Although the principle of origin in direct taxes is generally recognized, many exceptions turn up through the practice of treating the various components of the income stream differently. When this is done, reciprocal uniform treatment is provided for in the treaty. There is no good reason for not treating all income alike and there is little, if any, justification for not applying the unitary concept of income to income arising from foreign sources.

Tax conventions in the future are likely to give greater consideration to indirect taxes, maybe as a product of the efforts of the EC to harmonize indirect taxes. The pressure to include indirect taxes can be expected to expand as tariffs and various direct controls affecting international capital and commodity flows are reduced. Such reduction will make the impact of indirect taxes relatively greater and will also highlight the effect they have always had. In addition, the current trend in Western Europe to move toward a very intensive use of the value-added tax, which in Europe is considered an indirect tax, will require recognition of indirect taxes in tax convention provisions.

INTERNATIONAL TAX AVOIDANCE

The tax convention can be used to prevent tax avoidance as well as to reduce tax burdens. Some of this has been done by provisions that deny benefits of the convention to businesses operating in a certain fashion, but these possibilities have been developed in only a very minor way. The need for this type of action on the part of the United States will be particularly urgent if direct tax rates of Western European nations tend to fall through replacement with the value-added tax. Also, greater international stability generally makes tax haven operations of one sort or another more attractive. And the provision of a high withholding rate on income arising in a country and the establishment of refunding arrangements would reduce tax avoidance through nonreporting of income to tax authorities of the country of residence. Under existing provisions many receivers of foreign income do not take advantage of convention provisions because failure to report makes it possible to completely evade income taxes of the country of residence.

TAX SPARING

The effectiveness of the tax treaty tool, particularly in underdeveloped countries, will be expanded if the tax-sparing provision becomes an accepted part of U.S. tax conventions with underdeveloped nations. Under this provision, foreign income tax forgiven to attract U.S. investment can be counted as taxes paid and included in dollar-for-dollar tax credit in calculating U.S. tax liability.

The tax-sparing provision in tax treaties might be used to negotiate with Panama, Liberia, and Greece, for example, that ships owned directly or indirectly by American capital would pay the same taxes as they would pay if registered under the U.S. flag but that taxes forgiven on other U.S. investments would be credited as if paid. Under a tax-sparing tax convention, Panama, Liberia, and Greece would benefit, but they would, in turn, somewhat reduce their attractiveness as a foreign flag registry for American-owned vessels.

CONCLUSION

The OECD model tax convention was written in the hope that multilateral tax conventions could be negotiated. The member states of the EC are in the process of developing a draft convention out of the Neumark Report, which can be used to make additional progress in tax harmonization within the EC. This same development can be expected within EFTA and the Central American Common Market. Although the United States has not been agressively working toward the development of multilateral tax conventions, the provisions included in tax conventions with underdeveloped countries, particularly the tax-sparing provision, provide possibilities in this direction. Also, it is quite possible that the United States could negotiate a tax treaty with EC after tax harmonization has been established among the member states. This might also be possible with EFTA and the Common markets of Africa, Caribbean Islands, Central America, and South America. In this fashion the United States could, in effect, negotiate multilateral tax conventions without actually participating in a multilateral tax convention conference similar to the Kennedy and Tokyo rounds of tariff negotiations.

The tax tool, although frequently considered to be a method for the elimination of international double taxation of income, has never been able to accomplish this original goal. Despite shortcomings, however, it has been helpful in accomplishing a number of additional things. It may become the basic technique for international tax harmonization, the prevention of international tax avoidance, and the encouragement of capital flow from capital-rich to capital-poor areas. These are big jobs and useful ones, and they are within the theoretical capabilities of tax conventions.

THE U.S. TARIFF BASE

The individuality and perhaps rather expensive nonconformity of the United States shows up in its failure to use a general product tax at the national level and in its taxation of corporate incomes. Another area in which the United States fails to conform is in the base it has chosen for the application of its customs duties. In this instance, also, nonconformity is perhaps to the economic disadvantage of the country.

Four acceptable general bases can be used in the valuation of goods for the levy of a customs duty or a border tax assessed on an *ad valorem* basis. The lowest value is the free on board (FOB) or free alongside ship (FAS) price. The middle value is the cost, insurance, and freight (CIF) price, and the highest is the wholesale price within the country of importation. The fourth value is CIF plus import duty and maybe also plus border taxes.

The FOB or FAS price is the cost of bringing the goods alongside the carrier that is to bring the goods from the border or port of debarkation of the exporting nation to the port of entrance of the importing nation. The United States and a few other countries, including Canada, use this base.

The CIF price is the value of the item when it arrives at the customs house of the country of the importer. The value includes all the costs of bringing the product up to the point of paying import duties. This base is used by nearly all commercial nations. In addition to the CIF cost, the selling price of a foreign article within the importing country includes customs duties, border compensatory taxes, if any, and the markup of the importer.

The final value of CIF plus import duty is exactly as the description indicates. It is used by the United States and other leading trading nations as the base on which compensatory (border) taxes are levied. France uses a base that includes TVA when it applies its border tax. This is done because domestically the TVA is levied on a tax-on-tax basis.

Each of these valuations utilizes the price that the product will fetch at the time and place when the value is set. It is the price arising through the free working of the "forces of supply and demand."[56]

THE EVOLUTION OF UNIFORM VALUATION METHODS

When import duties were largely imposed to raise revenues, they were best if levied at a fixed rate per unit of quantity except where the market value of the goods was very easy to determine. Rates levied as so much per unit are specific rates. The introduction of protection as the principal element in setting customs legislation led to wide use of the *ad valorem* system because it could take account of quality variation and price fluctuations. This type of rate placed much greater valuation burdens on the customs officials of a nation.

One aspect of this burden was the desire of some governments to have legal tariff rates that were low but that would effectively keep out international competition through high and fictitious valuations. Administrative protection of this sort is effectively eliminated by the Brussels Convention and the provisions of GATT. It was a long road to this goal, however. The road started with the economic conferences sponsored in Geneva in 1927 and 1930 by the League of Nations. The results were meager and did not amount to much more than a statement that further work on the problem was necessary. It was not until 1947— after fifteen years, the world's worst depression, and the war—that another international conference to consider the problem was convened. This time the United Nations was the sponsor ,and the meeting place was again Geneva. It was called the United Nations Conference on Trade and Employment, and, maybe for the first time in history, international customs valuation policy was set and became the basis of GATT.

The momentum gained in setting up GATT was continued through the definition of value produced in 1949 by the U.N. study group. The definition was swiftly included as the basic concept of the Convention on the Valuation of Goods for Customs Purposes. This in turn became the Brussels Convention of December 15, 1950, which was accepted by the original fifteen signatory countries on November 3, 1953. The definition of value is for countries on the CIF basis. However, many of the basic principles are also appropriate to valuation on the FOB basis.

The setting of value for customs purposes has four basic elements recognizable by GATT and the Brussels Convention for valuation on the CIF basis and necessarily included in FOB valuation. The four elements are time, place, quantity, and level.

The *time* for CIF valuation is when "duty becomes applicable." For FOB or FAS valuation, it is when the goods are ready to be loaded onto the international carrier or are on the carrier.

The *place* for CIF is "the port or place where the goods are introduced into the country of importation." For FOB it is the point of export.

The *quantity* for CIF is flexible and account may be taken of commercial practices. To avoid abuse, however, a basic rule is that "where the normal price would depend upon the quantity in the sale, it shall be determined on the assumption that the sale is a sale of the quantity to be valued." The same general rules meet the needs regarding quantity for FOB valuation.

The term *level* refers to the commercial stage at which sales are negotiated. This means that the same product can have a different value for customs purposes at a given time, place, and quantity. The difference depends on whether the sale is negotiated at the jobber, wholesale, or retail level. This same concept is applicable to FOB valuation.

In all cases, it is the *bona fide* sale that is the basis upon which any goods are valued after proper adjustments are made to meet the value concept, whether it is CIF, FOB, or wholesale price in importing country.[56]

AN APPRAISAL OF THE FOB AND CIF VALUE BASES

The United States and a number of other countries, considerably fewer now than thirty years ago, use FOB or FAS value as the base to which *ad valorem* tariff duties are applied. However, the U.S. now reports its balance of trade data on a CIF basis.

A study completed by the Tariff Commission in 1932 found the following countries of the world used "foreign value of imported merchandise as the basis for *ad valorem* duties": Bolivia, Canada, Colombia, Cuba, the Dominican Republic, Ecuador, Guatemala, Honduras, Newfoundland, Nicaragua, Panama, Paraguay, the Union of South Africa, the United States, and Venezuela.

The data on international trade listed in *International Financial Statistics,* a United Nations publication, indicate in the January, 1976, issue that the following nations used an FOB value in their customs valuation: Australia, Canada, the Dominican Republic, Ecuador, Panama, Paraguay, South Africa, the United States, and Venezuela.

For some of the countries a designation of value base was not given. Generally, they were new nations where administrative procedures are in the formative stage and/or data on imports are not available. Of the nations using FOB as the basis of valuation in 1932, the following were reported to have changed to the CIF value basis by 1976: Colombia, Guatemala, Honduras, and Nicaragua.

None of the new nations established since 1932 have adopted FOB. They all have chosen the CIF basis of value. Also, Australia, which was reported in 1932 as using foreign value plus 10 percent (which must in that year theoretically result in an FOB classification), is considered an FOB country. All the other nations of the free world use the CIF basis.

There is a pattern discernible in the use of FOB as the customs valuation base. The FOB nations, with the exception of the few Latin American countries where the decision may have been influenced by American advisers, are geographically big and were largely colonized by the British.

The FOB countries are a minority group, and their number is declining. The United States, however, is the leading commercial nation of the world, and as long as she uses the FOB method, it must be considered important. The United States used the CIF method in the first tariff legislation of 1789 but then quickly abandoned it for the FOB basis.

STRENGTHS OF THE FOB BASIS

The basic arguments presented to justify the continued use of the FOB basis of valuation in the United States rather than CIF are as follows:

1. The value developed from import data is comparable to export data of the country of export.

2. Balance-of-payments data are not made less useful through the inclusion of transportation earnings that may accrue to neither the exporting nor importing country and are difficult to separate from other costs making up CIF value.

3. The price is a real price paid in the country of export.

Price is actually determined then and not when the goods land in the country of import, as must be assumed if the Brussels Convention for valuation is followed.

4. FOB avoids including in the foreign value base the cost of transportation and insurance which may be purchased from good domestic industries, and should not be subject to tariffs.

5. The tariff levied in dollars and cents is the same on an identical product with the same domestic price whether produced near or at a great distance from the importing company.

6. It is neutral in its impact on the choice of international transportation and insurance to be used, because these costs are not included in the base.

STRENGTHS OF THE CIF BASIS

There are several very persuasive reasons why the United States should shift from FOB to CIF valuation for levying tariffs. In the background is the assumption that U.S. tariff rates would be reduced by 10 percent to develop an equivalent tariff that used the CIF value base rather than the FOB or FAS base, and a statistical study by the author seems to indicate that this is the appropriate percentage.

Also, because of the complications of attempting to make adjustments between different country sources and different products within tariff schedules, a flat-rate adjustment would be the only sensible way to make a shift from FOB to CIF value base. Necessary later adjustments arising from proof of true hardship could be made by the President on the recommendation of the United States International Trade Commission.[2]

The basic considerations and changes that would be related to a shift to the CIF basis for the application of the U.S. tariff are as follows:

1. The businesses located in countries at a great distance would have the value to which the tariff was applied increased by more than the tariff was cut.

2. The tariff per dollar of foreign value of goods sold in our market would increase.

3. If producers in Canada and Mexico were in competition with those in Australia and South Africa to market a product in the United States, they would find their competitive position improved.

4. The change to a CIF basis would tend to stimulate regional international sales at the expense of worldwide sales.

5. Generally speaking, the tariff per dollar of foreign value would decrease on bulk raw material and nonbulky consumer goods

that can be cheaply placed in U.S. ports of entry, while it would increase on very bulky items and those that are expensive to ship for other reasons. This might result in increased imports of textiles, for example, and decreased imports of assorted fruits glacé. Generally, producers of luxury goods would find the tariff barriers a little higher than they had been and generally most consumer goods exporters to the United States would enjoy a tariff decrease. The impact might be some downward pressure on the U.S. consumer price index.

6. The adoption of the CIF base would make it somewhat more desirable to use the cheapest means of transportation and of getting goods to and through customs, for this would decrease cost more than the absolute decrease of the charges. This would tend to discourage use of air transportation and use of conference rates and American lines and also the full use of brokerage services. The impact would not be great and would tend to decrease as international competition became keener, for this would increase the value of time used in bringing goods from foreign producer to retailer.

7. The adoption of CIF would provide 10 percent additional bargaining power for the President under the Trade Act of 1974 that could be used in negotiating tariff reductions on American exports without actually reducing U.S. tariffs below the level contemplated by Congress.

8. Very likely if the United States moved to CIF the free world would shortly have uniformity in value bases and the effectiveness of international agreements such as GATT and the Customs Cooperation Council would increase. A shift in this direction could further expand the freedom of movement of goods and pull the free world closer together. Also, as long as two methods of valuation of goods for tariff purposes exist, there is a justification for the development of still another valuation base, as the strong "moral" argument of free world uniformity is lacking.

9. Another relationship to be considered when contemplating the desirability of the United States using a CIF basis is that our import totals are not statistically comparable with those of CIF nations. Our import totals are about 10 percent lower on a worldwide basis and considerably more when country-to-country comparisons are made with distant nations such as Japan and India. Also, of course, published U.S. tariff rates are higher relative to U.S. real rates. These official data make the United States appear to the casual observer to have higher tariffs than is the actual case. The fact that we are the world's leading international trading nation makes this undesirable "public relations angle"

more important to us than the same situation is to Canada, for example. The final result of the situation is to make it just a little easier for the high tariff groups of other nations to be successful in their efforts to keep tariffs up. On the other hand, the adoption of CIF valuation with rates equivalent to existing rates applied to FOB or FAS value would make it easier for those opposed to high tariffs to earn popular support.

10. Finally, the current trend in international transportation costs is up. A continuation of the existing trend would cause the CIF and FOB bases to move further apart. As this takes place, it causes relative effective U.S. tariff rates to decrease unless they are placed on an equivalent CIF basis.

CONCLUSION

Setting value for customs purposes is another area of taxation in which the problem of the United States is in being out of step with the rest of the world. As a result of this situation, the United States finds it very difficult to develop an accurate comparative statistical presentation of its international transactions. Also, the impact of the FOB system in use by the United States is to favor distant exporters to the United States, while the United States, which is a distant exporter in all cases except to Canada and Mexico, is put at a disadvantage by the CIF system. In January 1974 the Department of Commerce, at the insistence of Congress, initiated reporting of U.S. import data on the CIF basis as well as the FOB basis.

8

Tax Philosophy
for Today

Everyone is aware that rapid changes are taking place in the international and domestic economic, political and social environment. The next step is to decide on institutional changes appropriate to accommodate day-to-day activities to the new realities. One area where the character of change in the social environment needs to be reflected is tax policy. Government finance is the portion of the general area of finance most closely tied to the general social environment and the changing priorities.

The very size of tax collections has forced consideration of new approaches. The purchases and payments made from tax collections constitute over one-third of the GNP of the major industrial nations other than Japan. The nations of Western Europe in the adoption of their value-added tax to go along with their other taxes have provided new stable revenues to meet expenditure requirements without increasing the relative tax burden on incomes and profits.

COMPARATIVE TAX USAGES

In the United States, a very regressive payroll tax continues to finance what is called an actuarially sound social security program. The tax in 1971 collected about $3 billion more than was paid to old-age and survivors' insurance beneficiaries, but by the end of 1975 federal trust fund receipts had fallen behind outlays.[1] We stand alone among industrial nations in our approach to social security financing.

During the 1965–1971 period the United States collected a smaller portion of GNP from taxes and levies on goods and services than any other member nation of the Organization of Economic Cooperation and Development. The U.S. percentage was 1.7 percent. The percentage for France was 8.8 percent and Germany 5.6 percent. In 1972 about 6.2 percent of U.S. tax revenues came from taxes on general consumption. The percentage in France was 25.3 and in Germany 15.8.

The typical Western European nation uses taxes on goods and services to account for over 30 percent of tax revenues. The U.S. percentage in 1971 was 20.2 percent and in France 35 percent. It is also true that these European indirect taxes are a larger percentage of a tax total that is a greater percent of GNP.

Again in 1971, total taxes including payroll taxes amounted to 28.8 percent of GNP in the U.S. In Sweden, the total collected in taxes was 41.1 percent of GNP; in France the percentage was 35.4, and in Germany 34.3.

The indirect taxes collected in the United States are largely retail sales taxes and TAG taxes. In Western Europe, the indirect taxes consist of TAG taxes and the value-added tax. The VAT collections dominate the total.

The impact of this relationship is twofold. First, the higher indirect taxes permit lower personal income and corporate profits taxes. Second, the large portion of the high indirect taxes consisting of VAT can be refunded to exporters and can be levied on imports as border taxes. There can be little doubt that the result is a weakened market for products made in the United States and a stronger market in the United States for imports from both low taxing countries such as Japan and large users of VAT such as the Common Market countries.

The OECD fiscal data for 1971 (published in 1974) report that the United States gathers one-fifth of its total tax revenues from social security contributions. A wide variation exists in the relative importance of this revenue source among the non-communist industrial nations.

The sharp variation in the relative importance of social security contributions arises from differences in financing of social security and to some extent the completeness of the coverage of the programs of different nations. The data show, for example, that Australia does not use social security contributions to finance social programs; and in Canada, Denmark and Ireland, social security contributions are less than 10 percent of total tax revenue. France with a very complete social security system raises (1972) 26.1 percent of its total revenues from a value-added tax and 37.6 percent from social security contributions. However, about two-thirds of the French social security contributions are paid by the employer, who is also the one who writes out the check to pay the VAT.

POLICY CONSIDERATION FUNDAMENTALS

In meeting increasing revenue needs Western industrial nations have been wrestling with new revenue-raising approaches to meet the social welfare demands of their citizens. A consensus seems to have developed that any new revenue source adopted must minimize (1) development of inefficiencies arising from tax-determined economic decisions; (2) weakening the relationship between the wage bargain and take-home pay; (3) discouragement of saving; (4) inflation-caused economic disorganization; and (5) downward pressure on employment levels caused by payroll taxes.

Deficit financing continues to be important, but because of (3) and (4) its days appear to be numbered. The social security contribution is apparently at or near its ceiling if a general income tax is to be used and, in addition, its relation to (2) and (5) is being realized as very important in these days of rising unemployment and declining labor productivity. Finally, little growth can be recommended from highly graduated income taxes and high corporate profit tax rates that are so much a part of (1) and, as a result, to some extent of each of the situations to be minimized.

In facing up to immense transfer and service provision expenditure expansion pressures, industrial democracies have moved toward VAT. Undoubtedly VAT also gets worked into costs and prices, but this can be avoided in the international sphere through refunds and border taxes. And when VAT is related to each of the minimization goals it is found to be better than alternatives. And as R. M. Malt wrote in *Public Finance in Canada*, "Canada may be forced to adopt VAT simply in self defense."

More than likely VAT will continue to be used where it is now in effect and will continue to be adopted by other nations. Also, the tax collections of the United States for social security are expanding rapidly and are likely to continue to increase as a percentage of GNP. Under these circumstances, the desirability of seriously investigating a major VAT seems apparent; yet the United States has not really done this, and there is little indication of current interest in VAT.

BLURRING THE SEPARATION BETWEEN TAXES AND APPROPRIATIONS

The term *tax expenditures* has been coined to be used when talking about tax favors granted in the law. The words *favor, loophole,* or *breathing hole* possess emotional connotations. "Tax expenditures" is more neutral and perhaps an easier concept to discuss. The impacts of decisions in this area include technical complications and reduced revenues.

The concept of tax expenditure and an estimate of quantities from various sources is a portion of the 1976 federal budget. For fiscal year 1975 corporate tax expenditures are estimated at $19.3 billion, and for individuals the quantity is set at $81.4 billion. This adds up to a total about two-thirds as great as 1975 corporate and individual income tax collections.

Public finance writers have generally accepted the credo that if something or someone should be assisted by the government, money should be voted to do the job. This way everyone has a chance to know what is going on. Obviously, this is nonsense—but perhaps it includes a kernel of truth and is a useful way to improve the benefit-cost ratio.

An example of a tax expenditure is to allow a tax credit of a percentage of the value of a new investment that meets certain established criteria. Another example is the exemption from the individual income tax of imputed rent. In both cases the same effect—more housing and more investment—could have been brought about by a direct expenditure subsidy rather than through a tax favor. (Investment credit is included in the federal budget concept of a tax expenditure but imputed rent is not).

In the two instances, most would agree that the goal was desirable. But why was a tax expenditure rather than a straightforward appropriation used? Why was the division of labor—taxes to raise funds and appropriations to finance government activities—breached?

Some light is thrown on the explanation for the decision if this question is asked: Would the procedure be used if VAT were the major revenue source? Perhaps not. Tax expenditures are used because high profit and income tax rates are needed to meet the popular expectation of these taxes, but, on the other hand, the economic impact of these rates needs to be modified in selected areas. Therefore, tax expenditures and their shortcomings are tolerated because of the political nature of the income tax rate structure. However, one cannot be certain that a VAT in the United States would avoid tax expenditures. Sweden, for example, sharply reduces the applicable VAT rate on value added in the construction of a home.

The whole business of thinking of taxes as a procedure to permit the sharing of an economic abundance, stimulated and not destroyed by taxes, makes tax policy a key element of the new political and economic environment of the 1970s. The use of a major value-added tax by the federal government can surely be a giant step toward breaking up the current unproductive political game of justifying on one basis or another large federal deficits to finance general and specific economic benefits through government expenditures.

CONCLUSION

The introduction of VAT is a major element in the evolution of the change in the interrelationships between the public sector and the private sector that has arisen as a result of huge social expenditures. VAT can raise the large sums required without changing the effectiveness of the free market in nurturing the efficient and destroying the inefficient, while encouraging thrift and investment in productive capital.

A NEW TAX

The Revenue Act of 1975 and its many special provisions to give income tax relief to those earning low wages provides evidence of the pressures arising to reduce tax deductions from earnings. To make these wage tax reductions without provision for alternative revenues increases the size of the privately held interest-bearing federal debt.

Until this additional debt is retired annual interest payments must be met out of tax collections. Currently annual net interest payments of the federal government are running around $35 billion a year. It was only nine years ago that double digit interest payments were reached, and today $41 billion annual interest payments are just around the corner, maybe in 1977.

Thirty-five billion dollars is about 12 percent of the total receipts, including social security contributions and non-tax accruals as well as regular tax collections, of the federal government. The additional federal indebtedness of over $100 billion expected during fiscal years 1975 and 1976 alone will cost somewhere between $6 and $8 billion annually in additional interest payments.

One result of this approach to economic management is huge federal expenditures annually, a considerable portion of which will be paid to foreign investors, which will increase the international supply of dollars and tend to push down the international value of the dollar. And, in addition, higher taxes or more borrowing will be needed to meet the increasing cost of carrying the debt.

Much of this could be avoided with the introduction of a substantial national value-added tax. Tax collections would be used to hire pople and provide social welfare and not to make largely economically sterile interest payments on an expanded federal debt. Actually the interest payments may have a negative economic impact, because their payment prevents more productive use of incomes.

The federal government has not adopted a basic new tax since the 1930s, when the social security payroll tax was adopted. The use of special excise taxes and the excess profits tax of World War I was a reintroduction of the concept of war taxes used during the Civil War and World War I.

The growth of the payroll tax and the continuation of the personal income tax as a tax paid by the receivers of very modest incomes have combined to cause substantial double taxation of wage incomes. Under the system the income receiver is required to pay a payroll tax that makes no allowance for dependents and is not deductible from taxable income, and in addition to pay an income tax with graduated rates that has reached lower and lower real incomes during inflation.

The introduction in the United States of a VAT of sufficient productivity to sharply alleviate the payroll and personal income tax burden, to bring the corporate profits tax down to levels existing in other nations, and in addition to provide funds for a revenue-sharing system that would eliminate the retail sales tax, would be a major tax revolution; there is no doubt about that.

The process of introduction could work in a number of ways. For example, the tax as originally introduced could apply only to manufacturing corporations. A VAT introduced along these lines would familiarize domestic corporate management with the tax and would provide the maximum stimulant to the U.S. balance of trade. It might be desirable to give manufacturing corporations a choice of paying VAT or of paying the corporate income tax. This procedure would meet the basic GATT requirements for the refund of VAT on exports, but to make certain international difficulties did not arise, it might be well to prohibit the levy of a border tax on imports. (See pages 201–203 for consideration of the U.S. advantage.)

This modest VAT introductory procedure could continue the corporate income tax alongside VAT. The following scenario is suggested to minimize adjustment difficulties of two types: psychological ones, for those still believing CPT is a tax paid by the rich; and economic ones, for corporations with low export levels.

1. The value-added tax would operate alongside the regular corporate income tax and the corporation would be liable for the tax resulting in the highest tax liability.

2. For purposes of determining which tax to pay, the value-added tax refunds on exports would not be deducted from corporate VAT liability. Of course, if it turned out the corporation was liable for the corporate income tax, the tax refunds paid on exports would have to be returned to the Treasury.

3. The rate of VAT plus the deduction system set up in (2) would make most manufacturing corporations liable to the value-added tax, and set up pressures to move others in this direction.

The application of this type of VAT using the additive procedure is illustrated in Table 13.

The tax saving in Year II was possible because the value-added tax liability (in determining whether corporate income or value-added tax liability was the greater) is the liability before the rebate of the tax on exports.

A value-added tax limited to corporations and using the subtractive procedure would present difficulties as products moved from businesses organized as partnerships or cooperatives to corporations. However, any corporate seller following an unincorporated firm would become liable to the value added arising in unincorporated enterprises and therefore untaxed. Under the subtractive administration method, corporations would be required to list all purchases from corporate sellers and these would be deductible in arriving at taxable sales.

This type of value-added tax would be originally introduced in the United States largely as a means of retaining manufacturing investment in domestic production units. The reduced tax on domestic profits, the rebate of the VAT on exports from the United States, and the possible levy of the compensating tax on imports would expand the attractiveness of investment in U.S. manufacturing facilities for export and domestic sale. The Revenue Act of 1975 reduced the tax attractiveness of foreign production and sales by American companies, but it did not remove the exemption of this income, if not in tax-haven countries, from U.S. taxes until brought back home.

Although VAT of the type contemplated would be largely on cor-

Table 13

Application of Tax Proposal Using Additive Method of Applying VAT

Year I

Employee Payroll	$1,300,000
Profits	200,000
Interest	20,000
Rents, Royalties, and Depreciation	280,000
Total Value Added	1,800,000
VAT Rate of 10 Percent Applied to Total Value Added*	180,000
Exports	200,000
CPT Rate of 48 Percent Applied to Profit Total	96,000
VAT Refund on Exports	20,000
VAT on Purchases from Unincorporated Sellers	1,000
Net VAT Liability of $180,000 Less $20,000 Plus $1,000 or	161,000
Tax paid by corporation is the value-added tax and the tax payment is $65,000 greater than under the corporate income tax	

Year II

Employee Payroll	$1,250,000
Profits	250,000
Interest	20,000
Rents, Royalties, and Depreciation	280,000
Total Value Added	1,800,000
VAT Rate of 8 Percent Applied to Total Value Added	180,000
Exports	700,000
CPT Rate of 48 Percent Applied to Profit Total	120,000
VAT on Purchases from Unincorporated Sellers	1,000
Net VAT Liability of $180,000 Less $70,000 (10 percent of exports) plus $1,000 or $111,000 (tax paid by corporation as VAT is $15,000 less than the CPT liability)	111,000

*The 8 percent rate was selected as reasonable; it is only about two-thirds the rate used in Western Europe, yet it is high enough to make a real impact on export decisions.

porations, this would not always be the case if the subtractive procedure were used. For, as indicated above, noncorporate firms selling to manufacturing corporations would indirectly bear the tax; they would have to sell below the price offered by corporate suppliers to compensate for the fact that purchases from them are not deductible from the VAT base as are purchases from other corporations. If the French experience is repeated in the United States, the VAT will expand until it becomes a broad-based tax covering nearly all economic activities.

CONSIDERATION OF PROBLEM AREAS

Manufacturing by noncorporate enterprises is not included under the limited value-added tax considered above. This could result in a situation in which one exported shirt, for example, benefited from a tax rebate and another exported shirt did not. Such a situation, plus the possibility of avoiding a considerable portion of personal income taxes, would develop additional tax pressures to incorporate.

The single proprietorships and partnerships not able to see any export prospects and finding the personal income tax rates as applicable to their operation preferable to the value-added tax would continue to pay taxes as at present. The average manufacturing corporation with small exports will be paying more taxes than would be the case under the corporate profits tax. If the market is dominated by corporate production, as is the case in all areas of mass manufacture, prices would tend to rise if corporate profits as a percent of value added were average or below average, and perhaps fall if corporate profits measured in this way were substantially above the average, particularly if the area had an export potential.

GENERAL VAT

Let us start thinking about setting down a procedure for introducing a VAT like that of the EC by looking at a paragraph from the recent British study, *VAT*, prepared by the National Economic Development Office. The paragraph I have in mind goes like this:

> As has been suggested earlier, the introduction of a VAT in the UK would involve major social, economic and administrative policy decisions which cannot be anticipated, and which can only be discussed on a tentative and hypothetical basis. It is possible, however, to draw attention to some of the major issues which would be involved, and on which these necessary decisions would have to be made.[3]

The exercise that follows considers the introduction of a national U.S. VAT with a single 10 percent rate and a base as broad as that which exists generally in Europe and hopefully as broad as that in Denmark. The 10 percent rate is tax exclusive and payable monthly.[4]

If only one VAT rate is used, VAT liabilities can be reduced or increased on certain products by applying a percentage to the VAT taxable base. Sweden has made considerable use of this procedure. If automobiles were to be taxed at a higher rate, the selling price would be multiplied by 120 percent and the 10 percent rate applied to the artificially increased price. If a lower tax were desired, the price would be multiplied by 30 percent, for example, before the rate was applied.

An average VAT rate of 10 percent of market price assuming taxable expenditures—that is, a VAT payment base—of $1000 billion has a $100 billion revenue-raising potential. (See pages 53–57.) Hopefully, avoidance of the American VAT would be less than the $400 billion assumed here where GNP is taken to be $1,400 billion.

TAX ADJUSTMENTS

These $100 billion of collections from a national VAT could be divided in a number of ways. For example, the take would be well allocated if it were divided as set down here:

1. Allow a 50 percent reduction in corporate income tax collections. The cost would be about $20 billion, but $5 billion of additional individual income taxes would be collected because of higher dividend payments and resulting higher personal incomes, so the cost to the U.S. Treasury of a 50 percent reduction of the corporate income tax would be about $15 billion. This could be expected to encourage investment at home and the return to America of foreign earnings.[5]

2. Eliminate from the income tax all persons with gross incomes below the maximum wages included in the social security tax base. Currently, this is $15,300. This increase in minimum taxable income could use up about $50 billion of VAT revenues. The only federal tax withheld from the wages of these income receivers would be the social security tax. About 60 percent of the current payers of the income tax would be free of the tax.

3. Eliminate excises other than those on tobacco, alcoholic beverages, and gasoline. This would cause about $5 billion of revenue losses. The reduction in the prices of goods subject to selected excise taxes by the amount of the excise tax eliminated can be assumed with reasonable assurance and was the actual American experience in 1965.

4. Make some $25 billion available for distribution to the state and local governments in a federal revenue-sharing program. (State and local retail sales taxes would be eliminated).[6]

CONCLUSION

The large federal deficits, local government fiscal problems, and unemployment during the 1975–1977 period point to the need for a new approach to federal tax collections. The problems being encountered in maintaining a stable dollar and a modern production system demonstrate a need for greater international competitiveness. These serious and chronic economic shortfalls can be largely corrected through tax legislation in the United States that would be basically a VAT similar to EC's broadly based business tax.

The alternative VAT or CPT taxation proposal is a way to introduce the concept of VAT, and to do this in a manner that would give maximum international economic benefit from given increase in revenues. It could also be introduced as a replacement for DISC and avoid the revenue loss arising from the use of this complicated approach to improvement of the U.S. international posture.

INFLATION AND EMPLOYMENT

A considerable portion of the philosophical opposition to the introduction of taxes to meet the costs of government has been related to the belief that the level of employment was increased by government deficits and the related inflation. In the 1960s this seemed to be a tenable position in developed countries such as the United States and England, even though inflation and unemployment had expanded together in the less developed countries of the world. Current thinking that is based on U.S. data concludes that under current conditions of inflation expectation, additional inflation does not expand employment.[7]

The comparative economic stimulation of an expansion of government expenditures from tax collection increases and from borrowing increases is a portion of the process of selecting economic stimulation policy. In 1975, with the economy recently ravaged by inflation, and the liquidity of many financial and nonfinancial firms at very low levels, a belief that economic expansion can be hastened through the accumulation of huge inert government deficits requires faith that the private demand for funds to increase security will be great enough to overcome the weakness of the demand for money as a store of value. This position also requires confidence that once the normal liquidity needed for security is reached, private spending of all types will increase in a normal manner to stimulate production and sales.

On the other hand, a program of government direct or supportive spending on production-stimulating projects financed by a tax like VAT places less faith in the beneficial effects of liquidity on levels of production and sales. Rather, funds collected from previous savings and current sales and production are seen to be the wiser revenue-raising policy. Under the tax-and-spend approach reliance is placed on the multiplier impact of new government-stimulated projects—for example, the modern highway system of the 1950s financed with the gasoline tax. Therefore, the choice of projects to be stimulated is of great importance.

U.S. TAX INNOVATION PARALYSIS AND THE INFLATION CRISIS

The serious inflation experienced worldwide is now being attributed to America's huge budgetary deficits since 1968, and particularly to the back-to-back deficits of $23 billion in fiscal years 1971 and 1972, and a $14 billion deficit in fiscal year 1973. The failure to finance the Vietnam War with a tax increase had previously created a $25 billion deficit in fiscal year 1968 that clearly kicked off the series of events that has led to the destruction of the World War II Bretton Woods arrangement for stable exchange rates and the U.S. stockmarket crises of 1969–1970 and 1974.

These events and their impacts are now being outweighed by the $43.6 billion deficit in fiscal year 1975 and a $76 billion deficit in fiscal year 1976. The total of $119.6 becomes $129.5 when reductions of federal funds are included.

The economic advice of the 1965–1975 period was typified by analyses that were dominated by the idea of a trade-off between the rate of inflation and the level of unemployment. Also, various economists that have come to be known as the Brookings Group popularized a naive model called the "full employment balanced budget."[8] This economic environment has not been suitable to the development of a federal government revenue program providing for a new substantial source of tax receipts that would permit the politically required level of spending without an inflationary expansion of the money supply, and a federal debt with an annual carrying charge of $40 billion a year, or an average family cost forever and ever of $666 a year for each of our 60 million family units. Each twenty-year family generation must now dedicate $13,320 in earnings to pay interest on the national debt.

Too much good has been seen to exist in rising prices, an inflationary money supply, an expanding federal debt, and a tax system that avoided use of production and sales as a base on which to apply a major new tax.

To avoid production losses arising from a shortage of demand, there is a big temptation to stimulate demand through creation of investment funds or consumer subsidies. Efforts to do this run into a problem that has come to be called the Phillips Curve. The curve is constructed by plotting as in Figure 4 the percentage wage increase (vertical axis) against the percentage of the labor force that is unemployed (horizontal axis). When this is done a curve fitted to the points slopes downward to the right. This is true of curves *A* and *B*, as can be seen in Figure 4. More purchasing power to investors or consumers will make possible more production and more employment. This expansion is accomplished at the price of inflation, and not just once, but over and over again, as costs in relation to selling prices tend to return to their old relationship, causing unused productive resources (unemployment) as each group tries to preserve its real income.[9]

Figure 4
Phillips Curve

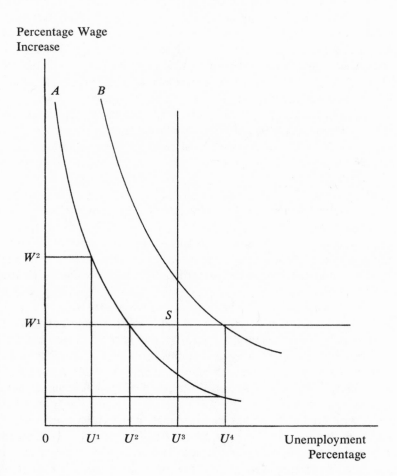

The Phillips Curve demonstrates that a trade-off exists between degree of inflation and degree of unemployment. To enjoy the benefit of less unemployment, the economy must suffer the disadvantage of more inflation. However, the fact that the historical record shows, for example, that a 1 percent increase in the rate of inflation decreases the rate of unemployment by 1 percent does not provide assurance that this will happen in the future.[10] The basic reason for this lack of assurance is that the Phillips Curve analysis does not provide an explanation of exactly what caused the historical relationship between the inflation rate and the unemployment rate. U.S. data seem to deny a long-run trade-off between inflation and unemployment.

One economist, at least, has speculated that as our economy becomes more affluent and able to "support" more unemployed, it will take more unemployment "to keep inflation down to any specific rate."[11] It is argued this is so because being unemployed will involve a smaller reduction of purchases when unemployment benefits are substantial. If purchases are not reduced when unemployment increases, the inflationary pressures are not reduced through unemployment. In fact, inflation could be expanded, because increasing unemployment would increase the pressure for reduced hours of work (in order to increase the number of jobs) without a reduction of pay to the person filling each job, despite the fact he worked fewer hours and produced less.

DEFICIT FINANCING AND TAX FINANCING

The highway program and the social security program are two examples of major government expenditures financed with tax collections paid into dedicated trust funds. Both the gasoline tax and the payroll tax are perhaps also income regressive taxes. Another similarity of the two taxes is that the base taxed is rather directly associated with the expenditure financed.

The regressivity of the gasoline tax is largely hidden in the impact it has on the prices of nearly all goods and services. The quantity of gasoline purchased is determined more by the portion of the country in which the buyer lives than by income levels. Also, gasoline is a product that possesses a very large satisfaction surplus. The existence of this surplus and the lack of a close substitute combine to make the gasoline tax an OK tax.

The payroll tax has benefited from the matching payment by the employer. In a way the employee got $2 for $1. The relationship between wages earned and provision for old age has also seemed proper. As a result the tax has not needed to be supported by provision for progressive rates, dependency deduction, or the inclusion of all income in the base. In both cases the relationship between revenue source and expenditure benefit has been viewed as sufficiently close to make the revenue-expenditure package acceptable. In both instances, need for tax revenues to finance what was to be done and the relation of the revenue source to expenditure benefit enjoyment were understandable to the electorate.

In the case of general government expenditures this basic fiscal logic provided by the relationship of the tax to the expenditure satisfaction does not exist. The situation was not always like this. General expenditures of the federal government were formerly expected to be met with tax receipts, largely as is the current practice among the states. The abandonment of the practice arose somewhat from the Congressional committee organization, which is now partially remedied. Economic teachings related to the cyclically balanced budget, excess savings, the full employment balanced budget, and the Phillips Curve concept also combined to weaken the practical citizen's conviction that what is bought must be paid for.

The economic troubles of the past several years have highlighted several basic shortcomings of conventional fiscal policy wisdom developed thirty-five years ago. The one shift that current economic conditions make most obvious is that in developed nations as well as in LDCs, expansion of liquidity is inflationary although unemployment is high. The realization of the accuracy of this one basic observation of the current scene sharply reduces the economic support of federal deficits financed out of revenues provided by the expansion of central bank credit.

The large 1975 and 1976 deficits in the federal budget were partially the result of the decline in revenues directly related to the heavy reliance on income and profits taxes. Another substantial portion was caused by the tax reduction legislation of 1975. The final contributor was increased expenditures related largely to inflation and unemployment. Each of these major causes of a steeply rising federal government indebtedness will continue to be around when, and if, the normal real GNP annual growth rate is regained.

The income tax will surely fail to recapture a portion of its 1974 ability to raise revenues. Also, new expenditure areas that were slowed by the crisis will be demanding attention. The economic leadership required of the federal government in the mixed economy of the United States to guarantee progress will be shackled by fiscal weakness.

CONCLUSION

The full-employment balanced budget is no longer a useful concept—if it ever was—for setting tax and expenditure goals of the federal government. The rising tax revenues expected as the economy approaches full employment are the result of inflation combined with graduated tax rates and higher profits arising from inventory adjustments. In other words, the doctrine is not useful in setting policy for stability at high levels of economic activity.

The Phillips concept of a trade-off between the inflation rate and the unemployment rate does not exist in the United States. Therefore, the stimulus thought to exist in the sharp drop of revenues and inflationary budget deficits of the U.S. fiscal system when a business recession arises, becomes a weakness and not a strength, once the public has adjusted to the inflationary environment.

POTENTIAL DIFFICULTIES IN THE INTRODUCTION OF A
VALUE-ADDED TAX

The fair way to begin a discussion of the administrative problems related to the introduction of VAT in the United States would be to reproduce all the regulations and court decisions required to carry out the income tax. It would also be appropriate when discussing individual justice of VAT to explore the horizontal tax equality of average income receivers that is provided by the income tax and also the special provisions provided by the law to allow breathing holes for the receivers of high income. The point at issue does not require lengthy belaboring. It can be satisfactorily handled through operation on two very generally accepted premises: (1) that the federal government's fiscal maneuverability is seriously handicapped by its nearly complete reliance on revenue sources using as a base a legal definition of personal income and corporate profits, and (2) that there isn't any particular divine or economic principle that supports the favors and disfavors extended under the existing federal tax system.

Justifiably, when a knowledgeable person considers the adoption of a new tax to produce billions in revenues, he wishes to explore the proposal in depth. This exploration would be of two major types—first, examination of the manner in which the VAT is being used now, and second, examination of the manner in which the somewhat unique U.S. situations would be handled under a VAT law. The simple underlying idea of VAT requires a carefully considered administration system.

The attributes of any tax exist only as they are a working portion of a tax system. VAT as a national tax is considered here as a major tax within a national revenue system that continues to use the corporate and individual income taxes. However, the lower-income receivers would be exempt from the income tax, and corporate income tax rates would be reduced. Also, revenue-sharing would be expanded to make elimination of the retail sales taxes possible. All this would be accomplished with a VAT rate below that used by several Western European nations.

DEPLETION

One thorny aspect of the federal income tax that should surely be questioned is the treatment of depletion under VAT. If depletion is seen as a using up of capital similar to depreciation, the basic treatment is that expenditures made to acquire and develop resource properties are eligible to enter into a presale tax payment only if the bill of sale showed tax payment. The sale of oil, or other resource products, would be subject to the value-added tax rate. The seller of the oil could deduct the amount of tax he had paid on purchases during the tax period.

An adjustment period is appropriate, because firms that had purchased mineral properties in the past would not have prepaid VAT to deduct from VAT liability arising from sales of minerals.

CAPITAL GAINS

Conceptually, VAT is concerned only with value added to a product through application of production factors. The increase in the sale price of assets that is not the result of additional productive activity is not a portion of GNP and therefore not a portion of VAT. It is the capital gains arising from inventory—or basically short-term capital gains, as the concept is used in the United States and other Western industrial nations—that could become the base of VAT even though these gains are not completely included in GNP. GNP and national income include the gains from inflation as they become a portion of wages, profits, dividends, and rents and as the incomes are used to save and directly purchase goods and services.

The economic problem in the application of VAT is to separate trading gains arising from the exchange of assets with additional value due to inventory service from monetary increases or decreases due to shifts in interest rates and prices. Basically, the same kind of problems and shortcomings encountered under the income tax arise here in the application of VAT. However, because of the much lower VAT tax rate, the degree of the difficulty is much less. And because VAT revenues permit a reduction of corporate income tax rates, the inherent difficulty in this area of profits taxation is reduced.

THE FINANCE INDUSTRY

Where administrative or political considerations made it appropriate, a VAT levied generally on the product base—that is, by the use of the subtraction method, could take advantage of the income or additive method to make it administratively easy to broaden the VAT base. In the area of finance this generally may be the appropriate procedure. It appears likely that this approach would be helpful in the application of VAT to capital gains. The general exemption of the finance industry from VAT in France, Germany, and also Michigan was not due to a theoretical or administrative weakness of VAT but seems to have arisen largely from traditional procedures of taxing finance that the respective legislative groups did not wish to dislodge.[12]

The provision of the new German VAT providing basic exemption to the finance industry is found in Paragraphs 8 and 11 of Section 4. Section 4 has the title "Exemptions from Taxation." Paragraph 8 provides for exemption from VAT of the following transactions: "granting of credit, transactions in securities, security shares in corporations and other associations, legal currency and domestic official stamps, the assumption of liabilities, guarantees and similar securities, the arrangement of transactions in securities and legal currency, the administration of credits, the depositing and administraton of securities, transactions in the deposit and current account business including payment and transfer transactions, the collection of trade paper as well as other services in the underwriting business." Paragraph 11 exempts "transactions resulting from activities of agents of savings and loan associations and insurance companies and of insurance brokers."

BUSINESS TAX PAYMENTS AS COSTS

The VAT tradition as developed in France and Germany uses as its base the difference between selling price and purchases from taxable vendors. Taxes are included as a factor of production and as a portion of the VAT base in two principal ways: (1) payments to labor, capital owners, and landowners are increased because the receivers are subject to a general income tax; and (2) the selling prices of the firm are higher because of the national, state, and local taxes the firm must pay.[13]

Administrative advantages of a VAT using the product or subtractive method include the elimination of most of the problems related to double taxation of income and the definition of income. Selling price includes all income distributions and all costs. Government costs represented by taxes fall into place as just another expense of getting the product or service to the final user.[14] Also, the taxes paid directly by the firm are no different in this respect from taxes paid indirectly by the firm through having to pay higher prices for raw materials and capital equipment. The assumption of the forward shifting of taxes concludes that the result is a higher price for the productive factors used and goods and services sold.

The relative economic burdens of these tax payments by individuals and firms, whatever the incidence assumption, vary depending on the products and services produced from the government expenditure of the payments it receives. The burdens of price payments vary similarly.

GOVERNMENT EXPENDITURES

For example, payments that support those above sixty-two years of age in enforced idleness, which is one of the purposes of the social security system, do not add directly to productive efficiency. On the other hand, payments that support education to make the population literate directly contribute greatly to the productivity of people as members of the economy.

Everything that is produced has a cost, whether the good or service is sold on the market, used, cast aside, consumed by the maker, or given to another, and whether the action results in dissatisfaction or satisfaction. This is true of actions that are organized within government, the business firm, and the family. The type of organization or the use to which a good or service is put does not change its cost.[15] This we all know, but somehow we become confused when looking at the real economic world.

When the selling price is used as the base to which the VAT rate is applied, it has been assumed that all costs are covered by price—that is, the cost of the care of the man living in idleness and the cost of setting land aside as hunting preserves as well as the wages of the worker. The important difference is not where the costs occur, but the effects of the costs on the efficiency of the economic process. Therefore, the inclusion of taxes in the base of VAT is the correct approach. More than likely, all attempts to exclude one cost or another from any economic base are certain to fail through definitional problems and market forces.[16]

RENTAL INCOME

Rent is charged and facilities are rented by large and small economic units. The rent required is a price charged for sale of a service and is taxable under VAT. Owner-occupied facilities that do not produce rent as a payment are also a portion of the base of VAT. However, they are excluded from the VAT base in France and Germany. The procedure used in France and Germany is to include the costs of construction as a portion of the VAT base.[17] In France "real estate transfers are usually excluded from the value-added tax as a noncommercial transaction."[18]

The inclusion of the cost of production gives structures constructed before VAT an economic advantage. This windfall could be picked up by the levy of a special tax equivalent to VAT on the undepreciated value of all physical capital and all durable consumer goods. However, the efficient functioning of VAT does not require this type of retroactive action. This is the case because the renter not currently buying goods will not have tax prepayments to deduct from tax liability. Also, if properties that were produced before VAT do enjoy an economic advantage, a considerable portion will be recaptured in the income tax.

The owner will receive invoices from those VAT-paying firms from which he makes purchases. These will be deductible from VAT liability on rent charges. If he has no rent receipts, he gets no deductions. This is the technical position of the owner who rents property before VAT was introduced. It is the usual situation in France because of exemption.

VAT in both Germany and France considers the home or industrial plant built for the owner as an end-use product. VAT is paid by the contractor and is included in the invoice. The owner treats this VAT charge in the same manner as a VAT charge made when inventory or capital equipment is purchased (under one concept of VAT).[19] The German VAT (Section 4, Paragraph 12) provides limited exemption of rents and property transfers: "Accommodation in apartments and bedrooms made available by an entrepreneur for the temporary accommodation of guests and the leasing of machinery and other equipment of any description which forms part of an industrial plant (even if they are essential elements of real estate) are *not* exempt."

DEPRECIATION

The economic sense of the capital cost included in productive activity has been twisted and abused beyond recognition in its treatment under the taxation of business income in the United States and other industrial nations. Under VAT, depreciation has become the basic difference in the popular presentation of the three basic methods of levying VAT.[20] (Two other differentiating elements are treatment of indirect taxes and inventories.) Some of the points developed in the consideration of depreciation under VAT are closely related to the treatment of capital gains.

The value added used as the base of VAT can consist of the net sales of a firm. The base is calculated by deducting from current sales the intermediate purchases on current account and depreciation and depletion correctly allocated to current sales. The base is equal to payments to factors of production, assuming that sales totals do not include indirect taxes and inventories remain constant. This is the income variety of VAT base, or IVA.[21] The problem of trying to calculate depreciation has not been avoided. Also, because of the problems of treating indirect taxes, inventory changes, and depreciation and depletion, the IVA type of VAT base is best administered through withholding the tax from factor payments. However, the problem remains of treating depreciation to calculate profits that are not distributed as dividend payments. If the income that remains is a major source of federal revenue, the problem of treating depreciation must be continued. Whether or not depreciation is deducted in developing the VAT base, as it must be if IVA is used, does not pose a new difficulty.

The consumption-type VAT (the CVA) levies the tax on net sales, as does the IVA, but no depreciation deduction is permitted. Instead purchases of capital goods are treated like purchases on current account. This means that capital purchases are treated the same as raw material purchases—all interfirm purchases are treated alike. This approach is sometimes called instant depreciation.[22] Because capital is excluded from the base of CVA in this way, in a simple capital-labor dividend economy, VAT becomes a tax on wage productivity only as capital is treated as congealed labor.

The introduction of a CVA-type VAT requires an adjustment period during the early years of the tax. The period is required to give old capital equipment a position approaching the instant deductibility given the new capital. This could be accomplished by permitting a deduction from net sales for a five-year period of 20 percent of the undepreciated values (the value not already deducted in arriving at income by the federal government).

When the VAT base approximates GNP, the tax is a GVA-type VAT.[23] In this approach neither depreciation nor interfirm purchases on capital account are deductible from sales. However, the VAT paid on interfirm sales is deductible from the VAT liability on sales. An adjustment period, as under CVA, is not required because the price of interfirm sales includes the cost of old as well as new capital. Also, new capital purchased will include VAT as charged by the capital manufacturing firm, and therefore the larger reduction of the tax liability of a firm accumulating capital is compensated by a higher gross price of capital goods after the application of VAT. The German and French VATs operate on the GVA base with minimum differences.

APPROPRIATENESS FOR CURRENT CONDITIONS

The economies of the United States, the EC member states, and all modern nations are very complex, and the taxes of the world must reflect this complexity. The modern nation has also become the provider of a vast quantity of very expensive services required by modern life. The income tax as a producer of large revenues during war was able to appeal to the injustice of war profiteering. In addition, it functioned at its introduction in a period when large welfare expenditures and mass civilian social security improvement programs were not part of the economic scene. Finally, Keynesian economics, as a child of excess savings and underconsumption, found the high taxation of profits and the low taxation of consumer spending attractive. It is unquestionably true that the development of a new federal tax approach is appropriate when war profiteering is gone, when welfare expenditures and social security protection are expanding, and when a worldwide shortage of capital funds exists. It is also unquestionably true that to do this is a major undertaking.

The foregoing consideration of administrative problems and difficulties arising from the introduction of VAT has been included to demonstrate that the difficulties are not basic.[24] In many cases they disappear when VAT is considered as a tax to reduce the corporate income tax, to eliminate the applicability of the income tax to the lower portion of taxable income, and to eliminate the retail sales tax. In other cases, the problems anticipated for VAT in the United States are really shortcomings of the existing tax system. Because the United States does not have a general excise tax, the adjustments required to bring most of GNP into the tax base are relatively formidable. Canada, because of her major manufacturer's sales tax, can do this more easily.[25]

RETAIL SALES

The general procedure in Europe is to make VAT a portion of the quoted retail price. The procedure is generally not followed, however, in the case of restaurant meals and hotel bills.

When VAT is made a portion of the selling price, the cashier needn't calculate the different VAT rates applying to basic foods and luxury items. The calculations are all made by management, and prices are given to those marking the items.

In addition to the added efficiency of including VAT in the retail price, it is also a justified practice because (1) other taxes paid are not separated out and listed on the sales slip or calculated by the cashier, and (2) the amount of VAT paid is not needed for the vast majority of retail sales because the item or service is an end-use purchase. The problem arising from the procedure is that some sales at retail are made for business purposes.

The French have met this difficulty by requiring the retailer to keep a separate account for customers subject to VAT. It is generally agreed that this answer provides too much administration to meet a minor problem. In Sweden a business buying at retail keeps its cash slip or bill, and the portion of price consisting of VAT is deductible when the business calculates its VAT liability.

For a number of reasons, America, in the treatment of VAT at retail, should follow the lead established in Europe. To my mind, these reasons substantially outweigh those requiring separation of tax from price. Following is a list of the pros and cons of including all taxes in retail prices and not quoting any tax separately.[26]

Pro—Reasons for Not Listing Taxes Separately

1. The listing must always be partial, and this gives people the wrong impression of the portion of total cost consisting of taxes.

2. Nontax costs are not listed, and taxes deserve equal treatment.

3. Data do not show that taxes are lower in cases where taxpayers are aware of taxes paid.

4. Special legislation to provide exemption for certain groups is discouraged.

5. Income, profit, and property taxes are encouraged, and taxes tied to sales prices are discouraged.

6. Errors arising from calculation of tax by cashiers are avoided.

Con—Reasons for Listing Taxes Separately

1. Voters become more aware of costs of government and as a result insist on more economy in government.

2. Administration of exemptions granted to certain groups becomes easier.

3. This method assures that the tax and only the tax is added on to the price paid by the customers.

4. The use of sales taxes to meet government budgetary needs is discouraged.

VAT can be administered to encourage including the tax in the price, while this is not true of such taxes as the gasoline tax and the retail sales tax. If the sales slip includes VAT paid to sellers as well as VAT due from purchasers, the markup at retail can be calculated by the purchaser. The retailer generally hesitates to make this amount known. This same situation arises if the retailer is required to include all the VAT he has paid in the base to be deducted from the selling price in calculating the markup to which the VAT rate applies.

These considerations, added to problems that are certain to arise at the cashier's counter, make the European procedure of not quoting VAT separately on retail sales a very understandable choice.

COLLECTION AT EACH STAGE

Because VAT is collected at each stage of production, those about to introduce VAT express strong fears of administrative difficulties. The experience has not justified these fears. France, which has the most complicated of all VATs in effect, has been able to administer the tax with personnel released when small excises were repealed with VAT's introduction.[27] The changeover from the German turnover tax to VAT was remarkably smooth.[28]

Very useful economic forecasting and planning benefits arise from the multistage base of VAT and the Western European procedure of monthly tax payments based on invoices. Unmatched data of economic movements are provided. An analysis of all VAT returns, made possible by computer processing, "would provide a virtually complete transaction matrix by region as well as by industry and could replace much of the statisical material now collected on a less comprehensive and less reliable basis."[29] The serious 1975 inventory recession would have been largely avoided if data VAT could provide had been available.

SERVICE BUSINESSES

The small service firm is perhaps best treated in the same way as a small retailer. However, the Michigan VAT made special provision for service industries through special base allocation provisions. The law provided that if statutory deductions did not total at least 50 percent of taxable receipts, the taxpayer had the right to deduct a flat 50 percent. In addition, if payroll alone exceeded 50 percent of taxable receipts, an additional 10 percent, or one-half of the excess, whichever was smaller, could be deducted.

The result of these provisions was that any Michigan firm, including a service firm, with gross receipts of less than $25,000 was exempt. In the case of service firms, the exemption was greater if their payrolls made up more than 50 percent of taxable receipts.[30]

Because service firms have been widely exempt under state and local retail sales taxes, they are likely to protest being taxed. In Europe certain service industries have been granted the option of being exempt or taxed. If the industry opts for exemption, it is unable to recover the VAT included in cost of supplies and capital goods purchased from the VAT collected from its customers as a portion of selling price because the industry itself does not pay VAT on its value added. This disadvantage is considerable and has brought about an unprecedented situation in taxation. Some service industries have actually requested they be included under VAT.

In Europe liberal professions (dentists, lawyers, accountants, and so on) are exempt from VAT. The exemption, of course, really means that their liability is limited to the VAT included in their purchases from businesses paying VAT.

Although the application of VAT to the liberal professions, financial institutions, and other service businesses causes problems, the difficulties are not insurmountable. The different environment in this country suggests an American VAT that breaks away from European tradition in this respect. This approach would make a considerable addition to the VAT "retail" base.[31]

CONCLUSION

Some areas of economic activity do not fit readily into the strict economic concept of value added. The failure of nations using VAT to overcome some of these difficulties has been due more to a reluctance to change certain established practices and violate certain taboos than to administrative or economic fundamentals.

The very broad potential base of VAT is more likely to be realized than that of income, for example, because pressures internal to the tax continue to work toward expanding the base rather than reducing it. Also, as the base expands, additional revenues can be collected without raising rates so high that evasion becomes irresistible.

The EC has moved VAT through retail sales. Before this was accomplished, it was believed that great administrative difficulties would be encountered. This has not proved to be the case.

CONCLUDING COMMENTS

One volume cannot hope to cover all of the historical background and economic impacts of one tax, even when other relationships are neglected. In this book where VAT was considered as the keystone to basic tax reform, it was thus necessary to make many difficult choices.

The interrelationships between the tax system and the manner in which the economy of the nation functions to meet basic and not so basic human demands are very complex, and they are constantly changing with the ebb and flow of relative scarcities. As we considered the productivity of the public and private sectors, the dependence of each upon the other became obvious. It also became clear that the manner in which the public sector gained support from the private sector, and in turn encouraged business efficiency, was very important in establishing the level of economic activity and per capita consumption levels.

VAT as an American tax turns out to be largely a replacement tax domestically. In addition, the range of international economic impacts of VAT is very broad and includes a new approach to international exchange rate adjustment. VAT has more potential to favorably affect the American international competitive position, while staying within the international economic institutional framework, than do other taxes.

The discussions have demonstrated that VAT can be used to raise very substantial revenues without increasing the relative cost of labor as does the payroll tax, or decreasing the incentive to invest as does the income tax. In addition, because the introduction of a major VAT would harmonize the U.S. tax system more closely with the tax systems of other industrial nations, the investment of U.S. savings and foreign earnings of U.S. companies will be affected much less by tax considerations than is currently true. Under current conditions this would increase the availability of capital in the United States and the potential productivity and therefore the income level of American wage earners.

The U.S. public sector currently uses incomes and produces services and goods equal to approximately 35 percent of GNP and collects taxes equal to 28 percent of GNP. The raising of this huge a level of revenues has, from the very fact of its size, the potential of seriously harming the efficiency with which day-to-day economic activities are carried out. Although much can be said of the desirability of reducing the relative level of economic resources used by governments, this potential has not been examined. Rather, actual and expected expenditure levels are accepted, and financing sources are looked at with an eye to carrying the revenue requirement load in the most expeditious manner.

The value-added tax comes out as a tax which can be very helpful because of its stability, economic neutrality, and the freedom it gives to a domestic fiscal policy. Each of these points in a world of huge government expenditures to remove citizen hardships and to encourage human development is perhaps more important in maximizing welfare than the use of graduated income tax rates and therefore the appearance of taxation according to ability to pay.

A very important element of a tax system taking nearly one-third of GNP is its relation to an efficiently operating economy. If the tax system sharply reduces after-tax profits, many investments with considerable potential become uneconomic. Also, if a tax system increases the cost of hiring a worker considerably above the negotiated wage rate, the inducement to hire more workers has been cut back. Finally, if a tax fails to increase the price of imports to meet production plus tax costs of domestic goods, production for the domestic market tends to migrate to foreign based firms.

Each of these three basic elements of a successful private enterprise economy deserves serious consideration in setting fiscal policy. When they are examined, as they have been in the analyses of this study, the shortcomings of the taxes in use, of which we are all aware in a general way, become specific. Also, the need for reform becomes apparent and very important if conditions required for a major non-communist modern industrial society to function are to exist. The shortage of investment capital, the unemployment of labor, the deficit in the trade account portion of the international balance of payments, and the export of domestic savings plus the failure of foreign profits of U.S. multinational firms to be repatriated and the large federal government deficits, all combine to paint a miserable picture that can be improved through major taxation attention.

Sections of this discussion have demonstrated that the modification of established taxes and the introduction of VAT can provide a very useful, stable base of government revenue. The built-in cyclical instability of the income tax with graduated rates and the corporate profits tax has turned out to be a shortcoming and not a strength of these taxes.

The cyclical need is for a major tax that collects a constant portion of total production sold in the market. Income taxes of all types, and particularly those with graduated and progressive rates, fail to do this. VAT is capable of doing a pretty fair job of providing stable revenues and can be usefully employed to modify tax collection impacts arising from mass unemployment, sharply reduced profits and substantial capital losses.

When tax collections become one-third or so of GNP, it becomes necessary to consider taxation in a much broader sense than was required when the level was one-tenth or one-fifth of GNP. Also, the increased proximity of nations to each other as a result of rapid transportation and communication requires greater consideration of the difficulties arising from a failure to harmonize tax procedures. The multinational corporation which developed out of these new relationships is an institutional arrangement that also needs a worldwide tax uniformity if it is to avoid investment and marketing inefficiencies and serious international frictions. The current U.S. approach to these developments has been half-hearted, and as demonstrated, quite ineffective.

The United States as a mature economy destined to rely more and more on the skill of its people and the capital goods of its industries must look to government as a cooperating agent in these economic endeavors. A major element of the government's role is the manner in which it collects the taxes it uses to finance the functions allocated to it. To some extent ability to pay and related concepts of economic justice will always determine the tax approach used. However, when the application of these principles develops economic pressures unfavorable to efficient use of labor and capital, their appropriateness is questioned.

Political support should move toward a revenue source that can increase the total of economic goods and services available to be divided by corresponding more closely with the requirement of the economic processes of capitalism and its competitive market economy. It is at this stage that VAT can perform a very useful function by providing large revenues without changing the existing market-determined relationship between wages, profits, interest, and rents. Therefore, the requirements of economic progress at that stage of the business cycle or at that level of economic growth and efficiency are not disturbed because large amounts of revenues are required to support the pubilc sector.

Notes

CHAPTER 1

1. Richard W. Lindholm, "German Finance of World War II," *American Economic Review* 37 (March 1947): 121–34.

2. Richard W. Lindholm, "The Farm: Misused Income, Expansion Base of Emerging Nations," *Journal of Farm Economics* 43 (May 1961).

3. W. M. Flinders Petrie, *Arts and Crafts of Ancient Egypt* (London: T. N. Foulis, 1923).

4. Herbert Heaton, *Economic History of Europe* (New York: Harper, 1936), pp. 59–60.

5. G. M. Trevelyan, *English Social History* (London: Longmans, Green, 1944), pp. 1–13.

6. Henri Pirenne, *Economics and Social History of Medieval Europe* (London: Routledge and Kegan Paul, 1958), pp. 142–177.

7. Alvin H. Hansen, *Full Recovery or Stagnation?* (New York: W. W. Norton, 1938), p. 321.

8. Richard W. Lindholm, *Introduction to Fiscal Policy*, 2nd ed. (New York: Pitman, 1955), pp. 219–22.

9. The Council of Economic Advisers provides economic policy guidance to the President.

10. Steering Committee of the National Urban Coalition, *Counterbudget* (Washington, D.C.: Praeger, 1971).

11. *Wall Street Journal*, May 4, 1972, p. 11.

12. The taxpayer must buy the new residence within one year before or after the sale of the old residence and use the new house as his principal residence within the same period.

13. In Germany, gains from sales of shares or other capital interests are taxable only if the owner directly or indirectly owned 25 percent of the capital.

14. William Vickrey, *Agenda for Progressive Taxation* (New York: Ronald Press, 1947), p. 395. This book is dedicated to the development of a "really sound and leak-proof individual income tax."

15. These and related data were developed by George S. Sadowsky and Joseph A. Peckman.

16. Vickrey, *Agenda for Progressive Taxation,* p. 395.

17. The Department of Commerce composite construction cost index rose from 119 in 1966 to 152 in 1970. The medical care index with 1958 equaling 100 reached 164 in 1970.

18. Allen Schick, *Budget Innovation in the States* (Washington, D.C.: Brookings Institution, 1971).

19. Department of Commerce, Bureau of the Census, *Local Government Finances in Selected Metropolitan Areas and Large Counties, 1965–66 and 1969–70* (Washington: U.S. Government Printing Office, 1973), pp. 41–73.

20. Richard A. Musgrave, *The Pure Theory of Public Finance* (New York: McGraw-Hill, 1959), p. 13.

21. Alan A. Tait, *The Taxation of Personal Wealth* (Urbana, Ill.: University of Illinois Press, 1967), p. 102.

22. Christopher Green, *Negative Taxes and the Poverty Problem* (Washington, D.C.: Brookings Institution, 1967).

23. Windsor Davies, "Social Services in Britain," *Progress, the Unilever Quarterly* 51 (March 1966): 187. The U.S. Bureau of the Census reports that between 1969 and 1970 the number of persons living below the poverty level increased by 1.2 million. This reverses a year-by-year decline during the 1960s. The total number is now 25.5 million.

24. In 1966 slightly more than 40 percent of taxpayers submitted returns they had not prepared themselves. In 1969 the percentage had increased to over 50 percent. In the 1970s the rate of increase continued. Preparing income tax returns has truly become a growth industry. It is estimated that 200,000 persons and firms provide income tax preparation services for a fee. Between 1966 and 1969 the number of returns with adjusted gross income below $5,000 with a signature of a preparer other than the taxpayer increased by 40 percent. The increase for the $10,000 to $25,000 bracket was about 100 percent. *Taxes, the Tax Magazine* 49 (May 1971): 289.

25. *Fortune,* May 1971, p. 134.

26. Bert G. Hickman, *Growth and Stability of the Postwar Economy* (Washington, D.C.: Brookings Institution, 1960), p. 209. Hickman's observation for the twenty-year period from 1940 to 1960 has been even more true between 1960 and 1975.

27. *Economic Report of the President for 1974* (Washington, D.C.: U.S. Government Printing Office, 1974), pp. 77, 323, also for 1975, p. 326.

CHAPTER 2

1. Ursula K. Hicks, *Public Finance* (London: James Nisbet, 1955), pp. 248–51. The consideration of the impact of taxes on economic decisions, including the prices of goods taxed and the income level before taxes, is included under the term *effective incidence.*

2. Harry Gunnison Brown, "The Incidence of a General Output or a Sales Tax," *Journal of Political Economy,* April 1939, pp. 254–62. The analysis holds that prices do not increase if a general sales tax is levied because the tax itself does not provide the additional purchasing power to support a generally higher price level. Earl R. Rolph, "A Proposed Revision of Excise Tax Theory," *Journal of Political Economy,* April 1952, pp. 102–17. The analysis holds that the use of specific excise taxes will increase the price of the product taxed, but the higher price of the taxed product will use up more of a constant ability to purchase, causing the prices of other goods to decline, so that the general price level does not change.

3. U.S. Constitution, Art. 1, Sec. 9; *Pollock* v. *Farmer's Loan and Trust Co.,* 157 U.S. 429, 558 (1894); *Brushaber* v. *Union Pacific Railroad Co.,* 240 U.S. 1, 14 (1916). See discussion in Richard W. Lindholm, *The Corporate Franchise as a Basis of Taxation* (Austin, Texas: University of Texas Press, 1944), pp. 171–74.

4. *Revenue Statistics of OECD Member Countries, 1965–1971* (Geneva, Switzerland: Organization for Economic Cooperation and Development, 1973), p. 184.

5. *Pollock* v. *Farmers' Loan and Trust Co.,* 157 U.S. 429 (1894) rehearing, 158 U.S. 601 (1895).

6. The tax was the Business Activities Tax (BAT) of the state of Michigan, 1953–1967, and Single Business Tax, 1975.

7. Dan Troop Smith, James B. Webber, and Carol M. Cerf, *What You Should Know About the Value Added Tax* (Homewood, Ill.: Dow Jones–Irwin, 1973).

8. John Chown, *VAT Explained* (London: Kogan Page, 1972), pp. 25–27.

9. Bureau of International Commerce of the Department of Commerce, *Overseas Business Reports,* November 1967, p. 9.

10. Harvey E. Brazer and Marjorie C. Brazer, *State and Local Taxation of Banks*, Part III, Committee on Banking, Housing, and Urban Affairs, U.S. Senate, December 1971, pp, 412–14.

11. Arthur Becker, *Land and Building Taxes* (Madison, Wis.: University of Wisconsin Press, 1969), pp. 11–47.

12. Wesley Claire Mitchell is best known for his empirical work associated with the development of an explanation of business cycles. His emphasis was always on description of what happened rather than prediction of what would or would not happen under certain circumstances.

13. John Maynard Keynes, *The General Theory of Employment, Interest and Money* (New York: Harcourt, Brace, 1936).

14. The Council of Economic Advisers, which was established in the Employment Act of 1946, has never been given the responsibility of identifying what must be done to avoid unemployment. The concept of the government as the employer of last resort has never been accepted in America, as it has largely been in Europe.

15. Brookings Institution, *Report on a Survey of the Organization and Administration of State and County Governments of Alabama* (Montgomery, Alabama: Wilson Publishing Co., 1932), Vol. 4 Pt. 3, pp. 341–98; and *Report on a Survey of Administration in Iowa: The Revenue System* (Des Moines, Iowa: State of Iowa, 1933), pp. 120–54.

16. Gerhard Colm, "The Ideal Tax System," *Social Research* 1 (August 1934) : 319–42.

17. Paul Studenski, "Toward a Theory of Business Taxation," *Journal of Political Economy* 48 (October 1940): 621–54.

18. T. S. Adams, "Fundamental Problems of Federal Income Taxation," *Quarterly Journal of Economics* 35 (August 1921): 527–56.

19. Martin Bronfenbrenner and Kiichiro Kogiku, "The Aftermath of the Shoup Tax Reforms," *National Tax Journal* 10 (September 1959): 236–54.

20. Dr. Shoup was a student of the late Robert M. Haige and of E. R. A. Seligman, both from Columbia University. These three tax scholars form the bedrock foundation of American taxation thinking.

21. James A. Papke, "Michigan's Value Added Tax After Seven Years," *National Tax Journal* 13 (December 1960): 350–63.

22. "Finance: Proposed Reform of the Turnover Tax," *European*

Taxation 10, no. 8 (August 1965): 208. Since the 1963 reform the French TVA has included all operations of the housing cycle. In order to encourage housing construction, the TVA base under designated circumstances has been decreased by 50 or 80 percent. See also Martin Norr and Pierre Kerlan, eds., Harvard Law School International Tax Program, *World Tax Series, Taxation in France* (Chicago: Commerce Clearing House, 1966), pp. 981, 1003.

23. Maurice Lauré, *La Taxe sur la valeur ajoutée* (Paris: Recueil Sirey, 1952).

24. Wilhelm von Siemens, *Verdelte Umstatsteuer*, 2nd ed. (Siemenstadt, Germany [private], 1921).

25. Günter Schmölders, "Turnover Taxes" in *Developments in Taxation Since World War I* (Amsterdam: International Bureau of Fiscal Documentation, 1966) pp. iv-17.

26. Ibid., pp. iv-18.

27. Note from Clara Sullivan, October 2, 1965.

28. *Business Taxation: The Report of the President's Task Force on Business Taxation* (Washington, D.C.: U.S. Government Printing Office, 1970); Advisory Commission on Intergovernmental Relations, *The Value-Added Tax and Alternative Sources of Federal Revenue* (Washington, D.C.: U.S. Government Printing Office, 1973); George E. Lent, Milka Casanegra, and Michele Guerard, "The Value-Added Tax in Developing Countries," *IMF Staff Papers,* July, 1973, pp. 318–378; Michele Guerard, "The Brazilian State Value-Added Tax," *IMF Staff Papers,* March 1973, pp. 118–169.

29. Ibid., p. 61.

30. Department of the Treasury, *DISC: A Handbook for Exporters* (Washington: U.S. Government Printing Office, 1972).

31. A translation is available: *Neumark Report of the Fiscal and Financial Committee on Tax Harmonization in the Common Market* (Chicago: Commerce Clearing House, 1963). References to pages in succeeding notes are to this translation. The membership of the FFC Committee was chairman, Fritz Neumark, Frankfurt am Main; members, Willy Albers, Kiel; Alain Barrere, Paris; Cesare Cosciani, Rome; Joseph Kauffman, Luxembourg; Maurice Masoin, Brussels; Bernard Schendstok, the Hague; Carl S. Shoup, New York; G. Stammati, Rome; and George Vedel, Paris.

32. See *A Review of Balance of Payments Policies,* Hearings before the Subcommittee on International Exchange and Payments of the Joint Economic Committee, 91st Congress, 1st session (U.S. Government Printing Office, 1969), pp. 38 and 253–54.

33. Neumark Report, p. 20.

34. Ibid., p. 28

35. Ibid., p. 30

36. Ibid., p. 38

37. Ibid., p. 31

38. Ibid., p. 37

39. Ibid., p. 43

40. Ibid., p. 46

41. Ibid., p. 46

42. Ibid., p. 49, and L. S. Bartlett, "Tax Harmonization in the EEC: A Status Report," *European Taxation* 14 (August 1974): 272–80.

43. This has been the basic U.S. policy. It is developed particularly in *A Review of Balance of Payments Policies,* Hearings before the Subcommittee on International Exchange and Payments of the Joint Economic Committee, 91st Congress, First Session (Washington, D.C.: U.S. Government Printing Office, 1969), p. 38.

45. "Harmonization of Taxation," *European Taxation* 11, no. 4 (April 1966), provides a summary of the steps taken under Article 99 of the Treaty of Rome of 1957.

46. *European Taxation* 12, no. 2 (February 1967): 45.

47. Commerce Clearing House, *Common Market Report,* annex, explanatory notes to the commission's opinion on the structure and implementation of the common added-value tax system.

48. National Economic Development Office, *VAT* (London: Her Majesty's Stationery Office, 1969), p. 46.

49. Ibid., pp. 75–98. (Included in industry replies to questionnaires; also mentioned in other places.)

50. National Economic Development Office, *VAT,* p. 38.

51. Ibid., p. 37.

52. Rudolph J. Nichus, "The German Added Value Tax—Two Years After," *Taxes, the Tax Magazine* 47 (September 1969): 554–66; Manfred Schirm, "The Value-Added Tax in Germany," in *Value Added Tax: The UK Position and European Experience,* ed. T. M. Kybezynski (Oxford, U.K.: Blackwell, 1969), pp. 30–43; G. C. Hutbauer, "The Taxation of Export Profits," *National Tax Journal* 28 (March, 1975): 43–59.

53. Carl S. Shoup, "Experience with the Value-Added Tax in Denmark and Prospects in Sweden," *Finanzarchic* 28 (March 1969): 247.

54. "How EEC Integrates on the TVA Front." *Business International: Europe,* June 19, 1970.

55. Earl R. Rolph, "The Concept of Transfers in National Income Estimates," *Quarterly Journal of Economics,* May, 1948; 327–61.

CHAPTER 3

1. Andrew Hacker, *The End of the American Era* (New York: Atheneum, 1970), p. 133.

2. *Economic Report of the President for 1976* (Washington, D.C.: U.S. Government Printing Office, 1976), p. 172.

3. Ibid. pp. 247, 251. Federal debt increase is the increase in the amount held by the public.

4. Fiscal Year (Millions of dollars)

	1967	1968	1969	1970	1971
Federal Corporate Profits taxes	34.0	28.7	36.7	33.0	26.8
State Corporate Profits taxes	2.5	3.1	3.4	3.7	4.2

	1972*	1973*	1974	1975	1976*	1977*
Federal Corporate Profits taxes	32.2	36.1	38.7	40.6	40.0	49.5
State Corporate Profits taxes	5.0	5.7	6.7	6.8*		

*estimated
Source: Economic Report of the President, 1976, pp. 246–247, 251.

5. Richard W. Lindholm, "Value Added Tax vs. Corporation Income Tax," *Business Economics* 5 (January, 1970), pp. 62–65.

6. The Keynesian economic world was capable of over-saving. The situation could only be rectified by a reduced national income which in combination with a relatively constant rate of saving would bring actual savings in line with actual investment. The classical approach did not believe oversaving was possible because downward changes in interest rates would always bring about an equating of savings with investment.

7. The Committee for Economic Development (CED) supported VAT, *A Better Balance in Federal Taxes on Business* (New York,

N.Y.: CED, 1966) because it would reduce the biased tax treatment of equity earnings by permitting a reduction of CPT rates.

They point out that to the extent the incidence of CPT is on profits the before-tax rate of return on equity investment must be higher, and a larger cash flow is required by a firm aiming at a particular quantity of funds for investment expansion.

To the extent the incidence of CPT is in higher consumer prices, the prices of goods using most equity capital and earning most profits for producers would have their prices raised most. This would again reduce investment, particularly in the heavy equity capital-using sector.

The CED sees a reduction of equity capital leading to "less output in total, less corporate investment, less capital per worker, less output per worker, and higher prices."

Also see Robert Eisner's summary of arguments favoring taxing undistributed corporate profits as stockholder income, *Business Week*, December 14, 1974, pp. 18–19.

8. An analysis made by the Treasury and reported in 1962 was concerned with the outflow of capital. The Treasury analysis fails to determine the quantity of net capital export which the U. S. overall international and domestic economic position permits. Some mention is made of the stimulation of the domestic economy of switching investments made abroad to the U. S., but the case is not developed much beyond the statement that "A dollar invested in this country in new plant and equipment is normally thought to create a continuing stream of 40 cents worth of current output, if demand keeps up with capacity." The data presented supported a figure of 10 cents for each dollar of capital invested abroad. (*Revenue Act of 1962, Hearings of Senate Finance Committee,* Part I, p. 192.) Large outflows of capital from the U. S. in mid-1974 were undoubtedly reflected in the weakness of the U. S. economy.

9. In 1973, additional direct investments abroad from the United States totaled $12.9 billion and total sales of American owned affiliates were $221.0 billion and assets in foreign countries increased to $226.1 billion. All of these totals are new records and increased sharply between 1972 and 1973. *Survey of Current Business* 54 (August 1974): 1–6, 9; 10–24, 40; 25–40.

10. Also see pages 137–145.

11. Organization for Economic Cooperation and Development, *Company Tax Systems in OECD Countries* (Paris: OECD Publications, 1973).

12. Tax Foundation, *Facts and Figures on Government Finances,* 18th Biennial Edition, 1975, pp. 115, 184.

13. In Great Britain the VAT on gasoline was increased from 8 percent to 25 percent. The increase was expected to expand the consumer price index by 0.55 and will provide £20 million of additional revenues for general purposes. The gasoline tax provides 10 percent of Britain's budget. *Economist,* November 16, 1974, pp. 81, 103.

14. Carl G. Uhr, *Sweden's Social Security System,* Research Report no. 14 (Washington, D.C.: Social Security Administration, 1966).

15. The eight types of coverage of a complete social security program: old-age pensions, mother pensions, child care benefits, unemployment benefits, health insurance, illness benefits, prenatal and maternity benefits, and low-income benefits.

16. "Everyone wishes to be generous to old age: nearly everyone resents paying increased national insurance contributions." Davies T. Windsor, "Pensions for the Future," *New Society,* April 28, 1966, p. 13.

17. J. Henry Richardson, *Economic and Financial Aspects of Social Security (an International Survey)* (Toronto: University of Toronto Press, 1960), p. 62.

18. Ibid., p. 65.

19. James A. Brittain, *American Economic Review* 61 (March 1971): 123, concludes ". . . that labor bears the tax . . . that its burden on low income groups is greater than generally realized. It also implies that its impact on income distribution is typically regressive. The qualities of the payroll tax offer a solid basis for proposing that this form of taxation be curtailed or eliminated."

20. Elizabeth Deran, "Changes in Factor Income Shares Under the Social Security Tax," *Review of Economics and Statistics* 49 (November 1967): 627–30; R. F. Hoffman, "Factor Shares and the Payroll Tax: A Comment," *Review of Economics and Statistics* 50 (November 1968): 506–8.

21. Arnold C. Harberger, "Taxation, Resource Allocation, Welfare," in *The Role of Direct and Indirect Taxes in the Federal Revenue System* (Washington, D.C.: Brookings Institution, 1964), pp. 33–42.

22. Richard W. Lindholm, "The Value Added Tax: A Short Review of the Literature," *Journal of Economic Literature* 8, no. 4 (December 1970): 1178–89.

23. Günter Schmölders, *Turnover Taxes* (Amsterdam: International Bureau of Fiscal Documentation, 1966), p. 15.

24. Ibid., p. 71.

25. U.S. Department of Health, Education and Welfare, *Social*

Security Programs Throughout the World (Washington, D.C.: U.S. Government Printing Office, 1967 and 1973) and U.S. Department of Health, *National Health Systems in Eight Countries* (Washington, D.C.: Social Security Administration, 1975).

26. L. G. Sandberg, "A Value Added Tax for Sweden," *National Tax Journal* 17 (September 1964): 292–96; "A Further Word on Swedish Taxation," Ibid., pp. 319–20.

27. Martin Norr and Nils G. Hornhammer, "The Value Added Tax in Sweden," *Columbia Law Review* 70 (March 1970): 390.

28. Royal Danish Ministry of Foreign Affairs, *Economic Survey of Denmark, 1967* (Copenhagen, Denmark: J. H. Schultz Forlag, 1967), p. 49.

29. ". . . when pension goals are realized, the disposable income of pensioners will eventually be about 70 percent of that of childless couples in similar earnings brackets." Carl G. Uhr, op. cit., p. 135.

30. ". . . in no country reporting to the International Labor Office (ILO) is social security financed entirely through contributions from workers and their employers." Milledge W. Weathers, "Systems of Social Security and the Flow of International Trade," *Journal of Economic Issues* 5 (December 1971): 54–62.

31. Roy G. Blakey and Gladys C. Blakey, *The Federal Income Tax* (New York: Longmans, Green, 1940), p. 1.

32. Richard Goode, *The Individual Income Tax* (Washington, D.C.: Brookings Institution, 1965), p. 2.

33. Nicholas Kaldor, *An Expenditure Tax*, 4th impression (London: George Allen and Unwin, 1965), p. 24.

34. Gunnar Myrdal, *The Political Element in the Development of Economic Theory* (London: Routlege & Kegan, 1953), p. 185.

35. Nicholas Kaldor, *An Expenditure Tax*, p. 171.

36. Dr. Michael Taussig at the Massachusetts Institute of Technology is trying to isolate "the net effect of the taxpayer's marginal tax rate on the amount of charitable giving."

37. Al Ullman, while Acting Chairman of the Ways and Means Committee of the U.S. Congress, proposed a national uniformity in the state income tax by making the $14 billion paid as state income taxes a 5 percent credit on federal individual income taxes if the rates are sufficiently graduated to pick up the federal credit. *Portland Journal*, July 8, 1971, p. 4.

38. Sumner Benson, "A History of the General Property Tax," in *The American Property Tax: Its History, Administration and Economic Impact,* edited by George C. S. Benson (Claremont, California:

Claremont College's Printing Service, 1965), p. 71, also *National Tax Journal* 20 (March, 1967): 1–19. Martin Fieldstein concludes the deductibility from taxable income is more important to educational than to religious organizations. *National Tax Journal* 28 (June, 1975): 209–226.

39. Jens Peter Jensen, *Property Taxation in the United States* (Chicago: University of Chicago Press, 1931), p. 44.

40. Ibid., pp. 457–58.

41. Robert Murray Haig, *A History of the General Property Tax in Illinois* (Urbana, Ill.: University of Illinois Press, 1914), p. 227; Arthur D. Lynn, "Property Tax Development," in *Property Taxation— USA*, edited by Richard W. Lindholm (Madison, Wis.: University of Wisconsin Press, 1967), pp. 7–19.

42. Dick Netzer, *Economics of the Property Tax* (Washington, D.C.: Brookings Institution, 1966), p. 7.

43. Jensen, *Property Taxation in the United States*, pp. 326–30.

44. Ibid., p. 76.

45. Netzer, *Economics of the Property Tax,* p. 9.

46. Ernest L. Bogart, *Financial History of the General Property Tax of Ohio* (Urbana, Illinois: University of Illinois Press, 1912), p. 111.

47. *Excerpts from 1965 State Legislative Program of Advisory Commission on Intergovernmental Relations* (Washington, D.C., September 1964), pp. 14–18.

48. *The Role of the States in Strengthening the Property Tax,* vol. 1 (Washington, D.C., Advisory Commission on Intergovernmental Relations, 1963), p. 73.

49. Ibid., p. 75, and Jesse Burkhead, *State and Local Taxes for Public Education,* (Syracuse, N.Y.: Syracuse University Press, 1963), p. 43.

50. Henry J. Aaron, *Who Pays the Property Tax* (Washington, D.C.: the Brookings Institution, 1975), p. 93; Richard W. Lindholm (ed), *Property Taxation and the Finance of Education* (Madison, Wis.: University of Wisconsin Press, 1974).

51. Nicholas Kaldor, *An Expenditure Tax,* p. 53. Incidence and tax burden analyses continue to be very unsatisfactory. For example, state and local property taxes are assumed to rest 50 percent on consumption and 50 percent on housing expenditures. Tax Foundation, Inc., *Tax Burdens and Benefits of Government Expenditures by Income Class, 1961 and 1965* (New York: Tax Foundation, Inc., 1967), p. 44.

52. Henry George, *Progress and Poverty* (New York: Vanguard

Press, 1929), p. 132; Vernon T. Clover, *Property Tax on Houses and Concept of Justice* (Lubbock, Tex.: Texas Technological College, 1966), pp. 31–37.

53. The earliest retail sales tax was enacted by West Virginia in 1921.

54. Tax Foundation, *State and Local Sales Taxes* (New York: Tax Foundation, 1970).

55. Ibid, pp. 51–61. About one out of every six cities in 1970 used a local sales tax. The current trend is toward absorption by the state.

56. To reduce this difficulty, Louisiana collects the sales tax from suppliers, and retailers receive credit for this payment against remittances to the state later. The innovation sharply increased collections. As yet, this approach, which has aspects similar to VAT, has not been adopted by other states.

57. *National Bellas Hess, Inc.,* v. *Illinois* (1967).

58. James A. Papke, "Michigan's Value Added Tax After Seven Years," *National Tax Journal* 13 (December 1960): 350–63.

59. House Bill No. 588, passed February 4, 1970.

60. F. L. Largent wrote, "We must adopt a new concept in taxation. A broader base must be developed by eliminating exemptions and having the tax apply to more transactions and services." *Washington Evening Star*, February 14, 1970, p. B-2.

61. Walter H. Beaman, *Paying Taxes to Other States* (New York: Ronald Press, 1963).

62. Thomas F. Pogue, "Value Added vs. Property Taxation of Business: Effects on Industrial Location," *Land Economics* 58 (May 1971): 150–57.

63. For additional descriptive material concerned with the Michigan Business Activities Tax (Act 150, P.A. 1953) see Robert D. Ebel, *The Michigan Business Activities Tax* (East Lansing, Michigan: Michigan State University Press, 1972). For additional background on state use of VAT see Richard W. Lindholm, *Description and Analysis of Oregon's Fiscal System, Area 11*, "Value Added Tax" (Salem, Oregon: Oregon Department of Revenue, 1971).

CHAPTER 4

1. *Report of the Committee on Turnover Taxation* (London: Her Majesty's Stationery Office, 1964). Committee members were Gordon Richardson, Henry Benson, and Donald MacDougall.

2. Advisory Commission on Intergovernmental Relations, *The*

Value-Added Tax and Alternative Sources of Federal Revenue (Washington, D.C.: U.S. Government Printing Office, 1973).

3. Report of the Committee, p. 78.

4. Advisory Commission on Intergovernmental Relations, *The Value-Added Tax*, p. 3.

5. For example, the levy of the income tax has sometimes been identified as the spur for the general development of accurate accounting and bookkeeping systems that have made such an important contribution to the general efficiency of business.

6. The idea in a somewhat different form is being used when it is assumed that firms operating under oligopoly conditions will raise prices when taxes on their profits are increased. Here, the firm must have been charging less than the price that maximized profits. Ursula K. Hicks, *Public Finance* (London: James Nisbet, 1955), pp. 248–51.

7. Harry Gunnison Brown, "The Incidence of a General Output or a General Sales Tax," *Journal of Political Economy* 47, no. 2 (April 1939): 254–62. Under modern conditions with an active central bank and full employment an accepted goal, the analysis becomes much more complex.

8. E. A. Rolph, *The Theory of Fiscal Economics* (Berkeley, Calif.: University of California Press, 1954), chapters 6 and 7.

9. If it is assumed that full cost pricing is followed in most firms or if a profit target after taxes is the principal determiner of price policy, then one must also conclude that corporate profits taxes affect sales, prices, and profits in very largely the same way as VAT.

This is the position taken by Leon Walras, one of the great theoretical economists. He wrote that a tax levied on entrepreneurs prior to the distribution of the earnings to the factors of production will be added to the prices of products they sell to landowners, workers, and capitalists. An indirect tax like VAT is seen to increase prices directly, while a direct tax like CPT increases prices indirectly. Leon Walras, *Elements of Pure Economics*, trans. William Jaffe (Homewood, Ill.: Richard D. Irwin, 1954), p. 450.

10. Organization for Economic Cooperation and Development, *Report on Tax Adjustments Applied to Exports and Imports in OECD Member Countries* (Paris: OECD Publications, 1968), pp. 78–82. Price theory applicable to American business is considered in many studies. The following are examples: R. A. Gordon, "Short Period Price Determination in Theory and Practice," *American Economic Review*, June 1948, pp. 265–68; Robert F. Lanzillotti, "Pricing Ob-

jectives in Large Corporations," *American Economic Review*, December 1958, pp. 921–40; A. D. H. Kaplan, Joel B. Dirlam, and Robert F. Lanzillotti, *Pricing in Big Business: A Case Approach* (Washington, D.C.: Brookings Institution, 1958).

11. Ibid., p. 79.

12. Marian Krzyzaniak, ed, *Effects of Corporation Income Tax* (Detroit: Wayne State University Press, 1966). The book is comprised of papers presented at a symposium on business taxation (see note 18).

13. *Wall Street Journal*, August 25, 1967, p. 2. In 1975 there was a new steel export investigation "to decide whether the Common Market's value-added tax system . . . provide(s) unfair export subsidies to Western European steel producers." *Wall Street Journal*, January 9, 1975. The decision was that refund of VAT was not a subsidy under federal applicable law. U.S. Steel made its presentation to the Treasury on September 17, 1975. *Legal and Economic Brief: In Support of Countervailing Only Petitions Filed by United States Steel Corporation in Connection with the Value-Added Tax System.*

14. Gary L. Becker, "A Theory of the Allocation of Time," *Economic Journal*, September 1965, pp. 494–517.

15. Both E. A. Rolph and H. G. Brown come to the conclusion that the incidence of a completely general excise tax, such as VAT approaches, makes resource owners relatively worse off and non-resource owners relatively better off. James M. Buchanan, *Fiscal Theory and Political Economy* (Chapel Hill, N.C.: University of North Carolina Press, 1960), p. 139.

16. Joint Economic Committee, *The Federal Tax System: Facts and Problems 1964* (Washington, D.C.: U.S. Government Printing Office, 1964), p. 48. Under a number of assumptions of birth rates, inflation rates and real growth rates the payroll tax for 2030 is estimated from 15 percent to 32 percent. *Economic Report of the President, 1976* (Washington, D.C.: U.S. Government Printing Office, 1976), pp. 116–117.

17. Marian Krzyzaniak and Richard A. Musgrave, *The Shifting of the Corporation Tax: An Empirical Study of Its Short-run Effect on the Rate of Return* (Baltimore, Md.: Johns Hopkins Press, 1963).

18. The materials considered in this section are based on *Effects of Corporation Income Tax.* Papers from the symposium are by Marian Krzyzaniak, Rice University; Arnold C. Harberger, University of Chicago; Richard A. Musgrave, Harvard University; Richard E. Slitor, Assistant Director at the Office of Tax Analysis, U.S. Treasury; and Richard Goode, International Monetary Fund.

19. In a discussion of the desirability of introducing the value-added tax in the UK, Nicholas Kaldor concluded his analysis with the statement: "This means that, allowing for the effects of the withdrawal of the purchase tax (previously allowance was made for reduction of income and profit taxes) a 10 percent value added tax may ultimately only raise prices to the general consumer by no more than 1 to 2 percent." "A Memorandum on the Value Added Tax," in *Essays on Economic Policy*, Vol. 1 (London: Gerald Duckworth, 1965), p. 288.

20. American Retail Federation, *The Value-Added Tax in the United States—Its Implications for Retailers* (Cambridge, Mass.: Cambridge Research Institute, 1970), pp. 65–97, 162–63.

21. "Sales and Use Taxes," *State Taxation of Interstate Commerce,* vol. 3, part 3. A report of the Special Subcommittee of State Taxation of Interstate Commerce (Washington, D.C.: U.S. Government Printing Office), pp. 637–38.

22. Daniel C. Morgan, Jr., *The Retail Sales Tax: An Appraisal of New Issues* (Madison, Wis.: University of Wisconsin Press, 1964).

23. Richard W. Lindholm, "Integrating a Federal Value Added Tax with State and Local Sales Levies," *National Tax Journal* 24 (September 1971): 403–11.

24. Milton Friedman, *A Theory of the Consumption Function* (Princeton, N. J.: Princeton University Press, 1957).

25. Five tax experts calculated federal income tax due on gross income of $13,962.69. Results varied from owed $652.04 to refund of $141.00.

26. *IMF* Survey, November 12, 1971, p. 337

27. Richard W. Lindholm, *New Tax Directions for the United States,* Committee on Ways and Means, U.S. House of Representatives, December 15, 1975 (Washington, D.C.: U.S. Government Printing Office, 1975), pp. 2–7.

28. An indirect tax is basically as just as a direct tax. I. M. D. Little, "Direct Versus Indirect Taxes," *Economic Journal,* September 1951, pp. 577–84. Analyses of VAT nearly always fail to point out that the sales of capital goods are taxed as they become a portion of the cost and therefore of the price of the end use, and that therefore the refunding of VAT paid on capital purchases is not a procedure to eliminate VAT from investment spending, but rather a procedure to eliminate double taxation.

29. Conference Board Economic Forum, *The Council of Economic Advisers: Retrospect and Prospect, Studies in Business Economics,* no. 38 (New York: National Industrial Conference Board), 1953.

30. John Cobbs, "The Limits on Economic Advice," *Business Week*, November 10, 1973, p. 36.

31. Sidney S. Alexander, "Opposition to Deficit Spending for the Prevention of Unemployment," in *Income Employment and Public Policy* (New York: W.W. Norton, Inc., 1948), pp. 177–98.

CHAPTER 5

1. Pierre Tabatoni, *Foreign Tax Policies and Economic Growth* (New York: National Bureau of Economic Research, 1966).

2. George E. Lent, *et al.,* "The Value-Added Tax in Developing Countries," *International Monetary Fund Staff Papers,* July 1973, pp. 318–378; and Michele Guerad, "The Brazilian State Value-Added Tax," *International Monetary Fund Staff Papers,* March 1972, pp. 118–169.

3. The tax due is determined by type of business, floor space, and number of employees. It is a business tax widely used in less developed nations influenced by French tax procedures.

4. A. Rubner, "The Irrelevancy of the British Differential Profits Tax," *The Economic Journal,* June 1964, p. 350.

5. *European Tax News,* 1964, p. 82. Great Britain initiated taxation of capital gains in 1965.

6. Frederick G. Reuss, *Fiscal Policy for Growth Without Inflation* (Baltimore, Md.: Johns Hopkins Press, 1963), p. 72.

7. *Tax Revision Compendium*, vol. 2 (Washington, D.C.: U.S. Government Printing Office, 1959), pp. 1203–99.

8. Richard W. Lindholm, *The Corporate Franchise as a Basis of Taxation* (Austin, Texas: University of Texas Press, 1944).

9. Stanley S. Surrey, "Definitional Problems in Capital Gains Taxation," *Federal Tax Policy for Economic Growth and Stability* (Washington, D.C.: Joint Committee on the Economic Report, 1955), pp. 404–18.

10. Letter to Hutches Trover (frequently quoted).

11. The arguments pro and con are well presented by Lawrence H. Seltzer in *The Nature and Tax Treatment of Capital Gains and Losses* (New York: National Bureau of Economic Research, 1951), pp. 281–318. Different treatments by nations are discussed on pages 254–80. The *Final Report* of the Royal Commission on the Taxation of Profits and Income, Cmd 9474 (London: Her Majesty's Stationery Office, 1955) summarizes on page 33 the basis for the conclusion that capital gains and losses should not be included in taxable income.

12. For example, see Philip M. Stern, *The Great Treasury Raid*

(New York: Random House, 1962), pp. 81–107.

13. Earl R. Rolph and George F. Break, *Public Finance* (New York: Ronald Press, 1961), pp. 128–29; Kul B. Bhatia, "Capital Gains, the Distribution of Income and Taxation," *National Tax Journal* 27 (June 1974): 328–30.

14. E. B. Nortchiffe, *Common Market Fiscal Systems* (London: Sweet and Maxwell, Ltd., 1960), p. 33. Also, Commission of the European Communities, *Corporation Tax and Individual Income Tax in the European Communities, Competition Approximation of Legislation,* series no. 15(Brussels: EC, 1970).

15. Robert Eisner, "Tax Incentives for Investment," *National Tax Journal* 26 (September 1973): 398–400.

16. Reuss, *Fiscal Policy for Growth,* p. 108. On page 98 Reuss writes, "But the very fact that taxable income is a legal fiction more than an economic concept offers perhaps the main manipulative tool, the lawmaker can quite freely manipulate the tax burden by declaring existing income non-taxable or by imputing taxable income where there is no economic income."

17. Ibid., p. 101.

18. Ibid., p. 101.

19. *Federation of British Industries Taxation Studies, Taxation in Western Europe* (London: FBI, 1962).

20. Peggy Brewer Richman, "Depreciation and the Measurement of Effective Profits Tax Rates in the European Common Market and United Kingdom," *National Tax Journal,* March 1964, pp. 86–91.

21. Marion H. Bryden, "World Tax Burdens, 1963," *Canadian Tax Journal,* 1966, pp. 49–53.

22. Norman B. Ture, *Tax Policy Capital Formation and Productivity* (New York: National Association of Manufacturers, 1973), p. 31.

23. Irving Fisher, "Income in Theory and Income Taxation in Practice," *Econometrica,* January 1937, pp. 1–55.

24. Nicholas Kaldor, *An Expenditure Tax* (London: Unwin University Books, 1955).

25. Nicholas Kaldor, *Indian Tax Reform, Indian Treasury,* 1956.

26. William Vickrey, *Agenda for Progressive Taxation* (New York: Ronald Press, 1947).

27. *Hearings before the Committee on Finance, U.S. Senate, Revenue Act of 1963,* p. 378, Table I: *Tax Reform Hearings:* "Tax Simplification," Senator Mark Hatfield: 20–25, Committee on Ways and Means, July 10, 1975 (Washington, D.C.: U.S. Government Printing

Office, 1975); William E. Simon, Secretary of the Treasury, "Simplicity, Fairness in Taxation," *Treasury Papers* (January, 1976): 21–22.

28. Frederick G. Reuss, *Fiscal Policy for Growth*, p. 82.

29. Robert Z. Aliber and Herbert Stein, "The Price of U.S. Exports and the Mix of U.S. Direct and Indirect Taxes," *American Economic Review* 54 (September 1964): 703–10.

30. Amotz Morag, *On Taxes and Inflation* (New York: Random House, 1965).

31. Carl Dietzel, *Das System der Staatsanleiben in Zusammenbung der Volkswirthsehaft betrachtet* (Heidelberg, 1855), in *Essays in Honor of Alvin H. Hansen* (New York: Norton, 1948).

32. *OECD Observer* 68 (February 1974): 5.

33. National Economic Development Office, *Value Added Tax* (London: Her Majesty's Stationery Office, 1969), pp. 27, 60–61.

34. Alan A. Tait, *Value Added Tax* (London: McGraw-Hill, 1972), p. 164.

35. *International Finance News Survey* 20, no. 10 (March 15, 1968): 83.

36. *New York Times*, October 1, 1967.

37. Carl S. Shoup, *Public Finance* (Chicago: Aldine, 1969), pp. 412–13; Paul A. Samuelson, "A New Theory of Nonsubstitution," in *The Collected Scientific Papers of Paul A. Samuelson*, Vol. 1 (Cambridge, Mass.: Massachusetts Institute of Technology Press, 1965), pp. 520–35.

38. In Latin America, for example, employers pay substantial payroll taxes. In 1971 the rates ranged from 5 percent in Honduras to 40 percent in Chile and Uruguay. An International Monetary Fund study found that in eleven of the eighteen Latin American countries studied, the employer payroll tax rates were in excess of 10 percent.

39. John A. Brittain, "The Incidence of Social Security Taxes," *American Economic Review* 61 (March 1971): 110–25.

40. American Retail Federation, *The Value Added Tax in the United States: Its Implications for Retailers*, appendix B (Cambridge, Mass.: Cambridge Research Institute, 1970), p. 17.

41. Herbert Stein, "Budget Policy to Maintain Stability," in *Problems in Anti-Recession Policy* (New York: Committee for Economic Development, 1954), pp. 82–101; Walter Heller, "CED's Stabilizing Budget Policy After Ten Years," *American Economic Review*, September 1957, pp. 634–51.

42. This is the concept of the full-employment budget surplus.

It holds that a government deficit is not really a deficit if the current tax rates and current spending rates would be in balance under full employment conditions. Our reliance on income and profits taxes causes tax payments to increase rapidly as full employment is approximated. This means a relatively large federal budgetary deficit when some unemployment exists. Under a tax system making considerable use of VAT, government revenues would decline less as unemployment increased and increase less as unemployment decreased. The *Economic Reports of the President* since 1962 have utilized the concept. It was dropped in 1970, but it reappeared in 1971.

43. Frederick G. Reuss, *Fiscal Policy for Growth Without Inflations.*

44. In 1971, as the federal deficit forced new government borrowing, banks expanded their holdings of government securities while term loans declined. This trend counteracted some of the stimulus provided by the introduction of accelerated depreciation. U.S. Treasury debt, which hardly grew at all in the late 1940s and in the 1950s, has soared by 100% since 1960. (1975)

45. Ronald I. McKinnon, *A New Tripartite Monetary Agreement or a Limping Dollar Standard* (Princeton: International Finance Section, 1974), pp. 7–9.

46. John Kenneth Galbraith, "Let Us Begin: An Invitation to Action on Poverty," *Harper's*, March 1964, and in *American Fiscal Policy,* ed., Lester C. Thurow (Englewood Cliffs, N. J.: Prentice-Hall 1967), p. 128.

47. Tibor Barna, *Redistribution of Incomes Through Public Finance in 1937* (Clarendon: Oxford University Press, 1945). The book is a basic effort to tie together tax sacrifice and expenditure benefit.

48. William Fellner, "Taxation, Resource Allocation, Welfare," in *The Role of Direct and Indirect Taxes in the Federal Revenue System* (Washington, D.C.: Brookings Institution, 1964), p. 79. This entire monograph deals tangentially with aspects of moving toward indirect taxes—that is, impersonal taxes.

CHAPTER 6

1. Lewis Meriam, *The Cost and Financing of Social Security* (Washington, D.C.: Brookings Institution, 1950), p. 180.

2. Willford I. King, *The Right Way to Provide Security Against Illness and Old Age* (New York: Committee for Constitutional Government, 1950), p. 17. In 1971 this idea found support from the studies of John A. Brittain, "The Incidence of Social Security Payroll Taxes,"

American Economic Review 6 (March 1971): 110–25. Health expenditures have increased from 4 percent of GNP in 1940 to 8.3 percent in 1975. *President's Economic Report, 1976*: 118.

3. Howard R. Bowen, *Toward Social Economy* (New York: Rinehart, 1948), pp. 124–200.

4. Rep. Robert H. Michel, "Uncle Sam's Feverish Medical Spending," *Nation's Business*, October 1972, pp. 25–28. State and local government medical expenditures in 1973 are estimated at $13 billion. Tax Foundation Inc, *Problems and Issues in National Health Insurance, Research Publication No. 30* (New York, 1974), p. 10.

5. *Social Security Bulletin* 37 (August 1974): 48, and 38 (June 1975): 49.

6. Each one percentage point of the combined social security tax rate will provide about $7 billion with $14,000 of wages covered.

7. *Social Security Bulletin, Annual Statistical Supplement, 1970,* pp. 24, 26.

8. Jonathan Spivak, "Social Security Tax Boost and Restraints on Benefit Rises Urged," *Wall Street Journal*, January 2, 1975, p. 2.

9. In Western Germany, France, and the United Kingdom, social security premiums as percent of total taxes were very stable between 1965 and 1969. *Aktuelle Skattetall* (Oslo: Central Bureau of Statistics, 1972), p. 22. This still permitted nearly a 100 percent increase of actual social welfare contributions in France and Germany between 1968 and 1972. *E.C. Tax Statistics Yearbook, 1973* (Luxembourg: European Community, 1973), pp. 74–76.

10. Vito Tanzi, "Tax Systems and Balance of Payments: An Alternative Analysis," and Richard W. Lindholm, "Rejoinder," *National Tax Journal* 20 (March 1967): 39–48.

11. This concept of John A. Brittain is not entirely shared by Martin S. Feldstein in "The Incidence of the Social Security Payroll Tax: Comment," *American Economic Review* 62 (September 1972): 735–38, but is largely supported by Benjamin Bridges, "Family Need Differences and Tax Burden Estimates," *National Tax Journal* 24 (December 1971): 437.

12. It is assumed that lower payroll taxes would mean lower wages and an improvement in the international competitiveness of U.S. goods and services.

13. Robert J. Myers, "The Future Role of Social Security," *Tax Review* 30 (November 1969). Myers makes a plea for continuation of the existing program as being the moderate approach.

14. Albert E. Burger, "The Effects of Inflation (1960–68)," *Federal Reserve Bank of St. Louis Review,* November 1969, pp. 25–30.

Also G. L. Bach and James B. Stephenson, "Inflation and the Redistribution of Wealth," *The Review of Economics and Statistics* 56 (February 1974): 1–13.

15. A tradeoff seems to exist between use of direct taxes and the level of transfer payments. Now that American transfer payments are increasing at a relatively rapid rate with prospects of continued growth, greater use of indirect taxes is appropriate. Vito Tanzi, "Approaches to Income Redistribution: An International Comparison," *National Tax Journal* 21 (December 1968): 483–86.

16. "The social security fund would have to equal $1.3 trillion for the interest to be sufficient to meet all the deficits of the U.S. social security system for the next seventy-five years." *Wall Street Journal,* November 26, 1974, p. 22. Also, *Wall Street Journal,* January 2, 1975, p. 2. The report of the Social Security Advisory Council sees a need to increase covered wages to $24,000 starting in 1976 and a combined 0.2 percentage point increase in the tax rate. The Council in its March 1975 report recommended general treasury financing of Medicare rather than payroll tax financing, pp. 81–82. Also, the Revenue Act of March 1975 provided for general treasury financing of a one-time $50 payment to social security recipients.

17. *Economic Report of the President,* January 1976, pp. 94–95.

18. Social Security Administration, Office of Research and Statistics, Research reports No. 40 and 0-733-902. Data for years 1971 and 1964 and *Social Security Systems Throughout the World, 1973.*

19. In Europe between 1968 and 1972 taxes on general consumption as a percent of GNP increased from 4.74 percent to 5.67 percent. In the United States (which includes state and local government retail sales taxes) the increase was from 1.35 percent to 1.75 percent.

20. Artikler, *Shattetall* (Oslo: Central Bureau of Statistics, 1973), pp. 20 and 21.

21. United Nations statistical *Yearbook,* 1971, p. 683.

22. *Taxes in Norway,* the Royal Ministry of Finance and Customs, The Tax Law Department, p. 100.

23. The tax as the taxe sur la valeur ajoutée (TVA) is by far the largest source of general French tax revenues. Also see A. B. Atkinson, *Poverty in Britain and the Reform of Social Security,* Department of Applied Economics, Occasional Paper 18 (Cambridge, UK: Cambridge Press, 1969).

24. Export subsidies are in violation of GATT principles. This results in "a corresponding impairment of the worldwide competitive position of countries relying heavily on employer payroll levies. . . ." George Break, "The Incidence and Economic Effects of Taxation," in

The Economics of Public Finance (Washington, D.C.: Brookings Institution, 1974), p. 175.

25. Jack Heller and Kenneth M. Kauffman, *Tax Incentives for Industry in Less Developed Countries* (Cambridge, Mass.: The Law School of Harvard University, 1963).

26. J. W. Barr, Secretary of the Treasury. Statement before Joint Economic Committee of the Congress (January 17, 1969). See especially supplementary statement on "Tax Expenditure: Government Expenditures Made Through the Income Tax System." Another summary was released in 1974 and is now required annually as a portion of the budget document.

27. CED, *Broad Based Taxes: New Options and Sources*, Richard A. Musgrave (Baltimore: Johns Hopkins Press, 1973).

28. Gerard M. Brannon and Elliott R. Morss, "The Tax Allowance for Dependents: Deductions Versus Credits," *National Tax Journal* 26 (December 1973): 599–609.

29. U.S. Treasury Department, "The Tax-Expenditure Budget: A Conceptual Analysis," Exhibit 29. *Annual Report of the Secretary of the Treasury on the State of Finance for the Fiscal year Ending June 30, 1968* (Washington, D.C.: GPO, 1969), pp. 326–40; *The Budget for Fiscal Year 1976, "Special Analyses"* (Washington, D.C.: GPO, 1975), pp. 108–9.

30. Raleigh Barlow, "Taxation of Agriculture," in *Property Taxation—USA*, R. W. Lindholm, ed. (Madison, Wis.: University of Wisconsin Press, 1967), pp. 93–100.

31. Douglas Y. Thorson, "Looking at Tax Choices in Statewide Finance of Education," in *Property Taxation and the Finance of Education*, R. W. Lindholm, ed. (Madison, Wisconsin: University of Wisconsin Press, 1974), p. 98.

32. Andrew Hacker, *The End of the American Era* (New York: Atheneum, 1970), p. 138.

33. Sweden is a large user of prices along with subsidy of service costs, particularly in the medical area.

34. *Wall Street Journal*, September 8, 1971, p. 1.

35. Report adopted November 19, 1960. The standardized definition of direct taxes settled upon by Richard Stone in a *Standardized System of National Documents*, OEEC, 1958, pp. 83 and 86, defines the term to include income taxes, estate and gift taxes, personal capital taxes and all social security contributions.

36. GATT, *Basic Instruments and Related Documents*, 9th Supplement (Geneva, Switzerland: GATT, 1961), p. 186. By "welfare

charges" is meant payroll taxes and social security contributions set aside to finance worker benefits.

37. Ibid., p. 32.

38. This states that those enjoying the satisfaction of consumption should pay the costs of government involved in production.

39. GATT, op. cit., p. 186.

40. Ibid., p. 33.

41. Clara K. Sullivan, *The Search for Tax Principles in the European Economic Community* (Cambridge, Mass.: The Law School of Harvard University, 1963).

42. John J. Carroll, *Alternative Methods of Financing Old-Age, Survivors, and Disability Insurance* (Ann Arbor, Mich.: Institute of Public Administration, University of Michigan, 1960), p. 5.

43. Robin Barlow et al., *Economic Behavior of the Affluent* (Washington, D.C.: The Brookings Institution, 1966), p. 7.

44. Franco Reviglio, *Social Security: A Means of Savings Mobilization for Economic Development* (Washington, D.C.: International Monetary Fund, 1966) (Mimeographed), p. 36.

45. The U.S. and other countries engage in exchange rate rigging activities. The float remains a dirty float.

CHAPTER 7

1. Executive Office of the President, Office of the Special Representative for Trade Negotiations, Press Release 120, December 3, 1968,

2. *Die Zeit*, January 7, 1969, p. 13.

3. Collections for fiscal year 1963 from BAT totaled $77.8 million, an increase of 232.91 percent since introduction in 1954. The original rate was 4 mills on each dollar of such adjusted receipts. The tax rate was raised in 1955 to 6.5 mills and in 1959 to 7.75 mills. Public utilities, whose rate charges were governed by regulatory agencies, received a special lower rate. See *22nd Annual Report of Michigan Department of Revenue,* pp. 17–21; and *Tax Policy,* October-November 1963, p. 13.

4. "The evidence we received did not provide much support for the view that the effect on prices might depend on whether the value added tax was assessed on invoices, or assessed on annual accounts. It was suggested that the showing of the tax on the invoice might help to overcome psychological resistance to higher prices on the part of the purchaser, and that it might result in the tax being taken into the price more quickly than would otherwise occur; but the presentation of costs to those who determine prices would be the same in either case, and

the general opinion was that any difference in the effect on prices between the two methods of assessment would be only transitory and not in the end less." *Report of the Committee on Turnover Taxation* (London: Her Majesty's Stationery Office, 1964), p. 75 (called the Richardson Report).

5. Conversations with Professor Carl S. Shoup, January 1965.

6. *General Statistical Bulletin*, no. 12 (Brussels: Statistical Office of the European Communities, 1968), Table 65.

7. Between May and December 1968, United States industrial prices increased 1.6 percentage points. During the same period in 1967 the increase was 1 percentage point. *Economic Report of the President*, January 1969, Table B-48, p. 282; and *Survey of Current Business*, June 1969, Table S-8. This relationship generally coincides with the findings of M. Krzyzaniak and R. A. Musgrave, *The Shifting of the Corporation Income Tax* (Baltimore, Md.: Johns Hopkins Press, 1963).

8. A. C. Harberger, "A Federal Tax on Value Added," in *The Taxpayer Stake in Tax Reform* (Washington, D.C.: Chamber of Commerce of the United States, 1968), pp. 21–32.

9. Article XVI, Section B4 of GATT bans the remission of taxes on exports "of direct taxes or social welfare charges on industrial or commercial enterprises." This means that a flat-rate corporate income tax could not be rebated as allocated to exports but that a value-added tax could be rebated.

10. Nicholas Kaldor, *Essays on Economic Policy*, Vol. 2 (London: Gerald Duckworth and Co., 1964), pp. 266–93.

11. A study (U.S. Bureau of International Commerce, April 1969, pp. 70–75, Table 12) showed that 122 or 77.2 percent of respondents considered tax incentives as measures the U.S. government could take to increase exports.

12. Fritz Neumark, *Neumark Report of Fiscal and Financial Committee on Tax Harmonization in the Common Market* (Chicago: Commerce Clearing House, 1963).

13. The distribution of the burden of the corporate income tax is of particular concern when the analysis centers on a reduction of corporate income taxes as a portion of the shift that includes the adoption of VAT. The location of the burden of the corporate income tax has been considered in many economic analyses. The conclusion of relatively recent studies seems to be that in the short run it rests on profits. Therefore, a reduction of the corporate income tax would tend to increase profits, and an increase would tend to decrease profits.

Marian Krzyzaniak and Richard A. Musgrave, *The Shifting of the*

Corporation Income Tax (Baltimore, Md.: Johns Hopkins Press, 1963); Eugene M. Lerner and Eldor S. Hendricksen, "Federal Taxes on Corporate Income and the Rate of Return on Investment in Manufacturing, 1927 to 1952," *National Tax Journal*, September 1956, pp. 193–202; John C. Clendenin, "Effect of Corporate Income Taxes on Corporate Earnings," *Taxes*, June 1956, pp. 389–98; Arnold C. Harberger, "The Incidence of the Corporation Income Tax," *Journal of Political Economy*, June 1962, pp. 215–40; J. A. Stockfish, "On the Obsolescence of Incidence," *Public Finance* 15, no. 2 (1959): 125–48; Richard E. Slitor, "Corporate Tax Incidence: Economic Adjustments to Differentials Under a Two-Tier Tax Structure," in *Effects of Corporation Income Tax*, ed. Marian Krzyzaniak (Detroit: Wayne State University Press, 1966), pp. 136–206.

14. Harold B. Malmgren, "Tax Harmonization in Europe and U.S. Business: The Border Tax Problem," in *Tax Policies and the Balance of Payments Problem*, Tax Foundation, 20th National Tax Conference, 1969, pp. 24–31.

15. Article XVI:4: "Contracting parties shall cease to grant either directly or indirectly any form of subsidy on the export of any product other than a primary product which subsidy results in the sale of such products for export at a price lower than the comparable price charged for the like product to a buyer in the domestic market."

16. Under existing practices under GATT this would mean that income taxes provided the revenues.

17. The impacts of the destination and origin principles with both applicable to the introduction of a new indirect tax are considered by Douglas Dossar, "Analysis of Tax Harmonization," in *Fiscal Harmonization in Common Markets*, vol. 1 (New York: Columbia University Press, 1967), pp. 99–104.

18. Country *A*, by moving to the application of the destination principle, has substituted a tax on transactions for its income tax. This shift would not involve making a choice that would cause country *A* great welfare damage. See William Fellner, "Taxation, Resource Allocation, Welfare," in *The Role of Direct and Indirect Taxes in the Federal Revenue System* (Washington, D.C.: Brookings Institution, 1964), p. 79.

19. Richard W. Lindholm, "The Value Added Tax: Rejoinder to a Critique," *The Journal of Economic Literature* 9 (December 1971): 1177.

20. Costs and prices would increase so that the relative international position of the devaluation nation would return to an approxima-

tion of the former position and another round of devaluation would be required.

21. John Maynard Keynes at various times wrote of the desirability of the world's leading commercial and credit nation (his reference was to Great Britain) making tax adjustments rather than exchange rate adjustments. John Maynard Keynes, *The World's Economic Crisis and the Way of Escape* (London: George Allen and Unwin, 1931), pp. 71–88.

22. J. Frank Gaston and William J. J. Smith, *Border Taxes and International Economic Competition* (New York: Conference Board, 1969), p. 53.

23. Using VAT as a major revenue source to meet national social responsibilities avoids adding to the cost of exports and prevents improvements in competitive positions of imports. The chairman of the board of General Motors had a point when he complained that meeting social responsibilities increased costs and prices. *Wall Street Journal*, March 26, 1971, p. 4.

24. A. H. Eskesen, "Border Taxes in GATT Negotiations," International General Electric Export Division, General Electric Co., August 18, 1964. The GATT Tokyo Round to reduce trade barriers initiated a ministerial meeting in September 1973; actual negotiations were initiated in Geneva in February 1975.

25. Federal Reserve Bank of Chicago, *International Letter* no. 159 (March 1, 1974).

26. Fritz Neumark, *Neumark Report.*

27. Raymond F. Mikesell, "The Lessons of Benelux and the European Coal and Steel Community for the European Economic Community," *American Economic Review* 48 (May 1958): 440.

28. G. G. Hufbauer and F. M. Adler, *Overseas Manufacturing Investment and the Balance of Payments,* Tax Policy Research Study no. 1 (Washington, D.C.: U.S. Treasury Department, 1968), p. 53.

29. Investment needs and tax stimulants in EC are considered in great detail in *Tax Policy and Investment in the European Community,* Taxation Series, 1975, Commission of the European Communities.

30. Lawrence B. Krause and Kenneth W. Dam, *Federal Tax Treatment of Foreign Income* (Washington, D.C.: Brookings Institution, 1964), p. 79.

31. L. S. Bartlett, "Tax Harmonization in the EEC, A Status Report," *European Taxation* 14 (August 1974): 272–80.

32. The crises in the foreign exchange markets in 1971, 1972, and

1973 amounted to a procedure to give the U.S. the same foreign exchange freedom that was enjoyed by other industrial nations. De la Giroday F. Boyer, "Myths and Reality in the Development of International Monetary Affairs," *Essays in International Finance*, no. 105 (June 1974): 20.

33. *Wall Street Journal*, November 20, 1968, p. 3.

34. Milledge W. Weathers (mimeographed paper), 1968.

35. This unnamed economist was expressing the generally held belief of German fiscal economists.

36. Internal Revenue Service, *Foreign Income and Taxes, 1964, 1965 and 1966* (Washington, D.C.: U.S. Government Printing Office, 1973), p. 7.

37. Ibid., p. 238.

38. Department of the Treasury, Internal Revenue Service, *Foreign Income and Taxes* (Washington, D.C.: U.S. Government Printing Office, 1973), p. 13. Also see *Ways and Means Hearings*, July 21, 1975, and *Staff Paper* of Committee on Finance, April 14, 1976.

39. Sherman J. Maisel, *Managing the Dollar* (New York: W. W. Norton, 1973). FOMC is the Federal Open Market Committee, the monetary policy-making group of the Federal Reserve.

40. Denmark had been attempting for a number of years to become a member of EC. Her efforts had been retarded by her need to export rather large quantities of dairy and other agricultural products that are already in surplus and being produced at higher prices by the EC member states.

41. An expanding U.S. welfare program under the existing tax system develops great pressures to devalue the U.S. dollar. Carl G. Uhr estimates that a fully matured pension and children's allowance program costs about 16 to 18 percent of GNP. Currently, the U.S. level is about 5 percent. *Sweden's Social Security System*, Research Report no. 14 (Washington, D.C.: Social Security Administration, 1966), p. 135.

42. General Agreement on Tariffs and Trade, *Basic Instruments and Selected Documents*, 9th supplement (Geneva: Contracting Parties to GATT, 1961), pp. 33, 186. Under the provisions, the refunding of direct taxes or the refunding of payroll taxes or other special types of welfare charges paid by businesses are an export subsidy if refunded to exporters.

43. The United States in 1954 made provision for businesses not allowed to incorporate to be taxed as corporations although operating as partnerships. The provision was seldom used and was repealed in

1969 with the expansion of the right to incorporate to the liberal professions.

44. Joint Tax Program, Organization of American States/Inter-American Development Bank/Economic Commission for Latin America, *Fiscal Policy for Economic Growth in Latin America* (Baltimore, Md.: Johns Hopkins Press, 1965).

45. William S. Vickrey, *Agenda for Progressive Taxation* (New York: Ronald Press, 1947), chapter 6; Harold M. Groves, *Federal Tax Treatment of the Family* (Washington, D.C., 1963), pp. 56–83.

46. Alan A. Tait, *The Taxation of Personal Wealth* (Urbana, Ill.: University of Illinois Press, 1967), p. 15.

47. Dan Throop Smith, "Improvement in the Quality of Environment, Cost and Benefits," address at Iowa Wesleyan College, April 3, 1970.

48. Committee for Economic Development, *A Better Balance in Federal Taxes on Business* (New York: CED, 1966).

49. Robert Z. Aliber and Herbert Stein, "The Price of U.S. Exports and the Mix of U.S. Direct and Indirect Taxes," *American Economic Review*, September 1964, pp. 703–10.

50. "The removal of institutional and psychological restraint on the movement of capital increases the response of international investment flows to direct tax differentials on business income." Peggy Richman, *Taxation of Foreign Investment* (Baltimore, Md.: Johns Hopkins Press, 1963), p. 34.

51. Joint Committee on Internal Revenue Taxation, *Legislative History of United States Tax Conventions,* vol. 2 (Washington, D.C.: U.S. Government Printing Office, 1962), pp. 4670–71. Sidney I. Roberts, "Force of Attraction: How the Foreign Investment Tax Act (1966) Affects Treaties," *Journal of Taxation,* May 1968, pp. 274–277.

52. Ibid., p. 4671.

53. Ibid., p. 4674.

54. Ibid., p. 4675. For detail of tax treaties of European countries see Section C of Supplementary Service European Taxation, International Bureau of Fiscal Documentation.

55. For example, the *Remarks* by Stanley S. Surrey, assistant secretary of the treasury, on September 21, 1964.

56. *Explanatory Notes* (Brussels: Customs Cooperation Council, 1960).

57. Analysis is based on discussions included in *Explanatory Notes,* and *IMF Balance of Payments Yearbook,* Vol. 23, 1972.

CHAPTER 8

1. *Economic Report of the President for 1976* (Washington, D.C.: U.S. Government Printing Office, 1976). Social insurance taxes and contributions totaled $86.4 billion in FY 1975 (p. 247); expenditures for programs financed from this source totaled about $79.7 for FY 1975 (p. 94).

2. *The OECD Observer,* December 1972, pp. 16–17. Other sources of comparative tax data include: Eurostat, *1973 Tax Statistics Yearbook;* OECD, *Revenue Statistics, 1965–71;* OECD, *Company Tax Systems in OECD Member Countries,* 1973.

3. National Economic Development Office, *VAT* (London, England: Her Majesty's Stationery Office, 1969), p. 46.

4. "If the tax rate is 10 percent, then an article selling for $100 tax *exclusive,* attracts tax of $10, making the selling price, tax *inclusive,* $110, but the VAT element is $10, which is 1/11th or 9.1 percent of the tax *inclusive* price." Ibid, p. 31. The *Wall Street Journal,* December 23, 1970, p. 1, reported that the Treasury estimated that a 2 percent VAT would yield $11.6 billion annually. Since then the wholesale price index has increased by about 50 percent. The All Commodities Wholesale price index was 119.1 in 1972 and 171.9 in November 1974.

5. The West German corporate tax rate on dividends is 15 percent. However, because the 15 percent tax is considered to be undistributed earnings, the real rate becomes 23 percent.

"The existing 'lower' rate on distributed earnings gives a strong edge to the Common Market countries in relation to Canada and the United States for corporations which retain relatively little of their earnings." Peggy B. Musgrave, "Harmonizing Direct Business Taxes: A Case Study," in *Fiscal Harmonization in Common Markets,* vol. 2, ed. Carl S. Shoup (New York: Columbia University Press, 1967), p. 243.

6. I have speculated in print on procedures for introducing VAT into America. "A Value-Added Tax for the United States," *The Commercial and Financial Chronicle,* February 15, 1968; "An Approach to the Introduction of the Value Added Tax by the U.S. Federal Government," appendix to chapter 25 in *A Business Approach to Taxation* (Eugene, Ore.: School of Business Administration, University of Oregon, 1966), pp. 204–8; "An Approach to the Introduction of the Value Added Tax by the Federal Government," *Proceeding of the 58th Annual Conference of the National Tax Association* (Harrisburg, Pa.: National Tax Association, 1966), pp. 517–30.

7. *Economic Report of the President, 1975*, pp. 94–97.

8. Arthur M. Okun and Nancy H. Teeters, "The Full Employment Surplus Revisited," *Brookings Paper, Economic Activity, 1970* (Washington, D.C.: Brookings Institution, 1970), pp. 77–110. The problems encountered in working with the concept of revenues and expenditures under full-employment budget assumption are discussed in the *Economic Report of the President, 1975*, pp. 62–65.

9. The basic analyses of the relationship between inflation and employment are found in A. W. Phillips, "The Relation Between the Level of Unemployment and the Role of Change of Money Wage Rates in the United Kingdom from 1862 to 1958," *Economica*, November 1958, pp. 283–99; G. L. Perry, *Unemployment, Money Wage Rates and Inflation* (Cambridge, Mass.: Massachusetts Institute of Technology Press, 1966).

10. Milton Friedman, "The Role of Monetary Policy," *American Economic Review* 58 (March 1968): 1–17.

11. Abba P. Lerner, "Employment Theory and Employment Policy," *American Economic Review* 57 (May 1967): 1–18.

12. Eric B. Nortcliffe, *Common Market Fiscal Systems* (London: Sweet and Maxwell, 1960), p. 60.

13. John Lindeman, "Income Measurement as Affected by Government Operations," in *Studies in Income and Wealth*, vol. 6 (New York: National Bureau of Economic Research, 1943), pp. 8–11.

14. Clark Warburton, "Discussion," Ibid., pp. 26–33.

15. M. A. Copeland, "Discussion," Ibid., p. 40.

16. Gerhard Colm, "Public Revenue and Public Expenditure in National Income," *Studies in Income and Wealth*, vol. 1 (New York: National Bureau of Economic Research, 1937), pp. 179–94.

17. Clara K. Sullivan, "Indirect Tax Systems in the European Economic Community and the United Kingdom," in *Fiscal Harmonization in Common Markets*, ed. Carl S. Shoup (New York: Columbia University Press, 1967), p. 134.

18. Ibid., p. 137.

19. Richard W. Lindholm, "The Value Added Tax: A Short Review of the Literature," *The Journal of Economic Literature* 8 (December 1970): 1178–89.

20. William Oakland, "The Theory of the Value-Added Tax: A Comparison of Tax Bases I & II," *National Tax Journal* 20 (June 1967): 119–36; and (September 1967): 270–81.

21. Ibid.

22. Ibid.

23. Ibid. The tax base is GNP under GVA. It is GNP minus depreciation under IVA and GNP minus investment under CVA.

24. Francesco Forte, "On the Feasibility of a Truly General Value-Added Tax: Some Reflections on the French Experience," *National Tax Journal*, December 1966, pp. 337–61; Stanley S. Surrey, "Taxation for Stabilization," *Canadian Tax Journal* 14 (May-June 1966): 248–49.

25. *The Canadian Report of the Royal Commission on Taxation* of February 24, 1967, recommended replacement of the manufacturer's sales tax with single-stage sales tax at the retail level. Paragraph 651 provides that "only if the problems of administrative control of a single-stage retail tax become too great should a value-added tax be adopted." In 1975 the Canadian government recommended use of wholesale level rather than manufacturing level.

26. The analysis of this section is largely based on a study completed for the American Retail Federation. This study follows the U.S. retail sales tax practice and recommends separate listing of VAT on retail prices. American Retail Federation, *The Value-Added Tax in the United States—Its Implications for Retailers* (Cambridge, Mass.: Cambridge Research Institute, 1970). Phillips Lifschultz in a paper before the Tax Foundation's state and local government finance seminar, Chicago (May 4–5, 1974), said that only Denmark of VAT countries states VAT separately at the retail level.

27. National Economic Development Office, *VAT*, p. 37.

28. Rudolph J. Mehus, "The German Added Value Tax—Two Years After," *Taxes, The Tax Magazine* 47 (September 1969): 554–56.

29. National Economic Development Office, *VAT*, p. 54.

30. Clarence W. Lock, "The Michigan Value-Added Tax," *National Tax Journal* 8 (December 1955): 360.

31. Walter Missorten, "Some Problems in Implementing a Tax on Value Added," *National Tax Journal* 21 (December 1968): 396–411.

Glossary of
Technical Terms

Acceleration principle. The change of investment arising from a given change of consumption expenditures.

Accounts method. VAT is applied to difference between total sales and total purchases. Sometimes called "sales less purchase" method.

Additive procedure. Calculating the VAT base by adding up the income of the factors of production correctly allocated to the taxpaying unit.

Ad valorem. See Excise tax.

Avoidance. Legal nonpayment of a tax.

Backward shifting. The movement of the incidence of a tax to the providers of products and labor used in producing the taxed product or service.

Balance of payments accounts. Record of payments between countries from private and public sources; includes all trade and financial transactions.

Base. The economic quantity to which the tax rate is applied.

BAT. Business activity tax. A value-added tax used by Michigan from 1953 to 1967.

Belasting Over De Toegevoegde Waarde (BTW) Dutch name for VAT.

Block grants. A specific amount granted to one government by another government without requirements for matching or area of expenditure.

Border taxes. A tax assessed on imports limited by GATT to domestic tax that would be levied if the product were produced domestically.

Buffer rule. Used in France; it prohibits cash refunds of tax credits in

295

excess of tax due on domestic sales, but the excess can be carried forward to the next tax period.

Business consumption. Purchases by businesses that are not necessary to carrying out the activity (VAT is not deductible).

Canons of taxation. Adam Smith's four maxims of taxation given in *Wealth of Nations*: equality, certainty, convenience, and economy.

Capital gains. Increases in market value of an asset. If the asset is sold, the gains are realized.

Capitalization. The value of an investment determined by dividing the annual net income flowing from the investment by the prevailing rate of interest. It is assumed that the income will flow indefinitely from the investment.

Captive use production. Goods manufactured by a firm for its own use and therefore not directly included in the sales total.

Cascading. Applying a tax rate to the tax-inclusive price at each sale.

CIF. Cost plus insurance plus freight; a value placed on goods at point of destination.

Common Market. Refers to European Economic Community, also called European Community.

Conjunctural measure. Provisions for modification of the basic tax measure under certain described circumstances. Usually concerned with investment levels and special provisions under the personal and corporate income tax.

Deduction physique. A French term for the right to deduct TVA paid in acquiring goods physically incorporated in the product on which TVA is due.

Depreciation. The amount set aside to cover cost of capital utilized in the production process.

Destination principle. The theory that a tax should be paid by the consumers rather than the producers of a product on the grounds that consumers are the ones enjoying the satisfaction of consumption.

Diffusion theory. The belief that the incidence of taxes is distributed throughout the economy.

Dirty float. Influencing exchange rates by government action when officially a free exchange market exists.

DISC. Domestic International Sales Corporation. Provided for in 1971 federal tax legislation to give indefinite deferment of about 50 percent of taxes on profits earned on exports if the profits are used for export expansion.

Double taxation treaties. Used by the United States since 1939 to reduce foreign taxation of income accruing to Americans.

EC. The European Community, also called the Common Market.

Elasticity. Refers to relative change in quantity offered or purchased in the market caused by price change.

End use. The consumption of a good or service by the purchaser. The good or service is not used to produce a marketable product.

Equalization levy. A charge collected by the seller of goods to exempt businesses. It is an amount in addition to the VAT due from the seller.

Equity capital. The capital provided by the owners of a business. The holders of common and preferred stock have provided equity capital.

Evasion. Illegal nonpayment of a tax.

Excess burden. Welfare cost of a tax system because it distorts choices from what would exist without the tax system.

Excise tax. A tax levied on a good or service. If levied as a percent of value, it is called ad valorem; if levied as so much per unit of some kind, it is called specific.

Externalities. Effects of economic action outside those experienced by the originator.

Factor payment. A payment to land, labor, or capital for carrying out a productive activity.

FAS. Freight alongside; value of goods at point of shipment.

Financial credit. Refers to the instant allowance as a cost of the purchase of capital goods.

Fiscal residua. The combined impact of a tax and the effects of the expenditure of the amount collected.

Floating exchange rate. National monetary units are valued by forces at work in the money markets of the world.

FOMC. Federal Open Market Committee, the monetary policy-making group of the Board of Governors of the Federal Reserve System.

Foreign tax credit. Profit taxes paid abroad are grossed up and deductible from domestic taxes due when foreign earnings are returned.

Forfeit system. Small taxpayers pay a tax based on number of employees, size of store, type, and quantity of inventory and are not required to keep records.

Forward shifting. The movement of the incidence of a tax to purchasers.

GATT. General Agreement on Tariffs and Trade. The GATT is responsible for setting the rules under which international trade takes place.

GNP. Gross National Product, the value of all goods and services produced for the market.

Grossed up. Taxes paid abroad are added to profits returned, and it is to this base the U.S. tax is applied.

Guideline life. The period of time over which an asset may be depreciated as established by the IRS.

Harmonization. The levy by different political units of taxes that are sufficiently similar that economic decisions are not affected by taxes.

Horizontal equality. Taxpayers receiving the same income make the same tax payments.

IMF. International Monetary Fund; the international agency concerned with exchange rates and the general condition of the money of the nations of the world.

Importa sul valore aggiunto. (IVA) Name given to VAT in Italy.

Incidence. The economic burden of taxation.

Income. In taxation refers to gross receipts of an individual or the profits of a corporation.

Income effect. The effect of a tax on effort to earn an income.

Inter-company pricing. The requirement that services and goods provided to foreign subsidiaries be priced to provide normal domestic profits.

Internalities. Impact on those directly affected by a fiscal action.

Investment equalization tax. A federal tax on dividends and interest received by Americans on foreign investments, in effect between 1963 and 1974. It was aimed at reducing the outflow of U.S. capital without increasing the domestic interest rates.

Invoice method. Basic to the subtraction VAT, used by EC. If the tax is not quoted on the sales invoice, the purchaser is not entitled to any VAT credit.

IRS. Internal Revenue Service, the tax administration agency of the federal government.

Marginal revenue. The addition to the total receipts arising from selling one more unit.

Measure. Legal designation of the economic quantity establishing the tax paid.

Mehrwertsteuergesets. (AVT) Name given to VAT in Germany.

Merverdiavgift. Name given to VAT in Norway.

MNC. Multinational corporation. These are mostly large U.S. corporations with production facilities outside the United States.

Money illusion. The tendency to believe that a monetary unit is worth more than it actually is during a period of inflation.

OECD. Organization for Economic Cooperation and Development.

Opportunity costs. Goods or satisfactions given up to have or enjoy other goods or services.

Origin principle. The theory that a tax should be paid where creation of value took place.

Overhead expenditures. Costs of supplies, advertising, and many services.

PAYE. Pay as you earn.

Patenté. French tax applied to businesses and based on evidences of level of business activity.

PIA. Primary insurance amount received under social security.

Physical-ingredient rule. Exemption from sales tax of items that are included in finished goods offered for sale.

Production tax. Introduced in France as a single stage tax on large manufacturers and importers at a rate equal to the sum of typical turnover taxes.

Progressive tax. The portion of the tax base collected in taxes increases as the base grows.

Purchase tax. A single stage tax levied at various rates at the wholesale level in the United Kingdom. Repealed when VAT was adopted.

Regressive tax. The portion of the tax base collected in taxes increases as the base decreases.

SET. Selective Employment Tax; a British tax on wages paid in the service industries. Repealed when the United Kingdom adopted VAT.

Second hand goods. Exempt from VAT because taxed when purchased new. However, the difference between the purchase price from the owner and the second hand sales price to a new end user is taxed in some countries.

SIC Code. Standard Industrial Classification, based on manual prepared by the federal government.

Single stage sales tax. A tax levied only on the retail sale or the wholesale transaction or, as in Honduras, on sales made by registered firms to nonregistered buyers.

Single tax. The taxation of land to allocate to the state all the potential net income arising from ownership alone.

Site value taxation. The property tax base uses only the value of land.

SMSA. Standard Metropolitan Statistical Area. Urban areas for which statistics are gathered.

Social balance. The relationship between the goods and services of the private and public sectors.

Spillover effects. The benefits or disutilities to persons and resources not directly participating in the activity.

Subject. The object taxed as stated in the title of a tax.

Substitution effect. The effect of a tax on the allocation of time between leisure and work.

Subtractive procedure. The determination of VAT either by subtracting purchases from sales or by subtracting VAT paid on purchases from VAT due on sales.

TAG. Excise taxes on tobacco products (largely cigarettes), alcoholic products, and gasoline.

Tax exclusive. Base to which rate is applied does not include tax paid previously.

Tax inclusive. Base to which rate is applied includes previous tax paid.

Taxe sur la Valeur Ajoutée. (TVA) Name given to VAT in France, Belgium and Luxembourg.

Transfer payments. Any income payment that is not made for services currently performed. Consists largely of welfare, pension, and social security payments.

Turnover tax. A tax based on the sales price and paid each time a sale is made.

Undistributed earnings. Profits of a corporation that are not paid out to stockholders.

Use tax. Equal to retail sales tax and levied on goods used in a state other than state in which purchased.

VAT. Value-added tax. A net turnover tax used by all member states of the EC and a number of other Western European nations and countries around the world.

Wealth tax. A tax using the net worth of a taxpayer as the base to which the tax rate is applied.

WHTC. Western Hemisphere Trade Corporation, a U.S. firm engaged in marketing activities outside the United States but in the Western Hemisphere, that benefits from reduced taxes on the profits made in this trade with customers within the Western Hemisphere.

Windfall. An unforeseen and unplanned improvement in economic well-being.

Zero rate. The receipts from sales are exempt from VAT, and VAT paid on purchases required for business purposes is refunded.

Bibliography

Aaron, Henry. "The Differential Price Effects of a Value-Added Tax." *National Tax Journal* 21, no. 2 (June 1968): 162–75.

Aboufadl, Nabil. "The Value Added Tax Theory and Background." *North Texas State University Business Studies* 11, no. 2 (Fall 1972): 13–21.

Aliber, R. Z., and Stein, Herbert. "U.S. Exports and Taxes." *American Economic Review*, September 1964, p. 704.

American Retail Federation. *The Value-Added Tax in the United States —Its Implications for Retailers*. Cambridge, Mass.: Cambridge Research Institute, 1970.

Arant, Roscoe. "The Place of Business Taxation in the Revenue Systems of the States." *Taxes, The Tax Magazine* 15 (1937): 191.

Arnold, J. A. "Value Added Tax in European Tax Structure." *Canadian Chartered Accountant* 97 (August 1970): 95.

Aslib. *Value Added—The Tax and the Concept*. London: Aslib, 1972.

Baldwin, Robert E. *Non-tariff Distortions of International Trade*. Washington, D.C.: Brookings Institution, 1970.

Barr, Joseph W. "Will the Value Added Tax Solve Our Foreign Trade Problems?" *Banking*, May 1969, pp. 43–44, 114.

Bauer, David. "A U.S. Value-added Tax?" *The Conference Board Record*, April 1971, pp. 29–32.

Bell, Philip W. "Private Capital Movements and the Taxation of U.S. Subsidiaries Abroad." *Hearings, 87th Congress Revenue Act of 1962* Pt. 1, April 2, 1962, pp. 177–217.

Berglas, Eitan. "The Effect of the Public Sector on the Base of the Value-Added Tax." *National Tax Journal* 24 (December 1971): 459–64.

301

"Bill for the Introduction of a Tax on Value Added" (Luxembourg). *European Taxation* 9, no. 6 (June 1969): 119–26.

"Bill for the Introduction of a Turnover Tax on Value Added" (Norway). *European Taxation* 9, no. 6 (June 1969): 127–33.

Bird, Richard M. "The Tax Kaleidoscope: Perspectives on Tax Reform in Canada." *Canadian Tax Journal,* September-October 1970, pp. 444–73.

Bird, Richard, and Oldman, Oliver, eds. *Readings on Taxation.* Baltimore, Md.: Johns Hopkins Press, 1964. Includes Clara K. Sullivan's "Concepts of Sales Taxation," pp. 319–58.

Bogan, Eugene F. "A Federal Tax on Value Added—What's Wrong With It? Plenty!" *Taxes* 49, no. 10 (October 1971): 600–619.

Boner, J. Russell. "Tax on Added Value Concept in Europe Produces Spiral, Second Thoughts." *Wall Street Journal,* October 14, 1969.

"Border Taxes, Five Misconceptions." *European Community,* July 1969, pp. 6–8.

Bossons, John. "The Economic and Redistributive Effects of a Value Added Tax." *Sixty-Fourth NTA Proceedings,* 1973, pp. 255–60.

Bratt, Harold A. "U.S. Traders Have Stake in GATT Border Tax Talks." *International Commerce,* October 7, 1968.

Break, George F., and Pechman, Joseph A. *Federal Tax Reform: The Impossible Dream?* Washington, D.C.: Brookings Institution, 1975.

Break, George F., and Turvey, Ralph. *Studies in Greek Taxation.* Athens: Center for Planning and Economic Research, 1964.

Brittan, Samuel. "Cuts in Government Spending and the Tax Illusion." *The Political Quarterly* 42 (January-March 1971): 7–19.

Bronfenbrenner, Martin. "The Japanese Value Added Sales Tax." *National Tax Journal* 3, no. 4 (December 1950): 306–7.

Bronfenbrenner, Martin, and Kogiku, Kiichiro. "The Aftermath of the Shoup Tax Reforms." *National Tax Journal* 10, no. 3 (September 1957): 236–54; 10, no. 4 (December 1957): 345–60.

Brookings Institution. *Report on a Survey of the Organization and Administration of the State and County Governments of Alabama,* vol. 4, pt. 3. Montgomery, Ala.: Wilson Printing Co., 1932, pp. 341–98.

————. *Report on a Survey of Administration in Iowa: The Revenue System.* Des Moines, Iowa: State of Iowa, 1933, pp. 120–54.

Brown, C. V. *Impact of Tax Changes on Income Distribution.* London: Political and Economic Planning (PEP) Institute for Fiscal Studies, Broadsheet 525, February 1971.

Brown, William J. "The Value Added Tax and the Balance of Payments." *Business Economics*, May 1970.

Burkhead, Jesse. "Fiscal Planning—Conservative Keynesianism." *Public Administration Review*, May-June 1971, pp. 335–45.

Buehler, Alfred G. "The Taxation of Business Enterprises—Its Theory and Practice." *The Annals of the American Academy of Political and Social Science* 183 (January 1936): 96–103.

Canadian Tax Foundation. *The National Finances, 1970–71*. Toronto: CTF, 1972, pp. 35–37.

Carter Report. Report of the 1970 Conference on the White Paper on Proposals for Tax Reform. Toronto: CTF, 1971.

Chown, John. *VAT Explained*. London: Kogan Page, 1972.

Christensen, Laurits R. "Tax Policy and Investment Expenditures in a Model of General Equilibrium." *American Economic Review* 60 (May 1970): 18–22.

Clark, Lindley H. "Better Alternatives Exist." *Wall Street Journal*, April 10, 1972.

Clendenin, John C. "Effect of Corporate Income Taxes on Corporate Earnings." *Taxes*, June 1956, pp. 319–98.

Colm, Gerhard. "Full Employment Through Tax Policy?" *Social Research* 7 (1940): 463–67.

———. "The Ideal Tax System." *Social Research*, August 1934, pp. 319–42.

Committee for Economic Development. *A Better Balance in Federal Taxes on Business*. New York: CED, 1966.

———. *Broad-Based Taxes: New Options and Sources*, ed. Richard A. Musgrave. Baltimore, Md.: Johns Hopkins, 1973.

Conservative (Party) Research Development. *Value Added Tax, Questions and Answers*, no. 17. October 2, 1972, pp. 278–88.

Cosciani, C., ed. *Studi Sull' Imposta sul Valore Agguinto*. Milan: Giuffre, 1968.

Cripps, Jeremy. "Stirring the VAT." *Financial Executive*, October 1973, pp. 88–91, 116–17.

Curzon, Gerard. *Multilateral Commercial Diplomacy. The General Agreement on Tariffs and Trade and Its Impact on National Policies and Techniques*. London: Michael Joseph, 1965.

Dale, Arthur. *Tax Harmonization in Europe*. London: Taxation Publishing Co., 1963.

Dam, Kenneth W. *The GATT: Law and International Economic Organization*. Chicago: University of Chicago Press, 1970.

Deadman, W. B., and Stewart, D. P. *Value Added Tax.* London: Farrington, 1972.

Denison, Edward F. *The Sources of Economic Growth in the United States.* New York: Committee for Economic Development, 1962.

Dooley, Oscar S. "Reactions of Selected United States Companies to the European Common Market." *Temple University Economic Business Bulletin,* June 1965, pp. 28–34.

Dorsa, Antonio. "A Tax Equal for All." *Successo,* July 1968, pp. 143–49.

Dosser, Douglas. "Indirect Taxation and Economic Development." In *Government Finance and Economic Development,* ed. Alan T. Peacock and Gerald Hauser. Paris: Organization for Economic Cooperation and Development, 1964.

————. *The Daily Telegraph,* September 30, 1971.

————. "Economic Analysis of Tax Harmonization." In *Fiscal Harmonization in Common Markets,* vol. 1, ed. Carl S. Shoup. New York: Columbia University Press, 1967, pp. 1–41.

————. "Welfare Effects of Tax Unions." *The Review of Economic Studies,* June 1964, pp. 179–83.

Drucker, Peter F. *The Age of Discontinuity.* New York: Harper & Row, 1969, pp. 63–65.

Due, John F. "Alternative Forms of Sales Taxation for a Developing Country." *The Journal of Development Studies* 8 (January 1972): 263–76.

————."The Proposal for a Federal Value Added Tax to Substitute for Local Property Taxes in Financing Education." *Taxation With Representation,* 1972, pp. 41–46.

Ebel, Robert D. "The Michigan Business Activities (Value Added) Tax: A Retrospective Analysis and Evaluation." *Proceedings of Sixty-First NTA Conference,* 1968, pp. 90–107.

————. *An Evaluation of a Value Added Tax for the State of Hawaii.* Honolulu: Economic Research Center, University of Hawaii, 1973.

————. *The Michigan Business Activities Tax.* East Lansing, Mich.: Board of Trustees of Michigan State University, 1972.

Ebel, Robert D., and Papke, James A. "A Closer Look at the Value Added Tax, Propositions and Implications." *Proceedings of Sixtieth NTA Conference,* 1967, pp. 158–59.

Eckstein, Otto, assisted by Vito Tanzi. "Comparison of European and United States Tax Structures and Growth Implications." In *The Role of Direct and Indirect Taxes in the Federal Revenue System.* Washington, D.C.: Brookings Institution, 1964, pp. 217–50.

Economic Community. *Yearbook of Tax Statistics, 1973.* Luxembourg: Statistical Office of the European Communities, Office of Official Publications, 1973.

European Coal and Steel Community, High Authority. *Report on the Problems Raised by the Different Turnover Tax Systems Applied Within the Common Market.* March 1953. Para. 44, p. 24.

European Communities Commission of Studies, *Tax Policy and Investment in the European Community, Taxation Series,* 1975, I.

Faxin, Karl-Olaf. "A Programme for Tax Policy, 1966–1970." Skandinaviska Banken, *Quarterly Review* 3 (1964): 79.

Feinschreiber, Lana F. "Final Regulations Affect DISC Requirements." *The International Tax Journal,* Fall 1974, pp. 77–82.

Fellner, William. "Comment" on "Taxation, Resource Allocation, Welfare" by Arnold C. Harberger. In *The Role of Direct and Indirect Taxes in the Federal Revenue System.* Washington, D.C.: Brookings Institution, 1964, pp. 75–80.

Floyd, Robert H. "The Very Controversial Tax on Value Added." *Monthly Review, Federal Reserve Bank of Atlanta* 57 (July 1972): 110–18.

Forte, Francesco. "On the Feasibility of a Truly General Value Added Tax: Some Reflections on the French Experience." *National Tax Journal,* December 1966, pp. 337–61.

"France: A New Value Added Tax to Curb Inflation," *Business Week,* October 5, 1974, pp. 39–40.

Giersch, Herbert. (In German. Deals with the question of the application of the origin or destination principle to the turnover tax in the EC.) Publications on economics and industrial policy of the Wirtschaftsvereinigung Eisen and Stahlindustrie, Brochure 1. Dusseldorf, 1962.

Gillespie, W. Irwin. "Effect of Public Expenditures on the Distribution of Income." In *Essays on Fiscal Federalism,* ed. R. A. Musgrave. Washington, D.C.: Brookings Institution, 1965, pp. 122–86.

Goldsmith, J. C. "About Problems Relating to the French TVA on International Services." *Commerce in France,* no. 265 (November 1969): 14.

Guerard, Michele. "The Brazilian State Value-Added Tax." *International Monetary Fund Staff Papers* 20, no. 1 (March 1973): 118–69.

Gumpel, Henry, and Boettcher, Earl. *Taxation in the Federal Republic of Germany.* Harvard Law School International Program in Taxation. Chicago: Commerce Clearing House, 1963.

Haberler, Gottfried. "Import Taxes and Export Subsidies, A Substitute for the Realignment of Exchange Rates?" *Kyklos* 20 (1967): 17–23.

Hall, R. E., and Jorgenson, O. W. "Tax Policy and Investment Behavior." *The American Economic Review* 57, no. 3 (June 1967): 391–413.

Hammer, Richard M. "The Taxation of Income from Corporate Shareholders: Review of Present Systems." *National Tax Journal* 28, no. 3 (September 1975): 315–334.

Harberger, A. C. "Let's Try Value-added Tax." *Challenge* 15 (November–December 1966): 16–18.

————. "The Incidence of the Corporate Income Tax." *Journal of Political Economy*, June 1962, pp. 215–40.

————. "Statement." In *Tax Changes for Short Run Stabilization.* Economic Committee, Subcommittee on Fiscal Policy. Washington, D.C.: U.S. Government Printing Office, 1966.

Harriss, C. Lowell. "Value Added Taxation." *Columbia Journal of World Business*, July–August 1971.

Heard, N. *How the Value Added Tax Can Boost Our Economy.* New York: Pilot Books, 1970.

Herber, Bernard P. *Modern Public Finance.* Homewood, Ill.: Richard D. Irwin, 1967.

Hicks, John B. *Essays in World Economics.* London: Oxford University Press, 1959. Chapter 2, "Devaluation and World Trade," pp. 251–59.

Hockley, G. C. "Incentives Under a Value Added Tax." *The Banker*, March 1968, pp. 237–42.

Horsman, E. G. "Britain and Value-added Taxation." *Lloyds Bank Review*, no. 103 (January 1972): 25–36.

"How EEC Integrates on the TVA Front." *Business International: Europe,* June 19, 1970, p. 195.

Hufbauer, G. L., and Adler, F. M. "Overseas Manufacturing Investment and the Balance of Payments." *Tax Policy Research Study*, no. 1 of the United States Treasury. Washington, D.C.: United States Government Printing Office, 1968.

Huiskamp, J. C. L. "Netherlands, A Draft Bill for a Turnover Tax on Value Added." Editorial. *Bulletin for International Fiscal Documentation* 20 (September 1966):1.

————. "TVA and Prices." Editorial. *Bulletin for International Fiscal Documentation* 22, no. 2 (February 1968): 46.

————. "The Dutch VAT Bill." *Bulletin for International Fiscal Documentation* 22(May 1969): 205–21.

Ilersic, A. R. "Value-added Tax for the United Kingdom?" *Canadian Tax Journal* 17, no. 6 (November–December 1969): 48–53.

"International Investment Position of the United States." *Survey of Current Business* 54 (August 1974):1–6, 9.

"Italian Tax Reform: Value Added Tax." *European Taxation* 13, no. 11 (November 1973):382–89.

"Italy Switches to VAT." *Economist*, January 6, 1973, p. 56.

Ito, Hanya. "Theorie und Technik der Nettoumsat Zaterier in Japan." *Finanzarchiv* 15, no. 3 (1955):447–78.

Jackson, John Howard. *World Trade and the Law of GATT*. New York: Bobbs-Merrill Co., 1969.

Jansen, Johannes. "TVA: 1970 and Beyond." *European Community*, April 1968, pp. 12–13.

Johnson, Harry, and Krause, Melvin. "Border Taxes, Border Tax Adjustments, Comparative Advantage, and the Balance of Payments." *The Canadian Journal of Economics* 3, no. 4 (November 1970): 595–602.

Joint Committee on Internal Revenue Taxation, *Estimates of Federal Tax Expenditures*. Washington, D.C.: U.S. Government Printing Office, 1975.

Joint Economic Committee, *The Value-Added Tax*, Hearings, 92 Congress, 1972.

Jones, Sidney L. "The Value Added Tax." *Michigan Business Review* 25, no. 4 (July 1972):8–13.

Joseph, Clifford. *Value Added Tax—The British System Explained*. London: Financial Techniques Ltd., 1972.

Kaldor, Nicholas. "A Memorandum on the Value-Added Tax." In *Essays in Economic Policy*, vol 1. London: Gerald Duckworth, 1964.

Kennedy, Thomas. "Excess TVA Credit—A Financial Burden Resulting from Fiscal Law." *European Taxation* 11 (March 1971): 60–68.

Keynes, John Maynard. *Committee on Finance and Industry Report*, addendum 1. London: Her Majesty's Stationery Office, 1931, pp. 199–203.

————. *The World's Economic Crisis and the Way of Escape*. London: George Allen & Unwin, 1931.

Knatz, Thomas. "Value Added Tax: Practice and Planning." *British Tax Review* 15, no. 5 (1970):292–303.

Krauss, Melvyn. "Tax Harmonization and Allocative Efficiency in Economic Unions." *Public Finance* 3 (1968):367–71.

————. "Indirect Currency Speculation and Border Tax Adjustments." *Western Economic Journal* 9 (March 1971):99–101.

Kriz, Miroslav A. "A Need for a Reappraisal of American Tax Policies." *Annals of the American Academy of Political and Social Sciences* 379 (September 1968):114–22.

Krzyzaniak, Marian. "The Burden of a Differential Tax on Profits in a Neoclassical World." *Public Finance* 23, no. 4 (1968):446–73.

Lawton, Philip. "Value Added Tax." *British Tax Revue*, no. 3 (1971).

Lent, George E.; Casanegra, Milka; and Guerard, Michele. "The Value-Added Tax in Developing Countries." *IMF Staff Papers* 20, no. 2 (July 1973):318–78.

Lexan, M. E. "The Recent Evolution of the French Tax System." *European Taxation*, November 1965, pp. 264–69.

Lindholm, Richard W. "Adaptation of Tax Policy to International and Great Society Requirements." Tax changes for short-run stabilization, hearings before the Joint Economic Committee, 89th Congress, 2nd. sess., March 1966. Washington, D.C.: U.S. Government Printing Office, 1966, pp. 288–91.

————. "Adjusting the Posture of the U.S. Economy to Facilitate Corporate Freedom in International Actions." *The Journal of Finance*, May 1966, pp. 258, 263–64.

————. "The Arguments in Favor of a Value Added Tax." *Taxation With Representation*, 1972, pp. 47–54.

————. "The Business Activities Tax." *Michigan Tax Study Papers*. Lansing, Mich.: Legislative Committee, House of Representatives, 1958, pp. 263–67.

————."A Comment on the Balance-of-Payments Deficit and the Tax Structure." *Review of Economics and Statistics* 68, no. 1 (February 1966):98–99.

————."The French Value-Added Tax." *Oregon Business Review* 37, no. 2 (February 1968):1–4.

————. "International Tax Disharmony: A Basic Cause of United States International Payments Restraints." *Western Economic Journal* 4, no. 3 (Summer 1966):268–80.

————. "National Tax System and International Balance of Payments." *National Tax Journal* 19, no. 21 (June 1966):163–72.

————. "National Tax Systems and International Competitiveness." *Taxes and International Business*. National Association of Manufacturers, 1965, pp. 50–64.

————. *New Tax Directions for the United States.* Committee on Ways and Means U.S. House of Representatives, Washington, D.C.: U.S. Government Printing Office, 1975.

————. "A Plea for the Value Added Tax." *Tax Review* 30, no. 5 (May 1969):17–24.

————. "Rebuttal of Stanley S. Surrey." In *A Review of Balance of Payments Policies.* Joint Economic Committee, 91st Congress, 1st sess., January 1969, pp. 253–54.

————. "Some Value-Added Tax Impacts on the International Competitiveness of Producers." *The Journal of Finance* 23, no. 4 (September 1968):659–65.

————. "The Sophisticated Swedish Tax Policy." *California Management Review* 15, no. 1 (Fall 1972):75–78.

————. *Tax Changes for Shortrun Stabilization.* Hearings before the Subcommittee on Fiscal Policy of the Joint Economic Committee, 89th Congress, 2nd sess. Washington, D.C.: U.S. Government Printing Office, 1966, pp. 288–92.

————. "Taxing Retailing and Service with the Value Added Tax." *The Conference Board Record* 9, no. 2 (February 1972):17–20.

————. "The Value Added Tax: A Short Review of the Literature." *The Journal of Economic Literature* 8, no. 4 (December 1970): 1178–89.

————. "Value-Added Tax vs Corporation Income Tax." *Business Economics* 5, (January 1970):62–65.

————. "Value-Added Tax for the United States." *Commercial and Financial Chronicle,* February 15, 1968.

————. "Value of Value-Added Tax." *AMS Professional Management Bulletins: Finance,* February 10, 1970, pp. 7–11.

Lock, Clarence W. "Administrative History of Michigan's Business Activities Tax." *Proceedings, 48th Annual Conference on Taxations of the NTA,* 1955, pp. 20–25.

————. "An Administrator's Point of View on the Value-Added Tax." In *Alternatives to Present Federal Taxes.* Princeton, N.J.: Tax Institute of America, 1964, pp. 55–63.

————. "Michigan's Most Unique Tax." *Michigan CPA,* October 1956.

Loeb, Charles W. "Value-Added Taxation in States." *Proceedings, Sixty-first NTA Annual Conference,* 1968, pp. 117–24.

Machinery and Allied Products Institute. *Manufacturing Abroad: The Role of the U.S.* Washington, D.C.: 1968.

McKinnon, Ronald I. "Export Expansion Through Tax Policy: The

Case for a Value-Added Tax in Singapore." *The Malayan Economic Review* 11, no. 2 (October 1966):1–27.

————. "Protection and the Value-added Tax." In *Effective Tariff Protection*, ed. H. Grubel and H. G. Johnson. Geneva: General Agreement on Tariffs and Trade, 1971, pp. 287–93.

————. "The Value-added Tax for Singapore: Rejoinder." *The Malayan Economic Review*, April 1967, pp. 36–46.

Mclure, Charles E. "Taxes and the Balance of Payments: Another Alternative Analysis," *National Tax Journal* 21 (March 1968): 57–69.

————. *Value Added Tax, Two Views*. Washington, D.C.: American Enterprise Institute for Public Policy Research, 1972.

Mahler, Walter, Jr. "Elimination of the Sales Tax Burden on Exports." *Asian Economic Review* 11, no. 2 (February 1969):228–32.

Mainprice, H. H. *VAT: A Concise Guide*. London: VAT Planning and Publications Ltd., 1972.

————. "Some Grey Areas in VAT." *Accountancy* 83 (May 1972): 14–20.

————. "VAT: Still More Grey Areas." *Accountancy* 83 (June 1972): 88–90.

Maital, Schlomo. "Some Aspects of a Value Added Tax for Israel." In *Israel and the Common Market*. Jerusalem: Weidenfeld & Nicholson, 1971, pp. 133–211.

Malmgren, Harold B. "Tax Harmonization in Europe and U.S. Business: The Border Tax Problem." In *Tax Policies and the Balance of Payments Problem*. Tax Foundation, Twentieth NTA National Conference, 1969, pp. 24–31, 32.

Malt, Richard M. "A Value-added Tax for Canada." In *Public Finance in Canada*, ed. A. J. Robinson and J. Cutts. London: Methuen, 1968.

————. "Some Aspects of a Value-added Tax for Canada." *Queens University Papers in Taxation and Public Finance*, no. 5. Canadian Tax Foundation, 1966.

Martinère, D. de la. Ministry of Finance. "France, Comment." In *Foreign Tax Policies and Economic Growth*. New York: National Bureau of Economic Research, 1966, pp. 332–35.

Matthiasson, Björn. "The Value-Added Tax." *Finance and Development* 7, no. 1 (March 1970):40–46.

Messere, Kenneth. "Border Tax Adjustments." *The OECD Observer*, no. 30 (October 1967):5–11.

Meyer, John, and Glauber, Robert. *Investment Decisions, Economic*

Forecasting, and Public Policy. Division of Research, Graduate School of Business Administration, Harvard University, 1964.

Michas, Nicholas A. "The Value Added Tax." *Taxation With Representation*, 1972, pp. 55–60.

"Miracle Levy Goes Awry." *Wall Street Journal*, October 14, 1969.

Missorten, Walter. "Some Problems in Implementing a Tax on Value Added," *National Tax Journal* 21, no. 4 (1968):396–411.

Moray, Amotz. *On Taxes and Inflation*. New York: Random House, 1965.

Morgan, Carlyle. "French TVA Problems." *Christian Science Monitor*, January 10, 1968.

Morris, Alf. *Value Added Tax*. London: Fabian Society, Fabian Research Series no. 264, February 1970.

Mundell, Robert A. "The Monetary Dynamics of International Adjustment Under Fixed and Flexible Exchange Rates." *Quarterly Journal of Economics*, May 1960, pp. 227–57.

Munnell, Alicia. H. *The Effect of Social Security on Personal Saving*. Cambridge: Ballinger Publishing, 1974.

Musgrave, Peggy B. "Tax Preferences to Foreign Investment." *The Economics of Federal Subsidy Programs, Part 2*. Joint Economic Committee, 92nd Congress, 2nd sess. June 1972, pp. 176–219.

Musgrave, Richard A. "Tax Policy Under Decentralized Socialism: A Summary." *Public Finance* 23, no. 1–2 (1968):202–11.

Nasini, Pietro. "Harmonization of National Systems of VAT." *European Taxation* 13, no. 2 (February 1973):39–43.

National Bureau of Economic Research and the Brookings Institution. *The Role of Direct and Indirect Taxes in the Federal Revenue System*. Princeton, N.J.: Princeton University Press, 1964.

National Economic Development Office. *Value Added Tax*. London: Her Majesty's Stationery Office, 1969.

National Industrial Conference Board. "Border Taxes and International Economic Competition." *Studies in Business Economics*, no. 108, New York, 1969.

Neumark, Fritz. *Fiskalpolitik und Wachstumsschwankungen*. Wiesbaden: Franz Steiner Verlag, 1968.

———. *Neumark Report of Fiscal and Financial Committee on Tax Harmonization in the Common Market*. Chicago: Commerce Clearing House, 1963.

Niehus, Rudolf J. "The German Added Value Tax—Two Years After." *Taxes*, September 1969, pp. 554–66.

————. "The New German Added Value Tax Law." *Taxes*, November 1967, pp. 727–57.

Norr, Martin S. "The Value-Added Tax in France." *Canadian Tax Foundation*, 16th Annual Conference, 1962, p. 243.

Norr, Martin S., and Hornhammer, Nils G. "The Value-Added Tax in Sweden." *Columbia Law Review* 70 (March 1970):380.

Norr, Martin S., and Kerlan, Pierre. *Taxation in France.* World Tax Series, Law School of Harvard University. Chicago: Commerce Clearing House, 1966.

Oakland, William H. "A National Value-Added Tax," *Taxation With Representation*, 1972, pp. 61–66.

————. "Automatic Stabilization and Value-Added Tax." In *Studies in Economic Stabilization,* ed. Albert Ando et al. Washington, D.C.: Brookings Institution, 1968.

————. "The Theory of the Value-Added Tax." *National Tax Journal* 20 (June 1967):119–36.

Oething, Robert. "Britain Eyes New Tax System." *Bankers Monthly* 84 (December 1967):38–40.

Ohlin, Bertil. "Taxation and Foreign Trade." Annex II to the export report on *Sound Aspects of European Economic Cooperation.* Geneva: International Labour Office, 1956.

Organization for Economic Cooperation and Development. "Changing to TVA." *OECD Observer* 44 (February 1970):13.

Papke, J. A. "Michigan's Value Added Tax After Seven Years." *National Tax Journal* 13 (December 1960):350–63.

Peckman, Joseph, and Okner, Benjamin. "Individual Income Tax Evasion by Income Class." Joint Economic Committee, *Economics of Federal Subsidy Programs, Part I—General Study Papers.* Washington, D.C.: U.S. Government Printing Office, 1972.

Peloubet, Maurice E. "European Experience With Value-Added Taxation." In *Alternatives to Present Federal Taxes.* Princeton, N.J.: Tax Institute of America, 1964.

Penn, J. B.; Irwin, G. D.; and Richardson, R. A. "The Value Added Tax: A Preliminary Look at Effects on the Agricultural Sector." *Southern Journal of Agriculture Economics,* July 1972, pp. 165–70.

Pepper, H. W. T. "Expenditure Tax: An Obituary." *British Tax Review*, March-April 1967, pp. 133–43.

————. "VAT in Europe and Elsewhere." *Accountant,* October 1971, pp. 519–22.

Peterson, Wallace C. "Transfer Expenditures, Taxes, and Income Redistribution in France." *Quarterly Review of Economics and Business* 5 (Fall 1963):5–21.

Philippine Joint Legislature Executive Tax Commission. "Replace Sales Tax With VAT." *The Tax Monthly* 10, no. 5 (November 1969): 5–12.

Pinder, John, ed. *The Economics of Europe*. London: Charles Knight, 1971.

Pommier, Paul and Aversa, Andre A. "Pros and Cons of a Tax on Value Added." Peat Marwick, Mitchell & Co. *World* 3, no. 4 (October 1969):20–26.

President's Task Force on Business Taxation. *Business Taxation*. Washington, D.C.: U.S. Government Printing Office, 1970.

Prest, A. R. "Proposals for a Tax-Credit System." *British Tax Review*, no. 1 (1973):6–16.

_____. *Public Finance: In Theory and Practice*. London: Weidenfeld & Nicolson, 1960.

_____. "Sense and Nonsense in Budgetary Policy." *The Economic Journal* 78 (1968):18.

_____. "Taxation and Growth." *The Political Quarterly* 42 (January–March 1971):66–74.

_____. "A Value Added Tax Coupled With a Reduction in Taxes on Business Profits." *British Tax Review*, September–October 1963, pp. 338–41.

Ray, Caldwell Lewis. "An Analysis of Value-Added Taxation With Special Reference to the State of Texas." 1967 University of Texas thesis (unpublished), Supervisor, Daniel C. Morgan, Jr. (Order No. 68-4333).

Ray, George F. "Post Mortem on the Import Surcharge." *Intereconomics*, no. 3 (March 1967):65–67.

Reinsel, Edward. *Farm and Off-Farm Income Reported on Federal Tax Returns*. ERS-383. Washington, D.C.: U.S. Government Printing Office, 1968.

Reuss, Frederick G. *Fiscal Policy for Growth Without Inflation*. Baltimore, Md.: Johns Hopkins Press, 1963.

Reviglio, Franco. "The Social Security Sector and Its Financing in Developing Countries." *International Monetary Fund Staff Papers*, November 1967, pp. 500–540.

Richardson, U. *Report of the Committee on Turnover Taxation*. Cmnd. 2300. London: Her Majesty's Stationery Office, 1964.

Roets, Perry. "The Personal Income Tax: A Study in Justice." *Marquette Business Review*, summer 1965, p. 70.

Rybezynski, T. M., ed. *Value Added Tax: The UK Position and the European Experience.* Oxford, U.K.: Blackwell, 1969.

Sagendorph, Kent. "Truth About the New State Tax. It's Fair—Plays No Favorites." *Inside Michigan,* May 3, 1953.

Sandberg, Paul A. "Value Added Tax for Sweden." *National Tax Journal* 17 (September 1964):292-96.

Sanden, B. Kenneth. "New Look at Value-Added Taxation." *Timber Tax Journal* 7 (November 1, 1971):25-33.

————. "Value Added Tax: Substitute or New Source of Revenue." *The Tax Executive* 24 (April 1972):168-74.

Schiff, Eric. *Value-added Taxation in Europe.* Washington, D.C.: Enterprise Institute for Public Policy Research, 1973.

Schmölders, Günter. *Turnover Taxes.* Amsterdam: International Bureau of Fiscal Documentation, 1966.

Schulte, Maria-Dolores. "The Economic Theory of the Destination Principle and the Origin Principle." *Institute International de Finances Publiques,* Congres de Luxembourg, 19th session, September 1963.

Schultze, Charles L., et al. *Setting National Priorities: The 1972 Budget.* Washington, D.C.: Brookings Institution, 1971.

Schultzer, Martin. "The Swedish Investment Reserve: An Experience with 'Push Button' Fiscal Policy." *British Tax Review,* March–April 1968, pp. 98-108.

Seghers, Paul D. "Advantages of Manufacturing in Ireland." *The Tax Executive,* April 1969, pp. 201-11.

Shone, R. "Taxation, One Change That Would Be for the Better." *The Statist,* July 29, 1966, pp. 270-72.

Shoup, Carl S. "Consumption Tax, and Wages Type and Consumption Type of Value-Added Tax." *National Tax Journal* 21 (June 1968):153-61.

————. "Experience With the Value Added Tax in Denmark, and Prospects in Sweden." *Finanzarchiv* 28, no. 2 (März 1969):236-52.

————. "Export Incentives in the Context of the Indirect Tax Structure." *Bulletin for International Fiscal Documentation* 26, no. 11 (November 1972):413-15.

————. *Public Finance.* Chicago: Aldine, 1969.

————. "Tax Tension and the British Fiscal System." *National Tax Journal* 14 (March 1961):1-40.

————. "Taxation Aspects of International Economic Integration." *Travaux de l'Institut International de Finances Publiques.* Neuvième session, 1953. The Hague: W. P. van Stockeem et Fils, pp. 93–94.

————. "Theory and Background of the Value-Added Tax." *Forty-eighth NTA Proceedings*, October 1955, pp. 6–19.

————. "The Value-Added Tax." *Taxation With Representation*, 1972, pp. 67–72.

Shoup Mission, *Report on Japanese Taxation*. 4 vols. Tokyo: Supreme Commander for the Allied Powers, 1949.

Simpson, F. S. "The Concept of 'Fiscal Drag' and Its Relevance to the Tax 'Bulge' in South Africa." *South Africa Journal of Economics*, June 1968, pp. 143–55.

Sleeper, R. O. "Manpower Redeployment and the Selective Employment Tax." *Bulletin Institute Economic Statistics* 32, no. 4 (November 1970):273–99.

Slitor, Richard E. "The Role of Value-Added Taxation in the Tax Structure of the States: Prospective Developments." *Sixty-first NTA Proceedings*, 1968, pp. 107–24.

————. "The Value-Added Tax as an Alternative to Corporate Income Tax." *Tax Policy*, October–November 1963.

————. "Value-Added Taxation Exporting and Growth." *British Tax Review*, September–October 1963, pp. 314–35.

Smith, Dan Throop. "Federal Tax Reform." *Annals of the American Academy of Political and Social Science* 379 (September 1968): 102–13.

————. "High Progressive Tax Rates: Inequality and Immorality." *University of Florida Law Review*, spring 1968, p. 451.

————. "The Value Added Tax as an Alternative to the Corporate Income Tax." *Fifty-seventh NTA Proceedings*, 1964, pp. 424–31.

————. "The Value-Added Tax: The Case For." *Harvard Business Review* 48 (1970):77–85.

————. "When-If We Have the VAT." *Harvard Business Review*, January–February 1973, pp. 6–23, 130–33.

Smith, William J. J. "The Role of Border Taxes in Western Europe and the United States." *The Conference Board Record*, October 1969.

Snyder, Wayne W. "Measuring the Stabilizing Effects of Social Security Programs in Seven Countries, 1955–1965." *National Tax Journal* 23 (September 1970):263–73.

Soule, Don M. "Ability to Pay Taxation as Discriminatory Pricing of Government Services." *Land Economics* 43 (May 1967): 219–22.

Special Subcommittee on State Taxation of Interstate Commerce. *Sales and Use Taxes.* Washington, D.C.: U.S. Government Printing Office, 1965.

Stam, Jerome M. "Current Debate Over Value-Added Tax and Implications for Farmers." *Farm Real Estate Taxes, Recent Trends and Developments.* Economic Research Service, U.S. Department of Agriculture, February 1973, pp. 5–7.

Stein, Herbert. "Budget Policy to Maintain Stability." In *Problems in Anti-Recession Policy.* New York: Committee for Economic Development, 1954, pp. 82–101.

Stephenson, E. C. "The Michigan Business Activity Tax: A Retailer's Viewpoint." *Proceedings of 48th annual NTA conference,* 1955, pp. 29–33.

Stephenson, Peter. "Problems and Political Implications for the United Kingdom of Introducing the EEC Value Added Tax." *Journal of Common Market Studies* 8, no. 4 (June 1970):305–24.

Stoddard, William I. "Effect of a VAT on Service Industries." *Tax Policy* 39, October–December, 1972 pp. 59–65.

Stern, R. M., and Smith, R. J. "Transatlantic Differences on Trade and Tariff Policy." *Banca Nazionale del Lavoro Quarterly Review,* September 1968, pp. 239–75.

Stockfish, J. A. "On the Obsolescence of Incidence." *Public Finance,* 14, no. 2, 1959, pp. 125–48.

Stout, D. K. "Value Added Taxation Exporting and Growth." *British Tax Review,* September–October 1963, pp. 314–35.

Strauss, Franz Josef. "Problems of Finance and Taxation Currently Facing the Federal Republic of Germany." *European Taxation,* June 1967, pp. 122–26.

Studenski, Paul. "Toward a Theory of Business Taxation." *Journal of Political Economy,* October 1940, pp. 621–54.

Sturrock, F. G. "The Effect on Efficiency of Introducing a Value-Added Tax to Agriculture." *British Tax Review,* 1970, pp. 112–21.

Sullivan, Clara K. "Concepts of Sales Taxation," in *Readings on Taxation,* ed. Richard Bird and Oliver Oldman. Baltimore, Md.: Johns Hopkins Press, 1964, pp. 319–58.

_____. *The Search for Tax Principles in the European Economic Community.* Cambridge, Mass.: Harvard Law School International Program in Taxation, 1963.

_____. *The Tax on Value Added.* New York: Columbia University Press, 1965.

_____. "The Value Added Tax Proposal Under Consideration by the White House Staff." *Taxation With Representation,* 1972, pp. 73–80.

Surrey, Stanley S. "Implications of Tax Harmonization in the European Common Market." *Taxes,* June, 1968, pp. 398–412.

_____. "Taxation for Stabilization." *Canadian Tax Journal* 14, no. 3 (May–June 1966):248–49.

_____. "Treasury's Need to Curb Tax Avoidance in Foreign Business Through Use of Section 482." *Journal of Taxation* 29 (February 1968):75–79.

_____. "Value-Added Tax: The Case Against." *Harvard Business Review* 48 (1970):86–94.

_____. "A Value-Added Tax for the United States: A Negative View." *The Tax Executive* 21 (April 1969):151–72.

"Swedish Proposals of 1968 for an Added Value Tax System." *Bulletin for International Fiscal Documentation* 22, no. 3 (March 1968):118–21.

Tabatoni, Pierre. *Foreign Tax Policies and Economic Growth.* New York: National Bureau of Economic Research, 1966.

Tait, Alan A. "A Comment on Rates of Taxation Varied According to Consanguinity." *Finanzarchiv* 25, no. 2 (July 1966):263–67 .

_____. "Deflation and Income Policy: The British Budget 1968/69." *Finanzarchiv* 28 (October 1968):110–25.

_____. *The Taxation of Personal Wealth.* Urbana, Ill.: University of Illinois Press, 1967.

_____. *Value Added Tax.* London: McGraw-Hill, 1972.

Tanzi, Vito. "International Tax Burdens: A Study of Tax Ratios in the OECD Countries." In *Taxation: A Radical Approach.* London Institute of Economic Affairs, 1970, pp. 1–49.

"Tax Reform." *The Times* (London), April 13, 1970.

Teeters, Nancy. "Revenue Alternatives." *National Priorities.* Joint Economic Committee, 92nd Congress, 2nd sess., 1972, p. 21.

Thorson, Douglas Y. "Comments on the Administration's Expected Value Added Tax Proposal." *Taxation With Representation,* 1972, pp. 81–86.

Thurow, Lester C. *Poverty and Discrimination.* Washington, D.C.: Brookings Institution, 1969.

Titlow, Richard E. "International Double Taxation and the United States." *Taxes,* March 1968, pp. 135–43.

"The Trouble With the Value-Added Tax." *Business Week,* April 17, 1971, p. 100.

Ture, Norman B. *Value Added Tax: Two Views.* Washington, D.C.: American Enterprise Institute for Public Policy Research, 1972.

————. *Value Added Tax: A Special Analysis for Wholesaler-Distributors.* National Association of Wholesalers 1972 annual meeting.

U.K. Chancellor of the Exchequer. *Value Added Tax.* Cmnd. 4621. London: Her Majesty's Stationery Office, March, 1971.

U.S. Steel Corp. *Legal and Economic Brief: "In Support of Countervailing Duty Petitions Filed in Connection with Value-Added Tax System."* Pittsburgh: U.S. Steel Corp., 1975.

U.S. Trade Act of 1974, *Business International,* January 25, 1975 .

U.S. Treasury. "Considerations Respecting a Federal Retail Sales Tax." Hearings before the House of Representatives Ways and Means Committee on Revenue Revision of 1943, 78th Congress, 1st sess., 1943, pp. 1095–1272.

————. "Proposed Manufacturing Excise Tax, Revenue Bill of 1932, Ways and Means Committee Report." Hearings before the House of Representatives Ways and Means Committee on Revenue Revision of 1942, 77th Congress, 2nd sess., 1942, vol. 1, pp. 414–39.

Value Added Tax and the Bill Explained. London: Butterworth and Co., 1972.

"Value Added Tax in Europe." *Business Conditions: Federal Reserve Bank of Chicago,* February 1971.

"Value Added Taxation in Europe." *Guides to European Taxation.* Vol. IV International Bureau of Fiscal Documentation. (Amsterdam: the Netherlands, 1974) (Loose leaf tax service) J. van Hoorn, Jr., Executive Editor.

Varthdomeos, John. "Corporate Taxes and the United States Balance of Trade: A Comment." *National Tax Journal* 26 (December 1973):653–54.

"VAT Untidy Edges" *Economist,* July 15, 1972, p. 65.

"VAT for India." *Tata Quarterly* 20, no. 4 (October 1965): 89–110.

Vernon, Raymond. *Sovereignty at Bay.* New York: Basic Books, 1971.

Vukelich, George. "The Effect of Inflation on Real Tax Rates." *Canadian Tax Journal* 20, no. 4 (July–August 1972).

Waldauer, Charles. "A Federal Value Added Tax for Local School Tax Relief." *Taxation With Representation,* 1972, pp. 87–92.

Wallich, Henry C. "The Brewing Interest in VAT." *Fortune,* no. 4 (April 1971):94–95, 115–116.

Wallich, Henry C., and Weintraub, Sidney. "A Tax-Based Incomes Policy." *Journal of Economic Issues* 5, no. 2 (June 1971):1.

Wanniski, Jude. "An Idea Worth Considering." *Wall Street Journal,* April 10, 1972.

Weathers, Milledge W. "Some Implications of the GATT Rules Governing the Treatment of Domestic Taxes in International Trade: The Case of Germany Since the Currency Reform of 1948." *National Tax Journal* 23 (March 1970):102–11.

_____. "Systems of Social Security and the Flow of International Trade." *Journal of Economic Issues* 5, no. 4 (December 1971): 54–62.

Weinrobe, M. "Corporate Taxes and the United States Balance of Trade." *National Tax Journal,* March 1971, pp. 79–86.

Weintraub, Sidney. "Border Taxes and the General Agreement on Tariffs and Trade." *Taxes and International Business.* Symposium, National Association of Manufacturers, November 19, 1964.

Wheatcroft, G. S. A. *Encyclopedia of Value Added Tax.* London: Sweet and Maxwell, W. Green & Son, 1972.

_____. "Inequity in Britain's Tax Structure." *Lloyds Bank Review* 93 (July 1969):11–26.

_____. "Some Administrative Problems of an Added Value Tax." *British Tax Review,* September–October 1963, pp. 348–49.

_____. *Value Added Tax.* London: Cassell/Associated Business Programs, 1972.

Williamson, J. G. *Company Taxation—A Tax on Our Future.* London: Aims of Industry, 1963.

_____. "Public Expenditure and Revenue: An International Comparison." *The Manchester School of Economic and Social Studies* 29, no. 1 (January 1961):43–54.

Wonnacott, Paul. "Tax Adjustments on Internationally Traded Goods," in *United States International Economic Policy in an Interdependent World.* Washington, D.C.: U.S. Government Printing Office, 1971: 739–759.

Zurcher, Arnold J. *History of Value-Added Taxation.* Pamphlet. Harvard Law School, September 1953.

Index

Ability-to-pay, 15, 115, 142
Ad valorem, 229
Adams, T. S., 42
Additive approach, 34–40, 96, 101,
    146–47, 188, 242, 255
    coverage, 150
Administration, 113, 250–56,
    258–59
Advisory Commission on
    Intergovernmental Relations,
    44, 83, 99–100, 175
Africa, 228
After-tax situation, 141
Agriculture, 66, 130, 132, 199, 201
American Retail Federation, 112
Announcement effect, 104
Armco Steel Corp. vs. *Department
    of Revenue* (359 Mich. 430)
    (1960), 93
Australia, 237
Austria, 47, 180
Avoidance, 87
    breathing holes, 238
Backward. *See* Shifting
Balanced budget, 244–45
    theorem, 8
Banks. *See* Financial institutions
Barr, Joseph W., 77, 173
Base of VAT, 34–40, 251–59.
    See also Taxes
Bastable, C. F., 114
Belgium, 102, 177, 178, 215, 223

Benefit-cost ratio, 238
Benefit theory, 84–85
Bermuda, 212
Bibliography, 301–19
Bilateral tax treaties, 222–25
Blakey, Roy G. and Gladys C., 76
Border tax, 47, 49, 149, 151,
    217, 237, 241
    180–81, 189, 197, 201–3,
    alterations of, 207
Bowen, Howard R., 163
Brazer, Harvey, 42
Brazil, 128–29, 215
Broad based national tax, 260–62
Brookings Institution, 246
Brussels Convention, 229–30
Budgeting, 15–16
Business and government, 144
    business taxation, 136–39, 146
Canada, 136, 177, 178, 209, 218,
    232, 237, 256
Capital exporting, 200
Capital gains, 11, 222
    French treatment, 135
    German treatment, 134–35
    U.S. treatment, 135
Capital goods, treatment by and
    DC's, 130
Capital purchaser, 147
Capital restrictions, 191
Caribbean Islands, 228
Cascade turnover tax, 110, 178

Central American Common
  Market, 227, 228
Centralized financing, 112
Chamberlain, Neville, 136
Chile, 215
C.I.F., 151, 228–34, *passim*
City taxes, 16–18
  revenue crunch, 15
Collection of taxes and prices, 57
Colm, Gerhard, 41
Committee for Economic
  Development, 7, 143
  VAT proposal, 216–17
Common law, 214
Common market. *See* EC
Competitive advantage, tax
  caused, 194–95
Competitive conditions, 217
Constructive market value, 86
Consumer price index, 69, 233
Consumer prices, 177
Consumption, level of government
  services, 158
Consumption tax, 117
Consumption type VAT, 147, 255
Contracts and taxes, 13
Contributary principle, 170–72, 184
Cormick, A. L., 42
Corporate income tax. *See*
  Corporate profits tax
Corporate profits tax, 14, 34,
  59–66, 105, 107–9, 155–56,
  188, 191, 217, 240, 256
  refund of, 66
Cost-benefit analysis, 174
Cost of entry. *See* Border tax
Cost push, 144, 216
Council of Economic Advisers,
  8, 123
Countercyclical, 64
Countervailing duties, 199
Country of origin approach, 47
Customs Cooperation Council, 233
Customs duties, 228–34
Cyclically balanced budget, 9, 155
De Murville Couve, 70
Death taxes, 225–26
Debt, financing social security,
  183–85

Deduction physique, 36
Deficits, 24, 119, 149, 154–55,
  239–40, 248–50
Deflation, 189
Denmark, 50–52, 75, 102, 150–51,
  177–80, 212–13, 223, 237
Depletion, 251
Depreciation, 137, 256
  accelerated, 156
  France, 138
Destination principle, 74, 94–97,
  149, 151, 159, 179, 182,
  190–93
Devaluation, 157, 192, 198, 205–7
Dewez, Thomas E., 122
Dietzel, Carl, 144
Diffusion theory, 103
Direct taxes, 189, 226
  burden of, 14–15, 28–30, 209
  trade effects, 194–95
Dirigistic tax policy, 137
Dividends, taxation of, 133, 221,
  225
Domestic International Sales
  Corporation (DISC), 43, 50,
  157, 203–4, 207
Domestic shortages, 206–7
Domestic sourcing, 203
Double taxation, 218–19, 226–28
EC. *See* European Community
Ecological impacts, 69
Economic growth
  causes, 126–28
  comparison, 126–28
  consumer buying, 127
  public sector, 127
  rebates on exports, 126
Economic impact, 239
Economic security
  middle income earners, 167
Economic stabilization, 154–60
Ecuador, 131
Education finance, 85
Efate, 212
EFTA, 227
Egypt, 3
Employment, 73, 120
Employment Act of 1946, 123
End use purchase, 257

Energy crisis, 68–69
Entertainers, 222
Entity approach, 214–15
Equal treatment, 116–17
Equity capital, 217
Equity finance, 63
European Community (EC), x, 6,
    44–45, 74–75, 163, 199–201,
    225, 227, 236, 243, 256, 259
  development, 48–51
  social security financing, 170–72
European Free Trade Association,
    47
Evasion, 51
Exchange rates, 102
  floating, 165
Excise taxes, 14, 68–69
Exemption, 146, 251–53
Expenditure efficiency, 45
Expenditure tax, 140
Export, 38, 75, 91, 120
  quantity, 201
  subsidies, 178–82, 202, 205, 207
  tax refunds, 158–59
Family unit, 215
Farm workers, 19
FAS, 228
Federal debt, 239
Federal Reserve Board, 211
Feudalism, 4–5
Finance industry, taxations of, 252
Finance shortages, 24–25
Financial institutions, 37–38
Finland, 215
Fiscal and Financial Committee,
    44–47
Fiscal flexibility, 156–57
Fiscal policy, 249
Fiscal residua, 159
Fisher, Irving, 140
Flat-rate income tax, 13
FOB, 228, 230–32
Food, 143, 175
Foreign investment, 65, 154, 218
Foreign value. *See* FOB
Forfeit procedure, 129
Forward. *See* Shifting
Foundation programs, 84
France, 35–36, 42–43, 51, 70, 74,

    135, 149–50, 153, 157,
    177–80, 188, 207, 223, 233,
    236, 252, 254–57
  depreciation practices, 138
Free market, 239
Free trading block, 199
Friedman, Milton, 155
Full employment, 207
Full employment balanced budget,
    7, 250
Galbraith, John Kenneth, 159
Gasoline tax, 59–60, 66–69, 248
General agreement on tariffs and
    trade (GATT), 28–30, 65,
    73, 149–51
General fund revenues, 183
George, Henry, 114
Germany, 37, 51, 76, 102, 118,
    134–35, 143, 177, 180, 182,
    197, 207, 214, 223, 236, 252,
    254, 256
  depreciation, 137
  export growth, 188
  going concern value, 138
  stability and growth law, 154–56
Gillette, 208
Global income, 215
Glossary of technical terms,
    295–300
GNP, vii, 56. *See also* National
    income
  double counting, 56
Gold, 192
Goode, Richard, 76
Government
  deficit, 149
  productivity, 144
  purchase of goods, 55
Great Britain, 49–50, 65, 76, 79,
    99, 152, 177, 178, 190, 204,
    214, 243, 245
Great Depression, 62
Greece, 3, 227
Gross product VAT, 255–56
Gross-up, 208–9
Hansen, Alvin H., 8
Harmonization, 45, 47, 66, 133,
    176–77, 194, 201, 212–13,
    221, 224

Hazlitt, Henry, 7
Health, 163. *See also* Social
security
Heinz, H. J., 208
Heller, Walter, 155
Hidden taxes, 257–58
Highways, 248
Historic perspective, 2
Holland, 102, 171, 177, 202, 214,
223
Home owners, 79
Horizontal justice, 9, 13, 78–79,
141, 250. *See also* Justice
Human satisfaction, 128
Imports, 75, 217
quantity, 201
restriction, 178
valuation, 198
Imputed income, 9
Imputed rent, 238
Incidence, 37, 63–64, 74, 88–90,
103–9, 144, 150, 165, 182,
192–93, 205, 253
Income
definition, 78, 140–41
redistribution, 80, 142, 216
Income maintenance costs, 171
Income taxes, 10–15, 59–60, 76–80,
105, 118, 122, 142, 149, 169,
172, 201, 211, 226, 237–38,
243, 256
cut back, 50
flat rate, 188
integration, 64
progressive rates, 139
tax credit, 90
Income type. *See* Additive
approach
India, 233
Indirect taxes, 28–30, 47, 50,
59–60, 76–80, 151–52, 178,
186, 189, 226, 236
impersonal tax, 116
trade effects, 194–95
Inequality, 216
Inflation, 144, 216, 245
accounting, 138
control of, 132
cruelest tax, 149

impact, 167
tax rates, 19–21, 124
Instability, 22, 126–27
Insurance reserve system, 162–63.
See also Social security
Integrated income tax, 133
Interest, 11, 221, 223–25
equalization tax, 157, 210
International Chamber of
Commerce, 225
International flexibility, 154–58
competition, 196
Introduction problems, 48–51
Investment, 73, 90, 102, 119, 200
foreign, 204
Iran, 209
Ireland, 178, 180, 233
Italy, 180, 189, 215, 223
depreciation, 138
VAT, 41
Ivory Coast, 129, 131
Japan, 42, 177, 202, 214, 218, 233,
235
Jensen, Jens Peter, 82–83
Job development credit, 137
Justice, 67–69, 85–87, 114–19, 141,
174–76, 250–51
economic impacts, 262
Kaldor, Nicholas, 140, 190–91
Kennedy round, 192
Keynes, John Maynard, 7, 114
Keynesian economics, 1, 7, 256
King, Wilford I., 162
Korla, 214
Kuwait, 209
Labor costs, 70
Laissez-faire, 5–6
Land value tax, 14, 85–87, 145, 148
Lauré, Maurice, 42
Less developed countries, use of
VAT in, 128–32, 218, 227
Liberal professions, 259
Liberia, 227
Libya, 209
Liechtenstein, 212
Life cycle of income, 115
Local government finance, 82–87
Locked-in effect, 79
London Model Conventions, 218

Long, Russell, 13
Loopholes, 77–79, 173, 238
Lump sum tax, 149
Luxembourg, 177, 180, 214
Malagasy Republic, 131
Malt, R. M., 237
Manufacturing corporations, 240
Market determined relationships,
    262
Market signals, 18
Metropolitan finance, xi, 16–18
Metropolitan planning, 84
Mexican Model Convention, 218
Mexico, 215, 232
Michelin Tire Co., 199
Michigan, 42, 50, 92–97, 188, 259
Mikesell, Raymond F., 199
Mill, John Stuart, 28, 84, 114
Minimum sacrifice, 78
Mitchell, Claire, 40
Money illusion, 138–39
Money supply, 155–56, 249
Monopoly, 64
Morocco, 131
Multilateral tax convention, 227
Multinational corporations, 204,
    207–12
Multistage gross turnover taxes, 46
Musgrave, Richard A., 18, 114
Myrdal, Gunner, 78
National Economic Development
    Office, 49
National income accounts, 29, 31,
    40, 53–57
    savings, 56–57
    taxes, 56–57
National resource tax, 68–69
National Resources Planning
    Board, 122
Negative income tax, 90
Net turnover tax, 34, 149. *See also*
    Indirect taxes
Neumark, Fritz, 44, 198
Neumark Report, 45–47, 227
Neutral tax, 38, 41
New York, 81
Nixon, Richard M., 174
Norway, 47, 170, 214
Notes, 263–93

OECD Model Tax Convention,
    218–28
Ohio, 81, 83
Oil cartel, 192
Oil imports, 67
O'Mahoney, C. Joseph, 42
Organization for Economic
    Cooperation and Development
    (OECD), 176–77, 218–28
Origin principle, 95, 149, 190,
    200, 226
Owner occupied houses, 9, 254
Panama, 211, 227
Partnership, 214–16, 243
Payroll taxes, 20, 59–60, 69–76,
    164–65, 186, 244
    effect on employment, 152–53
    reduction of, 240
Permanent establishment, 220–21,
    224
Permanent income, 88–89
Personal approach, 214
Personal consumption, 53
Personal income, 222
Personal income tax. *See*
    Income taxes
Phillips Curve, 246–48
Pigon, A. C., 104
Political environment, 238–39
Pollution control, 216
Poor, 145
Populist influence, 20
Portugal, 177–215
Poverty elimination, 18
President's Task Force on
    Business Taxation, 43
Prices, 67–69, 100–109, 145, 189
    CIF, 151
    stability contribution of VAT,
    167
Primary products, export
    subsidies, 181
Private sector goods, 22–24
Producing units inefficient, 203
Progressivity, 11–12, 78, 118, 216
Property taxes, 28, 59–60, 80–87,
    175
Public grants economy, 173
Public sector characteristics, 22–25

Public services, 23
Purchase tax, 49–50
Puritan influence, 20
Quotas, 199, 210
Rate variation, 150
Rationing, 69
Raw materials, 202
  cost of, 205–7
Redistribution. *See* Income
Regional trade association, 228
Regressive, 61, 88–90, 145–48, 248
Regulation, 22
Rent payments, 9
Rental income, 254
Replacement tax, 260
Research and Development, 210
Residency, 222
Retail sales, 59–60, 175, 256–57
Retail sales taxes, 111, 143, 145,
  170
  use of VAT, 153–54
Revenue Act of 1962, xi
Revenue inadequacy, 2, 9
Revenue needs, 6
Revenue-sharing, 15, 109–13
Ricardo, David, 80, 114, 135
Richardson Report, 99
Roman Empire, 4–5
Rome, treaty of, 44, 198
Roosevelt, Franklin D., 20, 122
Royalties, 209, 221, 225
Rubner, A., 133
Russia, 199
Sacrifice, 117
Salary supplements, 184
Saudi Arabia, 209
Savings, 56–57, 60, 63, 116,
  144, 149, 154
  double taxation of, 141–42
  excess of, 256
  purchasing power of, 166
Schedular income tax, 215
Schiller, Karl, 188
School districts, 84
Section 482, 50
Segregation of tax sources, 82
Selected employee tax, 49–50
Self-policing, 32
Seligman, E. R. A., 103

Selling prices, inclusion of
  government costs, 252–53
Senegal, 129–31
Separation of business and
  state, 136
Service charges, 87
Service firms, 258–59
Services of government, 21–25
Shifting. *See* Incidence
Shoufs, Carl S., 42
Simplicity in taxation, 13, 50–52
  administration, 113
Single business tax, 96
Single proprietorships, 243
Small businesses, 259
Smith, Adam, 5, 80, 114
Social expenditures, 239
Social responsibility spending, 18
Social security, 69–76, 128, 142,
  148, 157–58, 161–86, 217
  EC financing, 171–72
  general revenue funds, 185
  generation transfer, 168
  growth of, 163–64
  indirect financing, 182–83
  new philosophy, 165–67
  pay-as-you-go, 185
  payment total, 165
  reserve financing, 162-63, 168,
  170–72, 184
  tax rates, 162–65
  VAT usefulness, 166, 168–72
South Africa, 232
South America, 228
Spain, 177, 215
Spacific rates, 229
Special Drawing Rights, 197
Speculation, 213
Spending effects, 158–59
Spending program, 213
Stability of revenue, 137
Standard deduction, 174
State and local finance, 15–18
State taxation of interstate
  commerce, 113
Stein, Herbert, 143, 155, 216–17
Store-of-value, 163
Studenski, Paul, 41
Students, 222

Subpart "F," 50, 212
Subsidy
  of industry, 190
  wage and salary, 191
Subtractive/accounts method, 32
Subtractive approach, 34–40, 188,
  241, 252–53
Subtractive/tax credit method, 32
Surcharge on imports, 181
Sweden, 47, 75, 90, 177, 223,
  236, 244
Switzerland, 212, 214
TAG groups, 50
Take-home pay, 73
Tariffs, 228–34
  Kennedy round, 197
Tax aids. *See* Tax expenditures
Tax and spend, 8, 244–46
Tax credit, 201, 204–5, 338
Tax expenditures, 173–75, 193, 238
Tax havens, 212
Tax on tax, 35–36
Tax-option corporation, 214–15
Tax sparing, 227
Tax treaties, 190, 217–18
Taxable base flexibility, 243–44
Taxable income concept, 20
Taxe occulte, 105
Taxes
  attitude toward, 60
  economic goals, 237
  CNP accounts, 56–57
  harmonization, 176–77
  havens, 227
  importance of type, 8
  neutrality, 206
  partnerships, 214–16
  rates, 19–21
  refunds, 201
  three factor formula, 92–93
  treatment of social security
    financing, 179–80
Tight money, 121
Tourism, 151–52
Trade Act of 1974, 233

Transaction type VAT, 147
Transfer payments, 161–65
  between income levels, 182
Transformation impacts, 103
Turkey, 218
Turnover tax, cascade, 146. *See
  also* Indirect taxes
Ullman, Al, viii
Unemployment, 102, 121–24, 248
Unified profits tax, 133
Uniformity, 150, 153
United Kingdom. *See* Great
  Britain
United States International Trade
  Commission (ITC), 232
Urban planners, 67
Uruguay, 131
U.S. Constitution, 29
U.S. Gypsum Co. vs. *U.S.,* 211
U.S. Steel, 199
Use tax, 91, 94–95
Valuation policy, 229–30
Value-added tax, *passim*
  state tax, 92–97
  U.S. 10% rate, 244–45
Veblen, Thorstein, 40
Venezuela, 209, 215
Verity, William, 105
Vertical justice, 9, 11, 13, 141.
  See also Justice
Vickrey, William, 12, 140
Voluntary Foreign Credit
  Restraint Program, 210
Votes economic priorities, 163
Wage levels, 128, 149
Wealth taxes, 28, 116, 118
Welfare spending, 128, 155, 175–76
West Virginia, 93–94, 96
Western Hemisphere Corporation,
  211–12
Windfall tax, 68
Working capital, 204
Zero rate, 36–37, 200, 202
Zerox, 208

ABOUT THE AUTHOR

Richard W. Lindholm is a nationally acknowledged authority on taxation who has been a consultant to the Federal Reserve Board, the U.S. Department of Commerce, the U.S. Department of State, the House Ways and Means Committee, and for seven years a consultant to the First National Bank of Oregon.

He also has undertaken research assignments to Pakistan, Vietnam, Korea, Papua-New Guinea, and Turkey. He has been an adviser to a number of state governments.

Lindholm is the founding dean of the graduate school of management and business at the University of Oregon and is a professor of finance on its faculty.

He has been a researcher, writer, teacher, and consultant in the area of taxation and fiscal policy since the publication in 1941 of his book, *Tax Delinquency in Texas Cities*. Since then he has written *Corporate Franchise as a Basis of Taxation, Public Finance and Fiscal Policy, Our American Economy, Property Taxation and the Finance of Education,* and *Principles of Money and Banking*.

In addition he has contributed articles to the major magazines and journals concentrating on taxation and fiscal policy and has written widely for university publications.

Dr. Lindholm has been a member of the board of directors of the National Tax Association from 1968 to 1972 and of the Taxation Resources and Economic Development from 1960 to 1975. He was selected as distinguished scholar for the year 1975–76 by the business honorary society, Beta Gamma Sigma.